The New Public Leadership Challenge

The New Public Leadership Challenge

Edited By

Stephen Brookes
Senior Fellow in Public Policy and Management, Manchester Business School

Keith Grint
Professor of Public Leadership & Management, Institute of Governance and Public Management, Warwick Business School

First published 2010 by
PALGRAVE MACMILLAN

Palgrave Macmillan in the UK is an imprint of Macmillan Publishers Limited,
registered in England, company number 785998, of Houndmills, Basingstoke,
Hampshire RG21 6XS.

Palgrave Macmillan in the US is a division of St Martin's Press LLC, 175 Fifth
Avenue, New York, NY 10010.

Palgrave Macmillan is the global academic imprint of the above companies
and has companies and representatives throughout the world.

Palgrave® and Macmillan® are registered trademarks in the United States,
the United Kingdom, Europe and other countries

ISBN 978-0-230-22417-9   hardback

This book is printed on paper suitable for recycling and made from fully
managed and sustained forest sources. Logging, pulping and manufacturing
processes are expected to conform to the environmental regulations of the
country of origin.

A catalogue record for this book is available from the British Library.

Library of Congress Cataloging-in-Publication Data
   The new public leadership challenge / edited by Stephen Brookes, Keith
   Grint.
       p. cm.
    Summary: "This book is drawn from the results of five seminars. This
   unique book draws on the four areas of public sector reform, essential
   features for public leaders, public leadership in action and the outline of a
   public leadership approach for the future. It seeks to give public leadership
   a firm foothold within the study of leadership in general"–Provided by
   publisher.
   Includes bibliographical references and index.
   ISBN 978-0-230-22417-9 (hardback)
     1. Leadership. I. Brookes, Stephen, 1955– II. Grint, Keith.

   HM1261.N49 2010
   303.3'4–dc22   2009046193

10   9   8   7   6   5   4   3   2   1
19 18 17 16 15 14 13 12 11 10

Printed and bound in Great Britain by
CPI Antony Rowe, Chippenham and Eastbourne

Stephen Brookes
To my wife Kate – for her empathy and encouragement
and my children, David, Anthony and Katie

Keith Grint
to Kris and Becky, Beki and Adam, Katy and Richie, and to Sandra

Contents

List of Tables and Figures

List of Abbreviations

ACPO	Association of Chief Police Officers
AFMC	Air Force Material Command
AGMA	Association of Greater Manchester Authorities
AMI	Ashridge Management Index
ARK	Absolute Return for Kids
BCS	British Crime Survey
BPR	Business Process Re-engineering
BSC	Balanced Score Card
CADMID	Concept/Assessment/Development/Manufacture/InService/Disposal
CDA	Crime and Disorder Act
CDS	Chief of Defence Staff
CFHR	Cultural Facilities and Historical Resources
CIPD	Chartered Institute of Personnel and Development
CMOCs	Context, mechanism outcome pattern configurations
CSF	critical success factors
DCRs	Department of Capability Reviews
DND	Department of National Defense
DoD	Department of Defence
DSC	Directory of Social Change
DTA	Defence Transformation Act
DTR	Defence Training Review
EMA	Educational Management and Administration
ENA	Ecole National
FG	Focus Group
FRC	Financial Reporting Council
FTs	foundation trusts
GAO	Government Audit Office
IdEA	Improvement and Development Agency
JSCSC	Joint Services Command and Staff College
LA	Local Authority
LAAs	Local Area Agreements
LSPs	Local Strategic Partnerships
MOD	Ministry of Defence
NAO	National Audit Office
NCVOs	National Council for Voluntary Organisations
NDC	National Development Centre
NDPBs	Non-departmental public bodies
NFB	National Film Board

NHS	National Health Service
NIE	New Institutional Economics
NIS	National Illness Service
NPL	new public leadership
NPM	new public management
NPR	National Performance Review
NR	Neighbourhood Renewal
NSG	National School of Government
NWS	neo-Weberian state
OCM	Organizational Change Management
OECD	Organisation for Economic Co-operation & Development
OGC	Office of Government Commerce
OTTO	One Term Training Opportunities
PCTs	Primary care trusts
PFLS	Policing for London Study
PIs	performance indicators
PIU	Performance and Innovation Unit
PMCs	Private Military Companies
PMI	Public Management Index
PPPs	Public-private partnerships
PRG	peer review group
PROCAS	Process Oriented Contract Administration Services
PSAs	Public Service Agreements
PSG	Professional Skills for Government
PUS	Permanent Under Secretary
PVM	Public Value Management
QTS	Qualified Teacher Status
RBA	Revolution in Business Affairs
RCT	randomised controlled trial
REME	Royal Electrical Mechanical Engineers
RMA	Revolution in Military Affairs
RUC	Royal Ulster Constabulary
SCP	Signal Crimes Perspective
SCP	Sustainable Communities Plan
SCS	Senior Civil Service
SHAs	Strategic health authorities
SOLACE	Society of Local Authority Chief Executives
SOPs	Standard Operating Procedures
SSAT	Specialist Schools and Academies Trust
TBU	True But Useless
TPS	Toyota Production System
TQM	Total Quality Management
VCOs	Voluntary and Community Organisations
VCS	Voluntary and Community Sector

Notes on Contributors

John Benington is Emeritus Professor at the Institute of Governance and Public Management at Warwick Business School, where he has led its work on public management for over 20 years. His research, teaching and publications focus on public value, public leadership, multilevel governance and inter-organisational networking. In addition to his academic career John has 20 years of prior experience as a senior manager in the public and voluntary sectors, mainly in the fields of community development and economic development. He is a member of the Sunningdale Institute at the UK National School of Government, and is national chair of the Local Authorities and Research Councils Initiative (LARCI). He is or has been an adviser to the governments of the UK, Sierra Leone, South Africa, and Southern Sudan.

Stephen Brookes is a Senior Fellow at Manchester Business School where he specialises in leadership, public management and performance across public services. He previously served as a senior police officer in a 30 year career and immediately prior to his appointment at Manchester was a founding regional Home Office Director.

Naomi Chambers is Professor of Health Policy and Management at the University of Manchester in 1999. She has a range of research and teaching interests including in primary care, comparative health policy and board governance. Naomi was elected president of the European Health Management Association (2007–2010), which is based in Brussels and represents over 150 academic and service delivery bodies across 35 countries. Naomi is also currently non executive director on the board of NHS North Staffordshire, following previous non-executive appointments to a mental health trust, primary care trust and health authority.

Merv Conroy is a Senior Fellow at the Health Services Management Centre at the University of Birmingham. He is a qualified NHS counsellor by background and has worked in mental health services management and research. His work at the centre spans teaching, consultancy, research and PhD supervision. In his teaching role he has module co-directorship responsibilities on the MSc Leading Public Service Change and Organisational Development, MSc Leadership for Health Services Improvement and MTS MSc/PG Diploma in Health & Public Leadership.

Mike Dunn is the Director of Research at Cranfield University. Prior to joining Cranfield in 1998, Michael was a senior manager in British Telecom and, before that, the Post Office. He holds an MBA from Bristol Business School and a doctorate from Bristol University Graduate School of Education. Michael's doctoral thesis examined the impact of gender on leadership styles within the British Army. He has published in leading peer reviewed journals, contributed to leadership texts and undertaken funded research for the UK MOD.

Gillian Forrester is Senior Lecturer in Education Studies in the Faculty of Education, Community and Leisure at Liverpool John Moores University. Her main research interests are in education policy and modernisation, teachers' work, performance management in schools and school leadership. Between January 2006 and December 2007 Gillian was Research Assistant to Professor Helen Gunter (School of Education, University of Manchester) on the ESRC project: Knowledge Production in Educational Leadership, which investigated the origins and development of school leadership in England.

Sue Goss is a Principal at the Office of Public Management (OPM). Sue has wide experience of working with local, regional and central government, specialising in leadership, governance and strategy development; over the years Sue has worked with scores of local authorities, Government Offices of the Regions and government departments. She is a member of the evaluation team studying the introduction of Local Area Agreements, Local Public Service Agreements, and Local Strategic Partnerships.

Keith Grint is Professor of Public Leadership and Management at Warwick Business School and was formerly Professor of Defence Leadership at Cranfield University and Professor of Leadership Studies at Lancaster Leadership Centre. He taught for 12 years at Oxford University and has published 14 books on leadership and related areas.

Helen Gunter is a Professor of Educational Policy, Leadership and Management at the University of Manchester. Helen has research interests in the modernisation of education as policy and practice at national and local levels. She has been involved in a range of projects on policy change in education and how these developments are being handled, and in particular how interventions in practice support learning and learners.

Jean Hartley is Professor of Organisational Analysis and heads the Institute of Governance and Public Management at Warwick Business School. Jean's research, teaching and publications focus on innovation and improvement in public service organisations; political and managerial leadership and leadership development; employee reactions to change and uncertainty; organisational and cultural change in public services. She has led several large-scale evaluations of government programmes (eg the Beacon Councils scheme) and is working with the National School of Government on Ministerial leadership, and with the Chartered Management Initiative on leadership with political awareness. She is a fellow of the Sunningdale Institute at the UK's National School of Government, and was lead fellow for the ESRC's Advanced Institute of Management (AIM) programme on public leadership and management.

Mike Hough is Director of the Institute for Criminal Policy Research. He joined the School of Law in 2003, bringing with him the research unit that he set up at South Bank University in 1996. ICPR now has a staff of around 15, carrying out policy research for central and local government and for independent funders. It is one of the major criminological research centres in Britain. He was previously Professor of Social Policy at South Bank University, and before that Deputy Director of the Home Office's Research and Planning Unit.

Peter John is the Hallsworth Chair of Governance and Co-Director of IPEG at the University of Manchester. He has held posts at Birkbeck College, University of Southampton, Keele University and the Policy Studies Institute. He specialises in civic renewal, local political and public management reform. His main research interests are urban/local politics, both UK and comparative; public policy; participation and civic engagement; and field experiments.

Dominique Lelievre recently completed a PhD student at Manchester Business School. She has worked as a part time lecturer with the Open University Business School since 2001 and is taking up a post as lecturer in Management at the University of Liverpool. Her main research interests are concerned with the governance and dynamics of partnerships.

Kate Moss is a Reader in Law at the University of Wolverhampton. Her current research interest is crime prevention and the law. Specifically her work centres on the interface between these two issues and particularly the debate about how legislation surrounds and drives the crime reduction agenda. Her most recent publications include Crime Reduction and the Law (2006) published by Routledge; Crime Reduction: Critical Concepts in Criminology (2009) published by Routledge and Security and Liberty (2009) published by Palgrave Macmillan.

Alex Murdock is the head of the Centre for Government and Charity Management at London South Bank University. He specialises in both teaching and research within the third sector. He has taught at Copenhagen Business School, University of Paris Sorbonne and is currently also a Visiting

Professor at two Norwegian Universities. He worked as a professional social worker and senior manager in Social Work. He has a strong interest in social enterprise and is Chair of an Emmaus Community in London.

Carina Paine Schofield joined Ashridge in 2007 as a researcher in the Public Leadership Centre, and is now a Research Fellow working on a number of applied research projects. Her research interests are in the areas of psychology (cognitive, social, developmental and forensic) and technology (in particular, issues surrounding trust and privacy and in the effective use of technology in enhancing learning). She also provides research advice and support to Ashridge faculty and has strong links to the wider research team at Ashridge.

Mark Pegg is a Director of Ashridge and Founder of the Ashridge Public Leadership Centre, which focuses on research and delivery for public and voluntary sector clients. He specialises in leadership, coaching and team development in the public sector. He also works with a wide range of international companies, sharing ideas between business and government. Mark's background includes senior management in industry and international management consultancy in the public and private sectors.

Colin Talbot is a Professor of Public Policy and Management at Manchester Business School. His main area of expertise is in public services and public management reform. He has recently completed major international comparative studies on the creation of arms-length agencies (for the UK government and ESRC); of the use of performance reporting systems (for the National Audit Office); and of budget participation and scrutiny systems (for the Scottish Parliament). Colin has advised Parliamentary Committees on performance and public spending issues for the Treasury, Public Administration and Welsh Affairs Committees. Colin has advised a wide range of international public sector organisations and/or carried out research in countries as diverse as Canada, Jamaica, Mexico, Tanzania, India, Bangladesh, Japan, Hong Kong, Malta and Sweden and spoken at conferences and seminars in over two dozen countries.

Paul Tarplett is a Director at OPM where he has worked since 1996. His main areas of interest are: large-scale organisational change, particularly organisation design, performance management and culture change; partnership working; leadership development for both politicians and officers; senior team development; executive coaching; and policy evaluation and implementation. Before joining OPM, Paul held posts in large private companies as head of human resources and as training and development manager. Earlier in his career, he was both a lecturer and a manager in further education and worked for BTEC, where he led the evaluation and redesign of the national curriculum in business and management.

Nick Tilley is a Visiting Professor at the Jill Dando Institute of Crime Science at University College London. He was until his retirement a Professor of Sociology at Nottingham Trent University and a consultant to the Research, Development and Statistics Directorate at the Home Office. His research interests lie in policing, crime prevention and programme evaluation methodology.

Irwin Turbitt is an independent consultant and Senior Associate Fellow at Warwick Business School's Institute of Governance and Public Management (IGPM). He was previously an Assistant Chief Constable in the Police Service of Northern Ireland, where for several years he was responsible for the policing of the Drumcree demonstrations. He was subsequently seconded to the Police Standards Unit in the UK's Home Office in London, where he worked closely with the Prime Ministers Delivery Unit on the tackling violent crime programme.

Lord Turnbull retired from the Civil Service in 2005, and has since taken up a number of Senior Advisor positions. After university, he worked as an economist for the Zambian government as a Fellow of the Overseas Development Institute. He joined HM Treasury in 1970, was seconded to the IMF between 1976–78 and during 1983–85 he was Economic Private Secretary to the Prime Minister. In 1988 he returned to Number 10 as Principal Private Secretary. Lord Turnbull was Permanent Secretary to the Department of the Environment from 1994–98 and to HM Treasury from 1998–2002. In 2002 he was appointed Secretary of the Cabinet and Head of the Home Civil Service. He entered the House of Lords in December 2005 and holds a number of non-executive Directorships.

Kieran Walshe is Professor of Health Policy and Management at Manchester Business School. He is a senior academic with experience in health policy, health management and health services research. He has previously worked at the University of Birmingham, the University of California at Berkeley, and the King's Fund in London, and has a professional background in health-care management. He is an experienced researcher, who enjoys working at the interface between theory and practice and values the opportunities it offers to engage with the policy and practitioner communities and to put ideas into action. He has particular interests and expertise in public services regulation; the governance, accountability and performance of public services; and policy evaluation and learning.

Acknowledgements

This volume was inspired and informed by the debates that took place during the ESRC Seminar Series 'The Public Leadership Challenge' (award grant RES-451-25-4273).

1

A New Public Leadership Challenge?

Stephen Brookes and Keith Grint

Introduction

There has been an increasing momentum in public sector reform in the UK since 1997 as part of the wider modernising government agenda (HMSO 1999). This chapter explores the impact of these reforms on public leaders and how the reforms embrace the traditional notion of new public management (NPM). One of the aims of the challenge is to identify what public leadership means, whether the term can be applied consistently across the public sector and whether public leadership can be evaluated.

This first chapter outlines what public leadership means within the context of reform of public services in the UK and – in setting a public leadership challenge – whether an accepted understanding of public leadership can lead to the improvement and evaluation of this form of leadership. For the purposes of this chapter public leadership is viewed as:

> A form of collective leadership in which public bodies and agencies collaborate in achieving a shared vision based on shared aims and values and distribute this through each organisation in a collegiate way which seeks to promote, influence and deliver improved public value as evidenced through sustained social, environmental and economic well-being within a complex and changing context.

New public leadership in context

Leadership context

It is often said that we know what good leadership is – but do we? Research has tended to focus traditionally on the individual rather than the collective nature of leadership (Conger 1989, 2004; Pearce and Conger 2003) and more recently to look at leadership as a social construct (Pastor 1998) rather than a real element of organisational behaviour.

1

This chapter seeks to turn attention to the collective nature of leadership rather than its individual construct and explore how and why leaders work together across organisations.

The chapter takes its lead from the challenges presented by new public management (NPM) which has been dominant for over 20 years. It also notes the principle espoused that 'managers often must operate across organisations as well as within hierarchies' (Agranoff and McGuire 2003: 1). This chapter suggests that the time is ripe to move beyond new public management and more towards new public leadership (NPL) and whilst aspects of management will remain, the real challenge for the public sector is to advance a stronger theory of public leadership that emphasises its collective nature.

The broad question that this chapter seeks to ask in presenting a public leadership challenge is:

How and why do public leaders engage collectively through partnership activity in the delivery of public services?

Six possible responses to this question can be offered. Three relate to *how* public leadership is expressed in practice and three to *why* it has been adopted. These six contentions will be considered throughout this book and will inform the final chapter that suggests a response to the public leadership challenge.

Table 1.1 Public Leadership Contentions

The How	1	Leader relationships will either be shared across public services or distributed within individual services; collective public leadership is likely to represent a combination of both.
	2	Leader relationships are likely to take place within four contextual conditions with varying accountability mechanisms; these are 'organisational', 'individual', 'community' and 'political' leadership
	3	Leader relationships will differ dependent on the type and scale of the problem; Using Grint's (2000) typology three types of problems will be evident; wicked, tame and critical problems.
The Why	4	Leaders will engage collectively if there is 'mutual benefit' to each and where the whole is considered to be greater than the sum of its parts.
	5	Leaders will engage collectively because of a climate which favours either the drive provided by central government performance regimes or publically valued outcomes, or a combination.
	6	Leaders will engage collectively because of the strength of networks within a climate that is conducive to 'trust'

Why 'new' public leadership?

The arguments presented in this book have high policy salience for three reasons.

First, 'strong leadership' and 'collaboration' – key components of public leadership – appear to be newly emerging bywords in government policy in support of the modernisation programme. This is evident in the wide range of white papers and legislation being published and enacted respectively. The need for 'strong visible leadership' and the encouragement of 'greater service collaboration' was included in the DCLG WP 'Strong and Prosperous Communities' (DCLG 2006: 10 and 14). Similarly 'strong enabling leadership at a local level' and 'encouraging collaborative working' was included in the DOH WP 'Choosing Health' (DoH 2004: 197 and 56). These concepts have since been included within the Local Government and Public Involvement in Health Act (HMSO 2007). There is also a stated need for 'leadership at all levels' and 'forging a new collaborative relationship between the police and the public' in 'Building Communities, Beating Crime' (Home Office 2004: 9 and 47) which was also incorporated into the National Policing Plan for 2006–2009 (Home Office 2006) and the most recent green paper published by the Home Office (2008).

Second, public leadership has potential to generate *new* knowledge attuned to the complexities of the politicised context of public services and the needs of management and leadership, as identified by the 'modernising government' agenda (HMSO 1999). The Cabinet Office has been critical of the leadership within published capability reviews of central government departments (Cabinet Office 2006: 9), a point that Talbot and Turnbull refer to in subsequent chapters. Other commentators have identified the importance of both leadership and collaboration. This includes the National College for School Leadership in relation to education (Bennet *et al.* 2003; Doyle and Smith 2001) and in relation to health (Ansari *et al.* 2001), criminal justice (Brookes 2006a) and local authorities (Chesterton 2002).

Third, there is considerable scope for increased cross public sector leadership development such as that suggested by Charlesworth *et al.* (2005) and Benington and Hartley in Chapter 12 of this volume. It is rare that public leaders come together to develop collective leadership skills within the same learning environment. Public leadership has potential to bridge this gap and encourage *new* approaches to collective leadership development.

A focus on new public leadership (NPL) has potential to lever a shift away from new public management (NPM). As Dunleavy *et al.* (2006: 468) argues, NPM 'is no longer new. Rather, it is now a two-decade-old set of public management ideas' and 'one which has died in the water'. They argue that the torch of leading-edge change has passed on from NPM and will not return. A similar argument has been advanced in a number of different countries. In Norway for example, Christensen and Laegreid (2007: 3) argue that NPM-related reforms 'seemed to have "peaked" in several of the "trail blazing" countries' and that some of the reasons for this are changing conditions. As a reluctant reformer Norway has had some difficulty in implementing NPM. Leadership and culture were viewed as critical in overcoming some of the main barriers.

In an earlier review of NPM (Ferlie *et al*. 1996) four models of NPM were identified. The first (and earliest) – *the efficiency model* – represented an attempt to make the public sector more business-like, led by 'crude notions of efficiency' (1996: 11). Critics such as Pollitt (1990) argued that it took no account of the distinctive properties of public sector organisations. As Ferlie *et al*. continue, the key driver was viewed as the Thatcherite political economy which viewed the public sector as underperforming. Setting of targets, monitoring of performance and tight accountability processes were introduced. The second model focused on *downsizing and decentralisation*. This sought greater flexibility and introduced increased decentralisation of strategic and budgetary responsibility and a split between the small strategic core and a large operating periphery. It was more dominant than model one and embraced strategic alliances and networking. This was followed by model three – *a model of excellence* – influenced by writers such as Peters and Waterman ('In Search of Excellence') and encompassed a dual approach of bottom-up and top-down with a focus on values, managerial styles and human relations approaches within the context of public sector agencies and 'learning organisations' (see Senge). However, critics considered that charismatic leadership virtues were preferred which acted against the bottom-up focus. The fourth and final model – *public service orientation* – sought to re-energise the public sector by outlining a distinct public service mission and put local users and citizens at its heart.

Although Ferlie *et al*. were writing in the mid-1990s and in contrast to Dunleavy *et al*.'s description that NPM 'is dead in the water', many commentators suggest that the focus continued unabated post the 1997 election. Hough argues from a policing and criminal justice perspective, that many aspects of this approach were retained – indeed developed and extended – by New Labour from 1997 onward. As with the previous Conservative administration, their basic approach has been to secure greater accountability through performance management regimes that rely on quantitative performance indicators and target-setting. The concept of competition as a lever on performance has also been retained, though the language of privatisation and 'market testing' has now been replaced by that of 'contestability'.

Different aspects of NPM and networked governance will be considered within a range of public sector organisations in subsequent chapters. In setting the scene this chapter argues that there is potential to move to a new way of thinking about new public leadership with an emphasis on conducive public value and trust climates (what Einstein referred to as 'counting what counts') rather than the traditional approach to NPM measures and targets ('counting what can be counted').

Difference between NPM and NPL

The chapter argues that there are three suggested distinctions between NPM and NPL:

- The role of public leadership in the context of reform
- The importance of relationships through networked management
- The overall goal of public leadership *vis-à-vis* the overall goal of public management

Role of leadership

There has been an increasing momentum in public sector reform post-1997. This forms part of the wider modernising government agenda which seeks to reinforce more open, transparent and customer-focused government (HMSO 1999) with a view to increasing the trust of the public in the provision of public services – much akin to the fourth NPM model described earlier as 'public service orientation'.

The National Health Service has moved through a number of change programmes having recently implemented the latest which was launched in July 2005. Its purpose was to streamline strategic health authorities, strengthen primary care trusts and engage GPs with practice-based commissioning – all in the cause of improving services to patients.

In the world of local government, a number of reform programmes have been implemented not least of which is that of the 'Every Child Matters' report which drew together the key responsibilities of education, social services and other public sector providers (including the police and health) in dealing with children. There is also the emergence of new organisational forms and institutions such as the Care and Children's Trusts both of which focus on better-integrated health and social care (plus education in the case of Children's Trusts) and the increasing emergence of social enterprises as agents of public service delivery.

Reform is neither always consistent nor accepted (by ministers). A (former) Home Secretary announced substantial and radical reform to policing – reform which was unprecedented in modern times – the aim of which was a dual approach of fewer, larger and more strategic police forces to deal with serious and organised crime but balanced with more locally responsive policing at neighbourhood level. Successive Home Secretaries halted the programme and significant reform seems as far away as it ever was with a focus more on improved collaboration across forces and improved communication. Within the criminal justice system the merger of the Prison and Probation services created the National Offender Management Service, the overall aim of which is to provide seamless management of offenders (Goode and Brookes 2006).

All of these reform programmes share common characteristics; they potentially put meaning behind the government's modernisation agenda with its emphasis on locally delivered services and greater accessibility and responsiveness; greater accountability to and stronger engagement with local communities; the need to work in partnership across agencies (with statutory support such as the Crime and Disorder Act 1998 and the Health Act 1999 in which Section 31 provides for flexibilities of pooled budgets, lead commissioning and integrated provision) and greater flexibility and freedoms but within a national framework which provides standards and accountability mechanisms through Local Area Agreements.

A number of key leadership challenges are presented by this plethora of reform programmes for both the public sector organisations and the academic community. First and foremost is that the various reform programmes are being implemented 'in silos' and – to date – research is predominantly focused within similar disciplinary silos. Where research explores collaboration and/or network management, there is a similarly narrow focus predominantly on health and social care or community safety rather than wider arrangements. The challenge suggests that the issue of leadership is more important than management in encouraging the sharing of learning across non-traditional sector institutions and in an increasingly networked environment.

There is also a need for leaders to encourage a greater engagement in problem solving activity (as opposed to managers transacting public business) and in accepting that the context and components of problems will differ not only from sector to sector but also from issue to issue. Grint (2005d) focused on the distinction between tame, wicked and critical problems and suggested that both leaders and managers had different roles dependent on the type of problem, timescale and space. In assessing recent leadership within the Iraq military arena he argued also that differing contexts are a critical element of the decision-making apparatus but such accounts appear incapable of explaining the decisions of those engaged in decision-making who can often 'construct' the context for public consumption.

Network management

Networks are increasingly important to both governance (Stoker 2006) and leadership and management. Agranoff and McGuire (2003: 35–36) argue that network management offers an important class of collaborative management models. Their understanding is derived mainly from theoretically examining, rather than empirically cataloguing, its tasks. They noted how some colleagues identified how managers intervene in existing interrelationships, promote interactions, and mobilise coordination and thus work within networks.

There is thus a need to observe functional interdependencies but this chapter argues that leadership is the one factor that is often overlooked when examining the importance of network leadership. As Agranoff and McGuire (2003: 28) argue the importance of collaborative working is not new and the authors point to earlier work (Dahl and Lindblom 1953) when the authors demonstrated the 'multiplicity of interventions available to modern societies, many of which necessarily involve more than a single hierarchical organisation'.

Public value as the outcome of effective public leadership

Public value as a concept was first espoused by Mark Moore (1995) and later expanded on in a UK context by Talbot (2007) and Kelly *et al.* (2002). It requires the identification of social goals, delivering those goals in a way that secures trust and legitimacy and ensuring that the public sector organ-isation has the capability and the capacity to deliver these stated goals. A consensus achieved during the seminar series was that all public leaders need to engage in understanding, creating and demonstrating public value. In contrast, traditional public administration functions well in a stable environment with the key aim of delivering public goods. NPM works well in a competitive environment when the key aim represents that of choice. But NPL works better in a networked governance environment where the overall aim is the delivery of public value.

Developing a new public leadership framework

In discussing the development of a NPL framework we refer back to our six contentions at the beginning of this paper, the first three of which concerns the 'how' of public leadership and the last three concern the 'why'.

A form of collective leadership

If we are faced in the public sector with complex (Wicked) problems that require a collective response then we argue that public leadership should reflect a collective leadership style in which the responsibility for leaders is distributed throughout each organisation and shared across other organisations or institutions.

Whilst theories abound in relation to the individual nature of leader-ship traits, characteristics and contingencies in both traditional leader-ship theory (for example, Stogdill 1974) and more contemporary research such as Kotter (2003), Collins (2001) and Grint (2000, 2005a,b,c) there is limited literature on 'collective leadership', which is both horizontal (shared between organisations) and vertical (distributed throughout each organisation) although both these dimensions are recognised within the public policy process more generally (Hill 2005) and in relation to accountability (Considine 2002). Within the context of leadership both terms have been used, but not together (representing what the chapter describes as 'collective' leadership) and the terms are often used interchangeably. For example, in education, Bennett *et al.* (2003) refer to the concept of 'distributed' leadership and Doyle and Smith (2001) to 'shared' leadership but both authors are describing leadership *within* the education system. Even where the term 'collective leadership' applies, this relates to horizontal leadership across pluralistic organisations rather than incorporating the notion also of vertical leadership (Denis, Lamoth and Langley 2001). There is an opportunity to clearly delineate between the two terms with horizontal (shared) leadership extending *beyond* organisations and vertical (distributed) being *within* organisations. The former requires us to think about how we lead when we are not 'in charge'.

Context is critical

Our second contention acknowledges that the context of leadership is important. Within the public domain leadership relations could take place within four contexts. These are first, community leadership (ODPM 2004) which involves developing a vision for the locality, working in partnership to deliver that vision and guaranteeing quality services for all (Clarke and Stewart 1999), and its link to building social capital (Putnam 2000–05), second is political leadership (e.g. Hartley and Pinder 2001; Leach *et al.* 2005; Morrell and Hartley 2006) in addition to the third and fourth contexts namely organisational and individual leadership in linking vertical to horizontal leadership. These four suggested forms of public leadership have not previously been discussed in this way. Each is likely to have differing styles within them and reflect differing accountability and governance requirements.

The type and scale of the problem

Our third contention suggests that public leaders need to tackle uncertainty. There is a tendency for leaders to focus on 'known' problems and 'known' solutions and develop expertise in relation to critical incidents and thus crisis management. As important as these issues are, the reality of public service is that problems are often more complex and intractable and thus require a leadership approach that is both creative and adaptive to the circumstances and which deals comprehensively with the intractable nature of these types of problems. It is an approach that would encourage leaders to 'ask questions' rather than implement 'off-the-shelf' solutions and acknowledge that the answers may lie with many people and not just the favoured few.

Collaborative advantage

Our fourth contention suggests that leaders will engage collectively if there is 'mutual benefit' to each member and where the whole is considered to be greater than its parts. This is what Vangen and Huxham would describe as achieving collaborative advantage (2003: 66) and where they identify what they consider to represent enacting leadership; embracing, empowering, involving and mobilising.

Performance and public value

Our fifth contention argues that leaders should keep in touch with the 'big picture' without getting into minute technical detail and thus allow others to lead but within a context of shared and distributed accountability. This aligns also with the inextricable links identified by Ogbonna and Harris (2000) between leadership style, culture and performance. What is often neglected is a focus on assessing leadership performance as well as organisational performance and within the context of the organisational culture.

We prefer the use of the term 'climate' as opposed to 'culture'. Although the two terms are similar they are often confused (Denison 1990). The term 'climate' describes a collective consensus held about certain facts of organisational functioning that impacts leadership, rather than describing the much wider organisational culture. By including this within a public leadership challenge we believe that it would be helpful in 'giving space' for effective leadership to develop among many leaders rather than employ 'knee-jerk' reactions by the few and to ensure that leaders actions are monitored within the context of this climate in the same way as actual performance. The focus for public leaders should be on the achievement of long-term strategies and targets rather than the short-termism that has typified NPM over the last two decades. As subsequent chapters argue, the focus is predominantly upon the quantitative targets set by central government rather than the publicly valued outcomes represented by social goals.

Reflecting trust

Our sixth and final contention closely aligns the relative climates of public value and 'trust' (Sako 1998; Brookes 2007; Coleman 2007). We believe that both offer opportunities to assess the drivers for public leaders motivation in asking the 'why' question. Moore has argued that trust and legitimacy are important components of developing public value. Benington and Moore (2010: 13 forthcoming) argued that 'thinking about public value has since moved well beyond its origin in neo-liberal American discourse of the 1990s, and is now at the forefront of cross national discursion about the changing roles of the public private and voluntary section in a period of profound political, economic, ecological and social change'. If we are suggesting that the creation and demonstration of public value is the key outcome of effective public leadership then the development of trust and legitimacy by public leaders must therefore represent one of the key determinants of a new public leadership framework. The importance of trust in engaging with stakeholders cannot be underestimated. As Stoker argues, 'instilling value in the actual processes of political and social inter-action with citizens, users and stakeholders who act as authorisers of an organisations finances, objectives and performance targets is the route to shaping and legitimising service delivery and improving trust' (Stoker 2006).

The issue of trust that appears critical to the emergence of public leadership today appeared just as critical to success (or otherwise) of NPM over 20 years ago. As Hood (1995: 94) argued 'NPM involved a different conception of public accountability [he was comparing NPM with the traditional public administration that preceded it] with different patterns of trust and distrust.' It could be argued that one of NPM's main change elements actually defeated trust. As Hood continued (1995: 97) A move was made 'towards more explicit and measurable (or at least checkable) standards of performance for public sector organisations, in terms of the range, level and content of services to be provided, as against trust in professional standards and expertise across the public sector.' He further argued that the old public administration style involved 'low trust in politicians and managers but relatively high trust in professional expertise, both in a vertical (*or distributed*) sense and in a lateral (*shared across a range of agencies*) sense'. [Sections in italics are our emphases] leading to the erosion of self-management by professionals.

Trust *per se* is difficult to measure but its determinants could be identified and measured. One could argue that trust within complex networks would be similar to trust between a buyer and a seller thus contrasting the aim of achieving collaborative advantage (as espoused by Vangen and Huxham) with achieving competitive advantage in the private sector. There have been some interesting studies in relation to the latter. Currall and Judge (1995: 153) emphasised two points – reliance upon another (in giving over a particular – [*shared or distributed*] responsibility) and accepting risk (that the other person will deal with that responsibility in the way in which it was intended) thus achieving mutual advantage. Smeltzer (1997) examined the meaning and origin of trust in buyer-supplier relationships. In addition to acceptance of risk and handing responsibility to another, Smeltzer argued that the extent to which buyers and sellers determined levels of trust relies on the antecedents of trust as evidenced through trust enhancing behaviours which could form the basis of independent variables for trust and, conversely, trust eroding behaviours. Examples include consistency and follow-up, sharing ideas, listening, mutual respect and honesty. Trust eroding behaviours would be the opposite and a clear eroding behaviour would be one of dishonesty, lack of commitment or poor attitude or arrogance.

Our six contentions provide a useful background to a new public leadership framework and we turn now to our final section in which we set out an emerging definition of new public leadership alongside a comparison to our *'old'* friend *new* public management.

Defining new public leadership

To define NPL should mean that one must also be able to evaluate it. Two schools of thought can be considered. The first, social constructionism, some have argued, helps illuminate 'understandings of leadership that see it as shared or collective rather than inherent in one or more visible individuals' (Ospina and Folde 2005: 1). This fits well with the collective nature of public leadership. However, both earlier realists (Rusch, Gosetti and Mohoric 1991: 4) and later (Hartley and Tilley 2007) suggest that constructionism can obscure the reality of leadership and (to quote Rusch *et al.*) that there is a need to 'see with new (realist) eyes'. Both approaches can be given equal consideration.

Realistic evaluation does offer interesting possibilities as Tilley outlines in a subsequent chapter. It focuses on the relationship between context, mechanism (intervention) and outcome, and explores the connections between the three. It aims to produce more contingent and qualified findings – not 'does leadership work?' but 'what style of leadership works, for whom, in what circumstances, and why?' Rather than evaluate the specific outcome that leadership activities are intended to achieve it concentrates more on identifying and then testing out the theories in use by policy-makers and leaders (at different levels) which underlie those activities (Pawson and Tilley 1997) and in building cumulative findings (Bryman 2004).

A similar distinction can be made between NPM and NPL in examining the context, mechanisms and outcomes of 'management' and 'leadership'. Both terms are distinctive and complementary systems of action. 'Management' is about coping with complicated but essentially tame problems. That is, problems that can be removed from their context, solved, and returned without affecting the context. It is a response to the emergence of large and complicated organisations. Leadership, on the other hand is about coping with wicked problems involving complexity and change. That is, problems that cannot be treated as isolated elements of a mechanical organisation but as embedded aspects of a system which is changed if any attempt is made to remove that element. So, more change always demands more leadership (Kotter 1999).

In dealing with complicated tame problems a manager (or NPM) sets targets and goals, plans how to achieve these goals and allocates resources. A leader (or NPL), facing a complex and Wicked problem facilitates a collective vision and strategies to produce the changes needed to achieve the vision and give due regard to personal impact within a shared vision. Even though there is a considerable amount of overlap between leadership and management, they are different concepts. Management is more of a mechanical concept whereas leadership is not. This does not mean that leadership (NPL) can substitute management (NPM). The best results in a change process would result from a successful integration between the two but with NPL encompassing the needs of NPM. Another important point to stress is that good managers need not necessarily be good leaders and *vice versa*. There can be a separation of roles in this sense, as long as managers and leaders work together in order to achieve collective goals and objectives. This applies as much across the public sector as it does to individual leaders and managers within. The alignment of leadership and management thus holds promise in linking shared and distributed leadership but also allowing leaders to emerge from any point within the organisation. We return to this in the final chapter.

A final word on public leadership

This chapter has summarised the government's modernisation programme. It has suggested that this has been driven by the 20 year old NPM. We have argued that the need to lead within complex networks requires a new way of thinking about leadership in the public sector and we counsel a shift away from NPM and towards NPL. It is not the aim of this chapter to 'throw the baby out with the bathwater' but rather to build on these earlier discussions to embrace this increasing complexity through a natural evolution of public leadership skills.

References

Agranoff, R. and McGuire, M. (2003) *Collaborative Public Management*. Washington DC: Georgetown University Press.

Ansari, W., Phillips, C. and Hammick, M. (2001) 'Collaboration and Partnerships: Developing the Evidence Base', *Health and Social Care in the Community*, 9(4): 215–227, Blackwell Science Ltd.

Benington, J. and Moore, M. (2010 forthcoming) 'Public Volume in Changing Times', in Benington, J. and Moore, M. (eds) *Public Volume Theory and Practice*. Basingstoke: Palgrave Macmillan.

Bennett, N., Wise, C., Woods, P. and Harvey, J. (2003) *Distributed Leadership: Summary Report*, NCSL, Spring.

Brookes, S. (2006a) 'Local Authorities, Crime Reduction and the Law', in Moss, K. and Stephens, M. (eds) *Crime Reduction and the Law*. London: Routledge.

Brookes, S. (2007) 'Bridging the Gap between Theoretical and Practical Approaches to Leadership: Collective Leadership in Support of Networked Governance and the Creation Of Public Value', paper presented at the 6th International Studying Leadership Conference, Warwick 2007.

Bryman, A. (2004) 'Qualitative Research on Leadership: A Critical but Appreciative Review', *The Leadership Quarterly*, 15: 729–769.

Cabinet Office (2006) *Capability Reviews: The Findings of the First Four Reviews*. HMSO.

Charlesworth, K., Cook, P. and Crozier, G. (2005) *Leading Change in the Public Sector: Making the Difference*, Chartered Management Institute, June 2005.

Chesterton, D. (2002) *Local Authority? How to Develop Leadership for Better Public Services*. London: DEMOS.

Christensen, T. and Laegreid, P. (2007) 'NPM and Beyond – Leadership, Culture and Demography', paper presented to the Third Transatlantic Dialogue, 'Leading the Future of the Public Sector', University of Delaware, USA. May 31 to June 2.

Clarke, M. and Stewart, J. (1999) *Community Governance, Community Leadership and the New Local Government*. Joseph Rowntree Foundation.

Coleman, A (2007) 'The Importance of Trust in the Leadership of Inter-Agency Collaborations in Schools', paper presented at the 6th International Studying Leadership Conference, Warwick.

Collins, J. (2001) *Good to Great: Why Some Companies Make the Leap...and Others Don't*. New York: HarperCollins.

Conger, J.A. (1989) *The Charismatic Leader: Behind the Mystique of Exceptional Leadership*. San Francisco, CA: Jossey-Bass.

Conger, J.A. (2004) 'Developing Leadership Capability: What's Inside the Black Box?', *Academy of Management Executive*, 18(3): 136–139.

Considine, M. (2002) 'The End of the Line? Accountable Governance in the Age of Networks, Partnerships, and Joined-Up Services', *Governance: An International Journal of Policy, Administration, and Institutions*, 15(1), January.

Currall, S.C. and Judge, T.A. (1995) 'Measuring Trust between Organisational Boundary Role Persons', *Organisational Behaviour and Human Decision Processes*, 64(2), November, pp. 151–170.

DCLG (2006) *Strong and Prosperous Communities: The Local Government White Chapter*. Presented to Parliament, October.

Dahl, R. and Lindblom, C.E. (1953) *Politics, Economics and Welfare*. Chicago: University of Chicago Press.

Denis Jean-Louis, Lamoth, L. and Langley, L.A. (2001) 'The Dynamics of Collective Leadership and Strategic Change in Pluralistic Organizations', *Academy of Management Journal*, 44(4): 809–837.

Denison, D.R. (1990) *Corporate Culture and Organisational Effectiveness*. New York: John Wiley.

DOH (2004) *Choosing Health: Making Healthy Choices Easier*. November.

Doyle, M.E. and Smith, M.K. (2001) 'Shared Leadership', *The Encyclopedia of Informal Education*, http://www.infed.org/leadership/shared_leadership.htm, accessed 23 August 2005.

Dunleavy, P., Margetts, H., Bastow, S. and Tinkler, J. (2006) 'New Public Management is Dead – Long Live Digital-Era Governance', *Journal of Public Administration Research and Theory*, 16: 467–494.

Ferlie, E., Ashburner, L., Fitzgerald, L. and Pettigrew, A. (1996) *The New Public Management in Action*. Oxford: Oxford University Press.

Goode and Brookes (2006) 'Managing Offenders and Reducing Crime', in Moss, K. and Stephens, M. (eds) *Crime Reduction and the Law*. London: Routledge.

Grint, K. (2000) *The Arts of Leadership*. Oxford: Oxford University Press.

Grint, K. (2005a) 'Leadership: Limits and Possibilities', *Management, Work and Organisations*. Palgrave Macmillan.

Grint, K. (2005b) *Leadership Ltd: White Elephant to Wheelwright*. London, Ontario: Ivey Publishing Journal Online, January/February.

Grint, K. (2005c) 'Public Opinion: Keith Grint', *The Times Newschapter*, March 8th.

Grint, K. (2005d) 'Problems, Problems, Problems. The Social Construction of "Leadership"', *Human Relations*, 58(11): 1467.

Hartley, J. and Pindu, K. (2001) 'Coaching Political Leaders', in Passmore, J. (ed.) *Leadership Coaching*. London: Kogan Page.

Hartley, J. and Tilley, N. (2007) 'Evaluating Public Leadership', presentation at the 4th ESRC Seminar in the Series 'The Public Leadership Challenge' at the 6th International Studying Leadership Conference, Warwick Business School, December.

Hill, M. (2005) *The Public Policy Process*, 4th edition. Harlow: Pearson Education Limited.

Home Office (2004) *Building Communities, Beating Crime: A Better Police Service for the 21st Century*. November.

Home Office (2006) *National Policing Plan for 2006–2009*. HMSO.

Home Office (2008) *From the Neighbourhood to the National: Policing Our Communities Together*. Green Paper published July 2008.

HMSO (1999) *Modernising Government*. London: HMSO.

HMSO (2007) *Local Government and Public Involvement in Health Act*, 2007 Chapter 28.

Hood, C. (1995) 'The "New Public Management" in the 1980's: Variations on a Theme', *Accounting, Organisations and Society*, 20(2/3): 93–109.

Kelly, G., Mulgan, G. and Muers, S. (2002) *Creating Public Value: An Analytical Framework for Public Service Reform*. London: Cabinet Office, accessed March 2005 on www.strategy.gov.uk.

Kotter, J.P. (1999) *John P. Kotter on What Leaders Really Do*. Boston, MA: Harvard Business School Press.

Kotter, J.P. (2003) 'The Power of Feelings', *Leader to Leader*, 27 (Winter 2003): 25–31.

Leach, S., Hartley, J.F., Lowndes, V., Wilson, D. and Downe, J. (2005) *Local Political Leadership in the UK*. Joseph Rowntree Foundation.

Moore, M. (1995) *Creating Public Value: Strategic Management in Government*. Cambridge, MA: Harvard University Press.

Morell, K. and Hartley, J. (2006) 'A Model of Political Leadership', *Human Relations*, 59: 483–504.

ODPM (2004) *The Future of Local Government: A Ten Year Vision*. London: Office of the Deputy Prime Minister.

Ogbonna, E. and Harris, L.C. (2000) 'Leadership Style, Organisational Culture and Performance: Empirical Evidence from UK Companies', *International Journal of Human Resource Management*, 11(4): 766–788.

Ospina, S. and Folde, E. (2005) 'Towards a Framework of Social Change Leadership', paper presented at the Annual Meeting of the Public Management Research Association, September 2005, Los Angeles.

Pearce, C.L. and Conger, J.A. (2003) *Shared Leadership: Reframing the Hows and Whys of Leadership*. Thousand Oaks, CA: Sage Publications.

Pastor, J.C. (1998) *The Social Construction of Leadership: A Semantic and Social Network Analysis of Social Representations of Leadership*. Ann Arbor, MI: UMI.

Pawson, R. and Tilley, N. (1997) *Realistic Evaluation*. London: Sage Publications.

Pollitt, C. (1990) *The New Managerialism and the Public Services: The Anglo American Experience*. Oxford: Basil Blackwell.

Putnam, R. (2000) *Bowling Alone: The Collapse and Revival of American Community*. New York: Simon and Schuster.

Putnam, R. (2003) *Better Together*. New York: Simon and Schuster.

Putnam, R. (2005) *Social Capital: What Is It?*. Accessed 10-1-06.

Rusch, E.A., Gosetti, P.P. and Mohoric, M. (1991) 'The Social Construction of Leadership: Theory to Praxis', chapter presented at the 17th Annual Conference on Research on Women and Education, November 1991. San Jose, CA.

Sako, M. (1998) 'Does Trust Improve Business Performance?', in Lane, C. and Bachmann, R. (eds), *Trust Within and Between Organisations*. Oxford: Oxford University Press, pp. 88–117.

Smeltzer, L.R. (1997) 'The Meaning and Origin of Trust in Buyer-Supplier Relationships', *The Journal of Supply Chain Management*, 33(1): 40–48.

Stogdill, R. (1974) *Handbook of Leadership: A Survey of the Literature*. New York: The Free Press.

Stoker, G. (2006) 'Public Value Management: A New Narrative for Networked Governance?', *American Review of Public Administration*, 36(1). Sage Publications.

Talbot (2007) *Democracy*, 'Bureaucracy and the Domains of Public Value Leadership', *presentation at the 4th ESRC Seminar in the Series 'The Public Leadership Challenge' at the 6th International Studying Leadership Conference*. Warwick Business School, December.

Vangen, S. and Huxham, C. (2003) 'Enacting Leadership for Collaborative Advantage: Dilemmas of Ideology and Pragmatism in the Activities of Partnership Managers', *British Journal of Management*, 14: S61–S76.

Part I

Public Sector Reform and the Impact on Leadership

2
Central Government Reform and Leadership

Colin Talbot

> Leadership in the British Civil Service is really for Ministers, civil servants do not become leaders....
>
> > (senior civil servant quoted in Chapman 1984 page xv)
>
> It is the absolute nonentity of the British administrator that is his chief merit.
>
> > (Sisson 1959)

Introduction

The above representative quotation (Chapman), from a senior British civil servant, shows that until quite recently the dominant view amongst this group was 'we don't do leadership'. Indeed, as the now famous 'Next Steps' review was to reveal only four years later, most senior civil servants didn't even 'do' management, let alone leadership (Jenkins, Caines and Jackson 1988) – a problem that had been identified as early as the Fulton Review of 1968 (Fulton Committee 1968).

Even as late as 2002, a permanent secretary was willing to say (off the record) that 'those who can do policy, those that can't run agencies' (private communication) – thus implying that policy-making was far preferable to managing or leading organisations. This sentiment maintains the historic divide between 'policy' and 'operations', with the latter in a distinctly second rate position compared to the former, that has dogged British central government. And 'policy' in this context was supposed to be purely about advising ministers, in a supposedly disinterested, objective and neutral manner.

In this context 'leadership' in the British civil service has always been somewhat problematic – it exists, as historical accounts of the civil service clearly demonstrate (Hennessy 1990), but it was for many decades denied as even a possibility.

In recent years things appear to have changed. In the 'Departmental Capability Reviews' (DCRs) conducted by the Cabinet Office between 2006 and 2008 the issue of 'leadership' was one of three key areas that were assessed (the others being 'strategy' and 'delivery'). Over £10m was spent assessing departments' leadership and other capabilities and the results were published, demonstrating the seriousness with which leadership, and the other two areas of capability, were now apparently viewed.

This was a considerable turnaround. Clearly, senior civil servants were very much now expected to 'do' leadership and not to just leave it to Ministers. This chapter will critically assess why this change has occurred, what progress has been made (drawing on the civil services' own assessments in the DCRs), and what 'leadership' does and should mean in a civil service context. This includes some of the critical 'role' issues for leadership in all democratic public services – the roles of elected politicians and public (non-elected) servants; of public servants at different levels of government; of public servants in relation to the citizens; to name but a few.

The chapter will start by reporting the findings of the capability reviews on the issue of 'leadership', which make for fairly disappointing reading – at least on the criteria established by the civil service itself.

Next, an alternative model of 'good leadership' will be offered which is more comprehensive and more accurately reflects the diversity, and contradictory nature, of leadership roles that senior public servants have to perform.

We will then proceed to critically examine the criteria of 'good leadership' that the civil service explicitly and implicitly established in the DCRs and how these relate to historical institutional factors which shape the British civil service.

Departmental capability reviews: Leadership

Departmental Capability Reviews began life in 2005 as an attempt to make some rigorous, and semi-independent, assessment of the performance of government departments. They succeeded a previous attempt at 'peer review' within Whitehall that was widely seen to have been weak and ineffective. They also ran in parallel to several other, highly relevant, initiatives.

The first of these were the 'Public Service Agreements' (PSAs), which set measureable targets for each Whitehall department at each 'spending review', starting in 1998 and then repeated, with revised PSAs, in 2000, 2002 and 2004 at the time DCRs commenced (a further spending review and revised set of PSAs was published in 2007). PSAs were supposed to focus not on departmental capability but on outcomes achieved, although in practice they were slightly more variable and included elements of internal processes, outputs and outcomes, although the focus gradually shifted to the latter in successive iterations (Comptroller and Auditor General 2001, 2005, 2006).

The second major initiative was the so-called 'Gershon' efficiency drive which was launched in 2005 and planned to save £21bn from public spending (Gershon 2004). Each government department demanded savings targets fixed by the Gershon programme.

A third initiative was the Prime Ministers' Delivery Unit, which was launched in 2001 in order to ensure that public services which were receiving substantial extra funding following the 1998 and subsequent 'spending reviews' actually 'delivered' (Barber 2007).

The reason for mentioning these other initiatives is to put DCRs into context: DCRs focus was entirely on, as the name suggests, capability. They did not address actual performance, in terms of efficiency, outputs or outcomes, or 'delivery', all of which were the subject of separate initiatives.

Capability reviews were based upon a model of capability developed by the Cabinet Office which looked at three key areas: leadership; strategy; and delivery. Each of these were in turn divided into several categories, which were further revised in the light of the reviews (HMSO 2009). In the case of 'leadership' the original categories were:

L1   Set direction
L2   Ignite passion, pace and drive
L3   Take responsibility for leading delivery and change
L4   Build capability

The revised model collapsed these further into three leadership categories which are illustrated in Figure 2.1.

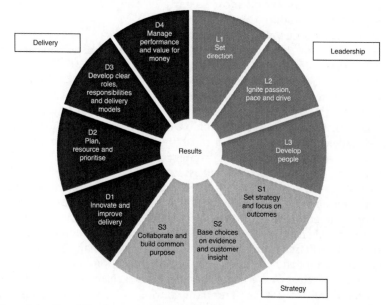

Figure 2.1   Capability Reviews: Revised Model
Source: HMSO 'Capability Reviews: Refreshing the Model of Capability', July 2009.

Each category was in turn sub-divided into a number of questions and criteria, which need not concern us at this stage. On the ten categories five possible assessments could be made:

- strong
- well placed
- development area
- urgent development area
- serious concerns

Actual capability reviews were carried out by teams appointed by the Cabinet Office, but including 'outsiders' – only 40% of review team members came from within central government, 33% from the private sector and consultancies, and 16% from local government (Comptroller and Auditor General 2009).

The first tranche of DCRs were published in July 2006 and came as something of a shock to many commentators (including the present author – see Talbot 2007) and to the civil service itself. The last tranche, bringing the total to 17 departments, was published in December 2007, with an additional review of the new Department of Justice in April 2008.

The present author took the step of applying a numerical scoring system (1–5) to the results of this first tranche (Talbot 2006), which has since been repeated (modified to 0 to 4) to rest of the DCR results by the *Financial Times* (Timmins 2007) and most recently by the National Audit Office (Comptroller and Auditor General 2009).

Using the Timmins/NAO scoring system, where '4' equates to 'strong' through to '0' for 'serious concerns', the 18 government departments covered present a pretty poor picture on 'leadership'.

The average 'score' is a '2' on leadership. This represents a 'development area' score and only half the available points. The leadership scores range from the best at 3.3 points (Department for International Development) through to the worst at 1.3 (both Home Office and Department for Health). Whilst leadership is bad, the other capability areas do not fare much differently with average scores of 2.4 for strategy and 1.9 for delivery.

This then is the civil services' own assessment of its leadership capability based on criteria it developed, applied through an assessment system it designed and by people it appointed. It is on average an area in need of 'development' and in five ministries of 'urgent development'.

Putting numbers onto the DCR outputs and creating 'league tables' can of course be criticised on many grounds, but no more than the same sorts of procedures applied by Whitehall to health, education, police and many other public services over the past decade. From a scientific point of view such procedures are just as potentially flawed and apt to be misleading wherever they are deployed, but of course they have the same strengths as well. However crude and potentially flawed, they do at least provide grounds for asking some questions about both the overall picture and relationships between the various actors. On leadership, despite the shift in Whitehall to seeing it as important and considerable resources having been deployed over the past decade and a half (at least), the picture is clearly less than positive.

The qualitative comments contained in the DCRs reinforce the message. There is no space here to repeat all the qualitative conclusions from all the DCRs, of which there are many, but the theme of leadership predominates much of the comment. Most startlingly, a survey of the 'senior civil service' (SCS) found that only about a quarter felt that departmental boards 'modelled a culture of effective teamwork' and only about a third thought they were 'good at managing change'. There is an even more serious aspect to the poor DCR scores however. It is reasonable to assume that the 'capability reviews' are supposed to diagnose not just capability, but to also point to future likely performance. Poor capability ought to lead to poor performance, and *vice versa*. Unfortunately the evidence does not support this.

The National Audit Office (Comptroller and Auditor General 2009), in its review of the capability review process, carried out a correlation between the scores in DCRs for 'delivery capability' and actual delivery as assessed by Public Service Agreements (PSAs). The result was that there appears to be virtually no correlation between them.

Table 2.1   Capability Review – PSA Correlations

Capability Review	Correlation with Actual Performance (PSA scores)
Delivery	–0.02
Strategy	–0.13
Leadership	–0.44
All	–0.35

Source: NAO and own calculations

These calculations have been extended (using figures supplied by the NAO) to include the 'strategy' and 'leadership' elements of the Capability Reviews, as well as overall DCR scores, correlated with PSA scores. This shows that 'leadership' scores correlated most negatively with actual performance, raising serious questions about the assessment of leadership, or the measurement of performance, or both. However, the setting of PSA targets was essentially a political process and represents, according to official accounts, the most important priorities for ministries. This does not mean the means of measuring their achievement might not be flawed – this is possible. Rather more likely though is that it does suggest that how the capability reviews assessed, or gave weight to, 'leadership' is more likely to be in error – in the sense that they did not assess what leadership capability was needed to achieve democratically set goals (as codified in PSAs) for ministries. This raises the issue of what a normative 'model' of performance for civil service leaders ought to look like, to which we now turn.

Towards a model of public leadership

The DCRs assessed leadership in the civil service against their own standards – but are they the right ones? In this section we will seek to offer an alternative model of leadership against which to compare both standards and achievements of the civil service in the leadership field.

The model proposed is in the form of a hypothesis, or normative theory, or conjecture, about the nature of leadership in the public domain. It is unproven, but should at least have, it is hoped, some 'face validity' and be rooted in what we do know about leadership in this area.

First, some limitations have to be placed on what this framework relates to. It is about non-elected public officials, not elected politicians. This distinction may seem an easy one to make but the boundaries between elected politicians, directly elected to executive office (presidents, mayors) or to legislatures which in turn appoint political executives

- elected 'non-political' executives (e.g. elected judges or sheriffs in the USA)
- politically appointed executives (e.g. again in the USA or 'special advisers' in the UK)
- non-politically appointed and non-elected public officials are not always easy to draw.

Only the last of these categories is unambiguously seen as a neutral public official and therefore the subject of the ideas advanced here. The two middle categories are somewhat more 'fuzzy' and may be at least partially covered by the leadership framework being suggested. Only the first category is definitely excluded because it is unambiguously about elected, political, executives.

Second, this framework is also therefore clearly about democracies. It makes no pretence to be applicable in non-democratic contexts, although some of the ideas may be transferable.

Third, the boundaries of the public domain are also notoriously hard to define (Bozeman 1987). The leadership framework suggested applies to what is commonly accepted as the 'core executive' of governments (Weller, Bakvis and Rhodes 1997) and it may apply less strongly the further one moves from the unambiguously 'public' into the farther reaches of multi-level governance, quangos, networks and quasi-public bodies.

Fourth, the framework suggested is meant as an analytical heuristic, not a definitive model. It does not claim to depict any specific 'actually existing' set of leadership roles but to serve as an analytical tool to unpack actual leadership practices.

The assumptions around which the framework is developed can be summarised as:

- the public domain is characterised by a great deal of goal and role ambiguity, which also applies to leadership roles
- this ambiguity often takes the form of actual contradictions and paradoxes in leadership roles – i.e. expecting public leaders to simultaneously perform mutually or contradictory exclusive leadership functions
- these functions relate strongly to the institutional structures of modern democracies and public agencies within them
- although the construct space of 'public leadership' is apparently infinitely variable – in a parallel way to that of the 'organisational effectiveness' construct which is also very variable – (Cameron and Whetten 1983) – in practice a limited set of (contradictory) roles can capture most of what 'leadership' in the public domain is really about.

The framework proposed has five elements – four leadership roles, strongly influenced by institutional and organisational contexts, and a fifth 'meta' role which is about balancing between the other four. The first four roles are:

- Counsellor
- Chief Executive
- Collaborator
- Conservator

We will examine each, briefly, in turn.

The counsellor

The role of Whitehall mandarins that is most familiar to the public, via the TV series 'Yes, Minister' and 'Yes, Prime Minister', is that of advisor and counsellor to elected politicians. In the TV series the urbane and wily Sir Humphrey Appleby was first the Permanent Secretary and then Cabinet Secretary to the hapless Jim Hacker MP, as first Minister and then Prime Minister. Whilst this was a highly amusing TV show it contained a very serious issue – what is the proper role of non-elected permanent civil servants in advising and 'guiding' elected politicians? How far can they seek to steer and how far merely advise?

In traditional Wilsonian public administration theory – often espoused if not practised by the British civil service – the role of the public administrator was mainly that of passive executor of the will of elected politicians (Wilson 1955[1887]). The quotation at the start of this chapter: 'leadership in the British Civil Service is really for Ministers, civil servants do not become leaders...' is very much in this tradition.

As 'Yes, Minister' humorously illustrated, the real role of the senior civil servant is far more active in advising and trying to steer ministers than the formal position would suggest. This has to be distinguished from the idea – which also has strong antecedents in public administration theory and research – that bureaucrats can/may act autonomously from, and even counter to, the wishes of elected politicians. The 'counsellor' role is not about bureaucratic *autonomy* (Carpenter 2001) but about bureaucratic *influence*, a far more subtle and, by its very nature, usually hidden process (at least in the British system).

The most recent discussion of this active but influencing, rather than autonomous, role for senior bureaucrats to influence British thinking has been the ideas of 'public value' promoted in the work of US-academic Mark Moore (1995) and taken up by the government's Strategy Unit (Kelly and Muers 2002; Kelly, Mulgan and Muers 2004).

Whilst most attention has been focused on the notion of 'public value' itself, Moore's work also promotes a view of public leadership that involves active attempts at influencing political decision-making. Indeed, it is this aspect of 'public value' that has come in for the most vociferous criticism from some academics and commentators who accuse Moore and his supporters of promoting some sort of Platonic elite that usurps democratic accountability (Rhodes and Wanna 2007).

Moore of course comes from a constitutional tradition (the USA) where public managers are accountable to more than one 'principal' – i.e. in the case of federal bureaucrats both the Presidency and the Congress. This dual accountability also involves a much greater degree of transparency and often more latitude for public officials to openly espouse particular policy options – although even here a bureaucratic leader who openly and persistently opposed both, or either, the Presidency and Congress would be likely to get into trouble. And unlike the UK, both President and the Congress can effectively dismiss public leaders.

The constitutional position in the UK is very different: in the famous words of Lord Armstrong the civil service has 'no constitutional personality separate and apart from that of the government of the day'. There is no dual accountability – although civil servants may be scrutinised by Parliament they are not accountable to and cannot be dismissed by it. Nor are their appointments (except in a very few cases more recently) approved by Parliament, as the US Congress approves many federal appointments.

The chief executive

The 'chief executive' role is primarily concerned with the actual running of ministries. Even where ministries are very small – as in 19th century Britain or modern Sweden – someone still has to run them. In modern Britain ministries are neither small – they employ ten of thousands – nor purely dedicated to policy-making – some manage large operations like revenue collection, prisons and employment services.

Since at least the Fulton Committee of 1968 'management' of ministries and services has been identified as major problem (Fulton Committee 1968; Keeling 1972). Probably the most extensive recent diagnosis was provided by the 'Next Steps' review of 1988, which launched the programme to create 'executive agencies'.

'Next Steps' followed from several attempts by the Thatcher government between 1979 and 1986 to improve management in the civil service. The report emerged from a review of these initiatives – such as the Efficiency Scrutinies and Financial Management Initiative – that had been less than successful (Jenkins, Caines and Jackson 1988; Hennessy 1990; Jenkins 2008). The key problem the report identified was the propensity of senior civil servants to spend their time looking 'upwards' towards ministers and policy issues (in our terms the Counsellor role) and very little time on the management of their ministries and services. It's prescription was for radical structural change – creating semi-separate, semi-autonomous 'agencies' that would have separate managements from the ministries, dedicated to implementation and running services. This became the 'Next Steps' programme (the reports title had been 'Improving Management in Government: The Next Steps') of Agency creation which between 1988 and 1996 created around 140 new bodies within the civil service, each with its own Chief Executive (Talbot 2004).

This policy is what I have elsewhere called the 'apartheid solution' – separate but (supposedly) equal management roles for policy-making and operational services – separating the roles of 'Counsellor' and 'Chief Executive'. This has been consolidated in the more recent 'Professional Skills for Government' (PSG) programme which includes separate streams for 'policy-making' and 'operational management'.

In practice it is of course impossible to completely separate these roles. Ministries still 'own' agencies (or quangos or public corporations) and have to play a role in setting policy and strategy and monitoring the 'performance contract' which often goes with such reforms. Conversely, managers of 'agencies' often have a detailed knowledge of implementation that is vital for successful policy-making (for extensive discussion of these issues see Pollitt and Talbot 2004; Pollitt, Talbot, Caulfield and Smullen 2004).

The 'Chief Executive' role is thus usually an inescapable one for senior civil servants – in some cases it may be more strategic and less operational but it can hardly ever be entirely free of some operational leadership alongside more strategic leadership responsibilities. In the British civil service tradition it is one that has been often neglected – both strategically and operationally.

The collaborator

A great deal has been written in recent years about various forms of collaborative leadership: including lateral, networked, and catalytic leadership just to name a few and this can be aligned to the discussion in Chapter 1 on shared and distributed leadership. These concepts have been applied to both the private and public sectors, and especially linked to various forms of networked production and innovation (Chrislip and Larson 1994; Luke 1998; Fisher and Sharp 2004; Bryson 2005; Blomgren Bingham and O'Leary 2008). Most recently in British central government these ideas have been linked to notions of 'joined-up government' (Performance and Innovation Unit 2000).

The issue of coordination, collaboration or 'joined-up' government has been a perennial subject in public administration. It is endemic to government because all state's divide and distribute responsibilities along some lines and then face the problem of how to coordinate the resulting plethora of ministries, departments, agencies and quangos – often also across multiple tiers of government.

Whitehall has traditionally exhibited two forms of leadership – one partly collaborative and one very hierarchical. The former relates to relations within the 'Whitehall Village' where there has long existed a somewhat paradoxical competitive and collaborative culture (Heclo and Wildavsky 1981). This centres on the role of the Treasury and the simultaneous competition and collaboration between it and spending ministries and also between the latter (Thain and Wright 1996). It is exaggerated in the British system because of the frequent moves of senior civil service between ministries, including the Treasury. One day a senior civil servant may be 'bowling' for a spending ministry and the next 'batting' for the Treasury (and this helps to explain the prevalence of cricketing metaphors in discourse within Whitehall).

The hierarchical aspect of Whitehall leadership has mainly related to the rest of the UK public services. Only about one in ten public servants in Britain are civil servants – 90% work in local government, health, policing, education and other services. Although we have local government (and more recently devolved administrations) the UK has always had a notoriously centralised system of government and control of public services (Clarke and Newman 1997; Stoker 2004). This has meant that senior civil servants have had an often far from collaborative attitude to other layers and tiers of government and services. This has been compounded by the almost total absence of people with experience of these other levels within the senior civil service, which has traditionally recruited and trained its future leaders 'in-house'.

Collaborative leadership has thus, until very recently, been constrained almost entirely to relationships within the senior civil service and even then has been of a somewhat ambiguous character. Recent policy initiatives in the past decade towards more 'joined-up' government both within Whitehall and across tiers of government and services (Performance and Innovation Unit 1999, 2000) may have started to break-down some of this lack of collaborative leadership. The existence of much more independent devolved administrations in Scotland, Wales and Northern Ireland may also force greater collaborative leadership upon Whitehall, but it is probably too early to tell to what degree this is happening.

The conservator

The word 'conservator' is borrowed by an interesting book by the late US academic Larry Terry (2002). Terry quotes another US academic saying that 'we do not really want administrative leadership: we want political leadership which requires a strong administrative underpinning' (Price 1962). Terry argues that this approach (which is very similar to the quotation at the head of this chapter) is highly ambivalent and in practice neglects an important aspect of a public administrator's role – that of what he calls the 'Conservator'. In British terms, this is the ability to say 'no, minister'. That is, administrators have an 'active and legitimate leadership role in governance... because they are entrusted with the responsibility of preserving the integrity of public bureaucracies....' (Terry 2002).

This relates to what political scientists have called 'losers' consent' (Anderson, Blais, Bowler, Donovan and Listhaug 2005) – that is the agreement of the losers' in democratic elections to accept the results. This idea can be extended to the consent not merely to accept the outcome of elections themselves but also the consequences of that – the laws, taxes and other policies that emanate from a government that the losers did not vote for. In order to maintain consent public bureaucracies have to have both a politically responsive (democratic) element and a 'universal' aspect.

In Britain the role of senior civil servants in this regard is substantial but often obscured – to such an extent that it forms part of what one constitutional historian has called the 'hidden wiring' of the British state (Hennessy 1995). The most obvious form this has taken recently has been the duty placed upon the head of the civil service to report to the Prime Minister on possible breaches of the 'Ministerial Code' of conduct. This places a civil servant in the position of making judgements on the actions of elected politicians that could potentially lead to the dismissal of the latter.

The term 'conservator' may be too negative – it suggests protecting and defending constitutional, legal and procedural propriety against the sometimes over-zealous aspirations of politicians. In recent years we have also seen a more active aspect to this role – that of creating and sustaining consensus around certain policies and strategies. The most obvious examples here have been at local rather than national level, where local government chief officers have played a key role in creating a 'vision' for their areas.

Role conflicts

This very brief tour of the four roles immediately raises a question – are these four roles not at least potentially in conflict with one another? Does the role of 'Counsellor' (yes, minister) not sometimes conflict with that of 'Conservator' (no, minister) for example? We have already briefly noted the tension between the 'Counsellor' and 'Chief Executive' roles. There are then tensions embodied in these normative roles. Successful leadership in this context would be a question of achieving some balance between the conflicting demands of these roles. This is an approach that has been extensively explored in the 'competing values' literature which, whilst not using these same four categories of leadership does explore how four conflicting roles can be managed (e.g. Cameron, Quinn, DeGraff and Thakor 2006; Quinn, Faerman, Thompson, McGrath and St. Clair 2007).

What is evident is that these four leadership roles are not given equal weight within the British civil service tradition. The role of 'Counsellor' dominates strongly, with a somewhat subterranean 'Conservator' role. The 'Chief executive' and 'Collaborator' roles are the ones which seem to have posed, and probably continue to pose, the biggest problems for senior civil servants. It is not at all clear that current policies and initiatives really address these problems. Senior civil servants may well 'do leadership' – but how well is doubtful.

References

Anderson, C., Blais, A. *et al.* (2005) *Losers' Consent: Elections and Democratic Legitimacy*. Oxford: Oxford University Press.

Barber, M. (2007) *Instruction to Deliver*. London: Politicos.

Blomgren Bingham, L. and O'Leary, R. (eds) (2008) *Big Ideas in Collaborative Public Management*. M.E. Sharpe.

Bozeman, B. (1987) *All Organizations are Public: Bridging Public and Private Organizational Theories*. Jossey-Bass.

Bryson, J.M. (2005) *Leadership for the Common Good (2/e)*. Pfeiffer Wiley.

Cameron, K., Quinn, R.E. *et al.* (2006) *Competing Values Leadership*. Cheltenham: Edward Elgar.

Cameron, K. and Whetten, D. (1983) 'Organizational Effectiveness: One Model or Several?', in Cameron, K. and Whetten, D., *Organizational Effectiveness – A Comparison of Multiple Models*. San Diego: Academic Press.

Carpenter, D. (2001) *The Forging of Bureaucratic Autonomy – Reputations, Networks and Policy Innovation in Executive Agencies 1862–1928*. Princeton: Princeton University Press.

Chapman, R.A. (1984) *Leadership in the British Civil Service*. London and Sydney: Croom Helm.

Chrislip, D.D. and Larson, C.E. (1994) *Collaborative Leadership – How Citizens and Civic Leaders Can Make a Difference*. San Francisco: Jossey-Bass Publishers.

Clarke, J. and Newman, J. (1997) *The Managerial State – Power, Politics and Ideology in the Remaking of Social Welfare.* London: Sage Publications.

Comptroller and Auditor General (2001) *Measuring the Performance of Government Departments.* London: National Audit Office.

Comptroller and Auditor General (2005) *Public Service Agreements: Managing Data Quality – Compendium Report* (HC 476). London: National Audit Office.

Comptroller and Auditor General (2006) *Second Validation Compendium Report – 2003–06 PSA Data Systems (HC 985).* London: National Audit Office.

Comptroller and Auditor General (2009) *Assessment of the Capability Review Programme.* London: National Audit Office.

Fisher, R. and Sharp, A. (2004) *Lateral Leadership (2/e).* London: Profile Books Ltd.

Fulton Committee (1968) *Committee on the Civil Service – Report.* London: HMSO.

Gershon, P. (2004) *Releasing Resources for the Frontline: Independent Review of Public Sector Efficiency (Gershon Review).* London: HM Treasury.

Heclo, H. and Wildavsky, A. (1981) *The Private Government of Public Money (2/e).* Macmillan.

Hennessy, P. (1990) *Whitehall.* London: Fontana.

Hennessy, P. (1995) *The Hidden Wiring – Unearthing the British Constitution.* London: Victor Gollancz.

HMSO (2009) *Capability Reviews: Refreshing the Model of Capability.* Published July.

Jenkins, K. (2008) *Politicians and Public Services – Implementing Change in a Clash of Cultures.* Cheltenham: Edward Elgar.

Jenkins, K., Caines, K. *et al.* (1988) *Improving Management in Government: The Next Steps.* London: HMSO.

Keeling, D. (1972) *Management in Government.* George Allen & Unwin.

Kelly, G. and Muers, S. (2002) *Creating Public Value – An Analytical Framework for Public Service Reform.* London: Cabinet Office Strategy Unit (www.strategy.gov.uk).

Kelly, G., Mulgan, G. *et al.* (2004) *Creating Public Value – An Analytical Framework for Public Service Reform.* London: Cabinet Office Strategy Unit (www.strategy.gov.uk).

Luke, J.S. (1998) *Catalytic Leadership – Strategies for an Interconnected World.* San Francisco: Jossey-Bass.

Moore, M. (1995) *Creating Public Value.* Cambridge, Mass.: Harvard University Press.

Performance and Innovation Unit (1999) *Reaching Out: The Role of Central Government at Regional and Local Level.* London: Cabinet Office.

Performance and Innovation Unit (2000) *Wiring It Up – Whitehall's Management of Cross-Cutting Policies and Services.* London: Cabinet Office.

Pollitt, C. and Talbot, C. (eds) (2004) *Unbundled Government: A Critical Analysis of the Global Trend to Agencies, Quangos and Contractualisation.* London: Routledge.

Pollitt, C., Talbot, C. *et al.* (2004) *Agencies – How Government's Do Things Through Semi-Autonomous Organisations.* Palgrave.

Price, D. (1962) 'Administrative Leadership', in Graubard, S. and Holton, G., *Excellence and Leadership in a Democracy.* New York: Columbia University Press.

Quinn, R.E., Faerman, S.R. *et al.* (2007) *Becoming a Master Manager – A Competency Framework (4/e).* New York: Wiley.

Rhodes, R. and Wanna, J. (2007) 'The Limits of Public Value, or Rescuing Responsible Government from the Platonic Guardians', *Australian Journal of Public Administration*, 66(4): 406–421.

Sisson, C.H. (1959) *The Spirit of British Administration.* London: Faber and Faber Ltd.

Stoker, G. (2004) *Transforming Local Governance – From Thatcherism to New Labour.* Basingstoke: Palgrave Macmillan.

Talbot, C. (2004) 'Executive Agencies: Have They Improved Management in Government?', *Public Money & Management*, 24(2): 104–112.

Talbot, C. (2006) 'Who's the Weakest Link Now?', *Public Finance*. London: CIPFA.

Talbot, C. (2007) 'Talbot: Oral and Written Evidence', *Skills for Government – Ninth Report of Session 2006–07 Volume II Oral and Written Evidence*. P.A.S. Committee. London: House of Commons.

Terry, L.D. (2002) *Leadership of Public Bureaucracies: The Administrator as Conservator (2/e)*. M.E. Sharpe.

Thain, C. and Wright, M. (1996) *The Treasury and Whitehall – The Planning and Control of Public Expenditure, 1976–1993*. Oxford: Clarendon Press.

Timmins, N. (2007) 'Whitehall Performance has a Long Way to Go', *Financial Times*. London.

Weller, P., Bakvis, H. *et al.* (eds) (1997) *The Hollow Crown – Countervailling Trends in Core Executives*. Macmillan.

Wilson, W. (1955[1887]) 'The Study of Public Administration' [originally published in *Political Science Quarterly*, June 1887]. Washington: Public Affairs Press – Annals of American Government.

3

Healthcare Reform and Leadership

Kieran Walshe and Naomi Chambers

Introduction

The British National Health Service (NHS) employs over 1.3 million people, and spends about £90 billion a year. Services are delivered through about 300 NHS organisations and 5,200 GP practices. The NHS sees about 1.5 million patients every day. It is a huge enterprise, which dwarfs most other areas of the public sector in scale and complexity, touches the lives of almost every citizen directly or indirectly, and operates under intense public, media and political scrutiny. In any terms, it presents a unique leadership challenge.

For many of the problems and ills of the National Health Service, a common prescription, especially in recent years, has been more – or better – leadership. Indeed, in the last decade a number of Department of Health policy papers have made much of the need for improved leadership, and have proposed a range of reforms or initiatives intended to tackle that perceived leadership deficit, as Table 3.1 outlines below (Department of Health 1998, 2000, 2001a, 2008). The rationale for many of the repeated reorganisations of the NHS in recent years such as the demise of health authorities in 2002 or the more recent mergers of over 300 PCTs into around 150 has been the alleged failures of or limited capacity for leadership of those organisations. In a series of capability reviews of central government departments undertaken by the Cabinet Office in 2006, the Department of Health's leadership and strategic direction were rated as causing serious concerns (the lowest rating available) or as an urgent area for development (Cabinet Office 2007).

There is good reason to question the quality of NHS leadership, not least because it has been so often found wanting in a succession of public and other inquiries into failures or scandals in care in NHS organisations. Table 3.2 provides a limited selection of examples of such failures where NHS leadership has been criticised, though regrettably it would not be difficult to offer a much longer list of such cases. Some common themes

Table 3.1 Leadership: Policy Problems and Solutions

Policy report	Leadership challenges	Proposed initiatives
The NHS plan: a plan for investment, a plan for reform (2001)	'We need clinical and managerial leaders throughout the health service. The best NHS leaders are outstanding. There are simply too few of them. NHS organisations should be led by the brightest and the best of public sector management. Leadership development in the NHS has always been ad hoc and incoherent with too few clinicians in leadership roles and too little opportunity for board members to develop leadership skills.'	'Delivering the Plan's radical change programme will require first class leaders at all levels of the NHS. A new Leadership Centre will be set up to develop a new generation of managerial and clinical leaders'. 'We will provide management support and training for clinical and medical directors to better equip them for their leadership tasks.'
Shifting the balance of power: securing delivery (2001)	'This challenge cannot be met from Whitehall. The improvements to services can only be delivered by frontline staff working with patients and the public – reform must come from within the NHS. The reforms will be achieved through decentralisation and empowerment.' 'We need to change the way we work at all levels. Structural changes to devolve power and responsibility to frontline organisations, and to PCTs led by clinicians and local people in particular. And changes to the culture and working practices within organisations to devolve decisions to frontline staff and encourage the development of clinical networks across organisations.'	'Strategic Health Authorities will provide strategic leadership to ensure the delivery of improvements in health and health services locally by PCTs and NHS Trusts'. 'Strategic Health Authorities will create capacity through the development of the workforce including managerial and clinical leadership.' 'Publication of a set of leadership competencies including an inclusive and involving style and include staff involvement in management development programmes'.

Table 3.1 Leadership: Policy Problems and Solutions – *continued*

Policy report	Leadership challenges	Proposed initiatives
Next Stage Review of the NHS (2008)	Clinicians are expected to offer leadership and, where they have appropriate skills, take senior leadership and management posts in research, education and service delivery. Formal leadership positions will be at a variety of levels from the clinical team, to service lines, to departments, to organisations and ultimately the whole NHS. It requires a new obligation to step up, work with other leaders, both clinical and managerial, and change the system where it would benefit patients.	'There will be investment in new programmes of clinical and board leadership, with clinicians encouraged to be practitioners, partners and leaders in the NHS.'
		'We will explore ways to ensure that the undergraduate curricula for all medical and nursing students reflect the skills and demands of leadership and working in the NHS.'
		'We will introduce a new standard in healthcare leadership, the Leadership for Quality Certificate.'
		'We will establish an NHS Leadership Council which will be a system-wide body chaired by the NHS Chief Executive, responsible for overseeing all matters of leadership across healthcare.'
		'At the most senior levels, we will identify and support the top 250 leaders in the NHS. This group will include both clinical and non-clinical leaders. They will get close support in their personal development, mentoring, and active career management.'

Table 3.2 Failures in Care, and the Findings of Subsequent Inquiries

	Key failings or problems
Bristol Royal Infirmary inquiry into poor quality paediatric cardiac surgery (2001)	'It is an account of people who cared greatly about human suffering, and were dedicated and well-motivated. Sadly, some lacked insight and their behaviour was flawed. Many failed to communicate with each other, and to work together effectively for the interests of their patients. There was a lack of leadership, and of teamwork.'
	'The highest priority still needs to be given to improving the leadership and management of the NHS at every level. Trust boards must be able to lead healthcare at the local level. Executive directors should be selected on agreed criteria and appropriately trained. Non-executives should play an active role in the affairs of the trust.'
Kerr/Haslam inquiry into the sexual abuse of female mental health patients (2005)	'It is a story of management failure, failed communication, poor record keeping and a culture where the consultant was all powerful. There was a lamentable lack of communication and leadership at regional and district levels – there was nobody in control, or prepared to take control, so that an investigation could be carried out.'
Maidstone and Tunbridge Wells NHS Trust inquiry into failures in infection control (2007)	'Many, including senior managers past and present, were critical of the chief executive's style which some described as 'autocratic' or 'dictatorial.' The style of management and leadership was said by many staff to be reactive. Clinical directors failed to attend the governance and risk committee, which provided little leadership to, or monitoring of, the directorates. The quality of nursing in terms of attitudes and leadership skills was a major contributor to poor care'.
Mid-Staffordshire Hospitals NHS Trust inquiry into poor clinical care in the accident and emergency department (2009)	'There were significant failings in the provision of emergency healthcare and in the leadership and management of the trust. There was a longstanding lack of medical and general leadership. Leadership of nurses was poor. Senior nursing staff, consultants, therapists and managers described the leadership of the wards on floor two as being weak. The leadership operated a closed culture. The trust's board clearly preferred to conduct much of its business in private.'

emerge across these inquiries (Department of Health 2001c, 2005; Healthcare Commission 2007, 2009). They usually find that the clinical failures have organisational origins or causes, which are often centred on failures of leadership. They find dysfunctional 'club' cultures in which unacceptably poor quality care is tolerated or ignored, problems are hidden rather than tackled, people who raise concerns are marginalised or ignored, senior clinicians abrogate their responsibilities to lead their clinical teams properly, chief executives are fatally distracted from their responsibilities by external targets or grandiose plans, and NHS boards exercise inadequate oversight and control of their organisations.

However, while the problematic – and often unsatisfactory – nature of NHS leadership may be well established, it is far from clear that the repeated policy initiatives some of which were summarised in Table 3.1 have had much positive effect or impact. Indeed, it could be argued that repeated reorganisation and restructuring has weakened NHS leadership capacity and capability, rather than strengthened it. In recent years the term leadership has come to be used so promiscuously and unthinkingly that it could be argued that it has rather lost its meaning – both for the policy-makers and politicians who create and shape the statutory framework and policy priorities which set the context for the NHS, and for the NHS management and leadership community, those people who work in NHS trusts, primary care trusts (PCTs), strategic health authorities and other healthcare bodies and whose job it is to manage and lead.

This chapter first sets out a brief chronological account of the development of leadership arrangements in the NHS, outlining the formal structures and management arrangements and exploring the informal, less tangible but equally important dimensions of those arrangements, such as the political and cultural context for leadership. It then draws from that account to focus on four key themes for more detailed consideration – the engagement of clinicians in the leadership of healthcare organisations; the roles of chief executives in NHS organisations; the roles and contribution of NHS boards in governance and leadership; and the challenges of leadership development and capacity building. The chapter closes by drawing some conclusions about strengths and weaknesses of leadership in the NHS and considering its likely future development.

Context: A brief history of leadership in the NHS

The National Health Service in England has been perhaps the most centrally-directed state-run health system in Europe. It is managed and led by the Department of Health in London, and the legislative framework gives the Secretary of State for Health extensive and largely unfettered discretionary legal powers over the statutory NHS bodies which manage and deliver health services at a local or regional level – for example to set their budgets, approve their plans, direct them to take specific actions, and to remove or appoint their leaders. As of 2009, there are ten strategic health authorities (SHAs) which are effectively responsible for the NHS in a region (for example, the North West, or London, or the West Midlands) and are accountable to the Department of Health. Primary care and community services are provided through about 150 primary care trusts (PCTs), which also commission or purchase secondary care services from NHS trusts or foundation trusts which run hospitals, mental health services, ambulance services and so on. PCTs and NHS trusts are accountable to SHAs, while foundation trusts (FTs) have somewhat greater autonomy, but are closely performance managed by their regulator, Monitor.

The history of leadership in the NHS can be cast in four main eras or periods, and the transitions between them represent shifts in thinking at both a political and an organisational level about how to organise, manage and lead in the NHS. From its inception in 1948, the NHS was essentially a traditional professional bureaucracy; in a major reorganisation in 1974 it became what might be characterised as a state or government corporation; in the 1980s further reforms began an era of managerialism (in line with the wider rise of new public management as an idea); and in the 1990s and 2000s a succession of changes have moved the NHS away from being a single organisation and towards a new era of autonomy, diversity and plurality. Each of these eras is now explored in turn.

The traditional professional bureaucracy is an organisation in which professionals have a high degree of control – hospitals, universities, law firms and the like (Mintzberg 1979). The work undertaken is highly specialised but often not formally specified which means assessing performance is complex, individuals and teams have high levels of autonomy in their decision-making, and collective professional knowledge and relationships are as important – or more important – as any organisational hierarchy and authority. Such organisations exist to serve the needs of the professionals on their staff and their clients or service users, rather than the staff existing to serve the needs of the organisation. In that triad, the organisation is clearly subordinate. Healthcare organisations are classic professional bureaucracies, and from the creation of the NHS in 1948, leadership was essentially vested in the medical profession – individually and collectively. NHS organisations were not managed but administered, by administrators whose job titles (such as hospital secretary or house governor) conveyed their purpose – as supporters and facilitators for the individual and collective will of the medical staff (Harrison and Pollitt 1994). At a national level, there was an implied contract between government on the one hand and the medical profession on the other in which while government set the overall budget for the NHS, the use of resources was left to professionals to determine, and clinicians had a high level of clinical freedom (Klein 2006). However, as healthcare delivery became both more costly and more complex, the weak

nature of collective and individual accountability was increasingly scrutinised. The fragmented and unmanaged nature of health services was increasingly at odds with the corporatist mood in government and industry in the
1960s, and after almost a decade of planning, the first major reorganisation
of the NHS was undertaken in 1974 (Brown 1979).

The second era of NHS management emphasised a new form of state
or government corporatism, in which the management and leadership of
the NHS was placed in the hands of teams of doctors, nurses and managers
at every level through a complex and formulaic public bureaucracy. A complex blueprint was drawn up for a multilevel hierarchy of regional, area,
district and unit level organisational structures and at each level control
was placed in the hands of this triumvirate, which was expected to work
through consensus (Marks 1972). A new nurse management structure, and
formal quasi-democratic consultative structures for involving doctors in
management were put in place. In practice, the administrator began to
emerge – informally – as first among equals in the leadership of NHS organisations, though they were only able to exercise leadership with the consent particularly of medical staff, and those managers who prospered were
those who had the political, diplomatic and intellectual skills to secure and
sustain their position. But the new management arrangements placed greater
emphasis on inclusivity and consensus than on managerial effectiveness,
and decision-making was slower and more bureaucratic than before. The
multiple level hierarchy resulted in much duplication and overlap, and
the need for consensus tended to delay and defer contentious or difficult
decisions (Brown 1979).

In the 1980s, the political climate shifted from state corporatism towards
an ideological belief in the virtues of the private sector, markets and commercial discipline and a distrust of public service ideals, values and organisations. The chief executive of Sainsburys plc, Sir Roy Griffiths, was asked
to carry out a management inquiry into the NHS, and his pithy, 24 page
report to the Secretary of State was caustic in its criticism of the pace of
change and leadership capacity of the NHS (Griffiths 1983). Memorably, he
declared that if Florence Nightingale were walking the corridors of the NHS
with her lamp today, she would be searching for the person in charge.
Griffith's prescription was the abolition of consensus management and its
replacement with a system of general management, in which a single individual would have responsibility and authority. He also advocated the
formal engagement of doctors in managing resources and services, greater
decentralisation and devolution of authority, a joint focus both on financial and clinical accountability, and proper measurement of clinical and
service outcomes. Griffiths report was the start of a new era of managerialism in the NHS, which reflected the wider rise of 'new public management'
across public services in the UK and internationally (Harrison and Pollitt
1994). A new breed of chairs and chief executives, often with more formal

business and management training and experience, was created. Increasingly, doctors, nurses and other clinicians were drawn into the new managerial arrangements not as representatives or delegates of the wider collective clinical community, but as clinical managers placed in authority over members of that community, a position which created strong tensions between clinical and managerial paradigms and conflicting loyalties between the profession and the organisation.

But these new, more powerful forms of managerial leadership were clearly at odds with the essentially centrally directed and politically controlled nature of the NHS. Slowly, over a period of ten years or more, the hierarchy of control which led upwards from every healthcare organisation to the Department of Health and the Secretary of State began to weaken. The NHS started to move from looking and feeling like one, enormous organisation in which individual NHS organisations were like operating divisions or wholly owned subsidiaries of a single large conglomerate, to looking and feeling more like an industry, with a network of many independent and autonomous healthcare providers linked into a loose collective whole by their shared interests, mutual dependence, and a regulatory framework and overall policy direction created and overseen by the Department of Health. These changes were part of an international trend away from direct government control of healthcare systems and provision (Preker and Harding 2003).

The first, faltering steps involved the creation of NHS trusts in the early 1990s, which were at first promised high levels of autonomy but were soon controlled almost as closely as the directly managed provider units they had replaced. Even so, important freedoms over staff employment and pay, capital spending, and service configuration were won. But it was in the current decade that government began to move decisively to create a more decentralised and autonomous NHS in England (following devolution, the NHS in Scotland, Wales and Northern Ireland have tended to revert to the state or government corporatism models of the 1970s described earlier). Four main reforms deserve to be mentioned. Firstly, the role of the Department of Health itself was reduced, its staff was more than halved, and responsibility for many areas (such as employer relations, technology assessment, quality monitoring, and performance improvement) was passed over to a range of other bodies, national or local, at arms length from central government. The Department of Health began to focus more on setting policy and overseeing performance, rather than managing and directing the NHS. Secondly, NHS trusts were encouraged to apply for a new status as legally independent not for profit corporations called foundation trusts, outside the statutory powers of direction of the Secretary of State for Health, and with a membership from the community they serve, which elects a board of governors who in turn chooses the foundation trust's leadership. Thirdly, a range of new healthcare providers were encouraged to start providing health services through the NHS. A deliberate policy aimed at creating diversity and plurality of supply resulted in a growing number of independent sector, for profit providers, and the creation of new social enterprises with strong roots in the voluntary and charitable sector was also encouraged. Fourthly, the necessary system architecture (like markets, competition, patient choice, activity-based funding, and service contracting) was put in place to allow this new NHS to work.

The clinical business of today's NHS is not so different from that of the NHS in 1948 – outpatients, inpatients, operations, pharmaceuticals and so on – but the scope and sophistication of clinical medicine now allows us to do far more to prevent and treat illness and to prolong life and health. Similarly, while the organisational structures and leadership arrangements might seem not too dissimilar, based around hospitals, community health-care providers, mental health services and so on, the realities of leadership are really profoundly different. Today's NHS leaders are more visibly and publicly accountable, have to work in a more challenging, fast-moving and competitive system environment, and have both more power over and more responsibility for the delivery of clinical care.

The next four sections of this chapter tackle four key themes which emerge from this context-setting introduction. The first is the place of clinicians, especially doctors, and their contribution to leadership in the NHS. The second is the evolving role and function of chief executives of NHS organisations. Thirdly, we explore the parallel evolving role and function of NHS boards (especially their non-executive chairs and members), and finally we turn to considering how the NHS has gone about developing its future leaders.

The clinical dimension: Clinicians as leaders

The roles of doctors, nurses and other clinical professionals in the leadership of NHS organisations have changed as the NHS itself has changed, though NHS organisations remain at a fundamental level professionally dominated and driven organisations in which legitimacy and authority are essentially largely derived from professional standing or status, and the organisational culture and values are mostly determined by professional norms and socialisation processes. It is practically impossible to enact change in the NHS without securing professional support for and engagement in the change process. For this reason, the positional and professional authority of clinical leaders is crucial to NHS performance (Davies, Hodges and Rundall 2003; Denis, Lamothe and Langley 2001).

However, as the account above shows, the nature and terms of professional engagement in the leadership of NHS organisations has changed, as they have shifted from being traditional professional bureaucracies to being what some have called managed professional businesses (Dickinson and Ham 2008). The corporatisation of medicine has involved a shift away from clinician leaders as representatives of the collective group of professionals, often elected or appointed on a short term rotational basis and expected largely to watch over professional interests and values and act as a check on management. Instead, clinician leaders have been increasingly expected to oversee and manage the performance of clinical colleagues, have been appointed by the organisation for their management capacity and skills, and have increasingly seen management as a legitimate long term career pathway for senior clinicians (Robinson 1999; Smith and Walshe 2004).

For clinicians, particularly doctors, the transition from clinical practice to a managerial role can be a challenging one. While senior doctors certainly 'manage' in their clinical practice (they manage a clinical team of junior doctors, nurses and other professionals, and manage use of resources such as wards, theatres and diagnostic facilities), they have little or no formal accountability and function more as foreman/supervisor than as a manager. The first real managerial engagement for most doctors is the role of clinical director, where they take on responsibility for managing a clinical department or directorate, usually working in collaboration with both a nurse manager and a business manager. Most doctors in those roles continue with their clinical practice alongside their managerial responsibilities. Some then look to take on a more extended managerial role, usually as a medical director for an NHS trust where they then assume a much broader range of managerial responsibilities, across specialties and departments apart from their own, often have line management responsibilities for key functions such as clinical governance, and will be a member of the organisation's board alongside other directors such as the chief executive, finance director and director of nursing. For nurses, there is a much more established professional/managerial hierarchy, and most have their first significant management experience when they become a ward sister or charge nurse (now often termed a ward manager), from which they may progress to be nurse manager for a department, specialty or directorate, and then to be director of nursing for a NHS trust. Some nurse managers go on to have successful careers as chief executives in NHS organisations, but very few doctors move on from being medical directors to taking on the role of chief executive.

Clinical leaders often experience a profound clash of cultures and paradigms between their professional and managerial identities, and have to find ways of reconciling conflicting loyalties and ideologies (Degeling, Hill and Kennedy 2001; Degeling, Maxwell, Kennedy *et al.* 2003). Their clinical training and socialisation emphasises the primacy of science and evidence in decision-making, their responsibility to the individual patient, and their professional autonomy and responsibility. However, their managerial function often demands decision-making on the basis of complex and incomplete information, requires them to trade off costs and benefits for different patient groups and other stakeholders, and involves collective decision-making, negotiation and working within political and other constraints on their freedom to act (Fitzgerald 1994; Exworthy and Halford 1999).

The traditional medical or nursing educational curriculum provides little or no coverage of topics concerned with organisations, management, leadership or health policy and politics. However, there is often a presumption that senior clinicians have, by virtue of their extensive clinical experience, the skills and capacity for senior managerial posts (Dopson 1994). In practice, many clinicians feel unprepared for the management and organisational leadership roles they take on, and are expected to learn through personal experience and endeavour in a fairly unsupported and unplanned way. Medical management is not recognised professionally as a specialism in itself (as it is in some other countries), and taking on such roles can be seen as an unhelpful diversion from the mainstream career options of clinical practice and research. As a result, many clinician managers either struggle to continue with their clinical work alongside their management role, or take on management responsibilities only towards the end of their clinical career.

However, the last few years have seen a renewed focus on involving clinicians – and especially doctors – in management and leadership. The recent Darzi review of the NHS (Department of Health 2008) has placed great store by developing clinical leadership and investing in new programmes designed to support the development of clinical and medical directors and to encourage doctors to take up roles as chief executives. The NHS Institute for Innovation and Improvement has recently developed a medical leadership competency framework in collaboration with the Academy of Medical Royal Colleges which sets out in detail the competencies which medical leaders need at each level from doctors in training through to consultants, clinical directors and medical directors, and which will be used both by those involved in medical education and training nationally and regionally and by NHS organisations locally to plan their development activities (NHS Institute 2008).

Senior leaders: The roles of chief executives

Previous sections have shown that the dominant organisation cultural contexts for leading in the NHS have shifted, across four broad eras, from traditional professional bureaucracy (1940s–1960s), government corporatism (1970s), managerialism (1980s–2000) through to the current era, which is characterised by fast pace and a greater degree of local autonomy. The notion of path dependency however (Wilsford 1994; Bevan and Robinson 2005) extends to the framing of management practice as well as to policy framing: elements from earlier times can clearly be discerned in the current imperatives for chief executives. So, for example, a primary care trust chief executive today (2009) will have to be mindful of ensuring buy-in from local general practitioners through the Professional Executive Committee for any envisaged major strategic changes to services (a nod to professional bureaucracy), will have to abide by the guidance laid down by the Department of Health in the operating framework (in accordance with government corporatism), is urged by the 'World Class Commissioning' policy to strengthen market stimulation and procurement capabilities (managerialism) as well as being enjoined, by the chief executive of the NHS, to look out to local communities, not upwards to the Department of Health. Likewise, a chief executive of a hospital foundation trust is encouraged to ensure 'clinical engagement' for policies, has to conform to national standards for quality (albeit no longer set by the Department of Health but by an arms length body, the Care Quality Commission), must abide by a code of governance drawn up by Monitor, the regulator of foundation trusts, that is derived from the combined code for the private sector as well as being accountable to local people as represented by the governors and members.

The roles of chief executives in the NHS have nevertheless ostensibly changed significantly, and not least the terminology used to describe the executive leader. They have developed from the administrator or hospital secretary role alluded to earlier, where the emphasis, from the inception of the NHS to the 1960s, was on providing administrative support to ensure the smooth day to day running of the service. Between 1974 and 1984, the administrator was a *de facto primus inter pares* in the consensus management team which also consisted of a nurse manager, finance manager and a doctor. The team had significant delegated authority but the model was severely criticised for slowness and the 'lowest common denominator' consequences of its decision-making processes (Harrison, Hunter and Pollitt 1990). In addition, by the 1970s, long term strategic planning was in favour in order to inculcate 'scientific' management and to secure orderly improvements in care. Planning inched the legitimate activities of senior administrators closer to a more strategic and influential set of responsibilities, which along with consensus management, paved the way for the enactment of the new public management reforms of the 1980s. The Griffiths Report (1983) gave rise to the new term and the new role in the NHS of 'general manager' who held ultimate responsibility for the running of the service. The term was itself replaced by 'chief executive' with the arrival in 1990 of the smaller streamlined and business-like boards which replaced the larger, inclusive and stakeholder style membership of health authorities, about which more later.

Whilst the nomenclature and the range has indubitably altered, there are some enduring challenges for health service chief executives. These include the 24/7 operational provision of the service, internal and external communications, taking a lead on forward planning, management of the finances and staff, ensuring a productive relationship with the medical community and management of untoward and major incidents.

Added to the list more recently is a requirement to take responsibility for the overall performance including the quality of the clinical service and patient experience, to manage the local and national politics for the current and future benefit of the organisation and the service and to work closely with other partners who deliver health and social care. Increasingly, the focus and skills of the job have diverged with the advent of the internal market and the development of healthcare commissioning on the one hand, and the commercialisation of provision on the other. With budgets of typically up to £1 billion, primary care trust chief executives as the commissioners or purchasers of health and healthcare for their local population have to bear in mind the requirement to improve health and reduce health inequalities and to demonstrate the 11 organisational competencies expected of 'world class' commissioning, which are very different from the priorities for their colleagues leading the provision of health services. These competences include locally leading the NHS, assessing needs and managing knowledge, prioritisation and market stimulation and making sound financial investments (Department of Health 2008) and are typified by a type of leadership where the onus is on engagement and influence and whole system improvements in performance. A Foundation Trust chief executive on the other hand has to account to local members and governors, ensure compliance with the terms of authorisation of the trust with the regulator, Monitor, and has a role that is closer to the traditional challenges described above with a focus on business strategy, marketing, management and control and improvements in clinical quality, patient safety and overall institutional performance.

From this brief resume, it can be seen that the skills and attributes required of the two main types of current health service chief executive, especially those who are able to cross the divide between system and institutional leadership, are daunting. How do the various different theoretical models, frameworks and empirical evidence of effective leadership help to elucidate and explain the nature of the task? There is no space here to apply the leadership literature comprehensively to the challenges faced by health service chief executives. But three themes within the literature do have particular resonance and relevance in the case of NHS chief executives: the transactional approach, situational leadership, and the performance of leadership. A fourth is now emerging which has been tentatively termed 'leadership as orchestration' (Chambers 2007).

In simple terms, the transactional form of leadership belongs largely to an earlier era where the focus was on 'proper administration', and, latterly, on management by objectives with rewards and sanctions applied accordingly. It has been unfavourably compared with transformational leadership which provides inspiration and intellectual stimulation to create a climate for effective big change and improvement (Alimo-Metcalfe 1999). But transactional leadership also relates to a focus on high quality bureaucracy (in the Weberian sense) and on adherence to proper process, for example the production of well written board papers and good quality meeting minutes. Some of the recent failings in corporate governance (Chambers 2006) can arguably be related to weaknesses in transactional leadership. The recent trend in health services management to emphasise the use of project and programme management skills to steer big change initiatives, originally but now extending beyond information technology projects, may suggest a return to favour of a transactional approach but by another name.

Situational and contingency leadership ideas came out of a sense that the traditional trait and style theories did not adequately capture the range of skills and behaviours required from leadership in modern times (Bass 1990). The range of challenges for NHS chief executives today exemplifies this. Put simply, these ideas flow from the premise that ways of leading have to be matched to the qualities and experience of staff and to organisational and situational circumstances. In relation to the latter, Grint argues, in what he terms the social construction of leadership, that leaders do not merely respond to the context but proactively shape it. According to this perspective, leadership belongs explicitly to the world of theatre involving the enactment of identities, the adoption of roles and the giving of performances (Grint 2005).

Performance (in the sense of a witnessed and enacted performance) is a theme running implicitly through Goodwin's research which identified five interconnected variables including the quality of the chief executive's executive team as perceived by others, the history of local interorganisational relationships, the strength of interpersonal networks, the development of interorganisational alliances, and the extent of power sharing between organisations. Continuing the performance analogy, these are all dependent upon roles taken up and perceived by others to be taken up. In addition, Goodwin further argues that a track record of demonstrable local successes provides a local climate conducive to further change (Goodwin 2006).

The challenges for chief executives mirrored by developments in leadership theories and evidence add up convincingly to a move away from the traditional 'command' part of the 'command and control' form of leadership but retaining the 'control' element in order to ensure 'superb' execution (Collins 2001). The dominant theme is whole system leveraging which has elsewhere been tentatively termed 'leadership as orchestration' (Chambers 2007) but a convincing model which works for NHS leaders is still awaited. A recent paper written for NHS managers has argued that there is in practice a lack of strong underpinning theory to support the practice of leadership in the NHS which is holding back the design of effective leadership development interventions (NHS Confederation 2009).

Going by the board: NHS governance and leadership

It is increasingly argued that leadership in NHS organisations is expected to come from the board as much as from individuals including the chief executive, as was recently demonstrated by the injunctions to the board contained in the report into the failures of care at Mid Staffordshire NHS Foundation Trust (Healthcare Commission 2009). Boards in the NHS are relatively new entities, having been created in 1990 as a result of the influence of new public management approaches on the NHS from the 1980s onwards. They replaced the larger stakeholder model of health authorities, which managed the whole local health system from 1974, and which themselves displaced a four-part system, which had existed until then, of regional hospital boards, boards of governors for teaching hospitals, executive councils for family practitioners and local authorities that looked after community health services. In a simplistic summary, current boards are expected to lead, health authorities in the middle era were expected to manage, and the boards and councils in the early days of the NHS were expected to govern their hospital or administer independent family practitioner contracts.

Local boards in the English NHS are unitary boards of between 11 and 16 members, although with two distinct constituencies, comprising, on the one hand, the executive directors led by the chief executive, and on the other hand, the non-executive directors led by the chair, the latter being in the majority. Members of the board are expected to work jointly, and bear the same level of responsibility, individually and collectively, for the performance of the organisation, with a particular focus on strategic development, monitoring clinical and service performance and maintaining financial balance (Chambers 2006). An alternative governance model is now being developed with the introduction of NHS Foundation Trusts and over half of all NHS hospitals have now (2009) acquired Foundation Trust status.

NHS Foundation Trusts are independent public benefit corporations. Although subject to national targets and standards, they have greater freedoms than other types of NHS hospitals. Governance arrangements within the governance code laid down by the regulator, Monitor, are locally determined and board members are appointed by the governors of the hospitals, rather than by the NHS Appointments Commission. The financial regime underpinning Foundation Trusts is significantly more rigorous and the consequent expectations by the regulator, of board performance in ensuring financial control are also therefore markedly enhanced.

Whilst the evidence connecting boards to organisational performance is relatively weak (Chambers and Cornforth 2009) the contribution of boards is increasingly in the spotlight. There is some evidence that 'healthy' board dynamics is important and in particular having a climate of high trust, combined with high challenge and high engagement (*ibid*). There have been subtle changes in the description of the role of the non-executive director on NHS boards. The steward – ambassador – guardian descriptor was in vogue from the late 1990s. The education sector provided the term 'critical friend' to add to the mix. The influence of the Higgs Report in 2003 on non-executive directors in the private sector brought more edge and challenge to the role. Since 2003, the foundation trust application process has provided a reality check for many boards. All of this adds up to the likelihood of less comfortable board meetings although not necessarily less effective.

It is also possible that there may be some conflicting views about the essential purpose of the board amongst the members. Cornforth has described six different board models from the literature on board governance and the different roles and behaviours which flow from these. At one end, in the compliance model, non-executive directors control and supervise management decisions, and at the other end, in the rubber stamp model, board meetings are largely symbolic and tend to ratify decisions taken by management. In between there is a supporters club model where the focus is on the improvement of external stakeholder relations, a political model in which a democratic perspective holds sway with different members interests represented, a co-option model focused on boundary spanning, and finally a partnership model where, as experts, the executives and non-executives share interests and work closely together (Cornforth 2003). Uncreative conflict, or 'grumpy boards', occurs when individuals hold quite different beliefs about the purpose of their board and therefore exhibit behaviours which are congruent with their own beliefs but at odds with their colleagues. Board development in the NHS, still in its infancy, is now as a consequence focused on board dynamics as well as on knowledge and skills.

Leadership development and training in the NHS

In contrast with the relatively recent focus on boards, there is a long tradition of investment in NHS leadership development and capacity building, at both a national and a local level, going back at least to the establishment of the NHS in 1948 (Saunders 2006). No account of this topic would be complete without an exploration of the longstanding national graduate general management training scheme, which has been in place for over 50 years and is one of the few enduring features of the NHS organisational landscape, having survived many reorganisations or restructurings. Its longevity is perhaps a sign of its perceived success or effectiveness, or at least a signal that influential leaders in the NHS hold it in high enough regard to have protected and preserved it over the years. The scheme is broadly similar in some respects to the Civil Service 'fast track' management programme. It admits about 100 individuals a year on a 24 month programme of academic learning, management placements and development opportunities, and its modern structure is not too dissimilar in content and approach to that in place when it was established in 1956 with 12 trainees (Saunders 2006). With approaching 3,000 entrants over the last five decades, it is perhaps not surprising that its alumni have featured heavily among the senior leadership of the NHS. Alongside that scheme, more recent additions include a similar training scheme for finance managers, and one for HR managers. All three are intended to create the future leaders of the NHS.

A series of evaluations undertaken over the years have found that while the NHS management training scheme is very highly regarded, is competitive for the best talent in the graduate marketplace, and produces many future senior leaders, too little attention has been given to other parts of the leadership and management development landscape – such as the needs of a much wider and less elite-focused cadre of managers, the needs of clinician managers, the development of future board level leaders and chief executives, the needs of non-executive members of NHS boards, and so on. Over the last two decades since the introduction of general management in the 1980s, a number of reports have argued that NHS leadership development is too piecemeal, that levels of investment are too low for the size, scale and complexity of the NHS' leadership needs, that there is no coherent approach to managing and developing talent, and that a more comprehensive and integrated approach is required (NHSTA 1986; Department of Health 2009).

An important step forward in defining and framing the needs for development in the NHS has been the development of a competency based framework by the NHS Institute for Innovation and Improvement, which aims to provide a comprehensive and widely applicable way to describe the leadership attributes, qualities, skills or capacities needed at different levels by NHS leaders. Based on research by Hay Consulting with a wide range of organisations and individual NHS leaders, the NHS leadership qualities framework defines three main clusters of competencies (personal qualities, setting direction and delivering the service) each of which is then broken down into five qualities (Department of Health 2001b; NHS Institute 2003, 2006). It combines a cluster essentially concerned with personal qualities like self awareness, self belief, self management, personal integrity and drive for improvement with two clusters concerned essentially with direction and delivery. The framework is summarised in Figure 3.1.

In recent years, the NHS Institute has used the NHS leadership qualities framework to organise and integrate its increasingly wide range of leadership and management development programmes. As well as assuming responsibility for the longstanding management training scheme discussed earlier, it has run major programmes aimed at black and ethnic minority managers and women in NHS management and leadership roles, and has established a programme for managers with experience from other sectors entering the NHS. It has also recently developed an extensive portfolio of board level development activities, aimed at aspiring board level directors, future and current chief executives, and non-executive directors.

At the same time, the moves towards a much less hierarchical and centrally controlled NHS described earlier have made it, in some ways, more difficult to organise and deliver leadership development at a national level. In an NHS made up largely of autonomous NHS foundation trusts, with management appointments made at an organisational level, it is far from

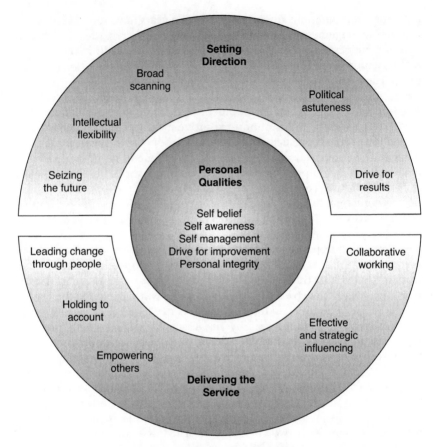

Figure 3.1   The NHS Leadership Qualities Framework

clear that the NHS Institute, Department of Health and SHAs can direct or control management and leadership development and their approach will have to be founded more on the collaborative development of agreed plans and strategies with the NHS community which are likely to then be delivered increasingly at a local level (Department of Health 2009).

Conclusions

It was noted at the outset of this chapter that the NHS presents a unique leadership challenge because of the sheer scale, complexity, professional control, political sensitivity and public scrutiny of the enterprise. Successful chief executives in the NHS are often very impressive individuals, equipped with the intellectual, political and emotional intelligence required to cope with this leadership challenge. But chief executives' careers can be extremely demanding – taking a high personal toll on their health and wellbeing – and they are sometimes cut short abruptly when internal or external problems are seen to require their ceremonial or symbolic removal from office. It is perhaps unsurprising that, despite high levels of financial reward for these positions, they are often difficult to fill.

Moreover, the centrally directed, politically controlled nature of the NHS has in the past created a rather toxic and brutal environment for senior leaders. Chief executives of NHS trusts, PCTs and strategic health authorities have been left in no doubt that their position depends on their absolute loyalty to the policy direction and national strategy set by the Department of Health, and their scope for freedom of thought and action has been quite limited. Chief executives and senior leaders have been expected to be faithful implementers of a constant and sometimes chaotic and conflicting stream of policy initiatives, reorganisations and reforms. The performance of NHS organisations has often been micromanaged by the Department of Health through its strategic health authorities, and there has been extensive interference in the operational management of health services. Perhaps the most successful chief executives in this environment have been those who were able to 'manage upwards' their relationship with the Department of Health, could ensure that they met all external expectations and performance measures, and were able to create a coherent narrative and consistent strategic direction for their organisation out of the rather incoherent and inconsistent national policy environment.

But the nature of the NHS is slowly changing – as it moves from being essentially controlled and directed by the Department of Health to having a more distributed, devolved and networked model of governance. Undoubtedly, the most interesting and exciting opportunities to exercise leadership arise from this slackening of the central reins, and from the new legal forms of organisation such as NHS foundation trusts and social enterprises. In the future, successful chief executives are likely to be so not because of their skill in managing their relationship with the Department of Health and the centre, but because of their skill as leaders in managing their organisations and their relationships with a host of other stakeholders. They will have far more opportunity to create and shape a new organisational destiny, and to set their own organisational strategy and direction. For some existing leaders in the NHS, this new era brings great uncertainty and some unfamiliar discomfort, but for others it is likely to be the start of a new era in NHS leadership.

References

Alimo-Metcalfe, B. (1999) 'Leadership in the NHS: What are the Competencies and Qualities Needed and How Can They Be Developed?', in Mark, A. and Dopson, S. (eds), *Organisational Behaviour in Health Care*.

Bass, B.M. (1990) Bass and Stogdill's *Handbook of Leadership Theory*. New York: The Free Press.

Bevan, R.G. and Robinson, R. (2005) 'The Interplay Between Economic and Political Logics', *Journal of Health Policy, Politics and Law*, 30: 1, 2: 53–78.

Brown, R.G.S. (1979) *Reorganising the National Health Service: A Case Study in Administrative Change*. Oxford: Blackwell.

Cabinet Office (2007) *Capability Review of the Department of Health*. London: Cabinet Office.

Chambers, N. (2006) 'Governance and the Work of Health Service Boards', in Walshe, K. and Smith, J. (eds), *Healthcare Management*. Maidenhead: Open University Press

Chambers, N. (2007) *Leadership in Social Care Settings: A Brief Review of the Literature*. www.talknet.eu accessed 1 May 2009.

Chambers, N. and Cornforth, C. (2009 in press) 'The Role of Corporate Governance and Boards in Organisational Performance', in Walshe, K., Harvey, G., Spencer, E., Skelcher, C. and Jas, P. (eds), *From Knowing to Doing: Connecting Knowledge and Performance in Public Services*. Cambridge: Cambridge University Press.

Collins, J. (2001) *Good to Great*. New York: HarperCollins.

Cornforth, C. (2003) *The Governance of Public and Non-Profit Organizations: What Do Boards Do?* Abingdon: Routledge.

Davies, H.T.O., Hodges, C. and Rundall, T. (2003) 'Views of Doctors and Managers on the Doctor-Manager Relationship in the NHS', *British Medical Journal*, 326: 626–628.

Degeling, P., Hill, M. and Kennedy, J. (2001) 'Mediating the Cultural Boundaries Between Medicine, Nursing and Management: The Central Challenge of Hospital Reform', *Health Services Management Research*, 14: 36–48.

Degeling, P., Maxwell, S., Kennedy, J. and Coyle, B. (2003) 'Medicine, Management and Modernisation: A "Danse Macabre"?', *British Medical Journal*, 326: 649–652.

Denis, J.-L., Lamothe, L. and Langley, A. (2001) 'The Dynamics of Collective Leadership and Strategic Change in Pluralistic Organizations', *Academy of Management Journal*, 44: 809–937.

Department of Health (2000) *The NHS Plan: A Plan for Investment, a Plan for Reform*. London: HSMO.

Department of Health (2001a) *Shifting the Balance of Power: Securing Delivery*. London: Department of Health.

Department of Health (2001b) *NHS Leadership Qualities Framework*. http://www.nhs-leaedershipqualities.nhs.uk/.

Department of Health (2001c) *Learning from Bristol: The Report of the Public Inquiry into Children's Heart Surgery at the Bristol Royal Infirmary 1984–1995*. London: Department of Health.

Department of Health (2005) *The Kerr/Haslam Inquiry*. London: Department of Health.

Department of Health (2008) *High Quality Care for All: Next Stage Review of the NHS*. London: Department of Health.

Department of Health (2008) *World Class Commissioning*. London: Department of Health.

Department of Health (2009) *Inspiring Leaders – Leadership for Quality, Guidance for NHS Talent and Leadership Plans*. London: Department of Health.

Dickinson, H. and Ham, C. (2008) *Engaging Doctors in Leadership: Review of the Literature*. Birmingham: HSMC, University of Birmingham.

Dopson, S. (1994) 'Management: The One Disease Consultants Did Not Think Exists', *Journal of Management in Medicine*, 8(5): 25–37.

Exworthy, M. and Halford, S. (eds) (1999) *Professionals and the New Managerialism in the Public Sector*. Buckingham: Open University Press.

Fitzgerald, L. (1994) 'Moving Clinicians into Management. A Professional Challenge or Threat?', *Journal of Management in Medicine*, 8(6): 32–44.

Goodwin, N. (2006) *Leadership in Health Care: A European Perspective.* Abingdon: Routledge.

Griffiths, R. (1983) *NHS Management Inquiry.* London: Department of Health.

Grint, K. (2005) *Leadership: The Heterarchy Principle.* London: Palgrave Macmillan.

Harrison, S., Hunter, D. and Pollitt, C. (1990) *The Dynamics of British Health Policy.* London: Unwin Hyman.

Harrison, S. and Pollitt, C. (1994) *Controlling the Health Professionals: The Future of Work and Organization in the NHS.* Buckingham: Open University Press.

Healthcare Commission (2007) *Investigation into Outbreaks of Clostridium Difficile at Maidstone and Tunbridge Wells NHS Trust.* London: Healthcare Commission.

Healthcare Commission (2009) *Investigation into Mid Staffordshire NHS Foundation Trust.* London: Healthcare Commission.

Klein, R. (2006) *The New Politics of the NHS*, 5th edition. Oxford: Radcliffe Publishing.

Marks, J.H. (1972) 'NHS Management: 1974 and Beyond', *Br Med J.*, 4 November (3528): 21–28.

Mintzberg, H. (1979) *The Structuring of Organisations.* Englewood Cliffs: Prentice-Hall.

NHS Confederation (2009) *Future of Leadership: Reforming Leadership Development... Again.* London: NHS Confederation.

NHS Institute for Innovation and Improvement (2003) *NHS Leadership Qualities Framework: Full Technical Research Paper.* Warwick: NHS Institute.

NHS Institute for Innovation and Improvement (2006) *NHS Leadership Qualities Framework.* Warwick: NHS Institute.

NHS Institute for Innovation and Improvement (2008) *Medical Leadership Competency Framework.* Warwick: NHS Institute.

NHS Training Authority (1986) *Better Management, Better Health.* Bristol: NHSTA.

Preker, A.S. and Harding, A. (2003) *Innovations in Health Service Delivery: The Corporatisation of Hospitals.* New York: World Bank.

Robinson, J.C. (1999) *The Corporate Practice of Medicine: Competition and Innovation in Healthcare.* Berkeley: University of California Press.

Saunders, G. (2006) *The NHS National Management Training Scheme in England: A Chronology.* Warwick: NHS Institute.

Smith, J. and Walshe, K. (2004) 'Big Business: Lessons from the Corporatisation of Primary Care in the United Kingdom and the United States', *Public Money and Management*, 24(2): 87–96.

Wilsford, D. (1994) 'Path Dependency, or Why History Makes It Difficult but Not Impossible to Reform Health Care Systems in a Big Way', *Journal of Public Policy*, 14: 251–283.

4
Education Reform and School Leadership

Helen Gunter and Gillian Forrester

Introduction

The beginning of the 2008 autumn term in schools in England has been accompanied by newspaper headlines declaring 'schools in crisis hunt for 1,000 new heads' because schools are without a permanent headteacher in place for the start of the new school year:

> Mike Stewart, headteacher of Westlands school in Torbay, Devon, and chair of the NAHT's secondary committee, said staff who would once have wanted to become heads were choosing not to because of rising levels of stress. 'Schools are now compared using 173 ranking methods – and if it is at the bottom on one of them the headteacher is sacked,' said Stewart. 'It's crackpot.' He argued that a lot of schools now had to advertise two or three times for a headteacher – something that would have been 'unheard of' five or six years ago (Lightfoot and Asthana 2008).

Such a situation seems to be far removed from the optimism of 1997 when New Labour staked a claim for rapid and sustainable school improvement based on a huge investment into headteachers as leaders. During the past decade heads have gained higher status and salaries, their own training college, the opportunity to lead national reforms in their schools and provide data to prove success in meeting national standards. However, it seems that headship, now rebranded as organisational and performance leadership, is not the role that it once was, and indeed the New Labour discourse is now about potential school leaders from the private, public and voluntary sectors. So headteachers as 'public sector' leaders are facing rapid and fundamental change generating the question: how is professional identity experienced through the practice of leadership? In this chapter we intend to explore this by beginning with the situation that New Labour inherited, before we go on to examine the more recent interventions they have made into the framing and practice of headship. We will draw on a range of primary and secondary sources, but in particular we will provide empirical evidence from the *Knowledge Production and Educational Leadership Project* (Gunter and Forrester 2008a) to allow headteachers to speak about their experiences and *their* voices be heard.

New Labour's eve

In taking up office in May 1997 the New Labour government colonised a field that had grown rapidly over the previous 30 years. They inherited a situation where those who practised leadership and management were headteachers together with teachers, middle managers (pastoral and curriculum/coordinator roles), and senior managers (deputy heads and staff with whole school roles). Structure was based on the historical legacy of the Victorian headmaster tradition which had produced the normality of the single person in charge of the school. Research suggests that the inherited 'public school' approach was autocratic with tensions between paternalism and professionality but with teachers as 'experts' in their own domains. While a 'first among equals' leading professional trend emerged in the post-World War Two period, the 1988 Education Reform Act turned schools into small businesses (right to hire and fire staff, open enrolment and formula funding) which Grace (1995) argues reworked the headmaster tradition into the entrepreneurial chief executive operating in a quasi-market:

> If school leadership, in the person of the headteacher, was expected to provide and articulate a moral mission in the nineteenth century and a professional and pedagogically progressive mission in the social democratic era, then it seems that contemporary headteachers in England will increasingly be expected to articulate a market mission (41).

While studies had taken place on the role and work of the headteacher (e.g. Coulson 1976; Hall *et al.* 1986) and heads had written about how best to undertake the job (e.g. Edmonds 1968), the tensions between the chief executive and leading professional roles remained.

The production of headteachers in the state system was by a trained and experienced teacher climbing the rungs of the ladder to head of subject/year/house, to deputy headteacher to headteacher. Hence the head as head*teacher* could lead on pedagogic and curriculum issues, as well as liaise with the local authority and other external agencies. The emphasis was on the preparation for the role through the experience and credibility of having been a classroom teacher combined with training by local authorities and postgraduate study. The 1988 Act shifted this professional identity from educational leadership towards school organisational leadership where the headteacher had to be separated from teachers in order to lead and manage staff work and performance. Hence heads had to manage budgets and generate income through bids, and, through a mandated system of performance management, reward and sack staff. Studies of heads and senior teams focus mainly on experiences and how they adjusted to business management (e.g. Hall 1996; Ribbins and Marland 1994; Southworth 1995; Wallace and Hall 1994). Training rather than preparation had grown (e.g. OTTO, One Term Training Opportunities) with courses coordinated 1983–1988 by the National Development Centre (NDC) (Bolam 1986), and towards the end of the Conservative period in office from the mid-1990s nationally controlled training emerged as an important feature.

By the time New Labour took office in 1997 headteacher professional identity had been reworked around secular New Public Management notions of market competition, audit through inspection, performance through league tables, and delivery through standards (Clarke *et al.* 2000). The study of headship had two main trends; first, those who sought to capture and understand career pathways and professional practice (e.g. Pascal and Ribbins 1998; Rayner and Ribbins 1999); and second, those who sought to promote private sector models of organisational efficiency and effectiveness through prescriptive advice about marketing, and team management (see Gunter 1997). Evidence from an ESRC seminar series (Bush *et al.* 1999; EMA 1999), a state of the art literature review by Hall and Southworth (1997), and an enquiry by the House of Commons Select Committee (House of Commons 1998) shows that on the eve of New Labour taking office the field was pluralistic in relation to knowledge production and claims (Gunter and Ribbins 2003). However, New Labour thinkers and policy-makers were determined to control the knowledge claims underpinning their reforms by using School Effectiveness and School Improvement research to argue for the primacy of headteachers as organisational leaders (Barber 1996) even though analysis of the evidence base was more circumspect:

> The idea that powerful and visionary heads enhance the school's effective-ness is thus a continuing belief in the research and the teacher profession generally. Yet beyond this assertion surprisingly little else is known. For example, it remains unclear in what ways heads actually influence and shape their schools. School effectiveness studies and more recently school improvement commentaries have offered some broad ideas about the nature of effective leadership, but these are relatively generalised and superficial. Longitudinal and observational studies of heads increasing the effectiveness of the schools they lead are presently lacking. Hence, we do not have a sophisticated understanding of how heads make a difference and how this might vary according to the school's context, size, development needs and the head's professional background, experience, skills and know-ledge. Although the centrality of the head is widely acknowledged, it has not been examined in very much depth (Hall and Southworth 1997: 164–165).

New Labour's approach was not to seek to know more about head-ship and teachers but to act as if an investment in headteachers was both the obvious and right thing to do in order to bring about radical reforms.

New Labour's decade

The translation into action of the famous commitment to 'education, education, education' by Tony Blair in the 1997 election campaign was by setting the agenda for national standards in the White Paper *Excellence in Schools* (DfEE 1997) and presenting a workforce strategy in the Green Paper, *Teachers: Meeting the Challenge of Change* (DfEE 1998). Significantly, policy texts gave no acknowledgement to field development, and did not see the pluralistic nature of the field as a strength (see PIU 2001). Teachers were told that peer appraisal had failed and hence performance management was needed, and that a division of labour based on a leadership hierarchy supported by role specific training was essential. The New Labour discourse located in ministerial speeches, government documents and the work of private consultants contracted to deliver changes was around heroic and charismatic transformational leaders (Gunter and Forrester 2008b). Hence like Clarke *et al.* (2000) we would acknowledge that the change was more than the installation of New Public Management roles and jobs but was about 'a set of shifts in organizational beliefs and practices' (8) where the strategy is to forge new power relationships. The power process embedded within such agenda setting was revealed in two main thrusts designed to encourage a New Labour disposition: first, the *strategic* approach to headteachers as leaders was through a symbolic and financial investment with the National College for School Leaders (e.g. Clarke 2003; DfEE 1999; Munby 2006) enabled through the nationalisation of training and control of the research agenda through commissioning and publishing (Gunter and Forrester 2008b). Branded 'designer-leadership' (Gronn 2003: 7) became a requirement (a contractual one for new heads) and this enabled a second interconnected *operational* thrust to further separate an elite of trained, accredited and accountable leaders from teachers, and the audit culture to permeate lives and work. Significantly the use of targets to manage the system, what Barber (2007) celebrated as 'deliverology', meant that required and preferred practices could be determined and reforms secured. In the revised National Standards (DfES 2004) headteachers were told that they had to implement reforms, and this was secured through training and accreditation, and compliance with a panoply of control mechanisms (e.g. OfSTED inspections, League Tables, Contextual Value Added statistics) that sought to structure language, behaviour, and importantly the 'teacher's soul' (Ball 2003).

By the end of the first decade in power New Labour had continued the modernisation of the public sector through neoliberal ideas and strategies to the extent that it does not exist as a distinctive sector (Ball 2007). Hence a school is a small business that is 'funded', and such funding not only comes from the taxpayer but also can come from voluntary support through 'in kind' activity, private sector profit through service and product development, and philanthropic donations as one off contributions or through strategic investment in, for example, Academy schools. A school may stay separate or form partnerships with, or be taken over by another school, and so the structure of educational provision with Federations, All-through schools, and Academies in addition to Local Authority schools has impacted on how leadership is to be conceptualised and practised. Within this restructuring the dominance of the single person (whether headteacher, principal, chief executive) remains, but what has shifted is the pool from which this person is selected. The former requirement to have Qualified Teacher Status (QTS) has disappeared, and so the emphasis is on the effective local leadership of national reforms, where the Prime Minister's Strategy Unit (2006) suggested that the interplay between national performance requirements with local user needs and demands be mediated through leadership. Such leaders can come from the traditional route of teachers who have risen up the ladder, but also from public services, voluntary organisations and private sector companies. Such changes are redesigning the role of the top person leading educational provision in a local area, and the combination of restructuring with the reluctance of trained senior leaders to apply for headship and the retirement of sizeable generation of serving head*teachers*, means that those who take over the running of schools may not be from the traditional teacher background.

Such changes to headship (or principalship as it is increasingly being labelled) fits with the neoliberal market agenda, where the chief executive needs to deliver and the workforce needs to be flexible and trained to do the delivery (DfES/PwC 2007). Indeed, the nationalisation of training is developing in interesting ways with emerging partnerships between government and the private sector. For example, the NCSL and the Specialist Schools and Academies Trust (SSAT) are working with Absolute Return for Kids (ARK) to deliver the Future Leaders programme. It seems that while the government's own commissioned research has confirmed that 'school leadership is second only to classroom teaching as an influence on pupil learning' (Leithwood *et al.* 2006: 3) the emphasis on leadership rather than teachership remains. While the rhetoric is of 'distributed', 'shared', and 'total' leadership, sug-gesting that others are involved in ways other than the follower of a charismatic leader, this is mainly hybrid thinking as the leader-centric nature of policy and the knowledge claims drawn from School Effectiveness and School Improvement remains a stable feature of policy design. Furthermore, those who have developed such models of leadership have a stake in retaining the basic purposes and features of the role, with regular rebranding in order to retain product advantage in the market.

Researching headteachers

Current research into the experiences of headteachers in the decade of New Labour remains limited, and it seems that little has moved on from Hall and Southworth's (1997) identification that claims are stronger than the empirical data. Research is dominated by government and its agencies, and following Raffo and Gunter (2008) we would argue that it tends to be functional. The rationale is about efficiency and effectiveness, and the narratives are about organisational change and increasingly wider systemic contributions (e.g. Bristow *et al.* 2007; Earley *et al.* 2002; Huber *et al.* 2007; Leithwood *et al.* 2006; NCSL 2007). Important challenges to the underlying assumptions and epistemology (e.g. Barker 2006; Coupland *et al.* 2008; O'Shaughnessy 2007; Thomson and Blackmore 2006) as well as the negative impact of functionalism (e.g. Barker 2005; Goss 2008) are taking place. However, there is little socially critical work, that in Raffo and Gunter's (2007) terms, focuses on rationales to do with social justice with narratives that are about inclusion, democratic participation and community equity. The dominance of functionalism where interventions are about making the system work smoothly in the interests of the economy means that there is little actual research with and by heads where pedagogy and curriculum are a central focus, and where the headteacher (with teachers, students and parents) work as policy-makers (Ozga 2000). Thomson (2001) researching in Australia argues for 'pictures of principals as embodied moral subjects dealing with complex and shifting situations' with 'deliberate efforts to construct more disruptive representations...of "principalling"' (5–6). Such socially critical analysis is emerging with Hollins *et al.*'s (2006) study of alternative school improvement, and Bottery's (2007a,b) portraits of headteachers in context. Notably Bottery shows that headteachers continue to ground their practice in relation to children and learning, but their policy-making capacity is limited with a failure to link what they do locally with wider policy strategies. Hence Thomson's (2001) call remains urgent so that research 'can represent principals as saturated in pedagogies and ethically involved with the ambiguities and complexities of life in schools then scholars and professional associations could not only disrupt totalising technical and managerial strategies of regulation, but also provide useful resources for the principal as moral subject...' (19).

We intend to make a contribution to this emerging socially critical agenda by presenting analysis from interviews with 25 headteachers who participated in the *Knowledge Production in Educational Leadership Project* (Gunter and Forrester 2008a). The details about the sample are shown in Table 4.1.

Headteachers were asked to talk about their professional biography, their approach to leadership combined with views about policy reforms and practices. The research revealed the leadership habitus of headteachers,

Table 4.1   Sample of Headteachers

Headteachers	Primary	Secondary	Special	Total heads
Recent (1–5 years)	3 males 2 females	1 male 3 females		9
Experienced (6–15 years)	3 females	2 males 1 female	1 male	7
Experienced (Retired) (6–15 years, now retired)	1 female			1
Veteran (over 16 years)	1 female	3 males	1 female	5
Veteran (Retired) (over 16 years, now retired)		3 males		3
Total schools	10	13	2	25

which is structured from past experiences and personal and professional knowledge, and is structuring through how each individual experiences their practice (Bourdieu 2000). We intend in our analysis to draw on this data to show how headteachers experience their professional identity as leaders through their practice. Our argument is that headteacher professional identity is located in how they position themselves as educational agents interplaying with the structuring impact of neoliberal education policies. While headteachers are technically positioned as being integrated into government policy, we will examine what headteachers say about handling the functionality agenda by *having to* implement reforms.

Talking heads

A strong feature of the data is the underlying commitment to children and their learning. For example,

> I love seeing kids faces when they achieve. I like to see the fact that you can impact, you can help to shape children's lives by giving them opportunities. And I really enjoy to see those opportunities taken by children. I like to see staff be promoted (Phil).

> What do I like about headship? I have lots of fun. I think it is a huge privilege to be a head. For instance we had a celebration authority-wide event on Thursday and Friday of last week, and we did an authority wide INSET and we had 500 pupils performing and you stand back from that and you look at what education means to them and how much it

raises their hopes in life; all their aspirations, what they can do and if they set the benchmark high they get there (Jane).

This child-focused rationale by the majority of the headteachers is the starting point from which decisions in the job are rooted. The visibility of a child orientation does locate most heads as moral subjects where their professional identity is an embodied commitment to children and their learning, generating strong emotional claims of personal achievement. This is further extended to include staff as colleagues where headteachers want to support and enable good teaching and career advancement. At the same time there is a disposition to do leading where 'making a difference' by taking on complex challenges in the school is relished. The interplay between the two is a key theme in our data and manifests itself both in accounts of their positive contribution to school improvement and arguments about how frustrated they are in the job.

Frustration is shown in how the headteachers articulate their responses to being positioned as the implementers of national reforms, and what this means for how they understand themselves and their disposition to put children and staff first:

I think we are assessment crazy, and that concerns me. We seem to want to be assessing children and not concentrating on teaching and learning, as much as I would like (Susan).

I think this is a government that wants to get involved in too much detail. So the primary strategy when it was initiated was massively detailed wasn't it, the four part lesson. We were almost getting to the stage where we were going to know which page you were on if it was Tuesday 11th November... But once you get to the primary strategy, once you get to the minutiae of detail that this government tried to impose, I felt that you took away professionalism, I felt you took away, to an extent, excitement... (Don).

I think also in terms of policy, it's the sheer weight of initiatives, the sheer number of initiatives. Again we've got lots and lots of intervention strategies for lower achieving children. And of course children only get one chance and you know they deserve the right to make as much progress as they can. But it puts an enormous amount of strain on staff to co-ordinate all the different initiatives that are going on. And actually still be able to measure the impact of each individual one. I think the other major issue is not one of policy necessarily but of attitude. And I feel it just gets worse and worse, that no matter what you do and no matter what progress you make, it's always not good enough. There is always progress to make and yes of course there is always progress to be made but it just seems so rare that there is ever any recognition of the work that people put in these days from the national perspective (James).

The frustrations are not temporary but are located in deep-seated concerns that reforms are too rapid, too many and do not take into account the local situation. One head talks about the plan to put computers into children's homes where the family cannot afford one, with the dilemma on his part of knowing that the computers may be sold to feed drug habits. Another talks about how plans to site an academy which could destroy a nearby successful school. Two heads talk about how remodelling the school work-force has affected professional relationships in schools, not least through the requirement to provide time for planning, preparation and assessment when crises (not least in staffing absence) might mean that old fashioned goodwill is needed to deal with an 'all hands on deck' situation. The causes of this are all located in the top down nature of permanent revolution where functional interventions may not have taken into account the realities of schools as social and relational communities that requires educational as distinct from business leadership:

> But why is there a shortage of heads? It's a job that nobody wants so they have to ask themselves why? And my answer would be because of this model. You go into teaching because you want to teach, you want to be with children and obviously with the children comes the families and... then suddenly it's a business model... it's a very remote analytical data-led role. You have to be very cost efficient, you know every child has to, obviously every child we want them to achieve their full potential but in life things happen and it impacts on performance. But the business model to my mind doesn't allow for that... Two years ago we had twin girls, their mother died... Last year another child, her father died suddenly, you know these events impact, they have to don't they?... But those children are still expected to perform and it just seems a very, a harder image of headship (Mary).

> ... I am a little bit concerned about what I read in the press about headship, about that it may be bursars that take on headship. [...] my bursar [and] she is very well qualified, she has got an MBA, and she is on training that is saying in the future bursars will be leading schools... I am concerned about that for the future, because I think there needs to be some understanding about children. Yes, we are a business. We run three businesses here, two cheque book businesses: nursery, after school care and then the school budget. And that is okay but there has to be some compassion and sensitivity and understanding about young people. So I think that would be a bit sad, and I don't let it keep me awake at night, because I shall retire before that change happens, but I do think it is likely (Susan).

... in terms of the post 90's agenda, I think headship has become much more a managerial system in which the forces of accountability are the ones that hit you large rather than the forces of restructuring and reculturing. And I think if you're restructuring and reculturing I think you're going to have a very different enterprise for your heads. Its really interesting I mean, take for example, up and down the country secondary schools [...] If you take 2004 then every secondary school head would have had their kids doing modern languages, 14–16. It you take 2002, every secondary school would have had every single child doing modern languages up to 16. You take 2006, well it's up to you whether kids take it or not. You take 2008 and we're encouraged that 60% should do it. How can all that be right, you got me? And then you have things like the three part lesson, so you take the clock back three or four years and there is this massive encouragement for three part lessons as the way to go forward. And then probably people like you research to show that the three part lesson is shown to be inadequate [...] But we all do it, we don't question it. [...] And it isn't right. So what I worry about headship is that we are part of a system in which the notion of being a profession [...] I don't mean independently, I mean working with our peers, our communities, but in which we ourselves will debate what it is that is most worthwhile for our young people or community does not occur and we somehow too easily give up. We haven't given up here, but people generally (Barry).

What this third quotation illustrates is how the challenges of the top down are handled by the headteachers, and analysis of our data shows that heads position themselves in three main ways.

Educational agenda setters

These heads are a quarter of the sample. While concerned with local problem solving these heads have a strong commitment to a local agenda for the educational purposes of public education and its impact on the national. They talk about the highs and lows of initiatives, but have a strong sense of how to bring people and children with them in what they regard as the educational purposes of schools. There is a strong sense of being political where local practice can impact and change the national scene. Heads associate with the social justice aim of New Labour but are concerned about the managerialism embedded in strategic thinking and delivery and are active in their opposition to this, not least through their practice. As one headteacher puts it:

... its still that thing about, (1) making sure that every child actually can thrive in terms of our social democracy, (2) making sure that you create a sense in which you open up what it counts to be successful in terms of a learner rather than just five A to Cs and, (3) that you have an absolute remit to work in a sense of social justice and community and to build up fairness and a model of community so that you model something in a sense which you yourself can approve, appreciate and enjoy (Barry).

Ambivalent implementers

These heads make up 50% of the sample. There is more of an acceptance of the official positioning, even though frustration (and some disillusionment) is evident. There is a local orientation to problem solving, as one heads states in response to workforce changes:

And I actually naively came into headship thinking, right it's a national programme so people will be finding solutions. And I suddenly realised the solutions are local to the school and you have to find them (Lisa).

There is a drive in some of these heads to take risks to protect the local situation, which is usually about filtering national demands in relation to school priorities, but can be more dramatic for particular schools where national standards and OfSTED inspections could threaten survival. For example, one headteacher talks about setting up a local nursery without local authority permission, and this combined with other changes to service provision has meant that there have been no redundancies.

Reform agenda deliverers

These heads are a quarter of the sample. These heads operate close to government in relation to policy advice and delivery, and as such reveal a New Labour disposition through focusing on failing schools and national standards. There is concern about reforms and the manner in which they are imposed, not least how one head talked about the patronising nature of headteachers being told that they don't know how to do things. However, the dominance of functionalism is accepted and these heads seek to ensure the right type of interventions are made in schools so that centralism does not cause dysfunctional processes and outcomes. They are actively involved in government consultations and training:

... I have been invited twice to Downing Street to discuss government policy and changes in educational practice. So I think they do listen [...] And I have been able to have telephone conversations with them to say, 'look I approve of this, but do you realise the implications of the other?' (Name of Government Advisor) has been to this school. I think they have made themselves available and they have not hidden in ivory towers, and I think that is very laudable (Linda).

There is a tendency to publicly accept the charismatic leader role demanded by the reform agenda:

> ... I was invited four years ago to a meeting in London by the DfES. I hadn't a clue why I was, and there were about 200 of us there nationally. And that was because we had been identified as being transformational leaders. And it had come through a whole variety of OfSTED reports, knowledge from the DfES of you, LEA recommendations and so on (Linda).

There is recognition that being close to government enables them to see and engage with the insider politics in the production of policy. In Bourdieu's (2000) terms there is a symbolic exchange taking place where heads gain an opportunity to shape and indeed lead on reforms, are rewarded with honours, and in return they provide legitimacy for government through policy based on consultation.

In summary, we would argue that Lingard *et al.*'s (2003: 74) notion of 'productive leadership habitus', encompassing the dimensions of reflexivity and moral preparedness of the educational leader ('do the most good and cause the right change') along with 'the capacity and disposition to deal with the wholeness of the school', applies to understanding educational leadership. The headteachers in our study demonstrate various leadership approaches and different responses to centrally determined policies and, arguably, their leadership habitus is revealed through the choices they make. Hence we have gone beyond the descriptive technical features of New Public Management towards the reported lived experience of how a group of professionals have responded to attempts to change their power relationships with teachers and children. Some feel constrained in their educational leadership work and by the unremitting torrent of government policy initiatives. Others are seemingly more acquiescent to the reform agenda and their involvement with various government agencies is experienced as enhancing their professional identity as school leaders. Our data shows however the complexity of leadership for while headteachers may appear to accommodate modernisation in the way advocated by government they do not necessarily subscribe wholeheartedly to the values, which underpin New Labour's managerialism. Indeed all headteachers in this study had their own moral purposes for education and their own ideas regarding the qualities required for 'effective' leadership. These have been formulated depending upon the nature of their leadership habitus and are usually based on child-centred principles.

Conclusion

Public policy in England over the last quarter of a century has drawn on neoliberal knowledge production processes in order to frame and intervene in the work of headteachers. Old ideas of the headmaster tradition have been recombined with normative models of the entrepreneur located as an empowered local deliverer of national reforms. However the market penetration of public services means that headteachers as leaders, while serving a purpose in the early part of the decade, are increasingly viewed as part of the problem. While New Labour inherited and strengthened the headteacher as local leader, the shift has been towards effective organisational leadership that is generic and open to all who can demonstrate the requisite knowledge, attributes and skills.

Like Beech *et al.* (2008) we are interested in the work and workings of identity and there is ample evidence in policy texts and discourses of a direct intervention to do identity work with headteachers. We have shown how headteachers are being positioned by policy and how they position themselves. Notably, the headteachers we have worked with have to varying degrees taken on board and seek to improve the received neoliberal identity promoted by New Labour, or have rejected it in favour of educational and moral purposes, or experience ambivalence regarding their aim to do no harm to children but at the same time knowing that technical implementation of externally determined reforms is a requirement. We have therefore not engaged with particular styles of leadership but with the politics of headteacher identity as leaders, doing leading and exercising leadership. This has enabled us to relate the professional practice of headteachers to the bigger picture of neoliberal reforms under both Thatcherite and Blairite regimes. Such a picture shows that while considerable symbolic and economic capital remains invested (where we can be forgiven for thinking that the normality of headteachers seems to be unassailable), policy discourse suggests that what is actually emerging is a trajectory where generic leaders are deemed to be the most effective in the market place.

We have been studying headship at a particular moment in time, and while studies are concerned with how heads are doing their job and how they might do it better through prescriptive models of leadership, this is, to use Silver's (1990) words, an example of being busy but blind. The opening up of public sector services to the market means that a neoliberal disposition is needed, and this may or may not come from those who remain as headteachers. Our position could be characterised as somewhat 'unmodern' because we want to make a case for education to be led by those who are immersed in teaching and learning. Hence we should not be distracted by low level debates about which leadership model to use or how to lead change, but about the professional expertise, values, and the particular knowledge of what it means to work with people and children in pedagogic processes.

Acknowledgements

The research on which this paper is based was funded by the ESRC through the Knowledge Production in Educational Leadership Project 2006–2007 (ESRC RES-000-23-1192). We would like to thank the ESRC for supporting this research, and we are deeply grateful to the people from all parts of the education system who have told us their stories and participated by giving generously of their time. In particular we would like to thank the headteachers who have participated and the MEd students in the School of Education at the University of Manchester for their analytical and professional perspectives. We would like to thank the members of the Project Advisory Group for their engagement with the research and for the productive dialogue.

References

Ball, S.J. (2003) 'The Teacher's Soul and the Terrors of Performativity', *Journal of Education Policy*, 18(2): 215–228.

Ball, S.J. (2007) *Education PLC*. London: Routledge.

Barber, M. (1996) *The Learning Game: Arguments for an Education Revolution*. London: Victor Gollancz.

Barber, M. (2007) *Instruction to Deliver: Tony Blair, the Public Services and the Challenge of Achieving Targets*. London: Politico's Publishing.

Barker, B. (2005) *Transforming Schools: Illusion or Reality*. Stoke-on-Trent: Trentham Books Ltd.

Barker, B. (2006) 'The Leadership Paradox: Can School Leaders Transform Student Outcomes?', *School Effectiveness and School Improvement*, 18(1): 21–43.

Beech, N., MacIntosh, R. and McInnes, P. (2008) 'Identity Work: Processes and Dynamics of Identity Formations', *International Journal of Public Administration*, 31(9): 957–970.

Bolam, R. (1986) 'The National Development Centre for School Management Training', in Hoyle, E. and McMahon, A. (eds) *World Yearbook of Education 1986*. London: Kogan Page.

Bottery, M. (2007a) 'Reports from the Front Line: English Headteachers' Work in an Era of Practice Centralization', *Educational Management Administration and Leadership*, 35(1): 89–110.

Bottery, M. (2007b) 'New Labour Policy and School Leadership in England: Room for Manoeuvre?', *Cambridge Journal of Education*, 37(2): 153–172.

Bourdieu, P. (2000) *Pascalian Meditations*. Cambridge: Polity Press.

Bristow, M., Ireson, G. and Coleman, A. (2007) *A Life in the Day of a Headteacher*. Nottingham: NCSL.

Bush, T., Bell, L., Bolam, R., Glatter, R. and Ribbins, P. (eds) (1999) *Educational Management: Redefining Theory, Policy and Practice*. London: Paul Chapman Publishing.

Clarke, C. (2003) 'Speech by Charles Clarke', NCSL conference, 13th November 2003.

Clarke, J., Gewirtz, S. and McLaughlin, E. (2000) 'Reinventing the Welfare State', in Clarke, J., Gewirtz, S. and McLaughlin, E. (eds) *New Managerialism, New Welfare?* London: Sage.

Coulson, A.A. (1976) 'The Role of the Primary Head', in Bush, T., Glatter, R., Goodey, J. and Riches, C. (eds) *Approaches to School Management*, pp. 274–292. London: Harper & Row Ltd.

Coupland, C., Currie, G. and Boyett, I. (2008) 'New Public Management and a Modernization Agenda: Implications for School Leadership', *International Journal of Public Administration*, 31(9): 1079–1094.

DfEE (1997) *Excellence in Schools*. London: The Stationary Office Limited. Cm 2681.

DfEE (1998) *Teachers: Meeting The Challenge of Change*. London: The Stationery Office Limited.

DfEE (1999) *National College for School Leadership: A Prospectus*. London: DfEE.

DfES (2004) *National Standards for Headteachers*. London: DfES.

DfES/PricewaterhouseCoopers (2007) *Independent Study into School Leadership*. London: DfES.

Earley, P., Evans, J., Collarbone, P., Gold, A. and Halpin, D. (2002) *Establishing the Current State of School Leadership in England*. London: DfES. Research Report RR336.

Edmonds, E.L. (1968) *The First Headship*. Oxford: Basil Blackwell.

EMA (1999) 'Special Edition: Redefining Educational Management and Leadership', *Educational Management and Administration*, 27(3): 227–343.

Goss, P. (2008) *An Investigation into the Possible Pressures on Headteachers – Particularly the Current School Inspection Arrangements in England And Wales – And the Potential Impact on Recruitment*. Haywards Heath: NAHT.

Grace, G. (1995) *School Leadership: Beyond Educational Management. An Essay in Policy Scholarship*. London: The Falmer Press.

Gronn, P. (2003) *The New Work of Educational Leaders*. London: Sage.

Gunter, H.M. (1997) *Rethinking Education: The Consequences of Jurassic Management*. London: Cassell.

Gunter, H.M. and Forrester, G. (2008a) 'Knowledge Production in Educational Leadership Project', Final Report to the ESRC. RES-000-23-1192.

Gunter, H.M. and Forrester, G. (2008b) 'New Labour and School Leadership 1997–2007', *British Journal of Educational Studies*, 55(2): 144–162.

Gunter, H.M. and Ribbins, P. (2003) 'The Field of Educational Leadership: Studying Maps and Mapping Studies', *British Journal of Educational Studies*, 51(3): 254–281.

Hall, V. (1996) *Dancing on the Ceiling*. London: Paul Chapman Publishing.

Hall, V., Mackay, H. and Morgan, C. (1986) *Headteachers at Work*. Milton Keynes: OUP.

Hall, V. and Southworth, G. (1997) 'Headship', *School Leadership and Management*, 17(2): 151–170.

Hollins, K., Gunter, H.M. and Thomson, P. (2006) 'Living Improvement: A Case study of a Secondary School in England', *Improving Schools*, 9(2): 141–152.

House of Commons (1998) 'The Role of Headteachers', Education and Employment Committee, Nineth Report, Volume I. London: The Stationary Office.

Huber, S., Moorman, H. and Pont, B. (2007) 'School Leadership for Systemic Improvement in England. A Case Study Report for the OECD Activity, Improving School Leadership', Improving School Leadership Activity, Education and Training Division, OECD. www.oecd.org/edu/schoolleadership.

Leithwood, K., Day, C., Sammons, P., Harris, A. and Hopkins, D. (2006) *Seven Strong Claims About Successful School Leadership*. Nottingham: NCSL.

Lightfoot, L. and Asthana, A. (2008) 'Schools in Crisis Hunt for 1,000 New Heads', *The Observer*. www.guardian.co.uk/education/2008/sep/14/teachershortage.school/print. Accessed 18/9/08.

Lingard, B., Hayes, D., Mills, M. and Christie, P. (2003) *Leading Learning: Making Hope Practical in Schools*. Maidenhead, Berkshire: Open University Press.

Munby, S. (2006) 'The School Leadership Challenges for the 21st Century', Speech at the NCSL. www.ncsl.org.uk/media/653/C4/school-leadership-challenges-for-the-twenty-first-century-speech.pdf

NCSL (2007) *What We Know About School Leadership*. Nottingham: NCSL.

O'Shaughnessy, J. (2007) *The Leadership Effect: Can Headteachers Make a Difference?* London: The Policy Exchange.

Ozga, J. (2000) *Policy Research in Educational Settings*. Buckingham: OUP.

Pascal, C. and Ribbins, P. (1998) *Understanding Primary Headteachers*. London: Cassell.

Performance and Innovation Unit (2001) *Strengthening Leadership*. London: www.number-10.gov.uk/su/leadership. Accessed 23/03/04.

PMSU (2006) *The UK Government's Approach to Public Service Reform – A Discussion Paper*. London: PMSU.

Raffo, C. and Gunter, H.M. (2008) 'Leading Schools to Promote Social Inclusion: Developing a Conceptual Framework for Analysing Research, Policy and Practice', *Journal of Education Policy*, 23(4): 363–380.

Rayner, S. and Ribbins, P. (1999) *Headteachers and Leadership in Special Education*. London: Cassell.

Ribbins, P. and Marland, M. (1994) *Headship Matters*. Harlow: Longman.

Silver, H. (1990) *Education, Change and the Policy Process*. Lewes: The Falmer Press.

Southworth, G. (1995) *Looking in Primary Headship*. London: The Falmer Press.

Thomson, P. (2001) 'How Principals Lose "Face" A Disciplinary Tale of Educational Administration and Modern Managerialism', *Discourse: Studies in the Cultural Politics of Education*, 22(1): 5–22.

Thomson, P. and Blackmore, J. (2006) 'Beyond the Power of One: Redesigning the Work of School Principals', *Journal of Educational Change*, 7: 161–177.

Wallace, M. and Hall, V. (1994) *Inside the SMT: Teamwork in Secondary School Management*. London: Paul Chapman Publishing.

5
Policing, New Public Management and Legitimacy[1]

Mike Hough

Introduction

This chapter charts the emergence – and subsequent decline – of New Public Management (NPM) on policing in Britain. I shall argue that it had a negative impact on the quality of policing in Britain, imposing an overly crude conception of 'policing as crime control' on government policy.[2] Over the period that NPM was most in evidence in government policy crime fell steeply; yet public confidence in the police also showed steep falls over the same period. The chapter will argue that policing policy of the period needed to pay much more attention to more subtle policy goals of building institutional legitimacy in order to foster public consent to the rule of law. It will trace the way in which policing policy is showing clear signs of moving in the right direction, away from NPM solutions and towards a more sophisticated conception of policing. But the chapter will also point to the risk that the pursuit of public confidence in the police could result in a form of policing that actually does little to build consent to the rule of law amongst those who are most at risk of engagement in crime.

In essence, it is argued that NPM attempts to 'modernise' the British police narrowed the police function in a way that damaged public satisfaction with, and confidence in, the police. Senior police picked up on this before central government, and initiated a new 'Reassurance Policing' policy to counteract the trend. The chapter concludes by suggesting that the new policy (or in some senses the reversion to an old policy) could serve as a means to revivify police legitimacy – but it could be hijacked by those who want to co-opt the 'law abiding majority' in a 'war against crime'. The crudity of thought in this sort of Manichaeanism is no less risky and counterproductive than the thinking that underpins the 'war against terror' that I associate with the Bush and Blair administrations.

Legitimacy and criminal justice

The idea of policing by consent – building the legitimacy of the institutions of policing – has a long history, whose origins can be traced to the establishment of the Metropolitan Police, and the stress laid by its founders on the importance of securing public cooperation.[3] And community policing principles, articulated by various senior officers over the post-war consistently emphasised policing by consent (see, for example, Alderson 1979, 1984). Criminologists, notably Robert Reiner (1992) charted the processes of legitimation pursued by the police. The centrality of police legitimacy was also implicit in the land-mark judicial enquiry chaired by Lord Scarman into the urban riots that occurred in 1981 (Scarman 1981). In the period following the riots of the early/mid-1980s, both government policy and senior police officers often articulated the assumption that good relations between police and public would yield cooperation and compliance with the law.

Thereafter the idea that police legitimacy was a crucial dimension to policing became increasingly less visible in public and political debate throughout the 1990s and into the 21st century. In part this may reflect the fact that relations between the British police and poor urban communities were much calmer over the 15 year period from 1990 than in the 1980s – reducing pressure on the police and policing academics to scrutinise the quality of consent to policing amongst the public.

However, it would be misleading to suggest that the problems of police/community relations had become solved over this period. Relations between police and public remained poor for some groups, particularly those minority ethnic groups who are at risk of social exclusion (see, for example, FitzGerald *et al.* 2002). Thus other explanations are needed for the lack of engagement in Britain in the 1990s with ideas about police legitimacy and public compliance, and for the retreat from principles of policing by consent that were commonplace in the 1970s and 1980s. The main theme of this chapter is that debate about policing was drawn away from these issues by the combined effect of the New Public Management (NPM) reforms of the British police, which can be dated to around 1990, and the related emergence at the same time of a crude political populism in relation to law and order. These interacted in such a way that political questions about criminal justice in general, and policing in particular, began to be cast more simplistically than previously. Political debate started to take for granted a narrowly instrumental model of crime control. Politicians across the spectrum tended to assume that the role of the police is to control crime, and that the criminal justice system works achieves its purpose largely through the deployment of a credible deterrent threat. More subtle conceptions of policing were lost from political debate until quite recently.

New public management in Britain

Other chapters in this part of the volume trace the emergence of the 'modernisation agenda' for public services that Conservative and Labour governments shared.[4] The tools of NPM are familiar to most public services:

budgetary cuts, applying private sector management methods to the public sector, the introduction of purchaser/provider splits (or quasi-markets) within bureaucracies and the introduction of new providers, usually from the private sector, to compete with existing ones. These were intended to yield both efficiencies and greater responsiveness to the consumers of public services.

If the Conservative administration introduced this approach, New Labour developed and extended it from 1997 onward, with a vigour that only began to wane in the late 2000s. As with the previous Conservative administration, their basic approach was to secure greater accountability through performance management regimes that relied on quantitative performance indicators and target-setting. The concept of competition as a lever on performance was being retained, though the language of 'privatisation' and 'market testing' was replaced by that of 'contestability'.[5]

The key feature of NPM was the centralised definition of ends and the decentralisation of decisions about means. Various further features emerge as a consequence. NPM's logic points inevitably to a particular emphasis on processes of *prioritisation*. It is hard to quarrel with the basic principle that organisations should identify their key priorities and focus their energies on them. The risk is that systematic and focused action against *misidentified* or *poorly identified* priorities can have worse consequences than poorly marshalled and ineptly implemented action against well-specified priorities. The chapter aims to show that British policing fell prey to this precise risk.

NPM and policing in Britain

The police initially managed to escape the reforming attention of the Thatcher and Major administrations. Throughout the 1980s the Labour opposition failed to offer any plausible challenge to the Conservatives on 'law and order' and there was little political capital to be made from 'taking on' the police – even though crime was rising quite steeply over this period. However, in the early 1990s, New Labour, still in opposition, began to promote policies that promised to be 'tough on crime, tough on the causes of crime'. Ever since then, criminal justice politics have been characterised by intense political competition, with the two main parties aiming to prove themselves tougher than their opponents at every opportunity. Political debate about crime has been marked – or marred – by intense populism (see Roberts and Hough 2002; Roberts *et al.* 2003). Politicians have wanted to see politically marketable results from the police, and as a consequence, the latter have fallen increasingly under the NPM spotlight. The key changes since the early 1990s have been changes in legislation, on the one hand, designed to provide central government with greater powers to direct local police chiefs, and on the other hand, the development of an extensive suite of quantitative performance management systems designed to hold local police to account. In other words, there was a considerable shift in power from the local – as represented by chief constables, on the one hand, and their police authorities, on the other – to central government, in the shape of the Home Secretary.

The targets set for the police by their local police authorities and by the Home Secretary were, at the height of the NPM period, very largely to do with crime. This led to a marked simplification of public statements about policing. The police had to formalise their organisational aims and objectives, and to state them publicly in a way that allowed quantitative targets to be set. This led to an emphasis on crime-fighting goals. These had the appearance, at least, of being readily quantifiable. At the same time they were able to command public assent because they embodied simple, common-sense objectives of public protection. The fact that these pressures were at work until the mid-1990s against a backdrop of rising crime and an increasingly populist political debate about 'law and order' meant that senior police officers initially offered little challenge to the form of managerialism to which they had been subjected. It was not until the turn of the century that reforming police chiefs began to offer an alternative vision of policing.

Trends in crime and public perceptions

Trends in crime in Britain can be simply described. With minor fluctuations most categories of crime increased, year on year, from 1950 until the

Figure 5.1   Trends in Perceptions of Crime Trends

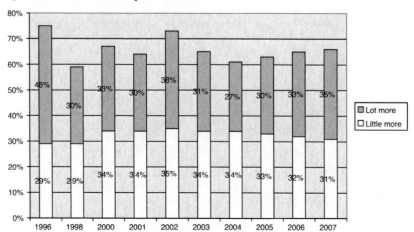

Notes: 1. *Source*: British Crime Survey (e.g. Kershaw *et al.* 2008).
2. Question wording: I would like to ask whether you think that the level of crime in the country as a whole has changed over the past two years. Would you say there is more crime, less crime or about the same amount since two years ago?

mid-1990s. Since then, with some exceptions, crime has fallen. This broad picture can be derived both from recorded crime statistics and from the British Crime Survey (BCS) though the interpretation of recorded crime statistics since 1998 has been complicated by successive changes to procedures for compiling the statistics (see e.g. Kershaw *et al.* 2008). It is clear, however, that people in Britain have not been sensitive to the trend. For some years the BCS has asked people whether they think crime has risen over the last years. Figure 5.1 shows the trend from 1996. In every year apart from 1998, over 60% thought that crime had risen – despite the fact that it had been consistently falling.

Equally or more worrying from the viewpoint of senior police managers, trends in ratings of police performance continued to decline over time. Figure 5.2 shows trends from 1982 until 2002 public ratings of local police. Clearly there is a long-run downward trend. The proportion of people who thought the police did a very good job in 2002/03 was a third of the figure in 1982. (Unfortunately, the BCS question was changed at this point, and so that a longer-run trend into the mid-2000s cannot be offered.)

The marked decline in ratings until 1996 is not especially surprising. After all, crime was actually rising over this period until 1995, and as mentioned earlier, the 1980s saw some of the worst riots that had ever occurred

Figure 5.2   Trends in Ratings of the Police Locally

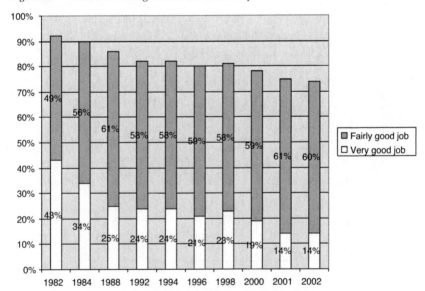

Notes: 1. *Source*: British Crime Survey (e.g. Nicholas *et al.* 2005).
2. Question: 'Taking everything into account, would you say the police in this area do a good job or a poor job?

in British cities, some of which were linked to tensions between the police and public. But the continued – and steep – decline thereafter was puzzling, because – for the first time in half a century – the underlying trend in crime had actually reversed.

The 'reassurance gap'

The survey data chimed with senior police officers' own perceptions that the police were rapidly losing ground in terms of public approval. At the turn of the century, senior officers associated with the reforming wing of the Association of Chief Police Officers (ACPO) were beginning to talk about the 'reassurance gap' as a way of referring to the divergence of trends in crime as perceived by the public and as measured by statistics. As one Chief Constable expressed it:

> Why has this [reassurance] gap arisen? Research suggests that it is because the incivilities that the public experiences in town centres and on housing estates belie the soothing message of criminal statistics. The police have become increasingly less visible and the public are sceptical about alternatives (O'Connor 2001).

The ACPO argument, in essence, was that reductions in crime had been bought at the expense of a retreat from the policing of less serious, but more visible, forms of disorder. Within it there was a submerged critique of the government's NPM approach to modernising the police – that the prioritisation of specific 'volume crimes' such as burglary and car theft had necessarily *deprioritised* other important police functions such as the policing of low-level disorder.

Falling police ratings may also reflect broader social shifts. For example, throughout the post-war period there has been a progressive decline in deference to authority, reflected for example in the rapidly falling popularity of the Royal Family and growing scepticism about the British Broadcasting Corporation. The long-run decline in ratings of the police seem likely to reflect generational differences, rather than a reaction to falls in the quality of policing. However, it should be stressed that the steepest falls in ratings of the police occurred over a five year period from the mid-1990s – at precisely the time when NPM 'modernisation' reforms were having their most marked impact.

The unintended effects of NPM target-setting

The Policing for London Study (PFLS) that this author mounted with colleagues in 2000–2002 provides ample support for the ACPO analysis. It also rendered explicit a series of unintended effects of NPM target-setting

(FitzGerald *et al.* 2002). PFLS found that these unintended consequences were a significant factor in falling public confidence in the Metropolitan Police. The study involved a large-scale sample of Londoners and analysis of administrative records, as well as extensive qualitative interviews and focus groups with members of the public and police officers.

The findings added to a growing body of evidence about the distorting effects of crude target-setting in other public services. Targets to reduce hospital waiting lists distorted access to treatment, favouring patients whose operations can be done quickly rather than those who are in greatest need. Similarly measuring schools' performance by the number of pupils getting a specified number of exams at a specified level has focused effort on those of middling ability whose performance can be raised across that critical threshold; to meet the target there is no need to put effort into the high-performers and no point in bothering with those of limited ability. This form of educational *triage* was certainly not foreseen by central government, and served to undermine their intention, of achieving improvements across the board in educational achievement.

In other words the bluntness of central government controls meant that they often failed to work as intended. The assumption behind setting such relatively crude targets is that agencies would tailor their work to the intention *behind* the target. The reality has now emerged very clearly that – where individuals' rewards and organisations' resources are at stake – organisations adopt a contractual approach to meeting targets, achieving them with scant regard to the unintended consequences of doing so. The PFLS suggests that this is just as true of policing as for other public services. A recurrent phrase in our interviews with police officers was: 'What can't be measured doesn't count and what doesn't count doesn't get done'.

The highly centralised management system with a heavy emphasis on compliance with numerical targets also appears to have disempowered middle managers and demoralised their staff. The targets that local managers had to deliver did not match with the workforce's understanding of what the job was actually about. This compounded the cynicism about management that is in any case inherent in 'cop culture', and undermined the workforce's sense of purpose.

Concerns about staff management and staff development were numerous. There are some reasons to believe that 'it was ever thus'; many studies of the police have found this, including the PSI study of which the PFLS was the sequel (Smith 1983). Cynicism about management has been an enduring part of the police occupational culture. However disaffection with managers was very explicitly linked in PFLS with the current performance management regime. These problems were compounded by the rapid turnover of senior staff at borough level, which made it hard to ensure sufficient continuity to provide for effective leadership. Senior staff also felt that their ability to provide this leadership was hampered by the plethora of demands relating to performance management and by other demands on their time. Cumulatively these factors appeared to have a serious impact on the morale of the staff who carried the main burden of responsibility for day-to-day contact with the public.

A changing tide: Reassurance policing and neighbourhood policing

From 2000 ACPO began to develop a Reassurance Policing Strategy to respond constructively to the 'reassurance gap', and plans for a pilot of the concept surfaced in 2001. Reassurance Policing drew on the 'Signal Crimes Perspective' (SCP) developed by Martin Innes, Nigel Fielding and colleagues. SCP suggests that particular acts of crime and disorder, and particular forms of social control, have a disproportionate impact upon how individuals and communities experience and construct their beliefs about crime, disorder and control (Innes *et al.* 2002).

SCP's implications for policing – if policing is constructed as the production of a public sense of security – is that the police should be as systematic as possible in identifying signal crimes and signal disorders, and in committing effort to tackling these in proportion to the impact they have on public perceptions of crime. Incivilities and anti-social behaviour are more common and more visible than the crimes in relation to which the government's NPM target regime measures impact. Innes and colleagues found that specific subsets of incivilities tended to function as 'signal disorders', including alcohol-related problems; drug-related problems and signs of drug use; young people loitering; aggressive begging; graffiti and vandalism. These findings go some way to explain the resilience of public concern about security and order – even if BCS measures of anxiety about the crime types that have shown the largest declines – burglary and vehicle crime – show a fall commensurate with the crime trends.

ACPO secured – initially lukewarm – government support for the reassurance policing pilot. Resources followed, and the pilot started in 2002. Originally set in two police forces (the Metropolitan Police Service and Surrey Police) it soon extended to several other forces. In practical terms it involved assigning small policing teams full-time to clearly defined neighbourhoods. They were tasked with auditing their area for signal crimes, and mounting appropriate problem-solving responses. There was also an emphasis on establishing a visible police presence, on responsivity to public concerns and on policing styles that would engender public trust and confidence.

The intellectual underpinnings of reassurance policing were thus rather more subtle than those on which NPM performance management in the 1990s drew. The latter presupposed that the task of the police is simply the control of crime, and that the police should concentrate their efforts on those crimes that deserve highest priority. By contrast, reassurance policing recognised that public perceptions of crime and of policing played a part in processes of social control. However reassurance policing adopted one dimension of the new Public Management agenda – a consumerist focus, in its very explicit orientation towards reducing citizens' sense of insecurity.

In practical terms reassurance policing had much in common with the community policing experiments that were tried in the 1970s and 1980s. An important difference, for our purposes, is that the idea of *policing by consent* was much less visible. In other words, public security was the primary police product of reassurance policing, rather than compliance with the law. The majority of the public were not to be *policed*, but to be *protected*. Reassuring the public and tackling crime were regarded as co-dependent, of course, but the public's compliance of the law was taken as unproblematic – with the exception, of course, of the minority of people engaged in criminality. Good relations between police and public were seen as supporting efforts to tackle crime by increasing the flow of intelligence, but not as a means of legitimating police authority and thus securing greater compliance with the law. Although there is no evidence beyond the anecdotal for suggesting this, the chapter suggests that it always appeared to be that the concepts of police legitimacy and legitimating authority infused the thinking behind reassurance policing, but that these were purposefully never rendered explicit – a point to which the chapter returns to.

After a positive Home Office evaluation (Tuffin *et al.* 2006) the reassurance policing pilots have been judged a success, and the programme was reshaped into a much larger Neighbourhood Policing Programme, launched in April 2005. This achieved national coverage of neighbourhood policing teams in local areas by 2008. The teams are typically small, and their composition is intended to be tailored to local circumstances. For example, the teams in London typically comprise a sergeant, two or three constables and two or three police community support officers – who as their name suggests are police ancillaries who operate without full police powers. Teams elsewhere may include wardens or youth workers.

The retreat from NPM in policing

At the time of writing, it seems that there has been a sea-change in the governance of policing, and that the government has turned its back on the micro-management of policing activity embedded in NPM. Following a review by a senior civil servant, Louise Casey (2008), the Government published a Green Paper on policing (Home Office 2008) that proposed the abolishing of all but one of the quantitative policing targets that had been imposed on the police. The remaining target was a survey-based one, designed to reflect public confidence in policing. The wording was as follows:

> How much do you agree or disagree that police and local councils are dealing with the anti-social behaviour and crime issues that matter in your area?

Leaving aside the technical merits of the question – which conflates police and council performance, as well as crime and anti-social behaviour – it is clear that this target will stimulate a responsiveness to local preferences, and should institutionalise the philosophy of neighbourhood policing in police management. There remains some scepticism whether the government will genuinely abandon the extensive panoply of policing targets that it has established over the last ten years. There is also a question-mark over the ability of this new approach to the governance of policing to survive under a new political administration – which at the time of writing looked a very likely possibility. However, the retreat for NPM managerialism has had the backing of all the main political parties, and it seems unlikely that we shall return to the excesses of NPM which occurred around the turn of the century.

It remains to be seen precisely what direction of travel is taken by the new policy for promoting 'confidence in justice'. At best it will provide the police and the courts with a new vocabulary for thinking about institutional legitimacy. It is to be hoped that politicians and criminal justice managers will pay more attention to identifying the drivers of legitimacy – and to finding ways of building trust in justice in those groups whose commitment to the rule of law is weakest. The result could be a set of progressive policies which paid more attention to the professional style and manner of law enforcement officials in their dealings with suspects, defendants and others. There is a growing body of evidence that 'procedural justice' is a key determinant of legitimacy in justice. That is, public compliance with the law increases when justice systems treat people fairly and with respect (cf Tyler and Huo 2002; Tyler 2003; Tyler 2007).

On the other hand, there is a risk that the 'confidence agenda' could easily degenerate into a set of intensely populist and punitive policies. The government's statements about public engagement have a Manichaean tendency to contrast the 'law abiding majority' with 'criminals':

> Crime is tackled most effectively when the law-abiding majority stand together against the minority who commit it (Casey 2008).

Promoting public confidence is seen as a means of securing public cooperation in the 'fight against crime', and confidence is pursued with a consumerist model of justice according to which the system should be responsive to the wishes and preferences of the law-abiding. The risk of this resulting in a set of highly illiberal policies that 'rebalance rights in favour of the victim' is only too obvious. The best way of mitigating this risk is to focus on building trust in justice amongst those groups whose commitment to the rule of law is most fragile. The parallels with the Bush/Blair 'war on terror' are obvious: the US and the UK pursued their war in a way that assumed that human rights could be traded for safety. This strategy seriously damaged the legitimacy of their enterprise, and served as a counterproductive 'recruiting sergeant' for those on the margins of radicalisation. Criminal justice policy needs to learn from this, no less than foreign policy.

Conclusions

One can only welcome the move away from the simplistic conception of crime control that was embedded in NPM thinking in the 1990s, and the removal of the straight-jacket of targets to which the police were subject. There are some signs that public concern about low level disorder peaked in the first part of this decade, and that it is now declining (see Nicholas *et al.* 2005; Flatley *et al.* 2008).

I have argued that the targets selected for the police in the 1990s narrowed the police function, and squeezed out both the capacity and the motivation of the police to respond to problems of low level disorder. This retreat from the policing of disorder was noticed by the public, but the falls in crime were not. The result was a fall in public ratings of the police. Whether one views the public as consumers of public protection services or as citizens whose consent to police authority is required, the downward trend is obviously undesirable.

Explaining how politicians allowed themselves to adopt such crude policing policies is complex. The nature of the current political process is such that politicians find themselves trapped in common-sense discourse even in those situations where more subtlety of thought and action might be preferable. Over the last two decades – in parallel with the development of the modernisation agenda – the British media have increasingly constrained politicians' room for manoeuvre on criminal justice issues. The press can define the terms of political debate, and they can force politicians to respond within the terms they set. Thus however subtle a grasp there may be in central government of the nature of policing, politicians' public pronouncements, including the targets that they pursue, have to be forced into a simple mould (see Roberts *et al.* 2003 for a fuller discussion).

A different explanation altogether is that government lacks skills and knowledge not in relation to the institutions it aims to control, but in the *processes* of control themselves. Thus the tools for performance management that are available to New Public Management modernisers are too crude for their ambitions. Experience of the modernisation agenda to date suggests that this has occurred in several public services. There are ample examples of the perverse effects of target-setting and of statistical performance management not only in criminal justice but in education, health and transport as similar chapters in this part of the volume have highlighted.

There is a further possible explanation of the crudity with which policing has been conceptualised by NPM modernisers. The institutions of the criminal justice system evolved in Victorian times into a shape that is still recognisable today, and many are struggling. The difficulty in finding any effective solutions is that there is no coherent political discourse about approaches to institution-building, and about strategies for achieving institutional legitimacy that will work in the 21st century. The NPM modernisation agenda has very largely framed the issues in ways that ignore the central requirements of institutions relating to legitimacy. Its concerns are to do with efficiency, effectiveness and with consumer satisfaction – none of which manage to encapsulate the subtleties of institutions' legitimacy.

We are now seeing, both in government and academia a resurgence of interest in issues of trust and legitimacy – both in policing and in broader issues of governance. It remains to be seen whether procedural justice perspectives will be incorporated explicitly in the thinking of those responsible for British police policy and management. One can see many possible benefits. If neighbourhood policing finds it feet, then there will be a need for sharper answers to questions about the purposes of engagement with, and responsiveness to, the public. Is the strategy simply designed to maximise cooperation and information flow? Or are there more fundamental underlying issues, about legitimating police authority and securing public compliance. If so, how is this best approached? The procedural justice literature provides a valuable set of concepts, and a growing body of empirical research, to help address these questions (cf Tyler and Huo 2002; Tyler 2003; Tyler 2007).

A new approach to performance management?

The more that a procedural justice perspective is adopted in thinking about police performance, the more there will be a need to re-engineer a new performance management framework. One of the central tenets of New Public Management is that conventional bureaucracies lose sight of outcomes in their obsession with process and that performance management systems should retain a clear outcome focus (cf Osborne and Gaebler 1992). Home Office managers would probably admit to the crudity of outcome measures applied up to the period of their own tenure. However, there has been a rumbling of dissent from performance measures based on outcomes for many years (see, for example, Joint Consultative Committee 1990; Horton and Smith 1988; Neyroud and Beckley 2001).

A common theme in these critiques is the need to improve performance by developing professional standards and focusing the efforts of managers on ensuring that their staff maintain these professional standards. Horton and Smith argue for the development of good practice standards; Neyroud and Beckley advocate a development of a 'professional model' of police practice that gives the individual officer greater personal responsibility within an ethical framework. American commentators such as Kelling (1999) have also argued for the development of good practice guidelines. The relationship between establishing professional and ethical standards and the legitimation of police authority is self-evident, of course.

These writers have conceptualised performance management as a two-stage process. Managers need to identify ways of working which achieve policing goals – to develop best practice. Best practice should be defined not simply in narrow instrumental terms, but in terms of behaviour that consolidates and supports police authority. Then they need to ensure that their staff meet best practice. What they should *not* do is expect a close-coupled relationship between delivering best practice and reducing crime. According to these perspectives, performance monitoring is not about the setting of targets for goal-achievement (or outcome achievement), but about monitoring policing practice against professional and ethical standards. Whilst policing needs to remain outcome-focused, it does not make sense to deny the complexity of the policing environment, and to expect to see a simple relationship between policing effort and the achievement of crime targets. The police – and their local partners – cannot be held directly responsible for the level of crime, and politicians should stop trying to do so.

Notes

1. This chapter is a shortened, revised and updated version of 'Policing, New Public Management and Legitimacy' published in 2007 in *Legitimacy and Criminal Justice* (ed. T. Tyler). New York: Russell Sage Foundation.
2. The chapter is almost entirely about policing in England and Wales. The Scottish and Northern Irish systems are separate and different, and were also less subjected to the excesses of NPM than England and Wales. With apologies to the latter, I refer to British policing simply in the interests of brevity.
3. See for example, the fourth of Rowan and Mayne's nine principles of policing, 'To recognise always that the extent to which the co-operation of the public can be secured diminishes proportionately to the necessity of the use of physical force and compulsion for achieving police objectives.' (quoted in Reith 1956)
4. Some, especially within New Labour, would take issues with the idea that modernisation is a variant of NPM, precisely because of the latter's identification with 'small government', in contrast to modernisation's commitment to social justice. However, the means to achieve these different ends look remarkably similar. There is something in the argument that NPM was exported from Thatcherite

Britain to the US, whence it was re-imported to Britain by Tony Blair during the Clinton administration.

5. Privatisation refers to the transfer of services from the public sector to the private sector, as has happened with British public utilities. 'Market testing' was the term used under the Conservative administration for arrangements whereby public bodies tendered in competition with the private sector for contracts covering the work over which they previously enjoyed a monopoly. Thus the Prison Service has for some time competed against private security companies for contracts to run prisons, and has often won these contracts. The Labour Government's preferred term for the same process is 'market testing'. See for example the Carter Review of the correctional services (Carter 2003).

References

Alderson, J. (1979) *Policing Freedom*. Plymouth: McDonald and Evans.

Alderson, J. (1984) *Law and Disorder*. London: Hamish Hamilton.

Carter, P. (2003) *Managing Offenders, Reducing Crime*. London: Prime Minister's Strategy Unit.

Casey, L. (2008) *Engaging Communities in Fighting Crime: A Review by Louise Casey*. London: Cabinet Office.

FitzGerald, M., Hough, M., Joseph, I. and Qureshi, T. (2002) *Policing for London*. Cullompton: Willan Publishing.

Flatley, J., Moley, S. and Hoare, J. (2008) 'Perceptions of Anti-Social Behaviour: Findings from the 2007/08 British Crime Survey', Supplementary Volume 1 to Crime in England and Wales 2007/08, *Home Office Statistical Bulletin*, 15/08. London: Home Office.

Home Office (2008) 'From the Neighbourhood to the National: Policing Our Communities Together', *The Policing Green Paper*. London: Home Office.

Horton, C. and Smith, D. (1988) *Evaluating Police Work*. London: Policy Studies Institute.

Joint Consultative Committee (1990) *Operational Policing Review*. Report published by ACPO, Superintendents' Association and Police Federation.

Kershaw, C., Nicholas, S. and Walker, A. (2008) 'Crime in England and Wales 2007/08', *Home Office Statistical Bulletin 07/08*. London: Home Office. Available at: http://www.homeoffice.gov.uk/rds/pdfs08/hosb0708.pdf

Innes, M., Fielding, N. and Langan, S. (2002) 'Signal Crimes and Control Signals: Towards an Evidence Based Conceptual Framework for Reassurance Policing', *A Report for Surrey Police*. Guildford: University of Surrey.

Kelling, G.L. (1999) *'Broken Windows' and Police Discretion. NCJ 178259*. Washington: National Institute of Justice [http://www.ojp.usdoj.gov/nij].

Nicholas, S., Povey, D., Walker, A. and Kershaw, C. (2005) *Crime in England and Wales, 2004/2005, Home Office Statistical Bulletin 11/05*. London: Home Office.

Neyroud, P. and Beckley, A. (2001) *Policing, Ethics and Human Rights*. Cullompton: Willan Publishing.

O'Connor, D. (2001) 'Civility First: The Reassurance Policing Concept', *Criminal Justice Management*, 26–27.

Osborne, D. and Gaebler, T. (1992) *Reinventing Government: How the Entrepreneurial Spirit is Transforming the Public Sector*. Reading, Massachusetts: Addison-Wesley.

Reiner, R. (1992) *The Politics of the Police (Second edition)*. London: Wheatsheaf Harvester.

Reith, C. (1956) *A New Study of Police History*. London: Oliver and Boyd.

Roberts, J.V. and Hough, M. (eds) (2002) *Changing Attitudes to Punishment: Public Opinion, Crime and Justice*. Cullompton: Willan Publishing.

Roberts, J.V., Stalans, L., Indermaur, D. and Hough, M. (2003) *Penal Populism and Public Opinion*. Oxford: OUP.

Scarman, Lord (1981) *The Brixton Disorders: Report of an Inquiry by the Rt. Hon. Lord Scarman OBE*. London: HMSO.

Smith, D.J. (1983) *Police and People in London: A Survey of Londoners*. London: Policy Studies Institute.

Tuffin, R., Morris, J. and Poole, A. (2006) 'An Evaluation of the Impact of the National Reassurance Policing Programme', *Home Office Research Study 296*. London: Home Office.

Tyler, T.R. and Huo, Y.J. (2002) *Trust in the Law: Encouraging Public Cooperation with the Police and Courts*. N.Y.: Russell-Sage Foundation.

Tyler, T.R. (2003) 'Procedural Justice, Legitimacy, and the Effective Rule of Law', in Tonry, M. (ed.), *Crime and Justice – A Review of Research*, 30: 431–505. Chicago: University of Chicago Press.

Tyler, T.R. (2007) *Legitimacy and Criminal Justice*. New York: Russell Sage Foundation.

6
Local Government Reform and Political Leadership

Peter John

Introduction

The administration of a wide range of local government services requires a similar kind of leadership to other public authorities. All public bodies, particularly to those with delivery functions, have to respond to policy changes introduced by Whitehall and in the European Union. They need to manage a complex environment, with many stakeholders and pressures on public services. But local authorities are different: they are led by elected politicians who draw their mandates from citizens living in their jurisdictions. The elected element creates a particular kind of leadership because a key pressure for policy change is directed by citizen voice and also by political parties with focused platforms. Most of all the leaders of local authorities are politicians rather than bureaucrats. They have an eye to the wider public and to managing political conflicts. Their careers do not depend on rising up the bureaucracy or transferring from place to place, but in making a difference locally, maintaining their reputations and keeping their rivals in their place.

In many ways having a politician in charge has many advantages even over and above the democratic arguments for having an elected element to local decision-making. Politicians have a broader source of legitimacy to manage public problems; they have the authority to bring the warring factions in partnerships together; they are able to aggregate interests into a coherent platform; they do not need to hide behind neutrality to get things done; and they should have clout to bring resources down from the central state. But the problem is that in the British context, local government has developed incrementally without much thought given to the political leader at the centre of the institution. Moreover, the national context has not been favourable to local political leadership, not allowing them the freedom and latitude to develop local policies. In all, this chapter identifies some weaknesses in the leadership that English local government has, which come from the institutional legacy, and a low equilibrium point for the local interest groups and organisations that make up the local political system. In all, this chapter identifies some weaknesses in the leadership that English local government has, which come from its institutional legacy and political history. In spite of some reforms during the last decade and a half that have pointed the way to the future, there is no sign that this weakness can be overcome.

The chapter begins by reviewing the historical context and the experience of the local government system as it has struggled to provide executive focus; it then reviews the changes in the policy environment of the 1980s and 1990s, before discussing the partially implemented reforms of the 2000s and suggesting which way local government leadership is going.

The historical context

Local authorities in England have tended to replicate both the structure and practice of parliamentary government, though with important differences. The 1835 Municipal Corporations Act, one of the foundational laws for local government, vested legal power in the elected council in much the same way as the British constitution gives parliament, or more precisely Crown-in-Parliament, the authority to act. Rather than cabinet and ministers, however, there was government by committee, which created a potentially more decentralised character to policy-making than at the national level of government, whereby the council's business was carried out by service-specific committees comprising elected representatives. As in the House of Commons, political leaders emerged when they headed the party with the ability to command a majority of seats on the council or at least when they led the largest party in a coalition. But there was no local equivalent to the prime minister, with formal powers of appointment, dismissal and the calling of elections. Whether they could appoint committee chairs was a consequence of the power relationships within the party group. With such trammels on their power, leaders could be vulnerable to challenge from discontented council members from their parties. The most famous example was just after the 1981 elections to the Greater London Council, when electors voted the Labour party into power, with Andrew McIntosh at its head, but a day later a backbench rebellion placed Ken Livingstone as leader. The more usual story is of leaders who cannot exercise power fully because they fear their colleagues will unseat them (Cole and John 2001). While leaders had ambitions to be like the long-serving mayors of French cities, in the end many were more tempted to abandon their posts after a couple of terms and to run for office to become members of parliament, severing their local roots and taking the backbencher role so as to position themselves for that elusive ministerial or opposition post. The rapid turnover of local politicians and the presence of former leaders of city governments in the House of Commons are familiar features of English politics.

Along with the tradition that administrative power in local government was decentralised to the service-dominated fiefdoms, the institutional framework before 2000 made for limited leadership or at least an invisible one. It has probably compounded the centralisation of English politics because there were no entrenched interests to overcome. Whereas the French executive faces a parliament stacked with elected mayors, especially in the Senate, both the Lords and Commons have happily voted through legislation to dismember local government. Critics suggested that the local executive was too weak and unaccountable (see Young 1994). Others believed that leaders were too consensual, a tendency that had became more marked over time (Norton 1978). None of this helped local leaders become barons with hitting power both in the centre and the locality.

The salience of party politics

Formal institutions do not tell the whole story. Parties, interest groups and political cultures have provided support for particular styles of local leadership. Local political parties have been strong organisations in Britain, especially when compared to their counterparts in other countries (John and Saiz 1999), which has meant that leaders can be decisive when they derived power through their parties. Rather than complete invisibility, the informal system produced some strong political figures: Herbert Morrison in London in the 1930s, John Braddock in Liverpool in the 1940s and 1950s and T. Dan Smith in Newcastle in the 1960s. However, scholars do not know whether these examples were exceptions from the bland uniformity of local political life or representative of a vibrant tradition. But charismatic local leaders emerged again in the politically turbulent decade of the 1980s: on the left there was Ken Livingstone in London, David Blunkett in Sheffield, Ted Knight in Lambeth and Derek Hatton in Liverpool; on the right there was Shirley Porter in Westminster, Eric Pickles in Bradford and Paul Beresford in Wandsworth. These leaders emerged in the vanguard of the radical movements that shook local party politics at that time (Gyford 1985).

Parties are a different type of organisation from political institutions. They are not as stable as formal arrangements; they also can also lack legitimacy in the eyes of the general public. While defenders of political parties argue that that the mechanisms of internal party democracy act as an effective check on political leaders, in the end such practices cannot be a substitute for formal democratic mechanisms because debates largely take place in secret, in what used to be called smoked-filled rooms, and decisions are not formally sanctioned by the democratic process. No matter how much deliberation occurs and how effectively the leaders' policies are developed and reviewed, there will always remain the suspicion that politics has taken place behind closed doors, a view that harkens back to the long suspicion democrats have of government by faction (cf. Madison *et al.* 1987). Even when the model works well, only a small proportion of the public has the chance to influence political debate directly. Thus the democratic function of parties, of aggregating and representing public opinion, needs to be complemented by formal and public procedures of scrutiny, review and challenge.

Before 2000 local government decision-making contrasted with its premodern legal framework. In most places majority party groups made the decisions, largely away from formal council and committee meetings, which made only the formal authorisation. Gyford *et al.* (1989) trace the gradual party politicisation of local government during the 20th century, where the leading national parties contested a greater number of council seats, more tightly organised themselves over council business and gave much greater definition of election manifestos. The early 1980s was the heyday of party organisation and control, giving way to less politicisation since that time. Parties also differ according to what part of the country they are in, and according to the ticket, with the Conservatives as the party where the leader is expected to lead. There are also differences according to whether parties are metropolitan or not, with greater tendency toward collective leadership in urban areas with Conservative authorities having more centralised patterns of leadership. In addition, there are local political cultures and traditions. Cole and John (2001) describe the emergence of a strong pattern of leadership in Leeds during the 1980s and 1990s, a development that owed a great deal to the well-organised Labour party, the acceptance of a clientelistic system of distributing benefits and a deferential political culture. These factors unified local politicians and elites behind the economic interests of the city. In Southampton the Labour leadership could not achieve such loyalty and obedience because of the power of factional interests in the party. A more diffuse political culture and less clear boundaries of the city did not stimulate such a strong articulation of political interests. Leach and Wilson (2000) find variations in political cultures according to the locality under study, which influence how the leader exercises power.

Such variations in the practice of political leadership occur in any political system, but where the leader has few formal powers, like the US president, power boils down to persuasion and the deployment of party resources (Neustadt 1960). When leaders used what weapons they had at their disposal, whether the party machine or financial leverage in the council itself, such techniques served only to underline the lack of authority in the exercise of power. Because of the lack of legitimacy and the goal of seeking nomination to secure a seat in the commons, leaders never fully developed in the their local public profile in the long term, so they could shape policy and effectively assert the interests of locality to central government bureaucrats and politicians.

The crisis of the 1980s

When local government was a settled, if rather neglected, institution of British democracy, the lack of executive potency and legitimacy did not matter much. Local government had established its role as the administrator of the services of the welfare state. The decentralised pattern of management in local government suited the professionalisation of services, where housing, education, social service and others had particular cultures and a selective officer corps based on professional norms and practices. But the rapid political changes of the 1980s highlighted the failings of local democracy. The attack on local government by the Conservatives, when in power in central government between 1979–97, was facilitated by weaknesses of accountability of local government, which undermined its authority when dealing with the centre. It is possible the Conservatives got away with removing functions and finance because local government was not greatly loved or respected by its electorates. When local authorities sought to resist or challenge such attacks on their powers, they did so from a weak level of public support and without entrenched and visible local and national champions who could have marshalled arguments and local resources with the self-confidence that derives from a fully articulated democratic mandate. In countries, such as France, where local mayors are powerful local and national politicians, central government could not have even contemplated let alone achieved the removal of a tier of government, as the Conservatives had managed in 1986 when they abolished the Greater London Council and the Metropolitan County Councils. Whereas France remains with its over 36,000 communes, created in the 19th century and each fiercely guarded by its mayor, Britain still suffers numerous local government reorganisations, such as the uncompleted local government review, the abolition of a tier of local government in Scotland and Wales before devolution, and a further round of abolitions, if the move to unitary status reaches its final conclusion with the abolition of district councils. In countries with strong local leaders, reformers added regions to the existing local government structure; in England, with its marginalised local leaders, central reformers could propose to replace a tier of local government with little controversy and effective opposition.

The return to local governance

Implementing the government's legislative and policy agendas required imaginative leadership, which could have ensured councils were ahead of the political game. As some of the municipal empires based around bureaucratically-provided and delivered services were removed or dramatically reduced, as in education and housing, so local government had to find a new role. It seized the European Union agenda, developed new policy arenas, such as on the environment, in such a way that many comment-ators came to believe that local government had reinvented itself (e.g. Atkinson and Wilks-Heeg 2000). But such changes needed coordination and encouragement from innovative political leaders. Where these experi-ments occurred it was often because of a local political champion, such as John Harman in Kirklees and Sir Peter Bowness in Croydon.

Not only was the political environment of the 1980s important – a linked set of economic and social changes meant that party machines could not govern localities quietly like they had done since the mid part of the 20th century. Economic competition imposed rapid changes in social makeup and prosperity of many localities, which needed local government to help lever in private investment and make cities and other areas attractive again to business. Political leaders were the obvious people local businesses and central government looked to for the implementation of these policies. The emergence of local governance required people who would be able to coor-dinate loose networks and inspire public-private partnerships (John 2001; John and Borraz 2004), and return local government to the governing of communities rather than guiding the provision of public services. Local councils had to work with stakeholders, such as Chambers of Commerce and voluntary sector organisation, which have different perspectives on the priorities of policy and often had long histories of rivalry with the town halls. Not only did local leaders usually lead these partnerships, they needed to represent these diverse interests to central government to lever in resources, which again required leadership skills and highlighted the need for locally elected people who have enough political legitimacy to carry out this task. When leaders succeeded in leading the partnerships, such actions highlighted their lack of formal legitimacy and the absence of a mechanism through which local politicians and electorates could hold them to account. They were caught in a double bind: either they remained invisible whilst embedded in their party groups or they seized the agenda but risked being accused of acting autocratically.

The debate about local political leadership

The changed political and policy contexts revived a long-standing debate about the role of locally elected leaders. In the 1960s and 1970s such delib-erations did not get far. But in the early 1990s the agenda for reform opened up. Secretary of State for the Environment, Michael Heseltine, had been impressed by the North American experience where strong leaders followed successful economic regeneration strategies, like the cities on the old industrial belt of North America. The 1991 Green Paper was an agenda for reform, which quickly ran out of steam (Stoker and Wolman 1992). But there was considerable interest from the national community of local gov-ernment. The Society of Local Authority Chief Executives (SOLACE) was particularly keen to review the options, and encouraged the Joseph Rowntree Foundation to sponsor research on the costs and benefits of different executive forms (Young 1994). The agenda for executive reform was stimulated by the research and report of the Commission for Local Democracy (Commission for Local Democracy 1995; Pratchett and Wilson 1996), which was picked up by the Labour opposition keen to adopt ideas promoting democratic government and alternatives to traditional party politics. Stronger leadership, involving vesting power in a directly elected mayor, appeared in a number of official pronouncements, linking together reform of management, democratic renewal and executive reform, in what was called the modernisation agenda (DETR 1998). The idea of direct election of mayors gained the support of the then prime minister, Tony Blair, and influenced the reform of London government, where the directly elected mayor was the centerpiece of the reform.

The introduction of mayors into English local government

The introduction of a strong leader into the Greater London Authority was largely a success in institutional terms, even if controversial politically. Even though some critics thought it would find it hard to promote effective policies (Pimlott and Rao 2002; Travers 2003), though the success of the congestion charge, the expansion of public transport, the role of the mayor in attracting the Olympic games, engendered greater confidence in the mayor's capacity to govern. But the story of London, as so often has been the case, was different to elsewhere. Policy-makers saw the mayor as a particular solution to the absence of a legitimate institution to represent the interests of the capital. Also it was easier to propose a radical option when the government had to create an institution from scratch. The history of its introduction into the rest of local government revealed more uncertainty in the decision-making process and more complex motivations of central government policy-makers. Whilst the government gave the electorate two choices in London – the electorate could either vote for a mayor or not in a referendum – such commitment to direct election was not so evident in the Local Government Act 2000. Here parliament allowed local councils to adopt one of three models – directly elected mayors, a council manager or a leader and a cabinet. There were different sorts of policy transfer at work – the council manager and directly elected mayors came from the United States and parts of Europe; the cabinet system derived from a Scandinavian innovation that had attracted the imagination of some reformers, but which offered local government close to what they thought was a no change option. Perhaps the government lost its nerve in the face of local government lobbies, as it allowed an even weaker version of the change option, the alternative arrangement for local authorities with populations of under 85,000 people, which could retain aspects of the committee system. In any case, the mayoral solution got a bad press as established interests in local government campaigned against it and indifferent local electors largely followed the public opinion leaders. The hurdle of a 5% nomination for a local referendum meant that only 30 were held in the first few years after the act, six of them on low turnouts of between 10 and 15%. In the end only 11 mayors were elected in May and October 2002.

Local populations sometimes demanded the mayoral option in order to express their dissatisfaction with local Labour party machines. The new system allowed independents to challenge the local apparatchiks, as in Middlesbrough, where the controversial ex-policeman Ray Mallon, who was known as Robocop because of his tough policing style, became mayor. In Hartlepool, candidate Stuart Drummond campaigned dressed as H'Angus the monkey, though he discarded his pantomime garb in favour of a conventional suit once elected. Independents defeated established Labour candidates in Bedford, Mansfield and Stoke-on-Trent. The other elections occurred where there was local attraction to the idea and strong links to central government policy-makers, which meant some Labour councils successfully promoted the idea, such as Newham and Lewisham. With these few exceptions and in London, the directly elected mayors only appeared on the margins of British local politics. Labour did not end up gaining from the reform, only winning four out of the 12 elections (including London) and even failing to secure the by-election in North Tyneside which went to the Conservatives on June 13 2003, following the resignation of the mayor who had been arrested on criminal charges.

It seems puzzling that a powerful government was not able to impose its will on local authorities. The government could have been less considerate of local democratic views and have introduced the reform in a time-honoured manner by imposing it on a reluctant local government as it has done in so many other areas. It may have believed that its ideas were so attractive and self-evident that councillors would willingly abandon the political structures that had served their interests for so long. This failure could be another example of New Labour's hubris. Or it could have reflected splits in the government, as some senior politicians, such as John Prescott, the then deputy prime minister, were strongly opposed to the mayoral option. In any case, the decision to give local government choice over its internal structures was never going to lead to an open debate.

The spread of cabinet government and the potential for organisational change

That 81% of councils opted for the cabinet model and a further 15% adopted the no change option of alternative arrangements might seem to be a victory for the forces of conservatism in local government. Some evidence suggests that many local authorities implemented the 2000 Act with little real change in their ways of going about business (ELG 2003: 14). Whilst the committees had been abolished and cabinet members had to take portfolios instead, cabinets appeared sometimes to be little more than extensions of the old policy and resources committees or at least of the party group meetings that occurred before them. In fact, some councils sought to replicate the old model by having pre-cabinet meetings and invited the opposition parties. Arguably, the new system consolidated the political practices of the past by abolishing opposition representation on the committees and allowing party groups to govern unchecked by the rather feeble scrutiny and overview committees. Where councils were keen on scrutiny and overview, they tried to ensure backbench members did similar kinds of business as they did on the old committees.

But such a view neglects two important features of the new system. The first is that the party-dominated account of local politics is only part of the story. Local councils varied in the extent to which the party exercised collective choices, the frequency with which the leader exercised independence, the amount of delegation to officers, and the degree to which the culture of the organisation fostered open debate about its policies. Moreover, one-party dominance is not as common as some stereotypes of local government imply with the frequency of party coalitions and where the largest party does not have a majority of seats. The number of councils that can be described as one party dominant, with over 60% of seats held by one party, was as low as 27%. The reform of executive arrangements was not purely a top-down affair and reflected the modest demand for a renewal of decision-making practices in the period before 2000.

The second reason why a conservative model of institutional changes does not capture the implementation of the Act is that its objectives are just as far-reaching with the leader and cabinet model as they are with the mayors. The legislation creates the separate executive that has close control over the policy-making and implementation. There is a clear definition and reporting of the executive's strategy, and the identification of portfolios through the responsibilities of cabinet members. These decisions have to appear in a forward plan, which is then updated on a regular basis by council officials. These groups meet much more frequently than their committee predecessors (ELG 2002). They tend to attract the younger and career-minded local politicians. There is the potential for a more dynamic and visible executive.

Some survey results bear this out (Stoker *et al.* 2006). Across all classes of authority respondents agreed that the 2000 Act changes has delivered stronger leadership with a majority of councillor, officer and stakeholder respondents agreeing that 'the role of the leader is stronger', and 'the leader has a higher profile'. The majority of officers agree that 'decision-making is quicker' (Stoker *et al.* 2006: 57, Table 5.3). Councillors and officers also believed that the new executives were effective in providing a vision for the area, leading a drive to service improvement, setting the policy direction, ensuring delivery, dealing with the budget process and lobbying for resources (Stoker *et al.* 2006: 59, Table 5.5).

Case studies of local authorities show a more focused executive and a stronger political leader more able to get things done, getting business through the council and having a more strategic orientation when formulating policy.

The variation in the leadership role

There are variations in the way in which leadership is exercised. In some authorities, decision-making flows through the leader or bilaterally between a portfolio holder and leader, in others decisions are taken collectively in cabinet (Stoker *et al.* 2004: 41). In the sample survey, respondents from mayoral authorities were more likely than other respondents to indicate that leadership aims had been met (Stoker *et al.* 2006: 58, Table 5.4). The case studies also suggest variation across authorities with respect to the ability to move resources, join up policy-making and manage party groups. Strategic management is perceived to be easier in authorities with concentrated leadership and party management plays a more important role in authorities with deconcentrated leadership forms (Gains 2006).

The legislation gives discretion about how these executives operate, allowing political leaders to act alone, to appoint the cabinet and to allocate portfolios, which together can create a formidable battery of powers, when backed up by a supportive political party. The irony is that local councils may have thought they were rejecting strong leadership with the demise of the mayoral model, but through the back door stronger leaders can emerge through these powers. Discretion to use executive powers increased: right from the first few months after the implementation, there was variation in the practice of leadership. In June 2002 a survey asked local councils to report on these leadership activities (ELG 2002). It found that 38% allowed the leader to act alone, 34% allowed the leader to select the cabinet members and 54% to allocate the portfolios. Taking these activities together by giving local authorities a score for each one, there is a continuum of leadership autonomy ranging from the 23% that give no freedom to act to the 16% that have all three attributes. Consistent with the idea that some councils always have had highly collective patterns of leadership whereas others, such as the Conservative controlled ones, developed a stronger role for the leader, the act and its implementation maintains this variety, and may have enhanced it.

Between 2002 and 2006 there was a gradual strengthening of leadership. The largest changes were in portfolio allocation where the proportion of all types of authority giving this power to their leader increased. For decision-making powers the picture is more stable. The proportion of unitary councils allocating this power was unchanged and the proportion of counties fell by four percentage points. In both London boroughs and metropolitan boroughs the proportion giving this power increased. On the selection of cabinet there has been a substantial increase in the proportion of metropolitan boroughs providing leaders with this power, less marked but still positive change in the London boroughs and unitary authorities and no change in the county councils. The most striking experience is the experience of the metropolitan boroughs. These authorities have seen the largest positive changes across all three powers.

Did the strengthening of leadership powers work? The official evaluation of the new council constitutions showed that councils that had adopted the stronger pattern of leadership powers tended to get higher satisfaction and formally measured performance as a result (Gains *et al.* 2009). Case studies of leadership seem to back up this position with stronger leaders setting up more effective management systems and finding that the officer corps happy to follow this pattern of leadership.

The Labour government was convinced that the failure of the intro-duction of the new system of local governance was marred by the lack of introduction of the mayoral options. They had read the report of their own evaluation of the Act and the policy-makers had been briefed about its contexts. This evaluation draws on surveys across England's local councils conducted in 2002 and again in 2006, sample surveys of officers and coun-cillors regarding attitudes, and 40 case studies. The team found that the evidence obtained showed the new arrangements had delivered on the government's intentions in 2000 to 'create more visible and effective leader-ship', 'enhance democratic legitimacy of local government' and 'provide sufficient checks and balances'. They also found that where councils accorded more power to the leader there was a visible trend in improving perfor-mance, as demonstrated by rising CPA scores in these authorities. Public satisfaction levels with councils is strongest where the leadership is stable and not subject to change. The report found that the new arrangements were favoured more by council officers than councillors themselves, with executive members more positive than non-executive members and Labour councillors more positive than other parties. Both councillors and officers felt that new executives were effective in providing a vision for the area, leading a drive to service improvement, setting the policy direction, ensur-ing delivery, dealing with the budget process and lobbying for resources.

In October 2007 the UK government's *Local Government and Public Involve-ment in Health Act* was finally approved by Parliament and overhauled the system of governance in most English councils, seven years after the land-mark 2000 act, which had introduced the elected mayor model for the first time. The new Act requires council leaders to be in place for four years. This is a significant change in the leadership position as it installs a leader who cannot be removed for a set period of office, perhaps creating a

Swedish-style indirectly elected mayor. Of course, in practice, it is easy to dislodge a leader by an internal coup, and a semi-forced resignation. But it may be easier for leaders to stay in place because of the effort required to dislodge the person, and by that virtue exercise more power than the leaders who were fearful of internal coups as described in Cole and John (2001).

But it may be the case that even the limited movement toward elected mayors may be reversed. Despite the hint that the government would exchange resources for a city-regional mayor for conurbations like Birmingham, Liverpool and Manchester, the city councils in these areas have resisted any such moves. They were divided and feared giving power to the central authority, such as Manchester – and even Manchester argued against such a reform. At the last referendum before the 2007 Act became law, in Darlington during September 2007, the opposition campaign's charge that elected mayors led to unstable mavericks getting elected (i.e. Ray Mallon in Middlesbrough) largely stuck, despite some local disaffection with the way in which the council was run. Campaigners in Doncaster and Lewisham seek to return their councils to the old system of having a council leader rather than having a directly elected mayor.

But in spite of these countertendencies, it is to be expected that councils would keep the basic structure of their political management arrangements at the beginning of the implementation of the Local Government Act 2000. There is no massive pressure for change. Even the experiences of scrutiny reflect different traditions for implementing legislation and different organisational and political cultures. It would seem likely that councils that had accepted the review principles of the act would be tempted to vest more powers in one person, so that the two branches of the local authority could be balanced, moving toward a fuller implementation of the aims of the act. In short, the leader and cabinet councils may be more willing to create stronger leadership patterns when they are checked by effective scrutiny committees. As much of the initial failure of the mayoral option arose from the fear of the unchecked leadership by one person, the leader and cabinet model offers the possibility of a slower evolution toward stronger leadership styles as it could build on the clearer definition of the executive function and a growing confidence in the scrutiny model. As the option of a move toward a mayoral system is open under the provision of the act, there remains the possibility that local leaders and councillors may wish to move away from leaders and cabinets and to encourage the local electorate to opt for direct election. In short, the critics of the new executives for local government may have emitted a sigh of relief much too soon.

Conclusion

This chapter has discussed the evolution of the system of political leadership in English local government. It shows the hand of history has continued to be strong. For a variety of reasons, mainly to do with the separation between institutions and the reality of party politics, England never institutionalised a system of local political leadership. This meant that political power was either exercised behind the scenes in party politicised local authorities with centralised local party organisations or was dispersed in service-based fiefdoms with a weak centre, both politically and administratively. This system of government could survive in the era when local government was a secure if neglected part of the British informal constitution, in the 1950s and 1960s. But when the pressures of centralisation, ideological party politics, a globalised economy, greater societal differentiation and more active forms of citizen and interest group politics, this lack of leadership became telling. It meant that local government found it hard to offer leadership to communities and to defend itself from incursion from other levels of government. Not that local government stood still. But it did not have the institutionalised power to act. The attempt by government to give leadership powers in the 2000 Act was only a partial success. Local governments now have a stronger more decisive executive, but they still lack visibility and sheer political clout. The factors that caused local government not to have strong leadership ensured that there was no local support for locally elected mayors so the project could not get off the ground. So local government continues as a neglected part of the public sector, and it finds it hard to offer the extra value that democratic leadership can give. For this reason, there is every reason to think the relative decline of local government will continue and that there will never be a revival of energetic and imaginative local political leadership in England.

References

Atkinson, H. and Wilks-Heeg, S. (2000) *Local Government from Thatcher to Blair: The Politics of Creative Autonomy*. Oxford: Blackwell.

Cole, A. and John, P. (2001) *Local Governance in England and France*. London: Routledge.

Commission for Local Democracy (1995) *Taking Charge: The Rebirth of Local Democracy*. London: Municipal Journal Books.

DETR (1998) *Modern Local Government in Touch with the People*. London: The Stationary Office.

Dicey, A.V. (1959) *An Introduction to the Study of the Law of the Constitution*. Basingstoke: Macmillan.

ELG (Evaluating Local Governance) (2002) Report of ELG Survey Findings for ODPM Advisory Group, 28 November 2002 by Gerry Stoker, Peter John, Francesca Gains, Nirmala Rao and Alan Harding, see http://www.ipeg.org.uk/research/elgnce/publications.php

ELG (2003) *Implementing the 2000 Act With Respect to New Council Constitutions and Ethical Framework: First Report*. London: ODPM. http://www.local.odpm.gov.uk/research/new.htm

Gains, F., Greasley, S., John, P. and Stoker, G. (2009) 'The Impact of Political Leadership on Organizational Performance: Evidence from English Urban Government', *Local Government Studies*, 35: 75–94.

Gyford, J. (1985) *The Politics of Local Socialism*. London: George Allen and Unwin.

Gyford, J., Leach, S. and Game, C. (1989) *The Changing Politics of Local Government*. London: Unwin Hyman.

John, P. (2001) *Local Governance in Western Europe*. London: Sage.

John, P. and Borraz, O. (2004) 'The Emergence of a European Urban Leadership?', *International Journal of Urban and Regional Research*, forthcoming.

John, P. and Saiz, M. (1999), 'Local Political Parties in Comparative Perspective', in Saiz, M. and Geser, H. (eds), *Local Parties in Political and Organisational Perspective*. Boulder: Westview Press.

Leach, S. and Wilson, D. (2000) *Local Political Leadership*. Bristol: Policy Press.

Madison, J. *et al.* (1987) *The Federalist Papers*. London: Penguin.

Neustadt, R. (1960) *Presidential Power: The Politics of Leadership*. New York: Wiley.

Norton, A. (1978) 'The Evidence Considered', in Jones, G.W. (ed.), *Political Leadership in Local Authorities*. Birmingham: Institute of Local Government Studies.

Pimlott, B. and Rao, N. (2002) *Governing London*. Oxford: Oxford University Press.

Pratchett, L. and Wilson, D. (1996) (eds) *Local Democracy and Local Government*. London: Macmillan.

Stoker, G. and Wolman, H. (1992) 'Drawing Lessons from US Experience: An Elected Mayor for British Local Government', *Public Administration*, 70: 241–267.

Stoker, G., Gains, F., Greasley, S., John, P. and Rao, N. (2004) *Operating the New Council Constitutions in English Local Authorities: A Process Evaluation*. London: Office of the Deputy Prime Minister.

Stoker, G., Gains, F., Greasley, S., John, P. and Rao, N. (2006) *Councillors, Officers and Stakeholders in the New Council Constitutions: Findings from the ELG 2005 Sample Survey*. London: Department for Communities and Local Government.

Travers, T. (2003) *The Politics of London*. Basingstoke: Macmillan.

Young, K. (1994) *Local Leadership and Decision-Making in London for LGC*. Joseph Rowntree Foundation.

7
Guns or Gantt Charts? – The Leadership Challenge for UK Defence

Mike Dunn

Introduction

This chapter addresses the question: what are the consequences of the New Public Management (NPM) for the leadership and governance of UK defence, in particular the UK Ministry of Defence (MOD)? The form and quality of the MOD's governance is important because, as the National Security Strategy of the UK (Cm7291 March 2008: 3) states: 'Providing security for the nation and its citizens remains the most important responsibility of government'.

However, and ominously for defence, Jones and Thompson (1999: 55) in a US context comment that: 'government's most important functions are inherently unmanageable, otherwise they could be performed quite satisfactorily by business' and then that: 'carrying out the efficient functions of (public) business necessarily gives rise to exceedingly large organisations, which inevitably leads to organizational inertia'.

The chapter first presents a limited review of the salient literature on NPM, and examines the evidence for its presence in defence. It continues with a brief overview of the MOD, its governance and current position. It then analyses MOD's experience of NPM using a two-lens model of principal-agent theory, and managerialism. It argues that NPM, in contrast to other major public service providers such as Health and Education, has had an appreciable, but ultimately superficial, impact on the operations of the MOD. The chapter suggests that this is because the MOD presents a complex instance of the principal – agent problem whose solution favours a traditional Weberian organisational model. The status of national security as a 'public good' also marginalises the 'customer as individual' dynamic in MOD, and so further attenuates the impact of NPM.

New Public Management – A review

The wicked issue that NPM addresses is: how should Governments go about their task in the 21st century? As the Organisation for Economic Co-operation and Development (OECD) comment:

> There is a persistent problem in public management reform recommendations – they are rarely based on empirical evaluations, and in practice, owe more to policy fashion than to evidence and with significant over-claiming about 'best practice'. (OECD 2007: 2)

So what is NPM? OECD (1996: 39) stated that: 'NPM tends to reject the image of government as a machine bureaucracy'. Hood and Jackson (1991) positioned it both as an administrative argument but also as an administrative philosophy. Hood (1991) states that NPM is a 'loose term' and is a descriptor for a set of broadly similar administrative doctrines. Pollitt (2003: 26) describes it as 'chameleon like and paradoxical' and concludes that it is customised for each different context in which it is introduced. Teisman and van Buuren (2007: 181) concur that 'the shape and effects of reform vary according to institutional contexts'. Using complexity theory as an analytical lens, they comment (*ibid*: 183) 'Implementing a NPM reform means adding a new element to a specific system and thus, not only changing the behaviour of this system but also the way the system is seen by and interacts with its environment'.

In many ways it is simpler to describe what it is held to be replacing. Hood (2000) positions this as 'old public management' stereotyped by:

> Weberian notions of general rule boundedness – rigid hierarchy often appears as a key element [...] and focuses on compliance with processes rather than results. In addition professional rather than corporate or managerial orientations, and an insulation of public from private management with an absence of business values and techniques in public service routines. (Hood 2000: 7)

However, some commentators (Gruening 2001; Pollitt and Bouckaert 2004; Pollitt 2007: 20) have identified a neo-Weberian state (NWS) model for NPM, particularly in continental Europe. This retains Weberian elements such as 'the preservation of public service as a distinctive status' but includes neo elements such as: 'shifting from an internal orientation to one towards meeting citizens' needs'. Is NPM important and how new is it? Hood (1991) describes its rise as one of 'the most striking international trends in public administration'. Drechsler (2005) refers to it as the most important reform movement of the last 25 years and, despite arguing that it is no longer a viable concept, concedes that that NPM is 'very alive and very much kicking'. Gruening (*ibid*) states that the NPM movement began in the late 1970s and early 1980s and that its first exponents were the UK Prime Minister Margaret Thatcher, characterised by her Government's programmes of privatisation, and US Municipal governments such as Sunnyvale California. Lynn (2005: 42) also ascribes NPM to this time, saying it was driven by the economic crises of the mid-1970s and that the Thatcher reforms, 'asserting the primacy of management over bureaucracy' became the foundation of NPM. In particular NPM saw an attack on the role and status of the professional in public services (Causer and Exworthy 1999; Exworthy and Halford 1999) with a particular target being the NHS (Harrison 1999). The governments of New Zealand and Australia then started reform programmes and it was their success, Gruening (*op cit*: 2) claims, that 'put administrative reforms on the agendas of most OECD countries and other nations as well'.

The US experience is important. Vice President Al Gore (1993) in developing the National Performance Review (NPR), later the National Partnership for Re-inventing Government set up a process that continued through the Clinton administration with the aim as President Clinton said: 'to make federal government less expensive and more efficient and to change the culture of our national bureaucracy away from complacency and entitlement toward initiative and empowerment'.[1] NPR asserted a set of principles empowering public employees to acquire and manage resources, cutting red tape and using common sense which it explained repeatedly and then left it to front line employees to figure out how these principles should be applied in their own organisations (Jones and Thompson 1999: 52–53). A key component of the NPR Programme was the establishment of around 300 re-invention labs in federal government, including the Department of Defence (DoD), where there was a freedom from administrative rules and regulations to experiment with new practice. Jones and Thompson (*op cit*: 53) comment that: 'NPR lost its focus after several years and support from Vice President Gore's office seemed to wax and wane'. Nevertheless Gore (1995, 1996, 1997) published several further influential reports on transforming government. The work was continued, at least in spirit, by President Bush's Management Agenda. President Obama's stance on the issue has yet to be established but the US current financial crisis is likely to intensify, rather than diminish, the need for efficient and effective public services.

The New Labour Government, despite political differences, took up where the Conservative Government left off. Their *Modernising Government* White Paper (Cm 4310 1999) set out the tone and scope of how the Government planned to go about 'renewing our country for the next millennium'. However there were practical issues. Blair by his second term had become frustrated by lack of progress in public service reform (Barber 2007). Michael Barber gives a detailed account in his work as head of the Prime Minister's

Delivery Unit from 2001–2005 where he was given an enforcement role for 'deliverology', and a clear list of priorities: Health, Education, Transport and the Home Office. He recounts how (2007: 33) his discovery of the utility of management theory came as pleasant surprise. He was particularly taken with the work of John Kotter (2006) on transformational change and used his theories extensively.

One of several paradoxes in this area is that the move by politicians to introduce a public management philosophy based, to an extent, on business practice has an inverted relationship with their own knowledge and understanding of business. Peter Oborne's (2007) polemic makes a strong case that we are witnessing, in the UK, the development of a political class which as he says:

> [...] is distinguished from earlier governing elites by a lack of experience of and connection with other ways of life. Members of the political class make government their exclusive study. This means they tend not to have significant experience of industry, commerce or civil society.
>
> Oborne (2007: 6)

Tony Blair and Gordon Brown are both examples of this phenomenon and I return to the point when examining the governance of the MOD.

Key writings on NPM

This is by necessity an abbreviated review. As Pollitt and Bouckaert (*op cit*: 20) comment: 'the academic literature on public management reform has become enormous'. Michael Barzelay identifies (2000a: 236) a chronological sequence of certain key texts on NPM. He holds that, along with Hood (1991) and Hood and Jackson (*op cit*), Aucoin (1990) although not using the term NPM, is a seminal piece on the subject. He argued that NPM is based on two 'fields of discourse "public choice and managerialism"'. Boston *et al.* (1991) in their conceptualisation of New Institutional Economics (NIE) by examining the New Zealand Government's policy choices in the 1980s located the intellectual foundation for NPM by identifying the use of public choice theory, transaction-cost economics and agency theory in the development of Government policy.

The popular work by Osborne and Gaebler (1992) *Re-inventing Government* used the term 'entrepreneurial government' to describe this new model of government as it was emerging across America. Their thesis was that the traditional Weberian model of bureaucracy that underpinned US government culture had been implemented largely to overcome the corruption and patronage endemic in the early 20th century and had now outlived its usefulness.

Moore (1995) in his seminal work discusses how:

> If private managers can conceive and make products that earn profits [...]
> then a strong presumption is established that managers have created
> value. [...] the aim of management in the public sector is to create *public*
> value just as the aim of managerial work in the private sector is to create
> *private* value.
>
> Moore (1995: 28)

He argues that what public management should do to create public value
ultimately is defined by, and derives, efficient and effective delivery of
the political mandate on which politicians are elected. He terms this the
'normative power of the preferences that emerge from the representative
processes' (*ibid*: 31) although he does acknowledge the complexity of this
task. Kelly *et al.* (2002: 6) comment that 'public preferences are at the heart
of public value. In a democracy only the public can determine what is truly
of value to them'.

Ferlie *et al.* (1996) describe and analyse the impact of NPM in the NHS in
terms of organisational behaviour and design. Pollitt and Bouckaert (2000,
2004), Barzelay (2001), and Ferlie, Lynn and Pollitt (2005) have also added
significantly to the growing scholarly body of work on NPM.

UK MOD – A contextual overview

The MOD is a high profile State Department, despite its relatively small
budget of approx £32bn (Edmunds and Foster 2007). It accounts for only
5.25% of Government managed expenditure compared to, say, Social
Protection, which accounts for 27% (HM Treasury 2006). However, it has a
significant external spend programme of approx £12bn, buying and supporting fighting equipment (HM Treasury 2007; CSR: D8.6). MOD's profile
is driven by several factors: a high level of public interest and concerns
about its activities, the extensive use (Kampfner 2003) that the New Labour
Government has made of the Armed Forces, and by its powerful and
diverse range of stakeholders. The military – industrial complex that supports its equipment programme, is a particularly important stakeholder.
The MOD directly employs a total headcount of 273,000 employees split
195,000 between the Armed Forces (Army, Royal Navy, and Royal Air
Force) and 78,000 Civilian personnel. This represents 15% of the Civil
Service (MOD 2007: 11).

The MOD is headed by the Secretary of State for Defence – currently (as
at March 2009) John Hutton. He is responsible for the formulation and
conduct of defence policy and is supported by three defence Ministers. The
Defence Ministers have two principal advisers, one military, the Chief of
the Defence Staff (CDS) and one civilian, the Permanent Secretary (PUS). A

number of senior committees underpin the management of defence, the most important of which are the Defence Council and the Defence Management Board. The Defence Council is the senior Departmental Committee. Chaired by the Secretary of State it provides the formal legal basis for the conduct of defence. As with other Government Departments (James 2004), the MOD has a Public Service Agreement (PSA) with the Treasury. This consists (MOD 2008) of three strategic objectives as shown in Table 7.1; these are underpinned by six top level performance indicators (PIs), which are not detailed here.

Table 7.1   MOD (2008: 5–7) Defence Plan 2008–2012

1	**Achieve success in the Military tasks we undertake at home and abroad**
2	**Be ready to respond to the task that might arise**
3	**Build for the future**

Additionally as part of the Comprehensive Spending Review MOD is committed to value for money reforms generating annual net cash releasing savings of £2.7bn by 2010–11, building on savings of £2.8bn during the 2004 Spending review period.

The objectives and PSA will be analysed later in the context of principal-agent theory. One of the New Labour Government's initial actions on assuming office in 1997 was to conduct a major review of all aspects of the UK defence organisation and policy. This led to the *Strategic Defence Review* White Paper (MOD 1998), which incorporated a number of key changes. It acknowledged and it was confirmed in a later White Paper (MOD 2003) that the UK was now in a post-Cold War environment, and detailed the major implications for the types of operations it would be engaged in.

The MOD has been subject to an initial Capability Review (MOD 2007) and a subsequent review (MOD 2009). The purpose of these reviews is to identify (MOD 2007: 1) 'the specific measures that are needed if central government departments are to play their part in enabling the UK to meet the considerable challenges of the future'. The report was a balance of praise and criticism. The paper commented (MOD 2007: 10) that: 'MOD's current structure and ways of working partly reflect the historic independence of the three Services [...] which were first brought together in a single ministry as recently as 1964'. Supporting this, Edmunds and Foster (2007: 16) report that: 'British Armed Forces are currently more active than they have been for decades'. They paint a picture of operational overstretch, lack of equipment and underinvestment to pay for rising personnel and housing costs and an incoherent management structure around the Chiefs of Staff organisation and civilian support structures.

NPM and defence

Most debate on the impact of NPM in the UK has focused on the provision of services in health, education and local government (Pollitt 2003; Clarke *et al.* 2000). This is possibly because they have most political appeal in terms of public choice theory and there is a clear definition of the 'customer as individual' for these services.

Before moving to a review of the literature on NPM and defence, it is appropriate to examine defence from an economist's viewpoint. Gravelle and Rees (2004) define a 'public good' as the provision of a good where the consumption by one person does not reduce the amount available for others to consume. Defence is an example as all the people in a nation must consume the same amount of national defence. So who is the customer for defence? In the UK, one could argue it was the Government, or the national population as a whole, but that would be a circular argument, as the MOD is the Government, which in turn represents the people as a whole. This is a confounding issue for NPM and defence because the absence of a 'customer as individual', removes the customer focus dynamic that energises so much NPM thinking.

There has been relatively little written on the role of NPM in the UK defence sector but an early start was made in the US (Thompson 1991). In the US there has been a claimed Revolution in Military Affairs (RMA). This comprises the impact of new technology and smart or precision-guided weapons. The increased capability of modern soldiers combined with this new weaponry has made a paradigm change in the way wars can be fought. The RMA has been paralleled by a Revolution in Business Affairs – or RBA (QDR 1997). This has included outsourcing and privatising support activities, reducing overhead cost and infrastructure cost.

Thompson and Jones (1994: xi) in a detailed analysis claimed that: 'the new public management provides some of the solutions the Department of Defense (which they describe as the world's largest and most complex organisation) needs to deal with the problems it faces'. ((Jones and Thompson 1999: 59–106) examine the performance of the DoD under the Gore NPR programme and identify a series of successful re-engineering projects including DoD worldwide travel re-engineering, Army Training support re-engineering and the Defense Logistics Agency's Process Oriented Contract Administration Services (PROCAS) initiative.

Barzelay and Campbell (2003) and Barzelay and Thompson (2006) present two case studies on the challenges faced in the DoD in implementing managerial reform in the USAF and Air Force Material Command (AFMC). McCaffery and Jones (2004) in their detailed analysis of the budgetary process for the DoD reveal many similar issues to the UK MOD including concerns over the acquisition process, personnel turnover cycles, political interference in spend programmes, or 'pork' as it is termed, turf battles between services, business process inefficiencies and leadership failure. Stringer (2007) explores the relevance of benchmarking, core competencies and outsourcing in a broad context but focusing on the DoD.

The US DoD continues to struggle with governance and management. McCaffery and Jones (*op cit*: 404) report on (then) Deputy Secretary of Defense, Paul Wolfowitz's planned Defence Transformation Act for the 21st century (DTA), 'a comprehensive reform addressing serious deficiencies in DoD's management'. Despite this, a Government Audit Office (GAO) report found that:

> The lack of adequate transparency and appropriate accountability across all of DoD's major business areas results in billions of dollars annually in wasted resources, in a time of increasing fiscal challenges.
>
> (GAO 2004: summary)

Detomasi (2002: 61), in a Canadian context, tests the central propositions of NPM partly because he states: 'it would be hard to find a government agency with an organisational culture as distinct as the armed forces; therefore examination of defence departments presents a rigorous test of the purported ubiquity of the NPM guiding principles'. He finds that although cost savings have been achieved, 'clear historical patterns of organisational behaviour and decision making remain intact' and that obstacles still remain to be overcome if NPM is to be translated into effective lasting reform within the Canadian Department of National Defense (DND).

Analysis of the impact of NPM on MOD

This section will examine some specific evidence for the presence of NPM in the defence discourse but will also identify a number of systemic issues that currently mitigate its impact. Given there is no agreed conceptualisation of NPM then the researcher has some latitude in a choice of theoretical framework. The analysis will use a framework consisting of two strands of thought identified in the literature: agency theory and managerialism. I consider the selection of these two lenses will reveal most about the unique nature of the defence enterprise.

Principal-Agent theory

Miller (2005: 203), in a political science context, argues that Weber identified the phenomenon whereby there is an asymmetric relationship comprising authority (the principal) located on one side but with informational advantage on the other (the agent). According to Barzelay (2000: 190), principal-agent theory is concerned with the economic analysis of relations between principals and agents. It concerns situations, endemic in organisations, where the principal for reasons, generally of cost, cannot personally conduct an operation, and so engages the services of an agent, who may be an employee or an external supplier, to do the work. The problem then is: how can the principal ensure that the agent acts in the interests and not at the expense of the principal, thereby incurring what are termed 'agency costs'. Examples might be using the office for ends incompatible with the original contract e.g. personal gain or dereliction of duty. Early works (Spence and Zeckhauser 1971) reviewed the issue focused on economics. Jensen and Meckling (1976) analysed the phenomenon in the context of commercial firms, although they comment that the issue has relevance in any organisation, including the public sector.

In the context of this chapter, I am positioning the elected UK Government in the form of the Prime Minister and Cabinet Ministers as principals, although of course, they are, in turn, only acting as agents to the electorate, who are the true principal in a political context (Miller *op cit*: 207). The agents then are the public service employees in these Ministries. Barzelay (*ibid*) points out that in typical principal-agent models, the principal does not observe the manner in which the agent achieves the output because it would be physically impossible or expensive. A typical principal-agent relationship is structured by means of a contract that specifies how agents will be rewarded economically or incentivised by their principals to conduct the intended task. He suggests care must be taken to avoid diluting the incentive effects of a reward scheme e.g. where the agent's output is specified unclearly and also the allocation and compensation of risk. If the agent will be exposed to risk because of factors outside their control then the rational agent will demand compensation for bearing such risk. In this sense it relates closely to game theory. He critiques the relevance of the theory to public management e.g. because the principal frequently can observe how the agent operates and also that incentives figure low in the discourse. I suggest the concept has more utility however in defence because that act of observation e.g. in theatre in Iraq or Afghanistan is both dangerous and difficult.

The Treasury – MOD PSA agreement (Table 7.1) can be understood in this context as the explicit contract or performance agreement and Capability Reviews form a type of compliance check or contract review mechanism. However the 'public good' nature of defence, coupled with the global reach and coalition nature of international security, makes the contract difficult to specify, and therefore it is more difficult to enforce responsibility and accountability – two pre-requisites of effective performance management. In confirmation, the Capability Review (MOD 2007: 17) said MOD had one of the most difficult briefs in Whitehall – to be prepared to rise to unpredictable challenges from an increasingly wide and sophisticated range of potential threats across the globe and, in exceptional circumstances, at home. MOD objectives exist within a complex and dynamic framework of Defence Strategic Guidance, Defence Planning Assumptions, Treasury budgetary pressures and exogenous events. As the Capability Review recorded (MOD 2007: 15): 'For seven out of the last eight years, the Department has operated at the limits of or exceeded these assumptions'.

An implicit aspect of principal-agent theory is that the principal should be competent to make and supervise the contract. Here I will revisit the paradox of the political class, identified earlier. The Minister of Defence is a transient politician. There have been five Ministers of Defence since 1997. The first George, now Lord Robertson (1997–1999) whose career prior to being elected an MP was as a GMB trade union official. Next was Geoff Hoon (1999–2005), a barrister by profession, then Dr John Reid (2005–2006) a Labour Party research officer and political adviser prior to becoming an MP. Des Browne 2006–2008 is an advocate by profession. The current Minister, John Hutton, was a senior law lecturer at the University of Northumbria before entering Parliament. This is partial confirmation of Oborne's thesis asserting the political class's lack of experience in the areas they are invited to lead. The sum of these incumbents' first hand military knowledge and experience appears to be zero. The combination of brevity in office and a lack of first order experience of the military operation must compromise the degree to which Ministers can make, and supervise, effective contracts.

The other problematic issue identified through this lens is the nature and structure of the UK's professional Armed Forces. A career in the Armed Forces, is vocational and 'bottom fed'. Individuals join either as officers, or as privates or equivalent, and then progress through the very hierarchical and tribal culture of their chosen service, often for a lifetime career. It is highly specialised with unique features in terms of the commitment it requires, the differentiated nature of its operations, the exposure to life threatening or otherwise traumatic situations – termed 'unlimited liability' and, in certain theatres of operation, the need to engage with and kill the enemy. It would certainly be classed as a 'closed system' in Hofstede's typology (1991) of organisational cultures.

Using a higher magnification, the issue is even more complex because the Armed Forces themselves, are highly 'stove piped' and tribal (Sampson 2004: 165) though the extent of joined up working between the three services is more advanced in the UK than any other major country in the world (MOD 2007: 23). Each of the three UK Armed Services has its own head, a post that according to policy, is rotated every two to three years. There is a line of command from Service Heads into the Chief of Defence Staff (CDS). He has responsibility for military operations; again, this post rotates every two to three years but, in addition and according to tradition, switches between the Armed Services, though not in any defined sequence.

The Capability Review (MOD 2007: 27) reflecting the unintegrated nature of MOD said: 'the Defence Management Board must become a more corporate body and find ways to communicate as one voice'. The follow up Review (MOD 2009: 10) observed that 'MOD needs a departmental strategy that spans all of its activities (operational and non operational) for the medium to long term'. One challenge for the military is that current operations require joint (i.e. all three services) operations, which is difficult in a 'stove-piped' organisation. Jones and Thompson (*op cit*: 25) identify this feature as hostile to NPM; 'Combat is the classic example of reciprocal task interdependence, a condition that has always justified tight centralization and detailed staff planning'.

So defence presents a nested example of the principal-agent challenge. There is a systemic problem of making contracts due to the constant rotation of personnel within both the principal and the agent's spheres of influence and the consequent absence of, to use the legal term, any 'guiding mind' apart from, possibly, the Permanent Under Secretary (PUS). This, in turn, impedes the formulation and delivery of a coherent and integrated strategy and change programme – corner stones of NPM. Of course, there may be a practical reason for this situation – the prospect of a truly integrated military may not be an altogether pleasing prospect to the body politic, or the citizenry.

A final point in this context is the public sector requirement for strict legal compliance. Several commentators (Lynn 1998; Behn 1998; Fesler and Kettl 1991) have made the connection between public management and the law. Most decisions made by public managers are subject to judicial review. Public organisations exist to administer the law, and 'every element of their being – their structure, staffing budget, and purpose is the product of legal authority' (Fesler and Kettl *ibid*: 9). This is even more acute in the military. Edmunds and Forster (*op cit*: 66) comment that: 'One of the major issues affecting traditional military structures of authority has been a steady flow of challenges to military law and its different legal procedures, standards of evidence and punishment'. This brings in the area of errors, mistakes and incentivisation. Savoie (1995) comments that: 'Public administration operates in a political environment that is always on the lookout for errors and that exhibits an extremely low tolerance for mistakes'.

This is particularly pertinent in the MOD with its high media and public interest profile. A recent example is the furore created by the decision to allow the 15 HMS Cornwall personnel captured in March 2007 by the Iranian Revolutionary Guard, to sell their stories to the press. Intriguingly, no one from the Minister down, could be publicly held responsible for that decision:

> A Ministry of Defence spokesman said: 'The independent report by Tony Hall looked very closely at whether an individual should be held accountable and concluded that it was a collective failure of judgment or an abstention of judgment rather than a failure of judgment by any one individual'.
> http://news.sky.com/skynews/article/0,,91211-1297013,00.html

A combination of these factors, the difficulty in specifying the task, the inability of the principal to manage the contract, combined with the high risk and lack of incentivisation, makes the principal-agent problem in MOD problematical to manage and contracts difficult to enforce.

Managerialism

Managerialism like many constructs in this field has not been conceptualised in any precise form. However Pollitt and Bouckaert (2004: 14) identify the essence of the issue when they say: 'Almost all writers about public management reform (including ourselves) acknowledge that, in many countries the last twenty years have witnessed extensive borrowing by public sectors of management ideas and techniques which originated in the commercial sector.' Lynn (1998: 117) further characterises this feature of NPM as being: 'an emphasis on quality and continuous improvement, devolution and expansion of managerial autonomy, and a commitment to customer satisfaction'.

Managerialism is contested in the MOD for both systemic and cultural reasons. One reason previously argued, is that given defence is a public good and with most of its work done outside the UK, there is no obvious 'customer as an individual' to provide the customer supplier/dynamic that underpins NPM in other areas such as Health and Education. Mulgan (2009: 24) states that: 'Generic methods [from the private sector] are equally unhelpful in guiding the core business of military organizations: they can help with improving logistics or recruitment, but not with winning wars'. His point is rather spoilt in that logistics is seen as a pivotal issue in combat success but the sentiment is clear.

Another reason, touched on in the previous paragraph, is the system of rotating officers through postings every two to three years. Deming's (1982) 14-point charter for successful management starts with: 'create constancy of purpose for improvement'. As Jones and Thompson (*op cit*) comment in the context of DoD's NPR re-invention labs:

> One of the factors that militates against consistent support for management effectiveness efforts in the DoD is management turnover. Several of the lab representatives complained that their bosses changed every two–three years. This inhibits initiative. As one lab representative asked: 'Why start something new when chances are it will be terminated by the next change of command?'
>
> Jones & Thompson (*op cit*: 76)

The MOD has had prior experience of such a managerialist approach, similarly driven by the need for efficiencies, with programmes such as the Options for Change programme (1990) and Frontline First (1994). Michael Heseltine, Minister for Defence (1983–1986) in the Thatcher era, said: 'the management ethos must run right through our national life' (quoted in Protherough and Pick 2002: 15–16). Total Quality Management (TQM) with its focus on identifying and meeting customer requirements (Peters and Waterman 1982) was also adopted in some areas in the 1990s, particularly the Royal Electrical Mechanical Engineers (REME). However the MOD has always been skilful in protecting its unique status. Sampson (*op cit*: 157), albeit in the Blair era, comments: 'The MOD is a non Treasury zone. The PM always defends it. It is impregnable'. A further example, and one which shows an early determination to resist any attempt to deprofessionalise the Armed Forces, is the Bett Report issued in 1995. This examined the Armed Forces Manpower Career and Remuneration Structures and was conducted at a time when many private sector companies were delayering and down-sizing. His recommendation on eliminating certain ranks was rejected on the grounds that the rank structure must be driven by operational con-siderations, including the need for continuity of command in the face of casualties (MOD 1996) plus the need for rank structures to fit with partner organisations, such as NATO.

However, I will take as my point of departure the New Labour Government period in office starting in 1997. Early work concerned the acquisition process reform and took the input of McKinsey consultants in developing Smart Procurement later retitled Smart Acquisition. They identified that the struc-ture of the current system meant there was no identifiable internal customer/ supplier relationship. One consequence of this was issues being passed within MOD with no one overall project ownership. They argued that this was a con-tributory factor to the time and cost overruns identified and the process required a customer dynamic. This concept is rooted back in the Total Quality Management (TQM) approach.

The consulting firm McKinsey developed the idea of a Customer 1 and Customer 2 framework within MOD. Customer 1 was the equipment budget holder and Customer 2 the end user or front line command. This frame-work was then built into an overall acquisition methodology known as the CADMID cycle. The acronym stands for the main stages in the acquisition process: Concept/Assessment/Development/Manufacture/InService/Disposal. This approach adopted commercial project management techniques to iden-tify, and embed, the key stages in the process. It is very similar in design to the Office of Government Commerce (OGC) Gateway model. The MOD equipment acquisition programme is of such significance that The National Audit Office (NAO) produces a regular report on MOD's acquisition perfor-mance. At this time, hopes of an end to cost and time overruns seem opti-mistic. NAO's report (NAO 2007) comments that overall the Department is in a similar position to the Major Projects Report 2006 for forecast cost and performance and there continue to be delays.

Despite the absence of an external 'customer as individual' in the conven-tional sense, there is strong evidence on use of other managerialist practice within MOD, generally supported by consultancy firms such as McKinsey and KPMG (Craig and Brooks 2006). Along with most Government Departments, the MOD has shifted its financial system to an accruals basis rather than cash accounting. However, there is significant flexibility in the funding mechanism. MOD budgets to recruit, train, retain and equip the Armed Forces to be ready to fight. The Treasury holds a Contingency Fund that provides the finance for Armed Services operations. However military operations are unpredictable and the Government simply could not put itself in the position where national interest was compromised, because the money ran out. Stiglitz and Bilmes (2008) in the context of how the Bush Administration has under reported costs for the Iraq war comment that: 'The British system is particularly opaque: funds from the special reserve are "drawn down" by MOD when required without the specific approval of Parliament. As a result British citizens have little clarity about how much is actually spent'. Considering Detomasi's view (*op cit*) that defence has a weak incentive to operate efficiently, this process could detract from a motivation to budget accurately. The separate funding route also opens up gaming possibilities to MOD (Hood 2006) for access to additional funds.

Further examples of managerialist practice include use of the Balanced Score Card (BSC) performance management tool (MOD 2006) first developed by Kaplan and Norton (1992). Indeed the Capability Review (MOD 2007: 26) is quite critical of the tool's utility stating: 'Production of the [BSC] is resource intensive and does not encourage decision makers to prioritise the most important areas'. Business Process Re-engineering (BPR), developed by Hammer and Champy (1996) has also been used to identify and re-engineer the key cross cutting processes that exist in MOD e.g. logistics, finance and management of civilian personnel. BPR was also used in 2003 to streamline the End to End Air and Land Logistics process, a project also supported by McKinsey. Furthermore MOD has been involved in a wide range of outsourcing and PPI/PFI deals. These include the Defence Training Review (DTR), which aims to outsource a significant element of services training including engineering, technology and personnel, and the construction of the Joint Services Command and Staff College (JSCSC) – a 30 year contract awarded to Defence Management (Watchfield) Ltd – now wholly owned by the Serco Group Plc.

Lean thinking (Womack and Jones 2003) has also been used heavily in the MOD logistics process and elsewhere (MOD 2006; NAO 2007a). This is an interesting vignette, further illustrating the dysfunctional nature of MOD. The use of this powerful philosophy, based on the Toyota Production System (TPS), and in many ways 'the new TQM' has been deployed in other UK public sector in areas such as the NHS and HMRC (Radnor and Walley 2006). Bhatiam and Drew (2006) and Scorsone (2008) point out some of the issues involved in transferring its use in the public sector. In MOD, it was pioneered initially by the RAF, who saw it as a means of achieving their contribution to the Defence Logistics Organisation's strategic goal of reducing operating costs by 20% of the total by 2005–2006 (around £1.862bn). As the NAO reports, the programme has been a major success but one of its recommendations (*op cit*: 11) Recommendation 11 was that 'The Department should adopt a common toolset and language for lean techniques across all areas of its business. The Department should make its lessons learned material more evaluative to provide information on how the methods were applied and quantify the results they achieved'. This is supporting evidence that there is no 'guiding mind' in MOD developing corporate strategy on cross cutting issues. Lean thinking has now escaped into, and is in use across, all Armed Services and the MOD civilian workforce but with no central policy driving it. One consequence is that Lean has gained the reputation for cost cutting, so participating in lean programmes is seen as a form of 'assisted suicide'. This has now reached the point where the term 'lean' is proscribed and is being replaced by 'continuous improvement'. The NAO report picks up on this in their Recommendation 8 which states that: 'the Department should make a proportion of the savings from transformation [...] available to teams to reinvest in future improvements. This could help embed the culture of continuous improvement by incentivising teams better to drive through change'.

The managerialist discourse in MOD has drawn a distinction between the 'business space', e.g. acquisition, where such techniques are considered appropriate, and the 'battle space' e.g. front line and support units, where they are not welcomed. Detomasi makes an interesting point in this context:

> The traditional separation of military and civilian society has been central to the organizational ethos of the armed forces. The criteria by which military personnel distinguish themselves from their civilian counterparts is through their legitimate authority and professional capacity to apply organised violence to protect the political interests of the state. (Detomasi *ibid*: 66)

He goes on to comment that the emphasis in NPM on efficiency might well be construed as a corrosive factor in trying to maintain the ethos of the Armed Forces. Indeed there is a strong cultural bias against managerialism in the Armed Forces, evidenced by the almost total absence of management in the education and development programmes for e.g. Army officers until they reach the rank of Brigadier or equivalent positions. At this point when: '[officers] receive responsibility for managing large organisations, their interest in private sector management practices seems to intensify' (Jones and Thompson *op cit*: 73).

Conclusions

The NPM philosophy reveals there is transformational potential open to the UK Armed Forces using radical options such as integrating the three services, delayering rank structures, and integrating living arrangements between officers and other ranks. MOD could also post officers for longer periods, or leave individuals to develop their own careers through making every post open for applicants. More extensive use could be made of out-sourcing to Private Military Companies (PMCs) such as Aegis – now prom-inent in Iraq, which would have the significant advantage of mitigating the political impact of troop losses or equipment shortages. MOD could also open up the Armed Forces at senior level to external applicants with the aim of breaking out the institutionalised culture endemic in such closed organisations. Additionally, management theories such as lean thinking and transformational change management, which have been shown to offer the prospect of significant gains in efficiency and effectiveness, could be embraced and implemented at corporate level.

However there would appear to be little real appetite at this time for such change. Why?

This evaluation has shown that the philosophy of NPM encounters major obstacles in the field of defence. Notably, the military task, other than near term, is difficult to define. It certainly requires a body of professionals in order to conduct it but has no end 'customer as individual' in the con-ventional sense. These factors combine to compromise any effective prin-cipal-agent model and leaves the principal (HMG) in a weak position to control the agent's (UK Armed Forces) contract. In organisational terms, the military's response, based on the operational need to maintain a chain of command in combat, is to insist on a traditional hierarchical structure; moreover this model is standard military practice – certainly in NATO. The military response is also to instil an ethos that privileges the military paradigm, particularly separation of services, and is hostile to any mangerialist discourse. This, coupled with the systemic issue of key personnel rotation, leads to the absence of any 'guiding mind' in the overall defence enterprise, conditions which are fatal to the managerialist agenda.

These factors, combined with a need to comply with a legal framework that is becoming increasingly onerous, continue to underpin and require the cultural paradigm of a Weberian model of governance. Jones and Thompson's comments about the unmanageability of key government functions, and the need for large organisations, are well founded. And yet, in a final paradox, the potential for improvement through NPM and subse-quent benefit to military capability seems to offer great potential. The abandonment of non value adding processes, the elimination of waste and the fostering of innovation could free up much needed resources for front line capability. As Edmunds and Foster (*op cit*: 79) comment: 'The British Armed forces are "running on empty" and conflicts in Iraq and Afghanistan have seriously diminished the ability of the armed forces to meet future challenges'.

Note

1. President Clinton announcing the initiative to streamline Government – March 3 1993.

References

Aucoin, P. (1990) 'Administrative Reform in Public Management: Paradigms Principles Paradoxes and Pendulums', *Governance*, 3: 115–137.

Barber, M. (2007) *Instruction to Deliver*. London: Politico's Publishing.

Barzelay, M. (2000) 'How to Argue about the New Public Management', *International Public Management Journal*, 2(2(A)): 183–216.

Barzelay, M. (2000a) 'The New Public Management: A Biographical Essay for Latin American (and Other Scholars)', *International Public Management Journal*, 3: 229–265.

Barzelay, M. (2001) *The New Public Management*. Berkeley: University of California Press.

Barzelay, M. and Campbell, C. (2003) *Preparing for the Future Strategic Planning in the US Air Force*. Washington, DC: Brookings Institution Press.

Barzelay, M. and Thompson, F. (2006) 'Responsibility Budgeting at the Air Force Material Command', *Public Administration Review*, Jan/Feb 2006, pp. 127–136.

Behn, R.D. (1998) 'The New Public Management Paradigm and the Search for Democratic Responsibility', *International Public Management Journal*, 1(2): 131–164.

Bhatiam, N. and Drew, J. (2006) 'Applying Lean Production to the Public Sector', *The McKinsey Quarterly*.

Boston, J., Martin, J., Pallot, J. and Walsh, P. (1991) *Reshaping the State: New Zealand's Bureaucratic Revolution*. Auckland, New Zealand: OUP.

Causer, G. and Exworthy, M. (1999) 'Professionals and Managers across the Public Sector', in Exworthy, M. and Halford, S. (eds) *Professionals and the New Managerialism in the Public Sector*. Buckingham: OUP.

Clarke, J., Gewirtz, S. and McLaughlin, E. (2000) *New Managerialism New Welfare?* London: Sage.

Cm 4310 (1999) *Modernising Government*. White Paper HMSO.

Cm 7291 (2008) *The National Security Strategy of the United Kingdom – Security in an Interdependent World*. March 2008.

Craig, D. and Brooks, R. (2006) *Plundering the Public Sector*. London: Constable and Robinson.

Deming, W.E. (1982) *Out of the Crisis*. London: MIT Press.

Detomasi, D. (2002) 'The New Public Management and Defense Departments: The Case of Canada', *Defence and Security Analysis*, 18(1): 51–73.

Drechsler, W. (2005) 'The Rise and Demise of the New Public Management', *Post Autistic Economics Review*, Issue no. 33, 14 September 2005.

Edmunds, T. and Forster, A. (2007) *Out of Step: The Case for Change in the British Armed Forces*. London: Demos.

Exworthy, M. and Halford, S. (1999) *Professionals and the New Managerialism in the Public Sector*. Buckingham: OU Press.

Ferlie, E. Ewin *et al.* (1996) *The New Public Management in Action*. Oxford: OUP.

Ferlie, E., Lynn, L.E. and Pollitt, C. (eds) (2005) *The Oxford Handbook of Public Management*. Oxford: OUP.

Fesler, J.W. and Kettl, D.F. (1991) *The Politics of the Administrative Process*. Chatham N.J.: Chatham House.

GAO (2004) Department of Defense. Further Actions are needed to effectively address Business Management problems and overcome key Business Transformation challenges, GAO-05-140T, 18.11.2004.

Gore, A. (1993) *From Red Tape to Results: Creating a Government that Works Better and Costs Less* – report of the National Performance Review.

Gore, A. (1995) *Common Sense Government: Works Better, Costs Less.* Washington DC: US Government Printing Office.

Gore, A. (1996) *The Best Kept Secrets in Government.* A report to President Bill Clinton. Washington DC: National Performance Review.

Gore, A. (1997) *Businesslike Government: Lessons Learned from America's Best Companies.* Washington DC: National Performance Review.

Gravelle, H. and Rees, R. (2004) *Microeconomics.* Third Edition. London: FT Prentice Hall.

Gruening, G. (2001) 'Origin and Theoretical Basis of New Public Management', *International Public Management Journal*, 4: 1–25.

Hammer, M. and Champy, J. (1996) *Re-engineering the Corporation – A Manifesto for Business Revolution.* London: Nicholas Brealey.

Harrison, S. (1999) 'Clinical Autonomy and Health Policy: Past and Futures', in Exworthy, M. & Halford, S. (eds) *Professionals and the New Managerialism in the Public Sector.* Buckingham: OUP.

HM Treasury CSR (2007) *Comprehensive Spending Review.* London.

HM Treasury (2006) *Budget 2006. A Strong and Strengthening Economy: Investing in Britain's Future.* March 2006.

Hofstede, G. (1991) *Cultures and Organisations.* London: McGraw Hill.

Hood, C.H. (1991) 'A Public Management for All Seasons?', *Public Administration*, Vol. 69, Spring 1991 (3–19).

Hood, C. (2000) 'Paradoxes of Public Sector Managerialism, Old Public Management and Public Sector Bargains', *International Public Management Journal*, 3: 1–22.

Hood, C.H. (2006) 'Gaming in Targetworld: The Targets Approach to Managing British Public Services', *Public Administration Review*, Jul/Aug 2006.

Hood, C.H. and Jackson, M. (1991) *Administrative Argument.* Dartmouth: Aldershot.

James, O. (2004) 'The UK Core Executive's Use of Public Service Agreements as a Tools of Governance', *Public Administration*, 82(2): 397–419.

Jensen, M.C. and Meckling, W.H. (1976) 'Theory of the Firm Managerial Behaviour Agency Costs and Ownership Structure', *Journal of Financial Economics*, 3(4): 305–360.

Jones, L.R. and Thompson, F. (1999) *Public Management – Institutional Renewal for the Twenty First Century.* Stamford: JAI Press Inc.

Kampfner, J. (2003) *Blair's Wars.* London: Free Press.

Kaplan, R.S. and Norton, D.P. (1992) 'The Balanced Scorecard: Measures that Drive Performance', *Harvard Business Review*, Jan/Feb, pp. 71–79.

Kelly, G., Mulgan, G. and Muers, S. (2002) *Creating Public Value: An Analytical Framework for Public Service Reform.* Issued as a discussion document by the Strategy Unit UK Cabinet Office, October 2002.

Kotter, J. (2006) *Leading Change.* Boston: Harvard Business School Press.

Lynn Jr., L.E. (1998) 'A Critical Analysis of the New Public Management', *International Public Management Journal*, 1(1): 107–123.

Lynn Jr., L.E. (2005) 'A Concise History of the Field', in Ferlie, E., Lynn Jr., L.E. and Pollitt, C. (eds) *The Oxford Handbook of Public Management.* Oxford: OUP.

McCaffery, J.L. and Jones, L.R. (2004) *Budgeting and Financial Management for National Defense.* Greenwich: IAP Information Age Publishing.

Miller, G.J. (2005) 'The Political Evolution of Principal – Agent Models', *Annual Review Political Science*, 8: 203–225.

MOD (Ministry of Defence) (1996) *Statement on the Defence Estimates*. CM3223.

MOD (1998) *Strategic Defence Review*. Government White paper HMSO.

MOD (2003) *Delivering Security in a Changing World*. Defence White Paper HMSO.

MOD (2006) *Annual Report and Accounts 2005/2006*. HMSO.

MOD (2007) *Capability Review of the Ministry of Defence*.

MOD (2008) *Defence Plan Including the Government's Expenditure Plans 2008–2012* (Cm 7385).

MOD (2009) *Civil Service Capability Reviews. Ministry of Defence: Progress and the Next Steps*. March 2009.

Moore, M.H. (1995) *Creating Public Value – Strategic Management in Government*. London: Harvard University Press.

Mulgan, G. (2009) *The Art of Public Strategy Mobilizing Power and Knowledge for the Common Good*. Oxford: Oxford University Press.

NAO (2007) *Ministry of Defence Major Projects Report*.

NAO (2007a) *Transforming Logistics support for Fast Jets*.

Oborne, P. (2007) *The Triumph of the Political Class*. London: Simon & Schuster.

OECD (1996) *Performance Auditing and the Modernisation of Government* (PUMA).

OECD (2007) 'Towards Better Measurement of Government', *OECD Working Papers on Public Governance*, 2007/1, OECD Publishing. doi:10.1787/301575636734

Osborne, D. and Gaebler, T. (1992) *Reinventing Government – How the Entrepreneurial Spirit is Transforming the Public Sector. From Schoolhouse to Statehouse, City Hall to the Pentagon*. Reading MA: Addison Wesley.

Peters, T.J. and Waterman, R.H. (1982) *In Search of Excellence: Lessons from America's Best Run Companies*. New York: Harper and Row.

Pollitt, C. (2003) *The Essential Public Manager*. Berkshire: OUP.

Pollitt, C. (2007) 'Convergence or Divergence: What has been Happening in Europe?', in Pollitt, C., van Thiel, S. and Homburg, V. (eds) *New Public Management in Europe – Adaptation and Alternatives* Basingstoke: Palgrave Macmillan.

Pollitt, C. and Bouckaert, G. (2000) *Public Management Reform: A Comparative Analysis*. Oxford: OUP.

Pollitt, C. and Bouckaert, G. (2004) *Public Management Reform: A Comparative Analysis*, 2nd ed. Oxford: OUP.

Protherough, R. and Pick, J. (2002) *Managing Britannia*. Denton: Brynmill Press.

QDR (1997) *Quadrennial Defense Review*. Washington: US Department of Defense.

Radnor, Z. and Walley, P. (2006) 'Lean on Me', *Public Finance*, July 28–August 3 2006.

Sampson, A. (2004) *Who Runs this Country – The Anatomy of Britain in the 21st Century*. London: John Murray.

Savoie, D.J. (1995) 'What is Wrong with the New Public Management?', *Canadian Public Administration*, 38(1): 112–121.

Scorsone, E.A. (2008) 'New Development: What are the Challenges in Transferring Lean Thinking to Government?', *Public Money and Management*, 28(1): 61–64.

Spence, M. and Zeckhauser, R. (1971) 'Insurance, Information and Individual Action', *American Economic Review*, 61: 380–387.

Stringer, K.D. (2007) 'Business Concepts for the Security Sector: Benchmarking, Core Competencies and Outsourcing', *Baltic Security and Defence Review*, 9: 210–235.

Teisman, G. and van der Meer, F. (2007) 'Implementing NPM: A Complexity Perspective on Public Management Reform Trajectories', in Pollitt, C., van Thiel, S. and Homburg, V. (eds) *New Public Management in Europe – Adaptation and Alternatives*. Basingstoke: Palgrave Macmillan.

Thompson, F. (1991) 'Management Control and the Pentagon: The Organizational Strategy-Structure Mis-Match', *Public Administration Review*, 51(1): 52–66.

Thompson, F. and Jones, L.R. (1994) *Reinventing the Pentagon*. San Francisco: Jossey-Bass.

Womack, J.P. and Jones, D.T. (2003) *Lean Thinking – Banish Waste and Create Wealth in Your Corporation*. London: Free Press Business.

Internet

http://news.sky.com/skynews/article/0,,91211-1297013,00.htmlU – accessed 1.03.08.

Part II

Essential Features of Public Leadership

8
What Do We Expect of Public Leaders?[1]

Lord Turnbull

Introduction

Raising the game of public leadership

In this chapter I raise three challenges for public leadership. The first, concerns the identity of the kind of leaders public institutions need; the second, how to develop those leaders and the third, asks what do public institutions need to do to raise the game of public leadership in a complex world. In addressing these challenges I provide my own reflections on leadership style and characteristics based on my long experience of both working within and, more latterly leading, the 'hub of government' – the civil service.

I address the three public leadership challenges against a backdrop of continual pressure for reform of the civil service and the wider public sector, but confine my discussion to the public leadership challenge. Government departments have been the subject of capability reviews that looked at three key areas: strategy, leadership and delivery. This chapter outlines what is considered to represent the future of public leadership and how those who lead the civil service and the wider public sector can respond to these challenges as well as influencing public leadership throughout the public sector delivery chain.

In raising the game of public leadership the first challenge suggests that we need to understand the nature of leadership in a public sector context. The second challenge requires an appropriate match between the kind of leadership that the situation requires and the efforts to develop appropriate skills at different levels and with differing levels of difficulty. The third challenge calls for new public leadership to be embedded within the public sector's way of working so that each and every member knows what is expected of them.

What kind of leaders do public institutions need?

The importance of leadership for successful organisations

The contribution that strong collective leadership makes to the success of an organisation is increasingly being recognised. This applies just as much to the public sector and the voluntary and community sector as it does to the private sector. So, whether it is in developing a successful company or in delivering better public services or in encouraging well minded people to work with and within the community, the importance of collective leadership cannot be ignored.

Some contributors will argue history has suggested that good leaders are born and not made, others that it depends on the situation in which leaders find themselves to be leading and yet others still, that it is the position that leaders occupy, or the results that they achieve or the influence that they hold that determines whether and how leaders lead.

We often assume that an organisation's leadership begins with recruiting and selecting the right people. But this can only be effective if we know what kind of leaders the organisation needs at that time and whether those who we do recruit or select will have the capability to ensure the success of the particular organisation.

Within the context of the civil service, we have come a long way from the days when fast stream entrants were recruited – not as future leaders – but as 'Administration Trainees' which calls into question how the role of public leaders and public institutions was perceived at that time. For many years the 'business' of the public sector was referred to as public administration and its incumbents as 'administrators'. From the early 1970s we began to see the emergence of public management as opposed to administration with those who serve the public viewed as managers rather than administrators. This volume is thus very timely in seeking to suggest that good public reform requires us to move on beyond administration or public management to leadership, where leaders motivate those who manage and those who administrate on behalf of us all and thus create outcomes that are valued by the public.

What leadership is (not) and from where does it (or could it) emerge?

Let me start by discussing some of the misconceptions about leadership. It is not just about those people who occupy positions at the top of public institutions or enterprises, still less the property of the single person at the top of each organisation. It is not just the Permanent Secretary, the Chief Constable, the Chief Executive of the local authority or the health trust or indeed the regional head of government agencies such as Job Centre Plus, but includes all of those leading all the component parts of the public institutions. This notion is not new. The Armed Forces have always recognised that the General and the Corporal are both leaders in their own ways; the law recognises, for example, that no person or no politician can tell a police officer what to do or convention suggests that no person or politician should tell a clinician not to take a particular course of action which he or she considers to represent the best interests of the patient. Senior leaders clearly have a role in setting direction but there are different levels and forms of leadership that can be identified and which need to knit together in a collective way.

It is equally important to affirm that leadership is not about individualism; it is really the opposite. Leadership is about making it possible for everyone in the institution or within a network of institutions to contribute. The essence of leadership at all levels is to give direction, and then to involve, inspire and motivate others.

Senior leadership development programmes often describe its participants as newly appointed strategic leaders. This begs the question; what does this word 'strategic' add? Is it one of those words inserted to make something more impressive than it really is? The Oxford English Dictionary describes 'strategy' as 'The art of a commander-in-chief; the art of projecting and directing the larger military movements and operations of a campaign. It is usually distinguished from *tactics*, which is the art of handling forces in battle or in the immediate presence of the enemy'. The significance of the word strategic therefore is the recognition that while much leadership is operational, working within a defined framework, e.g. the branch, the store, the platoon, there are wider dimensions to being a strategic leader:

- A person who finds themselves at the point where serious choices are to be made;
- A person who is operating with longer time horizons;
- A leader who does less themselves and more through others.

In terms of public leadership one attribute that thus distinguishes a strategic from an operational role is that such leaders have reached a level where operating in the mode which has made them successful to date will not necessarily guarantee success in the future. The most senior leaders in public service must be able to show how they can translate their skills to a higher level whilst still encouraging those who are entrusted with delivery to lead within an increasingly complex public landscape.

How to develop those who lead within public institutions

Levels of leadership and degrees of difficulty

It is important to recognise that there are different levels of leadership and each has its own degree of difficulty. Many of those who reach the top of their public professions unambiguously become the leader of their organisation, whether as CEO, Chief Constable or Permanent Secretary. Previously, each would have been a member of the leadership team. Paradoxically it is often easier to operate at the top of the organisation than at the next level down. The most difficult phase of my career was when for the first time, I became a member of the Treasury Management Board. That required juggling my responsibilities as a head of a business unit with the need, for the first time, to take a corporate view. But a leader has no choice but to operate through engagement with others at differing levels and across increasingly diverse networks.

The role of the most senior leaders in setting the right direction is critical, along with providing the right resources and support with a view to achieving the right impact. This is what John Kotter would refer to as establishing a sense of urgency, the creation of a guiding coalition to drive and sustain change and the development of a vision and a strategy as an investment in the delivery of a better future (Kotter 1999).

One of the biggest temptations for a leader on taking up a new senior appointment is to carry on doing the job that he or she previously did, resulting in a bias in the allocation of time and attention, leaving no space for others to develop and with the consequence that the leader would become a big tree beneath which nothing grows.

Leadership is therefore a distributed property throughout the organisation rather than the sole property of an individual. Indeed allowing leadership freedom to one individual alone can be dangerous. One needs to look no further than the first two principles of the Combined Code on Corporate Governance (FRC 2006) the first of which states that every company should be headed by an effective board, which is collectively responsible for the success of the company and the second which requires that there should be a clear division of responsibilities at the head of the company between the running of the board and the executive responsibility for the running of the company's business. No one individual should have unfettered powers of decision. Exceptions such as the recent appointment of Sir Stuart Rose as both Chief Executive Officer and Chairman of Marks and Spencer are permitted but have to be justified in time and place.

Let us examine this first principle of the code further as it also helps to illustrate some of the critical success factors of leadership. Principle one states:

> The board's role is to provide entrepreneurial leadership of the company within a framework of prudent and effective controls which enables risk to be assessed and managed. The board should set the company's strategic aims, ensure that the necessary financial and human resources are in place for the company to meet its objectives and review management performance. The board should set the company's values and standards and ensure that its obligations to its shareholders and others are understood and met. (FRC 2006: 3)

Through these principles, some of the key leadership activities at the most senior level of public leadership include:

- Encouraging innovation through entrepreneurial leadership
- Developing a framework of controls which support the assessment and management of risk
- Setting strategic aims which are clear to all, meaningful throughout the public sector and which are achievable
- Supporting the achievement of the aims through the provision of appropriate financial and human resources
- Reviewing performance as a means of organisational learning
- Setting the organisation's values and standards with the engagement of people at all levels
- Ensuring that its obligations to internal and external stakeholders are both understood and met.

How do we develop these skills within the public sector?

Though some of the principles of the Combined Code are relevant to the public sector, leadership in the public sector generally and the civil service in particular is very complex and leadership development must address this complexity.

We have shared leadership between Ministers and senior officials, each bringing something to the bigger picture. Officials bring professionalism, expertise and a longer term view; Ministers bring urgency and most precious of all political legitimacy and contact with citizens which should never be upstaged or usurped. A pre-requisite of public leadership development must be the acknowledgement that different forms of leadership are required. Already we are considering a distinction between organisational, individual and political leadership.

Having recognised the distinctive context in which public leaders lead – and that this is likely to change from situation to situation – it is then essential to ensure that the stewardship of public leadership is fit for purpose in that it achieves public value in return for significant public investment. The determination, achievement and measurement of outcomes is therefore central to the role of all public leaders.

As public leaders work mostly in a non-market environment a number of challenges are relevant:

a. the metrics for measuring public service activities are difficult;
b. Public leaders do not have full control over many aspects of what they do, for example they cannot decide to go 'up market' and pull out of serving the poorest customers or to close neighbourhood offices in difficult inner city or rural areas;

c. There is a great deal of ambiguity, with frequently conflicting objectives and the potential for perverse incentives;
d. Ministers are the ultimate leaders and – given their democratic mandate – can quickly change officials' priorities, with all the consequences being felt throughout the delivery chain;
e. Officials have constrained choices over the make up of their teams or the rewards they can offer.

In short, the civil service and much of the public sector are collective organisations providing collective goods. The integration of collective organisations delivering collective goods therefore requires effective collective leadership which draws into centre stage a different way of thinking about public leadership.

What type of leader do we want?

We accept that public servants are not mere advisers, or even courtiers with no leadership role. Far from it. The fact that leadership is exercised in a constrained context, that it is not appropriate for us to assume the Mr Big style of a corporate CEO (particularly the North American model), should not be an excuse for shrinking into the background and avoiding responsibility. It means that we should ensure that we equip our public leaders with the very best of public leadership skills to enable them to chart their way through these increasingly complex networks and to empower, negotiate with, and energise others.

We should not necessarily go back to the attractiveness of the great man theories or the idolisation of charismatic leaders. Not all of those who succeed in the private sector are all at the Conrad Black/Alan Sugar end of the spectrum of dominant controlling leaders. There are many intermediate places on the spectrum and leadership development must acknowledge this. Of the six commercial organisations I have worked for since I left the Civil Service, three are quoted companies, one is a genuine partnership, two are technically companies but operate effectively as partnerships. The dynamics of their decision-making is quite different from the PLC model.

In summary the key message in terms of leadership development is that different leadership styles are needed in different contexts and in different points in an organisation's history. Rather than advocate a particular model, leadership development should encourage prospective leaders to spend time thinking about what is required at any point in time and, potentially, in the future and to understand and appreciate the different ways in which leadership is practiced and with what impacts.

How public leaders can work better together in a complex world

Leading a winning team through a collective vision

Having defined the context how then should an organisation go about creating the leadership team and importantly the pipeline of future leaders to succeed them? It might seem natural to start by defining characteristics and competencies that leaders need. In my view, this is the wrong place to start for there is one important stage to go through first.

This is to define the organisation's strategy which can of course change over time. It is thus about purpose – what is it that the organisation is seeking to achieve? Vodafone may serve as an example. For several years its mission was expansion through acquisition. These years required the buccaneering spirit of Sir Chris Gent. Then came a phase of consolidation, during which a coherent whole was built out of all the businesses acquired. Now it is to continue the consolidation in Europe while seeking expansion in the new commercial world. Different times require different kinds of people and different leaders.

This is a clear message that emerges as the experience of organisational growth is examined. In a powerful description of the stages of organ-isational growth and development Larry Griener, writing in the *Harvard Business Review*, argued that as organisations grow in age and size the original founders and the original creative activities are not always the most appropriate to lead the organisation through predicted periods of both evolution and revolution. Both the original founders and their chosen ways of working – which were essential for the company to get off the ground – may become a problem as the company grows (Griener 1998: 60).

Outdated structures and over centralised procedures are often at the heart of the reasons for either failure or decline of profits but are held on to by key executives as it is often perceived to be the source of their power. This is equally applicable to a changing and turbulent public sector environ-ment when the assumption of continuous growth in the economy and continuous expansion of public services has been called into question.

From the strategic purpose expressed through a collective vision at any point in time one can derive the structure that is appropriate and the kind of leader that is appropriate. BP is a company that has been going through such a change in leadership and the issues Tony Hayward will need to address are very different from those John Browne faced a decade earlier. British Land, where I am a Non Executive Director has just completed a very successful transition from a dominant executive chairman to a Chair/CEO partnership, a transition which many companies have stumbled over.

This requirement to settle a strategic sense of direction of course creates a chicken and egg dilemma. You can't know what sort of leader you want until you have a strategy but it is the senior leader as an individual that is in a strong position to provide the sense of direction and create the sense of urgency required. However, this does not mean that you should set the direction and then build your team.

The genetics of public leaders: A case study from the civil service

The ability to think strategically is one of the key competencies a leader needs to have. It is to break this Catch 22 that the definition of strategy is not simply a CEO function but is shared with the board and then distributed within and across the range of networked public institutions. At this point we can consider further the definition of leadership characteristics, the career model and recruitment and training needed to develop the new style of leadership within the public sector. Different organisations will go about this in different ways but an example is used of an initiative I led in the Civil Service. This can be described as an exercise in genetic modification, retaining the genes we still value, removing the genes that are no longer appropriate and injecting some new genes.

We obviously wanted to retain the historic strengths of the civil service – integrity, objectivity, commitment, and its ability to manage government business. The genes we wanted to remove were excessive departmental focus, hierarchy, outdated processes, poor management of risk (though it is not to say the Civil Service is risk averse; it is more a case of risk myopia, often running horrendous but inadequately researched risks).

The genes to be injected were more creativity and innovation, customer focus, focus on outcomes, improved performance management, an ability to work through others and to communicate better. Far from creating a Frankenstein monster, the aim was to produce a new generation of leaders who are much more visible both to staff and to customers and partners, comfortable with taking personal responsibility for difficult decisions, better able to think strategically, and able to get results not just by personal endeavour but by influence and partnership.

The next step was to examine the career model. Some organisations may decide that they can simply recruit from the market for whatever kind of person they think they need at the time. This might work fine in a high reward, low loyalty, short time horizon business but it is unlikely to be as successful in the public sector which – some may argue (relative to the private sector) – is low reward, high loyalty and longer term time horizon bound! However, the shortcomings of this model have been dramatically exposed in the banking sector.

The Civil Service has been in a very different tradition of growing its own talent but probably too much so for a world in which skill requirements change very quickly. It now operates a mixed system, still relying at the senior levels on about two thirds for internally generated talent and one third on external recruitment. This latter aim provides access to new skills and people with experience of front line services while retaining a strong root stock, thereby providing continuity of values.

Another dimension is how far the service wants to develop a coherent leadership cadre across the whole of the civil service, or how far different businesses within the service are empowered to develop their own talent. Do people work their way up the organisation in one part of the business or do they expect to be cross posted? In all these dimensions – competencies, recruitment, career development there are choices. The Civil Service and Unilever are similar in being highly centralised in spotting and developing talent. The Prudential on the other hand has in the past developed its people mainly through the individual business units.

My message is that different approaches can work in different places, but those choices must be consciously made and be simply derived as the product of history. As the public sector is required to work ever more in partnership with other agencies so there will be a need to break even beyond the boundaries that this chapter suggests and consider cross public sector development.

Embedding public leadership

Sustaining our leaders

Having appointed public leaders what do public institutions do to support them? Leadership, particularly at the most senior level, can be a very lonely experience and, as Charles Handy implies, we are not very good at accepting that we are not very good at leadership (Handy 1999). So where do our senior public leaders go for advice and in what shape or form do they receive development as senior leaders? In a similar vein, Grint (2005) argues that all leaders have shortcomings. The clarion call to perceived problems of leadership are often rooted in the 'only those who can walk on water need apply' approach and attention is given to better recruitment criteria (2005: 34), such as that argued earlier. A better approach, Grint argues, might be to start from where we are, not where we would like to be. This is to concentrate on all leaders, as humans, as flawed individuals, not all leaders as the embodiments of all that we merely mortal and imperfect followers would like them to be: perfect. This has particular implications for ongoing leadership development within the public sector and the way that we develop teams so that one person's relative weaknesses are compensated for elsewhere.

The Civil Service approach for many years was to scoff at things like mentoring and coaching, viewing them as expensive fads. These approaches are now viewed as a valued tool for development. It is rare for a leader to arrive at the top with all competencies equally and fully developed. So an early task is to define strengths and weaknesses. Having someone to help in this and to help in working on a development plan can be

invaluable. It is often the case that the outcome of a recruitment or promotion process will award someone the job but recommend a programme of
mentoring/coaching.

The same goes for board evaluation. Once seen as 'money for old
rope' for head hunters, it is now part of the Combined Code. Individual
evaluation should aim to show whether each director continues to contribute effectively and to demonstrate commitment to the role (FRC 2006: 7)
including joint evaluation (2006: 24) and supported by processes to
regularly update and refresh these skills and knowledge (FRC 2006: 8). It
can seem like a chore and if external facilitators are engaged, an expensive
one. But it can be very helpful in getting a board to understand how
it works together, or does not, how it uses its time and whether it has
got the right balance between support and challenge. This will set the scene
for the development of leadership throughout the public sector where
development is both shared (at board level) and distributed within each
organisation (at the individual level) but within a collective framework that
supports collective effort in achieving collective outcomes.

The focus of this chapter has been primarily on the challenges facing
senior leaders and the examples used originate from my experience of
leading the civil service. However, it is important to point out that exactly
the same principles of public leadership would apply to partnership working through, for example, the community leadership role of local strategic
partnership boards, and the overall aim of those partnerships in delivering
improved and sustained social, environmental and economic wellbeing
through sustainable community plans. The concept of shared leadership
will apply as a critical link between the Whitehall end of the delivery chain
and the many public, voluntary and community sector institutions and
enterprises that support the local strategic partnerships.

Personal reflection on the role of public leadership

There are consistent challenges to public leaders across the spectrum of
public service delivery and the chapter will conclude with some reflections
that will apply throughout this chain. Reflection is a great virtue and one
that should be inherent in all leaders. Based on my experience in the civil
service, some points of reflection include the following:

It is important to exemplify values and integrity. The leader has to
be in the forefront in the establishment and protection of reputation, or
in private sector language, the brand. This involves defining the organisation's appetite for risk and how that risk is managed and supported
through effective governance arrangements.

Valuing diversity, including diversity of thought. Setting a tone in
which people of different backgrounds are valued and in which people are
encouraged to put forward different views and voice their concerns.

Improving Performance: Setting standards of performance, praising good performance (even more important where, as in much of public sector, we can't reward it very well) and confronting poor performance.

Maintaining optimism and energy and the mind set that problems are there to be solved. This is really dangerous when the leader disparages his organisation's people and products. This happily is rare in the private sector, Gerald Ratner being an exception, but alas all too common in the public sector. I know of no PLC chairman who would publicly label his company as 'not fit for purpose'.

Setting a tone of openness, readiness to listen and a willingness to engage with hostile audiences and thus building trust.

Setting a consistent course which is not deflected by minor setbacks.

An ability to take decisions, while not acting impulsively. A readiness to change one's mind and admit one was wrong in the face of evidence.

Encouragement of partnership and sharing; a willingness to delegate. Don't move in to take the credit, move in to help out and share successes.

Develop successors; don't see emerging successors as rivals. Be ready to leave the scene constrictively when the time comes and be honest enough to acknowledge that you might not be the right person to steer the institution or organisation through its next period of evolution and/or revolution.

Treat others as you would wish to be treated yourself: My least favourite people are those who are attentive to those more powerful but rude to those below them, and those who, far from supporting colleagues under pressure, dump blame on them while exonerating themselves.

At this point we come to the importance of stories. All organisations have them, and the importance of stories within the National Health Service is highlighted in a chapter within this volume. Most of the management text-books say the role of the leader is important in determining what they are, in developing stories of success. But the converse is also true. Many organisational stories are pernicious and it is as much part of the leader's role to eradicate them. It is about building reputation and reputation is an important aspect of public leadership.

I remember the stories that were prevalent within the Treasury which we worked hard to overcome:

- Like Millwall supporters, they all hate us but we don't care.
- They (i.e. departments) are all useless and only respond to being pushed about.
- Everyone is self serving.
- We are great in a crisis.

An important task of leadership is to replace these negative stories with more constructive ones, to be positive and develop a 'can do' rather than a 'cannot do' culture.

I think there are important lessons about the use of time. Leaders should not get sucked into energy absorbing, low output activities. It helps to stay a bit above the fray. Don't dive in at the first opportunity.

Many problems will be resolved by colleagues if you give them the chance. Billy Butlin once said the secret of his success was to be able to watch his colleagues do things that he would not have done while resisting the temptation to interfere. This of course left him with time to do the bigger things only he could do, and gave his colleagues the opportunity to develop their strengths.

There is agreement on the importance of the leader assembling and developing the leadership team. But one can be an effective leader without hogging the limelight and cherry picking the glamorous assignments.

Who are my role models for leadership? First, John, later Lord Hunt, whose aim was not to get to the top of Everest himself but to get men onto the top. Second, is Sir Ernest Shackleton, best known for leading the Endurance expedition of 1914–16. He was a meticulous organiser and a maintainer of optimism. Above all when the enterprise got into trouble he personally went off to get help.

As Kotter argues, during a process of change, having established a sense of urgency and delivered through a guiding coalition there is then a need to anchor the change in reality and embed it within the culture. Although the classic 'great man theories' are no longer the dominant theme in leadership theory today, senior leaders have an important role to play in creating the right climate for leadership to emerge throughout the public sector networks. The real challenge for public leaders is to create the conditions that enable those leaders to emerge and from any point in the delivery chain or the institution.

Note

1. Adapted from a speech originally delivered at the Windsor Leadership Trust, 26 April 2007, Windsor Castle.

References

FRC (2006) *The Combined Code on Corporate Governance*, published by the Financial Reporting Council, London.

Griener, L. (1998) 'Evolution and Revolution as Organisations Grow', *Harvard Business Review*, May–June.

Grint, K. (2005) *Leadership: Limits and Possibilities*. Basingstoke: Palgrave Macmillan.

Handy, C. (1999) *Understanding Organisations*. London: Penguin Books Ltd.

Kotter, J.P. (1996) *Leading Change*. Boston, MA: Harvard Business School Press.

Kotter, J.P. (1999) *John P Kotter on What Leaders Really Do*. Boston, MA: Harvard Business School Press.

9
Political Leadership

Jean Hartley

Political leadership in democratic systems

From one point of view, all organisations include a political dimension, in that those who lead, work for, manage, govern and contract to organisations have to deal with diverse and sometimes competing interests, with individuals and groups sometimes vying for power and influence and sometimes collaborating with others to achieve outcomes (Hartley and Fletcher 2008). This is politics with a small 'p'.

However, this chapter focuses on leadership in formal political systems – what might be called 'big P' politics. And the focus is on leadership in democratic societies, i.e. where political leadership is based on electoral legitimacy from, and accountability to, the population, rather than leadership based on military or totalitarian power.

Formal political systems are those organisations and institutions which are governed by elected representatives with public accountability. Some political institutions are about law-making and policy-making, while others plan and provide public services, such as education, healthcare and prisons, and some carry out both functions. Public organisations derive most of their funding from the state and their policies, their budgets and their practices are governed through boards, committees, councils or cabinets consisting wholly, mainly or partly of elected politicians.

The traditional view in the field of public administration that politicians (national and local) make policy while public managers implement it left little room for leadership (Denis, Langley and Rouleau 2005). For politicians in particular, leadership and leadership development were not seen as important because they saw themselves as exercising power, mandated by their political party, their election manifesto and the electorate (Hartley 2010; Behn 1998).

For their part, public managers, working within large bureaucracies, saw themselves primarily as 'clerks' (impassive officials implementing political directives) or 'martyrs' (holding private views about the policies they enacted but continuing to implement political decisions without comment) (Moore 1995). Thus, leadership was not much discussed in relation either to politicians or to managers (van Wart 2003; Behn 1998).

More recently, the worldwide interest in public sector reform (Pollitt and Bouckaert 2004) has been accompanied by a language more receptive to the idea of leadership. There has been a greater interest in 'entrepreneurial government' which includes a role for leadership. Initially, this was found under the rubric of 'new public management' (Hood 1991) which articulated a role for managerial leadership, though interestingly it failed to articulate a clear or prominent role for leadership by politicians. The emphasis on managerial (but not political) leadership was based on the importing of private sector management practices and ideologies into the public sector (Hartley and Skelcher 2008).

The interest in leadership has been given a further boost by the recognition of a newly emerging approach to public policy and public management which goes beyond 'new public management' and involves a paradigm shift to 'networked governance' (Benington 1997, 2000; Stoker 2006; Newman 2001). In a networked governance perspective, public sector renewal is resulting in a weakening of the hierarchically organised monolithic state in favour of more differentiated polycentric arrangements that cut across the boundaries of public, private and third sectors as well as across different levels of government (Benington 2000).

This means that political leadership, managerial leadership and community leadership may all have a place (or a voice) in how democracy is conducted, and public services created and produced (or co-produced). There are, of course, some countervailing tendencies. The new dynamic image of public leadership and the apparently enlarged opportunities for managerial discretion are counter-balanced by a strengthening of national interventions and centralised control, and explicit and rigorous inspections and performance regimes. Managing the tensions and paradoxes of these governance regimes has become the order of the day for politicians and public managers, strengthening the need for leadership (Pedersen and Hartley 2008). This chapter will therefore consider the complexities and challenges of political leadership in a context of polycentric, networked governance.

The chapter focuses on political leadership in the UK primarily, though it draws on a wider academic literature to understand this. The empirical base for the chapter is from research undertaken with UK elected politicians, across the political parties, at both local and national levels, and in three of the four nations of the UK.

Political leadership

Political leadership is substantial in numerical terms. In the UK alone, as noted by Hartley and Pinder (2010), there are about 120 Ministers in the

UK Government (in both Houses), 646 MPs in the House of Commons and over 700 members in the House of Lords, and 297 elected members of the devolved Parliaments and Assemblies of the UK. At UK local government level, there are over 22,000 councillors in England, 1,222 in Scotland, 1,264 in Wales and 582 in Northern Ireland (according to the Electoral Commission website) There are 78 European Parliament members representing the UK regions.

In decision-making terms, elected politicians are responsible for creating laws and by-laws, for providing policy and guidance to public service organisations, and for the disbursement of public funds. The public sector budget is substantial – in most post-industrial countries, politicians are responsible for taxation, fiscal policy and expenditure representing at least a third of GDP (Jackson 2003). Since the start of the recent recession, the percentage of public money as a proportion of GDP has soared to 51% in the UK (Treasury 2009). At the level of an individual government department or a local authority, politicians may individually be responsible for multi-billion pound expenditure. For example, the Department of Work and Pensions budget for 2007–8 was £130,417 million (www.dwp.gov.uk). At local authority level, the largest English council has a staff of about 50,000 (FTE), with a £1 billion budget.

Elected politicians use state authority to direct or even coerce citizens to engage in activities deemed to be for the public good. They make decisions such as going to war, taxation levels, police powers, and military conscription. Their decisions involve judgements based on political leadership.

Elected politicians are also involved in tackling complex and difficult choices facing society. Whether the issues are climate change, tackling childhood obesity, or sorting out transport infrastructure, the role of politicians is not only to use state authority and state resources. In some cases, their role is to tackle complex problems and to make tough choices, knowing that whatever decision is made it will not please everyone (Benington and Moore in press). It is increasingly recognised that not all societal choices can be addressed through market mechanisms, and that therefore the state, including its politicians, have a crucial role to play in creating, mobilising, orchestrating and leading inter-organisational coalitions to address these issues.

At the level of public service organisations, there is growing recognition of the role of elected politicians in setting strategic direction and creating a climate which supports the risk-taking often necessary for innovation and change. For example, Pandey and Moynihan (2006), in a US study, found that political support [i.e. from elected politicians] is associated with higher levels of organisational performance, including the reduction of red tape. Rashman and Hartley (2002) and Hartley and Rashman (2007) found that local government politicians are important contributors to inter-organisational learning, organisational change and performance improvement associated with the Beacon Council national initiative to improve local government.

The current paradigm shift from 'new public management' to 'networked governance' re-emphasises the importance of the political leadership role which had been downplayed or neglected in 'new public management'. If politicians are central not only to the effective functioning of a democracy but also to improving public services, what then does the academic literature have to say about political leadership?

The academic literature on political leadership

Leach, Hartley, Lowndes, Wilson and Downe (2005) note that there is only a small literature about political leadership from either a political science or an organisational behaviour perspective. The political science literature has tended to focus on political institutions, ideologies, structures and processes. Where leadership is discussed, it is often in terms of prominent leaders such as presidents and prime ministers, thereby conflating leadership with leaders and focusing primarily on 'top' leaders and on charismatic leadership (though see Wren 2007). Autobiographies and biographies of political leaders and case studies of high-profile crunch decisions (e.g. the Cuban missile crisis) are plentiful but the focus is rarely on general processes of leadership but rather on idiographic and historical analysis.

One writer who stands out from this is James McGregor Burns (1978), a political biographer and historian who focused not only on the detail of presidents' actions, but also conceptualised leadership in a processual way. He argued that leadership can be seen as a set of 'leadership acts', which are about actions and processes used by individuals and groups to mobilise support for a particular approach or decision. Burns was also the academic who distinguished between 'transformational' and 'transactional leadership' which has been so popularised and studied in the management field. Interestingly, most writing about transformational and transactional leadership has stripped the concepts of their originating context in political leadership.

There is also an emerging literature about the leadership qualities and styles of particular roles of elected politicians. For example, Greasley and Stoker (2008) analyse the directly elected local mayors in England and suggest that the institutional/constitutional arrangements affect outcomes and can encourage particular styles of leadership. By contrast, Leach *et al.* (2005) took an inter-disciplinary view of political leadership, arguing that it required attention to contexts, political constitutions, tasks and skills but that agency had greater explanatory power than structure alone. Kelman (1988), in the USA, examines the literature about the motivation of politicians both to take on the role and also in relation to the political choices they make while in power.

Political psychology has tended to be dominated by the US literature and focuses on personality, emotion and cognition of senior political figures, and on the voting preferences of citizens, rather than on theorising the nature and processes of political leadership (e.g. Jost and Sidanius 2004). Recent work has, however, applied organisational psychology to aspects of recruitment and selection of political candidates (Silvester and Dykes 2007).

Political leadership has scarcely been mentioned in the generic leadership literature. The index in most books does not include political leadership or related words, and the books themselves do not contain discussion or analysis of political leadership. Taking two widely quoted academic books provides an illustration: the definitive work of Yukl (2006); as well as the Sage Handbook of Organizational Studies with its review chapter on leadership (Parry and Bryman 2006). In relation to political leadership, therefore, organisational studies are context-blind – striving for a general theory of leadership without taking sufficient account of the political and economic context of leadership, or the societal or institutional authority which can form part of the basis of leadership. Where the word 'political' is used at all, it is generally in relation to organisational politics i.e. the informal 'small p' use of power in organisational settings – more about the politics of leadership than political leadership.

The management and organisational behaviour fields have closely studied and conceptualised leadership but this literature has only rarely analysed political leadership. A review of the literature on political leadership (Morrell and Hartley 2006) found scant material from an organisational behaviour perspective. Even in the management literature, there is relatively little research or commentary on the management challenges facing political leaders, or the need for managers to have political awareness skills to work with or alongside politicians.

Only the field of public management appears to have taken the concept of political leadership seriously – perhaps because public managers, particularly at more senior levels, encounter and work with elected politicians on a regular basis. However, even here, leadership is largely viewed from the perspective of public managers acting as leaders in a political context (e.g. Denis, Langley and Rouleau 2005; van Wart 2003; Behn 1998; Terry 1998). An exception is the work of Heifetz and Sinder (1988) and Heifetz (1994), who address political leadership directly, by arguing for the need to consider the work being undertaken by such leaders, the need to consider the role and power basis of political, managerial or community leadership, and also by providing analyses of leadership processes and problem identification and resolution through the work of political leaders working with formal authority (e.g. Lyndon Johnson) and without formal authority (e.g. Martin Luther King's social movement leadership). His work, thus, recognises that political leadership is distinct from managerial leadership.

What is formal political leadership?

In democratic societies, the electoral democratic basis for political leadership is so commonplace as to barely merit consideration – yet the authority base for leadership, it is argued, is crucial to understanding political leadership – and distinguishing it from managerial, professional or informal civic leadership.

Heifetz (1994) makes a crucial distinction between leadership *with* authority and leadership *without* authority. He argues that leadership research has made insufficient distinction between these, yet they affect the basis of leadership and the strategies of leading which are open to the person or group:

> I define authority as conferred power to perform a service. This definition will be useful to the practitioner of leadership as a reminder of two facts: First, authority is given and can be taken away. Second, authority is conferred as part of an exchange. Failure to meet the terms of the exchange means the risk of losing one's authority: it can be taken back or given to another who promises to fulfill the bargain. (Heifetz 1994: 57)

The conferring of power, in the quote above, emphasises that formal authority is given by other people, which in the case of political leadership is through election initially and then through continuing support. Formal authority is an important potential source of leadership though leadership and authority, while often connected, are not the same.

Leadership without authority, or informal leadership, has a different basis and therefore set of activities associated with it. These are individuals and groups who lead societies, communities, groups or particular issues and influence others without formal authorisation, for example, a campaigning group or an opinion leader. A leader acting without authority may be less constrained by the roles and rules, and by the expectations of others. Such leadership is likely to require political awareness but does not necessarily constitute formal political leadership.

There is a relationship between those in formal authority and those who accept (or resist or resent) authority. Authority is important in the analysis of leadership because the personal qualities of the individual are not the whole story, leadership may be a combination of personal qualities, positional authority, and the relationship(s) with the people who are being led or influenced.

If the basis of authority for an elected politician is then considered, the differences from managerial leadership become apparent. Political leaders are democratically elected through a legally defined voting system by an electorate which is also legally defined. Their claim to authority is a commitment to act as a representative of their electorate, and they are expected (at least in stable democratic societies) to represent the interests not only of all those in their constituency (not just those who voted for them) but also to take into account public interests for society as a whole, including non-voters and the needs of future generations. Given that politicians have access to the state's coercive powers of authority there is an expectation and legal requirement that such authority is used fairly, legally and proportionately (Benington and Moore in press).

Since political leaders gain their initial authority through election not appointment, and act as representatives, they require continuing consent from those whom they govern and serve. Political leaders gain their authority through the ballot box initially but their authority is potentially subject to challenge on a daily basis – from their political party (most operate within a political party structure and even those who operate as independents may need to construct a political coalition to reach decisions), from opposition politicians, the media, their constituents, and other stakeholders (e.g. business, voluntary and public sector organisations, lobby and advocacy groups etc). Support from particular stakeholders (e.g. the prime minister, the political party, the public, the media) may be withdrawn at any time over any issue and can become a matter for resignation if the politician judges that there is insufficient support to continue. A politician may move from being in power to being out of office literally overnight, as was the case with Margaret Thatcher.

This creates uncertainty in a way which appointed managers rarely experience. A politician may go from being Prime Minister one day to being a backbencher the next. Someone who worked for you may become your boss, and later you may again become more senior to that person. David Blunkett, when Secretary of State for Education, used to joke with Michael Bichard, the Permanent Secretary, that he, David, was only the Temporary Secretary.

Furthermore, the areas in which politicians have authority in which to make decisions are inevitably contested, because they are not only the concerns of private individuals but are also the concerns of society (Hoggett 2006; Marquand 2004) and these are inevitably uncertain, ambiguous, subject to different values, interests and priorities by different stakeholders and therefore open to debate and dispute. Political leadership therefore has to operate in conditions where decisions are not necessarily accepted but may be opposed, undermined and rejected by particular individuals and groups. Crick's (1993) view of politics as a means to achieve outcomes in situations where there are differences is central to this view of political leadership.

The sociological and psychological pressures on politicians are therefore often immense – both the threat of imminent loss of power and authority, and the continual contestation of ideas, decisions and actions associated with their role (Hartley and Pinder 2010; Simpson 2008), generally in the glare of the ravenous media.

One feature of the leadership challenges facing politicians is that actions and decisions may require the active mobilisation of different groups in order to build consent, and work to reduce the amount of opposition to policies and proposals. In this sense, leadership is constitutive (Grint 2000) – an interaction between the leader and the situation they are in.

Politicians may be in political control, in opposition or in coalition. If they hold different formal political roles they may experience control, opposition and coalition simultaneously, for example, if they are political representatives at county and district local authority level, whilst their political party is in opposition at national level.

Contexts, challenges and capabilities of political leadership

Given the evidence that political leadership is woefully under-researched (Morrell and Hartley 2006), there are a number of lines of enquiry and analysis which might be pursued. Here, we focus on three inter-related areas – contexts, challenges and capabilities (Hartley and Pinder 2010; Hartley and Benington 2010).

The contexts of political leadership

It is increasingly recognised that leadership in general is related to, or contingent on, context and that a key pre-requisite of effective leadership is the need to understand the context in which it is being exercised. Academics have looked at this from a number of perspectives, exploring both the influence of contextual factors on leadership and the influence of leadership in shaping context. Grint (2000) classifies theories about leadership according to the degree to which they pay attention to, or ignore, context, as an aspect of leadership. Porter and McLaughlin (2006) review the theoretical and empirical knowledge about the organisational context and leadership (across all types of organisation) and conclude that while leadership context is much discussed, in fact there is much less research which takes this into account as an analytical factor, rather than part of the description of the location of a particular sample. They argue for much more rigorous and systematic attention to understanding the impact of context on leadership and *vice versa*.

Taylor (1993) identified that local politicians have to operate in at least four arenas or contexts, and Hartley (2002) added a fifth arena:

1. Shaping and supporting the development of grass-roots communities
2. Negotiating and mobilising effective partnerships with other public, private and voluntary agencies i.e. lateral inter-organisational leadership

3. Voicing the needs and interests of the local community in regional, national, European and international arenas i.e. vertical inter-organisational leadership
4. Governing the public service organisation and giving its services clear strategic direction
5. Working within the political party group, both locally and within the governing body, and developing political coalitions as appropriate.

At the level of the national Parliament and the devolved assemblies (Scotland, Wales and Northern Ireland), the arenas are even more complex and varied, both due to the larger constituencies in demographic and geographical terms, and the need for a politician to keep in touch with local levels of democracy as well as regional, national and supranational ones. In the UK, with formal power at the national level but with power increasingly distributed between other spheres and levels, these arenas are complex and can be unpredictable. Arenas may partly be thought of as physical locations/spaces but they are also socially configured sets of actors and networks which whom the politician interacts or who operate as a stakeholder group in relation to the actions of political leadership.

Research into the contexts of political leadership at local level (Leach *et al.* 2005: 8) found that leaders face '...a shifting but always limited set of choices that stem from the internal and external context of the [organization], both current pressures and future trends'. However, context (the constitution, local political arrangements, traditions and cultures, the externally driven political agenda, the social, economic, geographical and demographic context) is not immutable. An effective political leader, in this research, was seen to be someone who could accurately read the context surrounding their political institution, and could adjust his or her leadership behaviour to respond to, but also help shape the context. As in the analysis by Grint (2005), context is shaped and articulated – constituted – not just adjusted to. Part of this is the sense-making or sense-breaking skills which characterise leadership more generally (Weick 1995; Pye 2005). Given that much of the work of politicians lies outside their own political institution, working with a range of stakeholders, then 'framing the narrative' (both inside and outside the organisation) is a critical aspect of the work of political leadership (see also Simpson 2008). Leach *et al.* (2005: 70) note that 'context is not immutable and there are opportunities for the role of political leadership in shaping...change, often over an extended period of time'.

The challenges of political leadership

What are the goals or purposes of political leadership? These tasks or purposes are here called challenges in line with an emerging literature which frames leadership purposes in this way (Morrell and Hartley 2006). Most definitions of leadership focus on some aspects of purpose such as influence towards a common goal, or mobilising others to tackle tough problems. The early definition of leadership from Stogdill (1974) is a reminder that the leader's role may be to find or frame the purpose not just implement goals or communicate a vision to others.

Leach and Wilson (2000) identified four key leadership tasks for political leaders, drawing on the organisational analyses of Selznick (1957), Kotter and Lawrence (1974) and Stone (1995). These leadership tasks were studied empirically in research on local political leadership in nine in-depth case studies of local authorities (Leach *et al.* 2005). These tasks were characterised as:

- Maintaining a critical mass of political support
- Developing strategic policy direction
- Seeking to further leadership priorities outside the organisation
- Ensuring task accomplishment.

Maintaining a critical mass of political support is the bedrock of political leadership, given the contested nature of the public decisions which have to be taken. Unless there is support from the political party, it will be impossible to win the argument for a cause or to carry the vote. Even independent politicians at local level find that they need to build political coalitions to create legislation or build support for change. When a Minister says that it is important to 'remember to go over for coffee in the House [of Commons] a couple of times a week', this is not about refreshment but about listening to, and lobbying support from, backbench MPs.

Developing and articulating strategic direction has always been a crucial part of military, political, organisational and social movement leadership. It is increasingly important as the complexity of the problems facing society have grown. Those in formal political leadership positions leading a government department or a local council report having to spend considerable time and energy ensuring that they stay focused on the big picture rather than getting caught up in the concerns of the various lobbyists, advocates and others with whom they deal on a daily basis. Working out how to be effective in strategic thinking and action as well as the crucial issues of today, without lapsing into micro-management is a challenge which some political leaders appear to have mastered while others struggle.

It can be tempting to become focused on activities inside the political institution (e.g. the government department, Parliament, the town hall) but seeking to further leadership priorities outside the organisation is increasingly important in the context of 'networked governance' (Benington 1997; Taylor 1993; Hartley 2002). There is a growing recognition of the limitations of government on its own in addressing complex, long-term political, economic and social issues, and the need to address declining trust in government and participation in representative democracy. This has led political leaders and public managers to place a greater emphasis on partnerships between the private, public and voluntary sectors as a means to plan, design and deliver services, and sometimes to fund services as well. The UK has been a particularly fruitful area for these ideas (Sullivan and Skelcher 2002). Some governments have also placed greater emphasis on citizen or user engagement in service planning and there is a greater interest in the co-production of services (e.g. Alford 2009). The implications for political leadership are considerable – to work through influence as well as through formal authority and to work with a range of partners and stakeholders in a variety of arenas (as noted above).

Finally, in terms of the four political leadership challenges noted above, there is the job of ensuring task accomplishment (e.g. legislation, service delivery). This is the work to be done, with and through appointed officials, to ensure that the political party manifesto is carried out, that strategic aims are accomplished, that promises are kept (or explained away) and that innovative ways of tackling complex problems are sought. The 'new public management' has led to a plethora of performance targets, performance indicators and measures and performance reports which can be used by the public and others to track the performance of the organisations and services for which the political leader has responsibility. 'Targets and terror' (Bevan and Hood 2006) and the recent emphasis on public services reform means that a political leader will ignore task accomplishment at their peril.

The four challenges, derived from analysis of local political leadership, may also be relevant at other levels of government, but further research is needed to establish this.

The work of Leach *et al.* (2005) noted that different political leaders placed different emphasis on each of these four challenges (depending on context, local traditions and the political leader's views about the needs and aspirations of the local community) but that each had to be addressed to some extent, and that there are tensions between them, given the width and depth of the workload.

The work of Heifetz (1994) is valuable for its emphasis on leadership as an active process of working with individuals, groups, communities and organisations to tackle tough problems. He makes the distinction between 'technical' and 'adaptive' problems or challenges, which require different approaches to the leadership task (see also Chapter 14). Technical leadership is appropriate where the problem is fairly well understood and where there is an agreed course of action. Here, leadership is based on bringing together and energising people and resources to achieve agreed goals. However, adaptive leadership is needed where the challenge is complex and where different individuals or groups may not agree either on what the problem is or how it can be tackled. Many of the complex cross-cutting problems of contemporary society are adaptive (e.g. crime and community safety, alcohol-related violence; climate change) and require the ability to lead and shape changes in attitudes, values and behaviours. A great deal of political leadership is concerned with adaptive leadership i.e. influencing individuals and groups to engage in difficult problem definition and problem-solving choices. Such choices often need the active engagement from those involved in the issue (e.g. crime will not be solved solely by legislation or by more police, but requires active work by citizens).

The strategic leadership of adaptive change is not just about rational decision-making, however persuasive the *posthoc* rationalisations of leaders. Complex change in an uncertain world can only be partially predicted and planned for. Sense-making becomes important in organisational change under conditions of uncertainty or ambiguity (Weick 1995). Sense-making captures the idea that people (individuals or groups) make sense of confusing or ambiguous events by constructing plausible (rather than necessarily accurate) interpretations of events through action and through reinterpretation of past events (see also Chapter 15). Pfeffer (1981) argues that a key role for leaders is to provide *'explanations, rationalizations and legitimations for activities undertaken'* (p. 4). The role of the political leader, in a sense-making framework, may be less to be fully clear about the future and rational plans for shaping it (i.e. providing a 'clear vision'), and more about being able to provide a plausible narrative that helps people understand what may be happening and mobilises their support and activity towards addressing the problem.

Capabilities of political leadership

Capabilities are the knowledge, skills, attitudes and other personal characteristics that are associated with skilful leadership. In shorthand, they are sometimes called skills though a broader concept is capabilities. The chapter defines capabilities as *the skills, knowledge, experience, attributes and behaviours that an individual needs to perform a job effectively* (e.g. Hirsch and Strebler 1995). Capabilities need to be set in the context both of job demands and of the organisational environment if models are not to be simplistic and over-generalised (see also Boyatzis 1982; Burgoyne 1993). Most work on capabilities has focused on managerial leadership and some has analysed political leadership (Hartley and Pinder 2010; Leach *et al.* 2005; Silvester 2008), linking these to context.

The chapter argues that political leadership capabilities need to be interpreted in their context as well as in the light of how the leader interprets their key priorities or challenges. This means that the specific combination of capabilities will vary according to the context and what the political leader aims to achieve. Capabilities are the skills of action and interpretation, within the political institution but also working with and influencing others, and mobilising organisations and networks.

A political leader has to be able to draw on a wide set of behaviours, self-awareness and attitudes in order to be skilful. The capabilities may also be manifest across a political group of senior elected members or leadership constellation (e.g. local authority Cabinet) (Leach *et al.* 2005). Indeed, the challenge of gaining, mobilising and maintaining political support suggests that political leadership will often be part of a leadership constellation.

Research with more than 400 elected members in local government led to the development of a framework of capabilities for political leadership at this level of government (Hartley *et al.* 2005), using an instrument called the Warwick Political Leadership Questionnaire. These dimensions are shown in Table 9.1. Research confirms the structure of these dimensions (Hartley and Morgan-Thomas 2003).

Table 9.1   The Capabilities Framework of the Warwick Political Leadership Questionnaire

1.	Public service values: service, integrity, courage
2.	Questioning thinking: skills of questioning, learning, challenging, creativity, lateral thinking, imagination
3.	Decision-making: making tough choices, seeing different possibilities for decision, balancing competing possibilities
4.	Personal effectiveness: self-awareness, managing emotions, persistence, handling difficult relationships
5.	Strategic thinking and action: strategising, planning the campaign, mobilising, gaining the high ground
6.	Advocacy and representation: shaping and voicing the needs and aspirations of the electorate
7.	Political intelligence: understanding collective responsibility, the boundaries of party discipline, building coalitions, negotiation skills, the art of judgement
8.	Communications: persuasion, engaging in dialogue, listening, understanding different perspectives
9.	Organizational mobilisation: inspiring and motivating, galvanising across boundaries and spheres, partnership working
10.	Systems and tasks: managing roles and organizational boundaries, implementing and tracking progress and performance

Research by Leach *et al.* (2005) shows that, notwithstanding context and the pressures from central government, there remains in all local authorities an interpretive space within which a leader's personal values, attitudes and other skills come into play. However, leadership capabilities are not divorced from context or challenges – we should not see leadership as a universal set of skills but rather capabilities interacting with context. Chapter 12 by Benington and Hartley outlines some of the capabilities for leadership across the whole system (encompassing capabilities for political and for managerial leadership) and this starts from the analysis of context and changes in the context. Hartley (2010) outlines an approach to leadership and management development which starts with the analysis of the context and challenges of public service organisations.

The Warwick research evidence on 400 local government elected politicians also suggests, on the basis of length of experience of being a political leader, that a number of leadership capabilities are acquired through experience in the role, rather than through maturity (age) or through being innate (Hartley *et al.* 2005).

Conclusions

Research from a leadership perspective has only scratched the surface of understanding political leadership. In this chapter we have outlined some areas to consider but they remain under-theorised and under-researched.

Political leadership is an important type of leadership, in both numerical and functional terms. Political leadership affects not only the work of public service organisations, but through public policy, regulation and the mobilisation of support, affects private and voluntary sector organisations too.

It is important theoretically too. While it is a particular type of leadership, located in a particular set of roles and governed by particular conceptions of authority, legitimacy and accountability, it raises questions about the context-blindness of much leadership research. A consideration of political leadership shows how much the leadership literature has been, perhaps unconsciously, influenced by models of leadership from the military and from large business organisations, where the majority of research is conducted. There are insights to be gained for leadership in other situations from examining political leadership.

Political leadership shows that careful attention to the sources of legitimacy is important, including clarifying the relationship between authority and leadership. In addition, the analysis of the arenas element of the context, shows that much of the time, attention and energy of political leadership is not inside the political institution, important though that is, but is about creating and mobilising support across diverse interests, through influence not just authority, and outside as well as inside the organisation. Some of these insights are now being used to consider the political awareness dimensions of managerial leadership (Hartley and Fletcher 2008).

The challenges of political leadership also remind us that leadership cannot be fully understood without thinking about the purposes of leadership. Political leadership has to try to be effective across a range of challenges, which are sometimes mutually conflicting but which each need to be addressed to some extent. Sense-making and sense-breaking lie at the heart of much political leadership activity, due to working in a polycentric governance arrangement. Such challenges are increasingly found in business environments, where public opinion and media views have to be addressed, not just shareholder views.

Capabilities only make sense when context and challenges are considered. Research suggests that these skills are about working with influence not solely authority, given that consent has to be won and rewon if power is to be retained. Conduct, not just context, is important. Some skills of political leadership appear to be learned.

While this chapter draws on empirical research with UK elected politicians, across all political parties and none, the field overall is under-researched. There is scope for work on all the areas above, plus others not covered here, including the impact of political leadership on outputs and outcomes. This is a difficult area, as the chapter on evaluating leadership in general shows (Chapter 20) but is important if we are to understand effective leadership.

References

Alford, J. (2009) *Engaging Public Sector Clients: From Service-Delivery to Co-Production.* Basingstoke: Palgrave Macmillan.

Benington, J. (1997) 'New Paradigms and Practices for Local Government: Capacity Building Within Civil Society', in Kraemer, S. and Roberts, J. (eds), *The Politics of Attachment.* London: Free Association Books.

Benington, J. (2000) 'The Modernization and Improvement of Government and Public Services', *Public Money and Management,* 20(2): 3–8.

Benington, J. and Moore, J. (in press) *Public Value: Theory and Practice.* Basingstoke: Palgrave Macmillan.

Behn, R. (1998) 'What Right Do Public Managers Have to Lead?', *Public Administration Review,* 58(3): 209–224.

Bevan, G. and Hood, C. (2006) 'What's Measured is What Matters: Targets and Gaming in the English Public Healthcare System', *Public Administration,* 84(3): 517–538.

Boyatzis, R. (1982) *The Competent Manager: A Model for Effective Performance.* New York: Wiley.

Burgoyne, J. (1993) 'The Competency Movement: Issues, Stakeholders and Prospects', *Personnel Review,* 22(6): 6–13.

Burns, J.M. (1978) *Leadership.* New York: Harper and Row.

Crick, B. (1993). *In Defence of Politics (4th edition).* Chicago: Chicago University Press.

Denis, J.-L., Langley, A. and Rouleau, L. (2005) 'Rethinking Leadership in Public Organizations', in Ferlie, E., Lynn, L. and Pollitt, C. (eds) *The Oxford Handbook of Public Management.* Oxford: Oxford University Press.

DWP (2009) www.dwp.gov.uk/publications/dwp/2006/dr06/annexa/table2.asp. Accessed 14 April 2009.

Greasley, S. and Stoker, G. (2008) 'Mayors and Urban Governance: Developing a Facilitative Leadership Style', *Public Administration Review,* 68(4): 722–730.

Grint, K. (2000) *The Arts of Leadership.* Oxford: Oxford University Press.

Grint, K. (2005) 'Problems, Problems, Problems: The Social Construction of "Leadership"', *Human Relations,* 58: 1467–1494.

Hartley, J. (2002) 'Leading Communities: Capabilities and Cultures', *Leadership and Organizational Development Journal,* 23: 419–429.

Hartley, J. (2010) 'Public Sector Leadership and Management Development', in Gold, J., Thorpe, R. and Mumford, A. (eds), *Gower Handbook of Leadership and Management Development*. Farnham: Gower.

Hartley, J., Fletcher, C. and Benington, J. (2005) 'Look at it from My Angle: The Development and Use of a 360 Degree Feedback Instrument for Political Leaders', *Working Paper*. Coventry: Institute of Governance and Public Management, University of Warwick.

Hartley, J. and Fletcher, C. (2008) 'Leadership with Political Awareness: Leadership Across Diverse Interests Inside and Outside The Organization', in James, K. and Collins, J. (eds), *Leadership Perspectives: Knowledge into Action*. London: Palgrave, pp. 157–170.

Hartley, J. and Benington, J. (2010) *Leadership for Healthcare*. Bristol: Policy Press.

Hartley, J. and Morgan-Thomas, A. (2003) 'The Development of the Warwick Political Leadership Questionnaire: Conceptual Framework and Measurement Properties', *Conference Paper*, International Studying Leadership Conference. Lancaster. December.

Hartley, J. and Pinder, K. (2010) 'Coaching Political Leaders', in Passmore, J. (ed.) *Leadership in Coaching*. London: Kogan Page.

Hartley, J. and Rashman, L. (2007) 'How is Knowledge Transferred Between Organizations Involved in Change?', in Wallace, M., Fertig, M. and Schneller, E. (eds), *Managing Change in the Public Services*. Oxford: Blackwell, pp. 173–192.

Hartley, J. and Skelcher, C. (2008) 'The Agenda for Public Service Improvement', in Hartley, J., Donaldson, C., Skelcher, C. and Wallace, M. (eds), *Managing to Improve Public Services*. Cambridge: Cambridge University Press, pp. 1–21.

Heifetz, R. (1994) *Leadership Without Easy Answers*. Cambridge, MA: Belknapp Press.

Heifetz, R. and Sinder, R. (1988) 'Political Leadership', in Reich, R. (ed.) *The Power of Public Ideas*. Cambridge, MA: Harvard University Press.

Hirsch, W. and Strebler, M. (1995) 'Defining Managerial Skills and Competencies', in Mumford, A. (ed.) *Handbook of Management Development*. Aldershot: Gower.

Hoggett, P. (2006) 'Conflict, Ambivalence and the Contested Purpose of Public Organizations', *Human Relations*, 59(2): 175–194.

Hood, C. (1991) 'A Public Management for All Seasons', *Public Administration*, 69(1): 3–19.

Jackson, P. (2003) 'The Size and Scope of the Public Sector: An International Comparison', in Bovaird, T. and Löffler, E. (eds), *Public Management and Governance*. London: Routledge, pp. 25–39.

Jost, J. and Sidanius, J. (2004) *Political Psychology*. New York: Psychology Press.

Kelman, S. (1988) 'Why Public Ideas Matter', in Reich, R. (ed.), *The Power of Public Ideas*. Cambridge, MA: Harvard University Press.

Kotter, J. and Lawrence, R. (1974) *Mayors in Action: Five Approaches to Urban Governance*. New York: Wiley.

Leach, S., Hartley, J., Lowndes, V., Wilson, D. and Downe, J. (2005) *Local Political Leadership in the UK*. York: Joseph Rowntree Foundation.

Leach, S. and Wilson, D. (2000) *Local Political Leadership* Bristol: Policy Press.

Marquand, D. (2004) *The Decline of the Public*. Cambridge: Polity Press.

Moore, M.H. (1995) *Creating Public Value*. Cambridge, MA: Harvard University Press.

Morrell, K. and Hartley, J. (2006) 'A Model of Political Leadership', *Human Relations*, 59(4): 483–504.

Newman, J. (2001) *Modernising Governance: New Labour, Policy and Society*. London: Sage.

Pandey, S. and Moynihan, D. (2006) 'Bureaucratic Red Tape and Organisational Performance: Testing the Moderating Role of Culture and Political Support', in

Boyne, G., Meier, K., O'Toole, K. and Walker, R. (eds), *Public Service Performance*. Cambridge: Cambridge University Press.

Parry, K. and Bryman, A. (2006) 'Leadership in Organizations', in Clegg, S., Hardy, C., Lawrence, T. and Nord, W. (eds), *The Sage Handbook of Organization Studies*. London: Sage.

Pedersen, D. and Hartley, J. (2008) 'The Changing Context of Public Leadership and Management: Implications for Roles and Dynamics', *International Journal of Public Sector Management*, 21(4): 327–339.

Pfeffer, J. (1981) 'Management as Symbolic Action', *Research in Organizational Behavior*, 3: 1–52.

Pollitt, C. and Bouckaert, G. (2004) *Public Management Reform: A Comparative Analysis*. Oxford: Oxford University Press.

Porter, L. and McLaughlin, G. (2006) 'Leadership and the Organizational Context: Like the Weather?', *Leadership Quarterly*, 17(6): 559–576.

Pye, A. (2005) 'Leadership and Organizing: Sensemaking in Action', *Leadership*, 1(1): 31–49.

Rashman, L. and Hartley, J. (2002) 'Leading and Learning? Knowledge Transfer in the Beacon Council Scheme', *Public Administration*, 80: 523–542.

Selznick, P. (1957) *Leadership in Administration*. New York: Harper and Row.

Silvester, J. (2008) 'The Good, the Bad and the Ugly: Politics and Politicians at Work', in Hodgkinson, G. and Ford, J. (eds) *International Review of Industrial and Organizational Psychology, volume 23*. Chichester: Wiley.

Silvester, J. and Dykes, C. (2007) 'Selecting Political Candidates: A Longitudinal Study of Assessment Centre Performance and Political Success in the 2005 UK General Election', *Journal Of Occupational and Organizational Psychology*, 80(1): 11–25.

Simpson, J. (2008) *The Politics of Leadership*. London: Leading Edge Publications.

Stogdill, R. (1974) *Handbook of Leadership: A Survey of Theory and Research*. New York: Free Press.

Stoker, G. (2006) 'A New Narrative For Networked Governance', *American Review of Public Administration*, 36(1): 41–57.

Stone, C. (1995) 'Political Leadership in Urban Politics', in Judge, D., Stoker, G. and Wolman, H. (eds), *Theories of Urban Politics*. London: Sage.

Sullivan, H. and Skelcher, C. (2002) *Working Across Boundaries: Collaboration in Public Services*. Basingstoke: Palgrave.

Taylor, M. (1993) 'The Four Axes of Civic Leadership', *Research paper*. Local Government Centre, University of Warwick.

Terry, L. (1998) 'Administrative Leadership, Neo-Managerialism and the Public Management Movement', *Public Administration Review*, 58(3): 194–200.

Treasury (2009) *Public Sector Finances*, March 2009. www.hm-treasury.gov.uk/d/psf. pdf. Accessed 26 April 2009.

Van Wart, M. (2003) 'Public-Sector Leadership Theory: An Assessment', *Public Administration Review*, 63(2): 214–228.

Weick, K. (1995) *Sense-Making in Organisations*. Thousand Oaks, CA: Sage.

Wren, J. (2007) *Investing Leadership: The Challenge of Democracy*. Cheltenham: Edward Elgar.

Yukl, G. (2006) *Leadership in Organisations (6th edition)*. Upper Saddle River NJ: Pearson Prentice Hall.

10
Telling the Story of Place: The Role of Community Leadership

Stephen Brookes

Introduction

This chapter continues the theme of thinking differently about public leadership. It focuses on community leadership as a distinct leadership style alongside organisational, individual and political leadership. These four styles combine and form what Chapter 1 describes as collective leadership. While the term 'collective leadership' is not new what this chapter argues is that defining public leadership as a form of collective leadership is unique.

The chapter describes research that sought to test for evidence of collective leadership at all levels of public sector activity through increased collaboration. A peer assessment and a series of interviews were held with director and policy leads in five local authority areas. Focus group interviews with senior officers from other public services in the same local authority areas followed. The chapter will argue that developing a collective leadership style poses several challenges for community leadership.

In Chapter 1 the argument was made for a form of collective leadership which differs from, but also builds on, earlier theories of leadership. Drawing upon the work of Ansari *et al.* (2001) in relation to the difficulties of developing an evidence based approach to collaborative partnership working and the work of Grint (2000, 2005a, 2005b) and Heifetz (1994) in relation to the nature and problem oriented focus of leadership, a model of collective leadership was offered. This suggested a dual focus on both shared and distributed leadership. The earlier chapter also argued that whilst both terms ('shared' and 'distributed' leadership) have been used in previous literature each has been used in isolation rather than in tandem. This certainly applies in the field of education (Bennett *et al.* 2003; Doyle and Smith 2001).

The chapter argues that to improve public leadership, shared aims and values and a shared commitment to delivery will help leaders rise to these challenges. The chapter will draw on both theory and practice. It will suggest that improved wellbeing lies at the heart of public value, which other chapters have suggested lies at the heart of collective public leadership.

The case for collaboration at the local level

Previous chapters have highlighted the dysfunctional impact of public sector reform. This is evident in examining a range of public services (Brookes 2006a, 2006b). With policing for example, Hough argues that governments' attempts to reform and modernise the police may themselves be responsible in part for the decline in public confidence through the centralising and quantitative nature of performance regimes (Hough 2007). Similar views are expressed about health (Stevens 2004; Walshe and Chambers Chapter 3) and education through performance regimes (Isherwood *et al.* 2007; Gunter and Forrester Chapter 4).

The chapter will briefly examine three issues in the first section:

- The nature of community leadership
- The role of networks
- The value of partnerships

Understanding community leadership

What is community leadership?

Several definitions are offered from different sources. For example, the local government Improvement and Development Agency (IdEA) suggest that community leadership differs from traditional notions of leadership and involves creating the right environment for others to act. Community leadership is less directing and controlling, and more stimulating, enabling and empowering (IDeA 2006) and they suggest a central role for local government. Given the role of local government as 'first among equals' (Woolas 2006), Martin (2002) questions whether this 'vision' and 'leadership' for their communities will take priority over the focus on 'value-for-money' that previous conservative administration stressed. In a later definition of the concept the IDeA were clearer. The agency defined community leadership:

> Community leadership is about councils, both councillors and officers, enabling local communities to steer their own future. It is not traditional, top-down leadership, but involves councillors and officers using all the tools at their disposal to engage communities in making their own difference. It promotes a partnership of shared commitment to promote a shared vision for the locality (IDeA 2009).

But it is more than this. It is also about encouraging the community to take responsibility as co-producers. Briefly, co-production brings technical experts (public leaders) with groups in society (community leaders) to create new knowledge and technologies (ways of tackling adaptive or wicked problems). This description is consistent with Gibbons and colleagues 'the new production of knowledge' (Gibbons *et al.* 1994). They argue that a new form of knowledge production started emerging from the mid-20th century which is context-driven, problem-focused and interdisciplinary. It involves multidisciplinary teams brought together for short periods of time to work on specific problems in the real world. In a broad sense community leadership is also a means of building social capital (Audit Commission 2003) and, in particular, the bridging and bonding aspects of social capital as described by Putnam (2000). As Burt (2007: 157) argues, the third sector plays a key role in building social capital.

Traditional approaches to community development link successful responses to community problems or issues with strong leadership (Peirce and Johnson 1998; Pigg 1999). Others argue there is a need to develop the leadership skills of community members (Williams and Wade 2002), considering factors such as the environment, community membership characteristics, process and structure, communication, purpose and resources (Mattessich *et al.* 2001).

The community and voluntary sector is also a key player as part of collective leadership approaches. As the National Council for Voluntary Organisations (NCVO 2009) point out, leadership within a community is both complicated and open to criticism. They suggest that as more people, with differing backgrounds, skills, interests and degrees of authority, claim to lead different communities within a growing number and complexity of arenas, e.g. from local strategic partnerships to community fun days, tension arises. This is the case with elected representatives and those, such as Voluntary and Community Organisations (VCOs) and community activists, who also believe they represent local communities (NCVO 2009). This presents a danger of creating a democratic deficit (Smith *et al.* 2006).

The chapter proposes that Community Leadership encompasses an interdisciplinary approach to collective leadership in which locally elected members, officers from public institutions, the public and community and voluntary groups work to produce tangible results that improve community wellbeing. It is therefore about people, places and public value; the people are the stakeholders, the place is the local community and the public value is the outcome of the collective leadership. The research described in this paper sought to test this proposition.

The Audit Commission highlighted five factors that it saw as being critical to community leadership. These are illustrated in Figure 10.1 and will be deployed to compare the critical success factors of community leadership that emerged from the research.

Figure 10.1   Factors Critical to the Success of Community Leadership

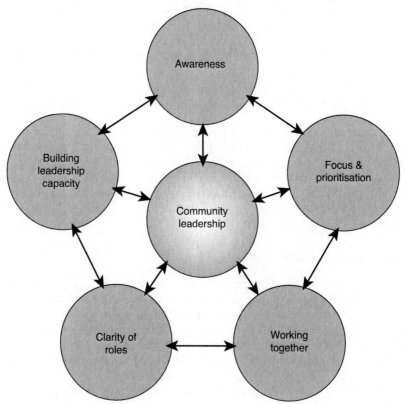

Source: Audit Commission 2003.

Networked governance

Networked governance is increasingly important given the intensive interdependencies of different organisations and individuals (Stoker 2006).

As previous chapters in Part I identified, the impacts of public service reform pose real challenges for leaders in achieving a suitable balance between the needs of the authorising establishment (central government) and the needs of the public. Stoker identifies the position succinctly when he states:

[Networked governance] ... requires the state to steer society in new ways through the development of complex networks and the rise of more bottom-up approaches to decision making. Established institutional forms of governance appear under challenge, and new forms of governance appear to be emerging. Networked governance is a particular framing of collective decision making that is characterized by a trend for a wider range of participants to be seen as legitimate members of the decision-making process in the context of considerable uncertainty and complexity. The pressure is on to find new ways to collaborate as the interdependence of a range of individuals and organizations intensifies (Stoker 2006: 41).

Stoker supports a shift towards public value management as opposed to new public management (NPM) and traditional public administration as it provides a greater opportunity in managing within the increased and dynamic networked environment. As Chapter 1 argues, whilst networks are not new (Agranoff and McGuire 2003), others suggest that not enough is made of organisational and community network analyses and how networks can be optimised (Stephenson 2007).

The value of partnerships

There has been increasing interest since the early 1990s in more coordinated approaches to public policy, particularly at the regional and local levels (Mawson and Hall 2000 and Goss and Tarplett Chapter 17). Across all of government delivery the value of partnerships is emphasised as a means of delivering effective public services. This includes health (Hewitt 2006), policing and criminal justice (Hough 2006), education (Dimmock and Walker 2002) and local government (Coulson 2004).

Coulson (2004) suggests the need for local authorities to engage in partnership is a result of the removal of various roles and responsibilities that 'obliged local authorities to work in partnership with other public and private agencies' (Coulson 2004: 468). In drawing these collaborative responsibilities together, the Local Government Act 2000 introduced the community leadership role for local authorities, described as the role of 'first among equals' (Woolas 2006). In support of this the white paper (DCLG 2006) gave a much stronger coordination role for local strategic partnerships.

Most acknowledge that partnership working is not easy. Huxham (1996) suggests that partnership working is both complex and problematic and this makes it difficult to achieve collaborative advantage through partnership activity.

In later work Huxham and Vangen (2003) saw an absence of 'challenge' as one of the weaknesses of partnership working. The Audit Commission – in recognising that community development is complex – said 'that local councils may need to lead and challenge communities as well as support them' (Audit Commission 2003: 3).

Leading places: Local area agreements

The Audit Commission has set out what it sees as the community leadership role of local authorities:

> The Councils bring people together, develop a vision for their areas, produce a community strategy and deliver improvements in the quality of life for local people. Central to this are the ideas of transparency of decision-making and accountability for the value for money and impact of local services, and to involve local people in political decision-making. (Audit Commission 2003: 4)

The community strategy is at the heart of this community leadership role with the local area agreement viewed as the delivery arm of the strategy.

The context and purpose of local area agreements

The primary objective of a local area agreement is defined as that of delivering 'genuinely sustainable communities through better outcomes for local people' (DCLG 2007a: 7). Other more secondary objectives relate to the creation of a more mature and constructive relationship between local and central government, enhancing efficiency, strengthening partnership and enhancing local government's community leadership role. The LAA represents the delivery plan of the wider Sustainable Communities Plan that all Local Authorities have to publish as part of their community leadership role (HMSO 2000).

Richards (2006) argued that the aim was to secure area based funding streams and to rationalise the bureaucracy surrounding them. The collaborative nature was emphasised with the need to 'share assets; systems; data; skills and knowledge'.

Local authorities as local leaders and enablers play a key coordination role in what has been described as 'first among equals' (Woolas 2006). Geddes (2006) has argued that the quality of LSPs – similarly described as the 'partnership of partnerships' – will ultimately determine the quality of its LAA and thus its delivery. Evaluation of the LAA process (DCLG 2007a) suggested that the process has strengthened partnership working in localities and provided a clearer role for LSPs and the Sustainable Communities Plan (SCP) although some weaknesses – more related to the process of policy implementation and lack of genuine discussion on freedom and flexibilities – were highlighted. The evaluations concluded that facilitating greater local input (from neighbourhood bodies, individual citizens and the third sector) has been difficult in part due to the focus on 'standardised and national targets' and that 'local ambition and uniqueness of place were being driven out of the process' (Department for Communities and Local

Government 2006: 3). Moreover, others have suggested that a critical account needs to be taken of the third sector to allow 'fundamentally important questions surrounding legitimacy, accountability, and trust to be confronted' (Burt 2007: 157).

Telling the story of 'place' – But is it democratic?

A single set of 198 indicators introduced a new performance framework for local authorities and local authority partnerships (DCLG 2007b). From these, each LAA comprise 'up to 35' targets which local authorities and their partners negotiate with Central Government, drawn from the new national indicator set (DCLG 2007a: 6). Negotiations are led by the local authority under its community leadership role. The LSP continues to coordinate activity which starts with 'the story of the place' building on the recommendations made in the Lyons report:

> The term place-shaping covers a wide range of local activity – indeed anything which affects the well-being of the local community. It will mean different things in different places and at different levels of local government, informed by local character and history. (Lyons 2007: 174)

The Local Government Association's report *Leading Localities* (Local Government Association 2005) rightly raises the issues of accountability in relation to LAAs. They recognise the role that the local authority has as the formal accountable body responsible for the 'regularity, propriety and value for money' in the use of funds. They argue that it is less clear how a more extended version of accountability is to be exercised. The LGA acknowledge that LAAs are ultimately a means for better governance in the locality and thus the delivery of public value but that it must reflect 'choice'. The report stated that:

> When difficult choices must be made, the public has a right to know who is making them, how they are being made, and what they can do to influence the outcome. (LGA 2005: 20)

There is a need, the LGA argue, to align the accountability structures with local democratic structures. To an extent this could be done through the LSPs. Although they are not direct democratic structures it could be argued that LSPs are at least democratic from the participatory democratic perspective. LAAs are neither. However, whilst LSPs are seen as the closest model to what is needed there are issues concerning whether many LSPs are fit for this purpose in terms of governance and accountability. The New Local Government Network suggests for example, that there remains a democratic and accountability deficit at a local level, where people still feel disengaged and lack the levers necessary to effect change or influence local outcomes (NLGN 2005: 7). Smith, Mathur and Skelcher (2006) also discuss a democratic deficit in terms of the rules and procedures of public governance. This is one aspect that the research subject of this paper refers to.

Leading places: LAA research in the North West

Outline of the research

The research sought to consider:

> To what extent constituent agencies were working towards constructive engagement for the agreement and delivery of LAAs and shared learning across the North West region.

A realistic evaluation framework was deployed based on its emphasis with contexts, mechanisms and outcomes (Pawson and Tilley 1997). A full analysis of the research has been published and the methodology described (Brookes 2007). This chapter draws conclusions from the research as it applies to community leadership.

Peer review

A peer review group (PRG) represented the first stage of the research to secure practitioner input.[1] The first task was to undertake an initial documentary analysis of all agreements from across the North West region. Strategic aspirations outlined in the LAA were identified and assessed against criteria identified through the research design. These aspirations were then tested for reality during the field studies in phase 2 through focus groups and interviews. All data from the field work was recorded, transcribed and coded. A full description is beyond the scope of this chapter other than to state that quantitative coding was undertaken of the qualitative data.[2]

The criteria for peer assessment were given overall weighted scores for a total of 29 potential critical success factors within five broad contexts. These are illustrated in Figures 10.2 and 10.3 respectively with the average given by assessors. Generally, it was concluded that all written agreements were 'fit for purpose' and set out a strong strategic direction but identified the key challenge as that of turning the aspirations into reality 'on the ground'. In terms of community leadership it is interesting that the LAAs were assessed as being strong in relation to shared and stated priorities but much less so in terms of engagement and capacity building.

Following the peer group analysis and with the full engagement of the participants, the research questions for the field work were further refined and deployed.

158

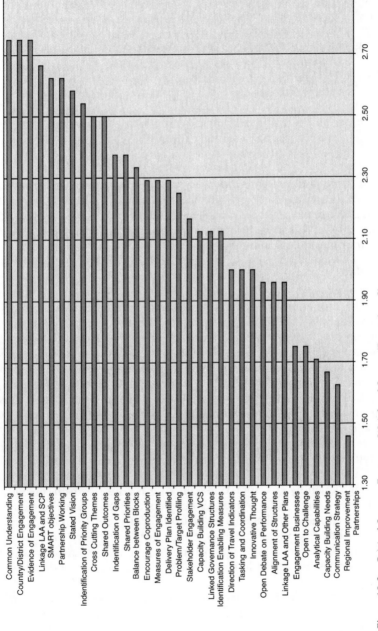

Figure 10.2 Critical Success Factors – Weighted Scores (From 1 to 3)

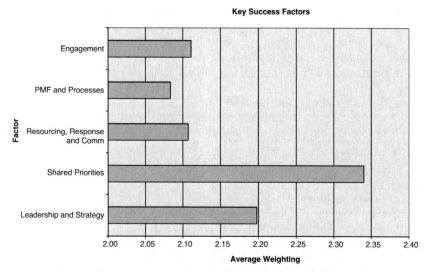

Figure 10.3   Contexts for Critical Success Factors of Partnership Working

Field research

The field research was conducted through the use of semi-structured interviews with Directors and Policy Officers and focus groups with cross agency partnership members on the LSPs or equivalent. Each comment or observation made during the interview or focus group was transcribed and then coded in relation to the research questions. Further coding was also developed to capture the perceived meaning of respondents using a combination of categories (based on the context of partnerships), sub-categories (representing the mechanisms or CSFs) and its perceived outcome at the time of the research (being coded as either a 'strength', 'weakness', 'opportunity' or 'threat'). It was additionally coded in relation to its relevance to the concept of shared and distributed leadership and the form of leadership ('individual', 'community', 'political' or 'organisational' leadership). Deploying some of the principles of grounded theory (Strauss and Corbin 1990) the coding was refined as the research progressed.

The interviews with directors and policy officers focused on the extent to which the Local Authority plays its part in leading improvement (using some of the factors for driving improvement identified in the original White Paper (DCLG 2006) and the observations of peer group practitioners) and in co-coordinating activity through their role as community leaders. The purpose of the later focus groups was to draw together senior representatives of partner organisations to reflect those who would generally represent their organisations on the LSP (or similar named body) and/or take the lead responsibility for the themed groups.

The three most and three least positive coded responses were analysed in relation to the broad research questions. A similar emphasis was given by both Directors and Policy Officers and Focus Group members (FG).

Table 10.1   Top Three Contextual Responses

Percentage of Responses classified as a 'Strength'	Policy Officers	Focus Groups
Capacity and vision of local leadership	53% (2)	31% (2)
If Public Service Boards Exist, how do they work	47% (3)	41% (1)
Exploring current and alternative means of commissioning and provision of services	54% (1)	31% (3)

Note: Numbers in brackets indicates ranking.

The most positive responses included leadership and governance (capacity/ vision and the way that Public Service Boards worked) and exploring current and alternative means of commissioning. This suggests that in each case both directors/policy officers and focus groups were more positive in relation to governance with some encouraging signs that alternative approaches were being considered. There were also similarities in the emphasis given to delivery.

Respondents in both groups were less enthusiastic about the role of LAA agencies as shapers and enablers of 'places', empowerment of citizens and users and the ability of peers to constructively challenge delivery arrangements. This is illustrated in Table 10.2 which highlights the three least positive responses the two least positive of which are factors critically relevant to community leadership.

Table 10.2   Least Positive Three Responses for Policy Officers and Focus Groups

Percentage of Responses classified as a 'Strength'	Policy Officers	Focus Groups
Willingness to Challenge/Change Delivery Arrangement	37% (4)	15% (8)
Experience of Empowerment of Citizens/Users	33% (5)	18% (5)
Role of Enablers and Shapers	23% (6)	5% (9)

Note: Numbers in brackets indicates ranking.

Critical success factor analysis

A detailed analysis took place of the contexts and mechanisms, the latter of which can be suggested as critical to success. The contextual factors emerged during the analysis and are illustrated in Table 10.3. In addition,

Table 10.3　Analysis of Contextual Factors and Form of Leadership

(a)　Critical Success Factors

	Total	Strength	%
Shared Vision	118	49	42
Decision Making	142	43	30
Governance	116	35	30
Trust	98	29	30
Capability	50	14	28
Capacity	34	9	26
Engagement	119	31	26
Legitimacy	196	44	22
Co-production	19	4	21
Review	37	6	16

(b)　Forms of Leadership

Individual Leadership	27	9	33
Organisational Leadership	156	51	33
Community Leadership	123	30	24
Political Leadership	66	11	17

the extent to which the statement or comment related to the perceived form of leadership (individual, organisational, community or political leadership) was also coded and illustrated in Table 10.3.

It is interesting to point out that less than half of all respondents identified any context as a 'strength'. However, of those that did, the responses were very similar to the earlier peer assessment. Respondents were relatively strong in their support of developing a shared vision, their decision-making processes and governance arrangements. They were less positive about those factors that this chapter argues are critical to community leadership, namely engagement, legitimacy, co-production and review of performance. Interestingly, there was a correlation between those responses coded as 'trust' and those of 'legitimacy' ($p > 0.001$) which suggests that trust and legitimacy are inextricably linked. This element of the analysis is now the subject of further research.

Given these findings it is not surprising that more emphasis is given to the strength of both individual and organisational leadership as opposed to either community or political leadership.

The underlying mechanisms were also examined. As with the broader realistic evaluation framework that was adopted the chapter suggests that the contexts described above will remain relatively static whereas the mechanisms (those factors that 'trigger' a response) will apply across

Table 10.4   Top and Bottom Five Mechanisms Based on Coding as 'Strength'

Top 5 Mechanisms	No.	%	Bottom 5 Mechanisms	No.	%
Leadership Maturity	6	67	First Among Equals Role	19	32
Shared Leadership	6	67	Relationships (National)	17	18
Accountability	11	55	Area Working	11	9
Performance Review	15	53	Operational Tasking	15	5
Trust	6	50	Information Management	9	0

the contexts and will be dynamic. To illustrate: 'accountability' – which is identified as one of the top five critical success factors – applies to the contexts of leadership and governance, shared vision and engagement and decision-making and co-production. The five most positive responses and the five least positive responses in relation to the underlying mechanisms are illustrated in Table 10.4.

The chapter argues that these findings suggest that LSPs are still predominantly transactional rather than transformational in nature. The critical success factors as represented by the mechanisms described above confirm the earlier peer analysis that partners are confident that they have developed a strong sense of a shared vision and governance arrangements to support it but are less strong in relation to those factors that transform strategic intentions into demonstrable deliverables. Community leadership relies upon a focused intention to work in local areas in delivering identified needs and to put in place those transformational factors that support this. Respondents were uniformly of the view that the partnerships had yet to ensure that operational tasking or commissioning were aligned to the strategic intentions and all respondents were unanimous that information management (as represented by the sharing of information and intelligence between partnership leaders) was a major weakness within networks.

A collective leadership analysis

In this penultimate section the chapter aligns the critical success factors (CSF) identified through this research with those identified by the Audit Commission (Audit Commission 2003), namely:

i.   Awareness
ii. Building leadership capacity
iii. Focus and prioritisation
iv. Clarity of roles
v.   Working together

Awareness

In describing this CSF, the Audit Commission state that community leadership roles will have good local intelligence about their local areas and communities including social, demographic, environmental and economic contexts of their locality. It is also suggested that information should be collected from a variety of sources which includes data from partner agencies. This should be accompanied by effective consultation and engagement which requires good networks both internally (in governance and performance management terms) and externally (in complimenting consultation and engagement).

Peers concluded that the LAAs were viewed as effectively highlighting the agreed priorities with strong evidence of consultation with other partners, the community and stakeholders but less so in terms of engagement. This was confirmed during the field work and, as highlighted above, the sharing of information and intelligence between partners is a major weakness.

Focus and prioritisation

The Audit Commission says that good community leaders provide a clear and ambitious vision for their communities with defined priorities based on widespread consultation. This should be linked to the community strategy which balances national and local priorities and which should be translated into targeted activity on the ground. Activity should be supported by clear targets and robust performance and risk management processes.

Peers found that strong links were made with the Communities Plan through the identification of shared priorities. They suggested that the agreements were considered less focused in terms of innovation and actions to achieve the longer term outcomes and in the arrangements for turning strategy into action. Given the main aim of the written forms of the agreements it is perhaps unsurprising that the main focus is on 'strategic aspirations' (where the agreements were strong) rather than delivery (where the agreements were less well developed). The field work also confirmed the peer assessments. Shared leadership, governance and performance management arrangements were a relative strength but there was a clear view that national priorities significantly overshadowed local priorities.

Working together

It is almost axiomatic to say – as the Audit Commission does – that community leadership recognises the benefits of joined-up working through shared responsibility at both the strategic and operational levels. The Commission also argues that there is a need for strong and mature partnership cultures where shared aims and priorities are encouraged. This is what this chapter describes as the shared element of collective leadership.

In relation to wider engagement (strong generally), peers felt that more could be evidenced in relation to engagement with the private sector and the voluntary sector as a means of enhancing shared learning. Peers also sought to assess the extent to which a commitment was given that the LAA will be delivered through a coordinated delivery plan with a description given of the main intervention approaches. Although most LAAs made implicit references to the needs of delivery and intervention, where delivery plans were referred to, they tended to emerge within the framework presented by the four blocks with less emphasis on overall coordination.

The field work confirmed this as the following respondent, who is describing the current challenges of the 'first-among-equals' role, highlights:

> We are in a position to make sure that it does appear in priorities, actions, or delivery tasks. Monitoring is the same – we have some control. We are less successful in being able to do this with partners – the willingness is there but it is aspirational. To ensure successful delivery – we need to see it and drive it through the council – where it is viewed as someone's delivery task. With other partners it is not so easy. They are not leading they are contributing – unless there is money in it.

Clarity of roles

The Audit Commission argue that stakeholders should be able to distinguish between their respective roles and ensure that each are fully understood and valued with appropriate governance arrangements in place. This is what this chapter describes as the distributed element of collective leadership.

Peers believed that desired 'SMART' (Specific, measurable, achievable, realistic and time based) performance targets and appropriate funding with evidence of shared leadership and partnership working at the executive level supported the clarity of roles. Peers found, however, that evidence of governance arrangements appeared to be loosely defined and there was no real reference to the opportunities presented by the overview and scrutiny arrangements. In relation to operational arrangements, the agreements were supported with little evidence of analysis other than what could be described as fairly routine and standardised with a similar approach taken to coordination, tasking and commissioning at the operational level of partnership working. The field work also confirmed this as Table 10.4 illustrates where operational tasking and effective information management were viewed almost unanimously as weaknesses.

Building leadership capacity

The Audit Commission believe that there is a need to promote the range of leaders' roles as community leaders and that these roles are recognised within the local authority, other partners and community stakeholders. It is argued that the council has a key role to play in encouraging other partners to take the leadership initiative by providing support and fostering empowerment. It also includes innovatively developing social capital by attracting traditionally excluded groups into the policy-making process through the creation of citizens' panels, youth parliaments and online debates. This should be supported by a common purpose and investment in training in which leadership development is a major component.

Peers felt that the capacity building needs of the voluntary and community sector (VCS) was given a reasonable emphasis but less so in relation to the capacity building needs of the partnership itself. The PRG analysis suggested that there is further scope for LAA authorities to be more open to challenge and to improve communication. The field work confirmed this. It is quite clear that there is a long way to go before community leaders will be in a position, for example, to build social capital. Area based activity is critical to this. However, during the field work, this was considered to be a major area for improvement. Most respondents saw the benefits of area based delivery but turning this into reality proved much more difficult and it tended to relate to the allocation of locally based funding. A number of respondents referred to the importance of the 'WIIFM' ('what's in it for me) factor, as this example illustrates:

> It is here that you engage people – when there is something in it for them – and money makes a difference. This is going to happen in my street – now I will talk to you! (Partnership Manager).

Towards a collective leadership approach?

A collective leadership approach suggests that a combination of shared and distributed leadership holds promise in developing public leaders within the context of networked governance. This chapter has sought to use the example of LAAs as a means of illustrating the challenges of collective leadership in practice as well as looking at the different forms of leadership that apply within a collective context. In this regard, the research subject of this chapter has clearly demonstrated a stronger degree of shared rather than distributed leadership with a key emphasis on organisational and individual leadership rather than community or political leadership which is much less in evidence.

Strong theories exist in relation to the first two forms of leadership such as that presented by Burns (1978), Kotter (1995, 1999 and 2003) and March (1980) concerning organisational (and transformational) leadership, Blanchard, K.H. and Hersey, P. (1999), Handy 1985) and Collins (2001) with regard to individual leadership, and Fiedler (1967 and 1976) in drawing these together within the 'situation'. Less emphasis has been placed on the needs of political leadership although Hartley and Branicki (2006) provide a strong insight on the factors necessary for increasing political awareness and Hartley builds on this in Chapter 9. There is a dearth of literature and research in relation to the relatively new role of community leadership. This chapter suggests that the four forms of leadership provide a useful focus for the further study of public leadership and that community leadership in particular should be central to this.

Notes

1. The Peer Review group comprised 16 LAA policy officers from across the North West Region in England. They analysed all 46 LAAs in the NW in pairs against set criteria based on a literature review and policy analysis. Each LAA was 'double-assessed' by two different pairs.
2. A bespoke database was created through Microsoft Access and data from interviews was transcribed and coded through the database. Each statement or observation was given a coding of between 1 (no evidence) to 7 (much evidence) in relation to its strength in support of partnership working. Further codings were related to the form of leadership and whether it represented 'shared' or 'distributed' leadership. This enabled quantitative analysis to be made of the qualitative data.

References

Agranoff, R. and McGuire, M. (2003) *Collaborative Public Management.* Washington DC: Georgetown University Press.

Ansari, W., Phillips, C. and Hammick, M. (2001) 'Collaboration and Partnerships: Developing the Evidence Base', *Health and Social Care in the Community*, 9(4): 215–227. Blackwell Science Ltd.

Audit Commission (2003) *Community Leadership: Learning from Comprehensive Performance Assessment: Briefing 1.* London: HMSO.

Bennett, N., Wise, C., Woods, P. and Harvey, J. (2003) *Distributed Leadership*, Summary Report, NCSL. Spring.

Blanchard, K.H. and Hersey, P. (1999) *Leadership and the One Minute Manager.* William Morrow.

Brookes, S. (2006a) 'Out with the Old, In with the New: Why Excellent Public Leadership Makes a Difference to Partnership Working', *The British Journal of Leadership in Public Services*, Volume 2, Issue 1.

Brookes, S. (2006b) *The Public Leadership Challenge*, ESRC Seminar Series Briefing Paper no. 2, accessible at http://www.esrc.ac.uk/ESRCInfoCentre/PSZ/News/News/Publeadership.aspx or http://www.publicleadership.org

Brookes, S. (2007) 'Bridging the Gap between Theoetical and Practical Approaches to Leadership in Support of Networked Governance and the Creation of Public Value', paper presented at the 6th International Studying Leadership Conference, Warwick Business School, 13 December, accessible http://www.publicleadership.org.

Burns, J.M. (1978) *Leadership.* N.Y.: Harper and Row.

Burt, E. (2007) *Voluntary Organisations in the Democratic Polity: Managing Legitimacy, Accountability and Trust.* Public Money and Management, April.

Collins, J. (2001) *Good to Great: Why Some Companies Make the Leap...and Others Don't.* HarperCollins.

Coulson, A. (2004) 'Local Politics, Central Power: The Future of Representative Local Government in England', *Local Government Studies*, 30(4): 467–480.

Department for Communities and Local Government (2007a) *Negotiating New Local Area Agreements.* London: DCLG.

Department for Communities and Local Government (2007b) *The New Performance Framework for Local Authorities and Local Authority Partnerships: Single Set of National Indicators.* London: DCLG.

Department for Communities and Local Government (2006) *Strong and Prosperous Communities*. London: White Paper.

Dimmock, C. and Walker, A. (2002) 'School Leadership in Context – Societal and Organisational Cultures', in Bush, T. and Bell, L. (eds), *The Principles and Practice of Educational Management*. London: Paul Chapman.

Doyle, M.E. and Smith, M.K. (2001) *Shared Leadership, the Encyclopedia of Informal Education,* http://www.infed.org/leadership/shared_leadership.htm, accessed 23 August 2005.

Fiedler, F.E. (1967) *A Theory of Leadership Effectiveness*. New York: McGraw-Hill.

Fiedler, F.E. (1976) *Improving Leadership Effectiveness: The Leader Match Concept*. New York: Wiley.

Geddes, M. (2006). *National Evaluation of Local Strategic Partnerships*. London: Department for Communities and Local Government HMSO.

Gibbons, M., Limoges, C., Nowotny, H., Schwartzman, S., Scott, P. and Trow, M. (1994) *The New Production of Knowledge: The Dynamics of Science and Research in Contemporary Societies*. London: Sage.

Grint, K. (2000) *The Arts of Leadership*. Oxford: Oxford University Press.

Grint, K. (2005a) *Leadership Ltd: White Elephant to Wheelwright*. London, Ontario: Ivey Publishing Journal Online January/February.

Grint, K. (2005b) 'Problems, Problems, Problems: The Social Construction of "Leadership"', *Human Relations*, 58(11): 1467–1494, The Tavistock Institute, London: Sage Publications.

Handy, C. (1985) *Understanding Organisations*. London: Penguin.

Hartley, J. and Branicki, L. (2006) 'Managing with Political Awareness: A Summary Review of the Literature', Chartered Management Institute and Warwick Business School.

Heifetz, R. (1994) *Leadership Without Easy Answers*. Harvard University Press.

Hewitt, P. (2006) *Better Services and More Choice, on Your Doorstep*. Press release 2006/0044. London: Department of Health.

HMSO (2000) Local Government Act 2000 (c.22).

Hough, M. (2006) 'Hands On or Hands Off? Central Government's Role in Managing CDRPs', *Community Safety Journal*, Volume 5, Issue 3, June 2006.

Hough, M. (2007) 'Policing London 20 Years On', in Henry, A. and Smith, D.J., *Transformations of Policing*. London: Ashgate Publishing.

Huxham, C. (1996) *Creating Collaborative Advantage*. London: Sage.

Huxham, C. and Vangen, S. (2003) 'Enacting Leadership for Collaborative Advantage: Dilemmas of Ideology and Pragmatism in the Activities of Partnership', *British Journal of Management*, Vol. 14, S61–S76.

IDeA (2006) *What is Community Leadership?* http://www.idea.gov.uk/idk/core/page.do?pageId=73211 accessed 2 May 2009.

IDeA (2009) *Community Leadership* http://www.idea.gov.uk/idk/core/page.do?pageId=1092358 accessed 2 May 2009.

Isherwood, M., Johnson, H. and Brundrett, M. (2007) 'Performance Management – Motivating and Developing Good Teachers? The Experiences of Teachers in a Small Special School', *Education*, 3–13, Vol. 35, No. 1. February, 71–81.

Kotter, J.P. (1995) 'Why Transformation Efforts Fail?', *Harvard Business Review*, March–April 1995.

Kotter, J.P. (1999) *John P. Kotter on What Leaders Really Do*. Boston, MA: Harvard Business School Press.

Kotter, J.P. (2003) 'The Power of Feelings', *Leader to Leader*, 27 (Winter 2003): 25–31.

Local Government Association (2005) *Leading Localities*. London.

Lyons, M. (2007) *Lyons Inquiry into Local Government: Final Report*. London: HMSO.

March, J.G. (1980) 'The Technology of Foolishness', in Leavitt, H.J., Pondy, L.R. and Boje, D.M. (eds), *Readings in Managerial Psychology*. Chicago: University of Chicago Press.

Martin, S. (2002) 'The Modernization of UK Local Government: Markets, Managers, Monitors and Mixed Fortunes', *Public Management Review*, 4(3): 291–307.

Mattessich, P.W., Murray-Close, M. and Monsey, B.R. (2001) *Collaboration: What Makes It Work*, 2nd edition. St. Paul, MN: Amherst H. Wilder Foundation.

Mawson, J. and Hall, S. (2000) 'Joining It Up Locally? Area Regeneration and Holistic Government in England, Regional Studies', *Taylor and Francis Journals*, 34(1): 67.

NCVO (2009) *The Changing Nature of Community Leadership*. http://www.3s4.org.uk/ drivers/changing-nature-of-community-leadership accessed 2 May 2009.

NLGN (2005) *Making Community Leadership Real*. London: New Local Government Network.

Pawson, R. and Tilley, N. (1997) *Realistic Evaluation*. London: Sage Publications.

Peirce, N. and Johnson, C. (1998) *Boundary Crossers: Community Leadership for a Global Age*. College Park, MD: The Burns Academy of Leadership Press.

Pigg, K.E. (1999) 'Community Leadership and Community Theory: A Practical Synthesis', *Journal of the Community Development Society*, 30(2): 196–212.

Putnam, R. (2000) *Bowling Alone*. London: Simon and Schuster.

Richards, G. (2006) 'Gail Richards on Local Area Agreements', *Health Services Journal*, 4th December.

Smith, M., Mathur, N. and Skelcher, C. (2006) 'Corporate Governance in a Collaborative Environment: What Happens When Government, Business and Civil Society Work Together?', *Corporate Governance: An International Review*, 14(3): 159–171.

Stephenson, K. (2007) 'Rethinking Governance: Conceptualizing Networks and Their Implications for New Mechanisms of Governance Based on Reciprocity', in Williamson, T., *The Handbook of Knowledge-Based Policing*. Chichester: John Wiley and Sons.

Stevens, S. (2004) 'Reform Strategies for the English NHS: Incentives and Local Accountabilities', *Health Affairs*, 23(1).

Stoker, G. (2006) 'Public Value Management: A New Narrative for Networked Governance?', *American Review of Public Administration*, 36(1): 41–57, March.

Strauss, A. and Corbin, J. (1990) *Basics of Qualitative Research: Grounded Theory, Procedures and Techniques*. Newbury Park, CA: Sage Publications.

Williams, M.R. and Wade, V.M. (2002) 'Sponsorship of Community Leadership Development Programs: What Constitutes an Ideal Partnership?', *Journal of the Community Development Society*, Vol. 33.

Woolas, P. (2006) 'Local Area Agreements: Key Messages and Lessons for Roll-Out', speech by Phil Woolas MP, Local Government House, 11 January 2006.

11
Wicked Problems and Clumsy Solutions: The Role of Leadership

Keith Grint

The problem of problems: Tame, wicked & critical

Much of the writing in the field of leadership research is grounded in a typology that distinguishes between Leadership and Management as different forms of authority – that is legitimate power in Weber's conception – with leadership tending to embody longer time periods, a more strategic perspective, and a requirement to resolve novel problems (Bratton *et al.* 2004). Another way to put this is that the division is rooted partly in the context: management is the equivalent of *déjà vu* (seen this before), whereas leadership is the equivalent of *vu jàdé* (never seen this before) (Weick 1973). If this is valid then the manager is required to engage the requisite process to resolve the problem the last time it emerged. In contrast, the leader is required to facilitate the construction of an innovative response to the novel problem, rather than rolling out a known process to a previously experienced problem.

Management and Leadership, as two forms of authority rooted in the distinction between certainty and uncertainty, can also be related to Rittell and Webber's (1973) typology of Tame and Wicked Problems (Grint 2005). A Tame Problem may be complicated but is resolvable through unilinear acts and it is likely to have occurred before. In other words, there is only a limited degree of uncertainty and thus it is associated with Management. Tame Problems are akin to puzzles – for which there is always an answer – and we might consider how F.W. Taylor (the originator of Scientific Management) epitomised this approach to problem solving – simply apply science properly and the best solution will naturally emerge. The (scientific) manager's role, therefore, is to provide the appropriate process – the veritable standard operating procedure – to solve the problem. Examples would include: timetabling the railways, building a nuclear plant, training the army, planned heart surgery or a wage negotiation.

A Wicked Problem is more complex, rather than just complicated – that is, it cannot be removed from its environment, solved, and returned without affecting the environment. Moreover, there is no clear relationship between cause and effect. Such problems are often intractable – for instance, trying to develop a National Health Service (NHS) on the basis of a scientific approach (assuming it was a Tame Problem) would suggest providing everyone with all the services and medicines they required based only on their medical needs. However, with an ageing population, an increasing medical ability to intervene and maintain life, a potentially infinite increase in demand but a finite level of economic resource, there cannot be a scientific solution to the problem of the NHS. In sum we cannot provide everything for everybody; at some point we need to make a political decision about who gets what and based on what criteria. This inherently contested arena is typical of a Wicked Problem. If we think about the NHS as the NIS – the National Illness Service – then we have a different understanding of the problem because it is essentially a series of Tame Problems: fixing a broken leg is the equivalent of a Tame Problem – there is a scientific solution so that medical professionals in hospitals know how to fix them. But if you run (sorry, crawl) into a restaurant for your broken leg to be fixed it will become a Wicked Problem because it's unlikely that anyone there will have the knowledge or the resources to fix it. Thus the category of problems is subjective not objective – what kind of a problem you have depends on where you are sitting and what you already know.

Moreover, many of the problems that the NHS deal with – obesity, drug abuse, violence – are not simply problems of health, they are often deeply complex social problems that sit across and between different government departments and institutions so attempts to treat them through a single institutional framework are almost bound to fail. Indeed, because there are often no 'stopping' points with Wicked Problems – that is the point at which the problem is solved (e.g. there will be no more crime because we have solved it) we often end up having to admit that we cannot solve Wicked Problems. Conventionally, we associate leadership with precisely the opposite – the ability to solve problems, act decisively and to know what to do. But Wicked Problems often embody the exact opposite of this – we cannot solve them, and we need to be very wary of acting decisively precisely because we cannot know what to do. If we knew what to do it would be a Tame Problem not a Wicked Problem. Yet the pressure to act decisively often leads us to try to solve the problem as if it was a Tame Problem.

When Global Warming first emerged as a problem some of the responses concentrated on solving the problem through science (a Tame response), manifest in the development of biofuels; but we now know that biofuels appear to denude the world of significant food resources so that what looked like a solution actually became another problem. Again, this is typical of what happens when we try to solve Wicked Problems – other problems emerge to compound the original problem. So we can make things better or worse – we can drive our cars slower and less or faster and more – but we may not be able to solve Global Warming, we may just have to learn to live with a different world and make the best of it we can. In other words, we cannot start again and design a perfect future – though many political and religious extremists might want us to.

The 'we' in this is important because it signifies the importance of the collective in addressing Wicked Problems. Tame problems might have individual solutions in the sense that an individual is likely to know how to deal with it. But since Wicked Problems are partly defined by the absence of an answer on the part of the leader then it behooves the individual leader to engage the collective in an attempt to come to terms with the problem. In other words, Wicked Problems require the transfer of authority from individual to collective because only collective engagement can hope to address the problem. The uncertainty involved in Wicked Problems imply that leadership, as I am defining it, is not a science but an art – the art of engaging a community in facing up to complex collective problems. The metaphor of the Wheelwright might be appropriate here. Phil Jackson (1995: 149–151), coach of the phenomenally successful Chicago Bulls basketball team, makes this point well. In the 3rd century BC the Chinese Emperor Liu Bang celebrated his consolidation of China with a banquet where he sat surrounded by his nobles and military and political experts. Since Liu Bang was neither noble by birth nor an expert in military or political affairs one of the guests asked one of the military experts, Chen Cen, why Liu Bang was the Emperor. Chen Cen's response was to ask the questioner a question in return: 'What determines the strength of a wheel?' The guest suggested the strength of the spokes' but Chen Cen countered that two sets of spokes of identical strength did not necessarily make wheels of identical strength. On the contrary, the strength was also affected by the spaces between the spokes, and determining the spaces was the true art of the wheelwright. In effect, leaders don't need to be experts to be successful and while the spokes represent the collective resources necessary to an organisation's success – and the resources that the leader lacks – the spaces represent the autonomy necessary for followers to grow into leaders themselves.

The leader's role with a Wicked Problem, therefore, is to ask the right questions rather than provide the right answers because the answers may not be self-evident and will require a collaborative process to make any kind of progress. Examples would include: developing a transport strategy, or a response to global warming, or a response to anti-social behaviour, or a national health system. Wicked Problems are not necessarily rooted in longer time frames than Tame Problems because oftentimes an issue that appears to be Tame or Critical can be turned into a (temporary) Wicked Problem by delaying the decision.

A Critical Problem, e.g. a 'crisis', is presented as self-evident in nature, as encapsulating very little time for decision-making and action, and it is often associated with authoritarianism. Here there is virtually no uncertainty about what needs to be done – at least in the behaviour of the Commander, whose role is to take the required decisive action – that is to provide the answer to the problem, not to engage Standard Operating Procedures (SOPs) – management – or ask questions (leadership). A commander resembles a White Elephant – in both dictionary definitions: as a mythical beast that is itself a deity, and as an expensive and foolhardy endeavour. Indeed, in Thai history the King would give an albino Elephant to his least favoured noble because the special dietary and religious requirements would ruin the noble – hence the connection between the god and ruination. Translated into Critical Problems I suggest that for such crises we do need decision-makers who are god-like in their decisiveness and their ability to provide the answer to the crisis, but the problem arrives when our decision-makers really come to believe that they are gods. And since we reward people who are good in crises – and ignore people who are such good managers that there are very few crises – Commanders soon learn to seek out (or represent situations as) crises. Of course, it may be that the Commander remains privately uncertain about whether the action is appropriate or the presentation of the situation as a crisis is persuasive, but that uncertainty will probably not be apparent to the followers of the Commander. Examples would include the immediate response to: a major train crash, a leak of radioactivity from a nuclear plant, a military attack, a heart attack, an industrial strike, the loss of employment or a loved one, or a terrorist attack such as 9/11 or the 7 July bombings in London.

That such 'situations' are constituted by the participants rather than simply being self-evident is best illustrated by considering the way a situation of ill-defined threat only becomes a crisis when that threat is defined as such. For example, financial losses – even rapid and radical losses like the run on Northern Rock in the UK or the difficulties of Fannie Mae, Freddie Mac and AIG in the USA in 2008 – do not constitute a 'crisis' until the shareholders decide to sell in large numbers or the government decides to step in. Even then the notion of a crisis does not emerge objectively from the activity of selling or the point of intervention but at the point at which a 'crisis' is pronounced by someone significant and becomes accepted as such by significant others.

These three forms of authority – Command, Management and Leadership – are, in turn, another way of suggesting that the role of those responsible for decision-making is to find the appropriate Answer, Process and Question to address the problem respectively. This is not meant as a discrete typology but an heuristic device to enable us to understand why those charged with decision-making sometimes appear to act in ways that others find incomprehensible. Thus I am not suggesting that the correct decision-making process lies in the correct analysis of the situation – that would be to generate a deterministic approach – but I am suggesting that decision-makers tend to legitimise their actions on the basis of a persuasive account of the situation. In short, the social construction of the problem legitimises the deployment of a particular form of authority. Moreover, it is often the case that the same individual or group with authority will switch between the Command, Management and Leadership roles as they perceive – and constitute – the problem as Critical, Tame or Wicked, or even as a single problem that itself shifts across these boundaries. Indeed, this movement – often perceived as 'inconsistency' by the decision-maker's opponents – is crucial to success as the situation, or at least our perception of it, changes.

That persuasive account of the problem partly rests in the decision-makers access to – and preference for – particular forms of power, and herein lies the irony of 'leadership': it remains the most difficult of approaches and one that many decision-makers will try to avoid at all costs because it implies that, (1) the leader does not have the answer, (2) that the leader's role is to make the followers face up to their responsibilities (often an unpopular task) (Heifetz 1994), (3) that the 'answer' to the problem is going to take a long time to construct and that it will only ever be 'more appropriate' rather than 'the best', and (4) that it will require constant effort to maintain. It is far easier, then, to opt either for a Management solution – engaging a tried and trusted process – or a Command solution – enforcing the answer upon followers – some of whom may prefer to be shown 'the answer' anyway.

The notion of 'enforcement' suggests that we need to consider how different approaches to, and forms of, power fit with this typology of authority, and amongst the most useful for our purposes is Etzioni's (1964) typology of compliance and Nye's (2004, 2008) notion of 'Hard', 'Soft' and 'Smart' power. Nye distinguishes between 'hard' power – brute force – and 'soft' power – ideological attraction – and argues that success often relates to the use of 'smart power' – the judicious use of hard and soft power depending upon the circumstance. Etzioni distinguished between Coercive, Calculative and Normative Compliance. Coercive or physical power was related to total institutions, such as prisons or armies; Calculative Compliance was related to 'rational' institutions, such as companies; and Normative Compliance was related to institutions or organisations based on shared values, such as clubs and professional societies. This compliance typology fits well with the typology of problems: Critical Problems are often associated with Coercive Compliance; Tame Problems are associated with Calculative Compliance and Wicked Problems are associated with Normative Compliance.

Again, none of this is to suggest that we can divide the world up objectively into particular kinds of problems and their associated appropriate authority forms, but that the very legitimacy of the authority forms is dependent upon a successful rendition of a phenomenon as a particular kind of problem. In other words, while contingency theory suggests precisely this (rational) connection between (objective) context (problem) and (objective) leadership style (authority form), I am suggesting here that what counts as legitimate authority depends upon a persuasive rendition of the context and a persuasive display of the appropriate authority style. In other words, success is rooted in persuading followers that the problematic situation is either one of a Critical, Tame or Wicked nature and that therefore the appropriate authority form is Command, Management or Leadership in which the role of the decision-maker is to provide the answer, or organise the process or ask the question, respectively. In effect, one particular skill that all three decision-modes require is that of reframing problems – seeing the problem differently so as to rethink how it might be addressed differently (Fairhurst 2005).

This typology can be plotted along the relationship between two axes as shown below in Figure 11.1 with the vertical axis representing increasing uncertainty about the solution to the problem – in the behaviour of those in authority – and the horizontal axis representing the increasing need for collaboration in resolving the problem. What might also be evident from this figure is that the more decision-makers constitute the problem as Wicked and interpret their power as essentially Normative, the more

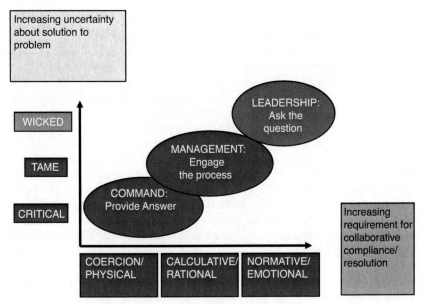

Figure 11.1 Typology of Problems, Power and Authority

difficult their task becomes, especially with cultures that associate leadership with the effective and efficient resolution of problems.

This might be regarded as obvious to many people – but if it is, why do we remain unable to effect such change? To answer that, I want to turn to Cultural Theory and explore some so called 'Elegant Solutions'.

Culture, elegance and clumsiness

Mary Douglas (2003[1970]) argued that we could probably capture most cultures on the basis of two discrete criteria: Grid and Group. Grid relates the significance of roles and rules in a culture – some are very rigid – such as a government bureaucracy – but others are very loose or liberal – such as an informal club. Group relates to the importance of the group in a culture – some cultures are wholly oriented around the group – such as a football team – while others are more individually oriented – such as a gathering of entrepreneurs. When these points are plotted on a two by two matrix the following appears.

Where a culture embodies both High Grid and High Group we tend to see rigid hierarchies, such as the military. Where the culture remains High Group oriented but lacks the concern for rules and roles in Low Grid we see Egalitarian cultures, epitomised by those organisations where the group meeting is sacred and the search for consensus critical. We might recognise this as the land where left wing political parties often live. Where the Grid remains low and is matched by an equal indifference to the Group, we tend to see Individualist cultures – the land of entrepreneurs, rational choice,

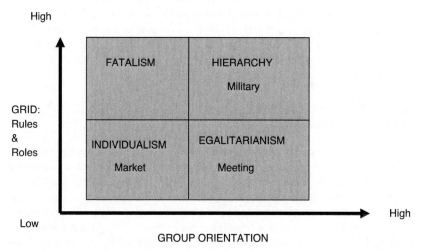

Figure 11.2   Four Primary Ways of Organising Social Life

and market loving politicians for whom any notion of the collective or rules is perceived as an unnecessary inhibitor of efficiency and freedom. The final category is that of the Fatalist, where the group dimension is missing but the isolated individuals believe themselves to be undermined by the power of rules and roles.

Douglas argued that these four cultural archetypes were heuristics rather than mirrors of society – most of us would find ourselves bordering regions or sitting across them rather than sitting wholly within one region but nevertheless she regarded the typology as a useful way for beginning a conversation about cultures. What is clear is that such cultures often tend to be self-supporting and internally consistent. In other words, hierarchists perceive the world through hierarchist lenses such that problems are understood as manifestations of the absence of sufficient rules or the enforcement of rules. In contrast, egalitarians see the same problem as one connected to the weakness of the collective community – it is less about rules and more about the community generating greater solidarity to solve the problem. Individualists would have little faith in this – the problem is obviously (for them) to do with the individuals. Fatalists, however, have given up.

Now the problem is that such internally consistent – or Elegant – modes of understanding the world are fine for dealing with Critical or Tame Problems because we know how to solve them and previous approaches have worked. Individualists can solve the problem of decreasing carbon emissions from cars – a Tame problem open to a scientific solution, but they cannot solve global warming – a Wicked Problem. Egalitarians can help ex-offenders back into the community – a Tame Problem – but they cannot solve crime – a Wicked Problem. And Hierarchists can improve rule enforcement for the fraudulent abuse of social services – a Tame Problem – but they cannot solve poverty – a Wicked Problem. Indeed, Wicked Problems don't offer themselves up to be solved by such Elegant approaches precisely because these problems lie outside and across several different cultures and institutions.

Why elegant approaches don't solve wicked problems but clumsy solutions might

If single mode (Elegant) solutions can only ever address elements of Wicked Problems we need to consider how to adopt all three in what are called Clumsy Solutions. In fact we need to eschew the elegance of the architect's approach to problems – start with a clean piece of paper and design the perfect building anew – and adopt the world of the Bicolour the do-it-yourself craftworker. Or to adopt the rather more prosaic language of Kant, we need to begin by recognising that 'Out of the crooked timber of humanity no straight thing was ever made'. Put another way, to get some purchase on Wicked Problems we need to start by accepting that imperfection and making do with what is available is not just the best way forward but the only way forward. In this world we must avoid alienating significant constituencies – but note that progress does not depend upon consensus – that would be too elegant and would take too long! We need to start by asking 'what do we all (or at least most of us) agree on?' We also need to assume that no-one has the solution in isolation and that the problem is a system not an individual problem and not a problem caused by or solved by a single aspect of the system. Let us take Global Warming to illustrate this (See Verweij *et al.* 2006 and Verweij 2006 for detailed accounts of this).

Figure 11.3 summarises the issue: Hierarchists consider the problem to be a result of inadequate rules and inadequate enforcement of rules. In effect a better Kyoto style agreement is necessary. But Egalitarians might argue that this misunderstands the problem – it isn't the rules that need altering and enforcing but our communal attitude to the planet that needs to change – we must develop more sustainable ways to live not just obey the rules better. But for Individualists both alternatives misunderstand the problem – and therefore the solution. The solution is to encourage the freedoms that will facilitate individual responses to the problem, including supporting the work of entrepreneurs who can generate the technological innovations that will save us. For Fatalists, of course, there is no hope – we are all doomed. The problem here is that none of these Elegant solutions actually generate sufficient diversity to address the complexity of the problem. Rules might facilitate safe driving but they would not prove adequate

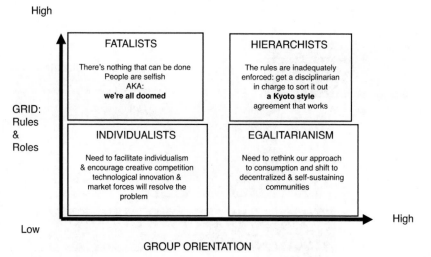

Figure 11.3   Elegant (Single Mode) Solutions to Global Warming

to saving the planet. Nor can we simply abandon our centralised cities and all live in self-sufficient communities in the countryside: that might have been a viable option if we were starting from scratch and we could have designed living space with a blank piece of paper to hand – but that architectural approach is no longer viable – we need to take the bricoleur's line and start from where we are. Similarly, although technological innovations will be critical and market pressures may help, we cannot rely on these to solve the problem. Indeed, global warming may not be solvable in the sense that we can go back to the beginning and reclaim an unpolluted world and because the 'facts' remain disputed and – more importantly – different interests are at stake in different approaches to the 'solution', the best we can hope for is a politically negotiated agreement to limit the damage as soon as possible. That calls for a non-linear, nay 'crooked', response to stitch together an inelegant or Clumsy solution combining all three modes of understanding and making use of the fatalists acquiescence to go along with the changing flow of public opinion and action. As shown below in Figure 11.4, what we actually need is to use all three frameworks to make progress here through the creation of a Clumsy Solution Space.

Wicked Problems are inherently political in nature not scientific or 'rational' and progress is likely to be via a Clumsy negotiation of the common ground. For this our bricoleur actually needs to acquire Aristotle's phronesis – the wisdom to acknowledge that the situation is not like any other, combined with the experience to recognise that such Wicked Problems require a qualitatively different approach from Tame or Critical Problems. So how do you address wicked problems?

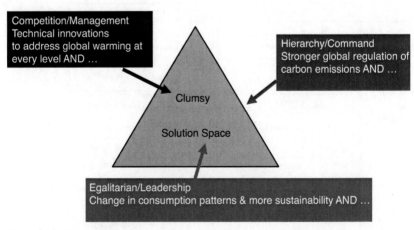

Figure 11.4   Clumsy Solution for Wicked Problem of Global Warming

Figure 11.5 below implies that a critical component of a necessarily clumsy solution is to combine elements of all three cultural types: the individualist, the egalitarian and the hierarchist, and within each of these types are techniques that, when combined, might just prise the Wicked Problem open enough to make some progress with it. Let us address each of these in turn.

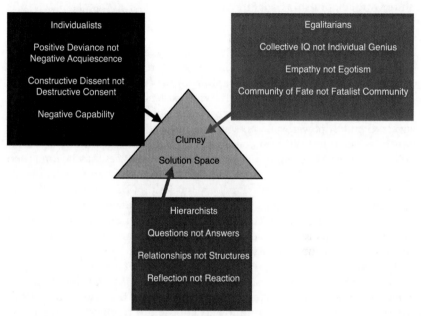

Figure 11.5   Clumsy Approaches to Wicked Problems

Hierarchists

H1: Questions not Answers

Since every Wicked Problem is slightly different from all others, and since we cannot know the answer initially (otherwise it would be a Tame or Critical Problem) there is no guaranteed method available, but the skill of the bricoleur (Gabriel 2002; Strauss 1966: 21) is in trying new things out, setting loose experiments to see what works and what doesn't, and all this requires an initial acceptance that you – our great esteemed leader – do not have the answer. Bricoleurs make progress by stitching together whatever is at hand, whatever needs to be stitched together, to ensure practical success. So the first step here is for the hierarchist to acknowledge that the leader's role has to switch from providing the answers to asking the questions. Such questions demonstrate that the problem facing the organisation is not of the common-garden variety – this is something different that needs a different response. In other words the leader should initiate a different narrative that prepares the collective for collective responsibility. Indeed, the reason that this sits within the Hierarchists' camp is that only the hierarchical leader has the authority to reverse his or her contribution from one of answers to questions. Linked to this switch in approaches from expert to investigator is a related requirement that Hierarchists are most suited for: Relationships not Structures.

H2: Relationships not Structures

Traditionally, change models imply that if failure occurs despite the model it must be because the leader has failed to pull the right levers in the right sequence. But this machine metaphor and its accompanying notion of power as a possession is precisely why leaders find change so difficult – because power is not something you can possess and thus there are no levers to pull. If power was a possession we would be unable to explain why mutinies occur in that most coercive of hierarchies, the military at war. If soldiers refuse to obey (and accept that the consequences may be dire) then generals are necessarily resistible in principle. Hence when you hear yourself saying the dreaded words 'I'm sorry but I didn't have any choice' – you are almost certainly lying to yourself because you can always say no – and take the consequences. Of course, sometimes the choice is merely one of two evils, but that remains a choice. Now all this means that change cannot be ordered from above by leaders who pull the right levers of power in the right sequence because power is a relationship and change depends upon the relationships between leaders and followers: in effect it is followers that make or break change strategies not leaders alone because organisations are systems not machines. If followers choose not to obey – or to comply is such a way that little progress is made – then the greatest strategy in the world will probably fail.

H3: Reflection not Reaction

The quest for decisive action is typically what we expect from our hierarchical leaders and this expectation has a long history back into the fabled past of heroes and gods. Indeed, being decisive is fine – if you know what to do... but if you know what to do then it isn't a Wicked Problem, it's a Tame or Critical Problem. However, if you don't know what to do such pressure may lead to catastrophe: you may have acted decisively but that may be decisively wrong. It isn't good enough to say that the best course of action in an ambiguous situation is to do something rather than nothing for two reasons. One, if you are very close to the cliff edge and the fog descends (metaphorically or in reality) then acting decisively might take you over the edge. If, on the other hand you just pause for as long as the mist persists then you might be late home but at least you will get home.

Two, we often conflate 'doing nothing' with 'reflection' but they are not the same thing. The former implies indecisiveness, indolence and weakness, while the latter implies a proactive philosophical assessment of the situation. Indeed, we could turn this issue around and note how often 'being decisive' actually can be reduced to mere reaction, being driven by somebody else's agenda or by the insecurity of an ambiguous situation to make a mistake. Again, the hierarchical leader can manage this best by the construction of a narrative explanation – to do otherwise is to risk being accused of weakness and indecisiveness.

Individualist

I1: Positive Deviance not Negative Acquiescence

In 1990 Jerry and Monique Sternin went to Vietnam for Save the Children to consider the utility of Maria Zeitlin's (1990) work on Positive Deviance: the idea that there are people within organisations who had already worked out the solution to many organisational problems often related to the role of culture. Why, the Sterns wondered, were some children well nourished in the midst of general malnourishment? Their answer was because the mothers of the well-nourished children were Positive Deviants – they deviated from mainstream culture in such a way that the outcomes were beneficial for their children. That mainstream culture generated a very conventional wisdom on malnutrition – it was TBU: True But Useless that malnourishment was the combined effect of poor sanitation, poor food-distribution, poverty and poor water. But since addressing all of these would take an inordinate amount of time it was True but Useless information. On the other hand, some children – and not the highest status children – were well nourished because their mothers ignored the conventional culture that mothers should:

- Avoid food considered as low class/common – such as field shrimps and crabs
- Not feed children with diarrhoea
- Let children feed themselves or feed them twice a day at the most.

Instead they:

- Used low class/common food
- Fed children with diarrhoea – it's critical to recovery
- Actively fed children many times during the day (self-fed children drop food on the floor so it's contaminated and children's stomachs can only take a finite amount of food at any one time so even feeding them twice a day was inadequate).

In short, the problems in organisations are often self-generated but the solutions are also often there too, it's just that usually we tend not to look.

I2: Negative Capability

The poet Keats called 'Negative Capability' the ability to remain comfortable with uncertainty, and Wicked Problems are inherently uncertain and ambiguous. Worse, since we seem to have developed an image of leadership that conjoins decisiveness to success we expect our leaders to cut their way through the fog of uncertainty with zeal. Yet by definition Wicked Problems remain ambiguous so the real skill is not in removing the uncertainty but in managing to remain effective despite it. Stein's (2004) comparison of decision-making in Apollo 13 and at Three Mile Island captures this issue well in situations where experience is critical to providing help in stressful situations. Thus the 'cosmology episodes' that strike both Apollo 13 and Three Mile Island – when 'the world no longer seems a rational, orderly system' provoke different responses from those responsible for decision-making, or rather, what Weick (1995) calls sense-making – imposing a framework of understanding upon a literally senseless world. 55 hours into the 1970 Apollo 13 mission a loud explosion – the 'cosmology episode' – left the astronauts short of food, oxygen, power, water and hope. But avoiding the natural temptation to jump to conclusions the ground crew through slow, careful analysis of the problems – and through the construction of a makeshift carbon dioxide scrubber (typical of the bricoleur's approach) – Apollo 13 returned safely. In contrast, in the 1979 Three Mile Island nuclear disaster the 'Cosmology episode' – led to instant actions being taken which unwittingly made the situation worse. In effect they were decisive but wrong and just to compound the situation they then denied any evidence suggesting that the problem had not been resolved. So the ability to tolerate anxiety and to ensure it does not become excessive (leading to panic) or denied (leading to inaction) generated different sense-making actions. Thus, the quest for the certainty of an elegant solution is sometimes a mechanism for displacing the anxiety of ambiguity that is a condition of Wicked Problems.

I3: Constructive Dissent not Destructive Consent

Finally, Individualists are excellent at resisting the siren calls of both hierarchists and egalitarians to fall in line, either to the rules or the group. Since Milgram's (1961) and Zimbardo's (2008) infamous compliance experiments in 1960s we have known that most people, most of the time, comply with authority even if that leads to the infliction of pain upon innocent others providing the rationale is accepted by the followers, they are exempt from responsibility, and they engage in harm only incrementally. Put another way, the difficulty for our Leader facing a Wicked Problem and seeking to use elements of the hierarchist and the egalitarian in a Clumsy approach is not of securing consent but dissent. Consent is relatively easily acquired by an authoritarian but it cannot address Wicked Problem because such consent is often destructive: subordinates will acquiesce to the enfeebling of their organisation rather than challenge their boss through Constructive

Dissent. Destructive Consent, then, is the bedfellow of Irresponsible Follower-ship and a wholly inadequate frame for addressing Wicked Problems. So what about egalitarians – why do we need them?

Egalitarians

E1: Collective Intelligence not Individual Genius

Typically, we attribute both success and failure to individual leaders. In fact the more significant the success or failure the more likely we are to do this, even though we usually have little evidence for linking the event to the individual (Bligh and Schyns 2007; Rosenzweig 2005). Yet when we actually examine how success and failure occurs it is more often than not a consequence of social rather than individual action. For example, Archie Norman, the British retail entrepreneur, rescued Asda from near bankruptcy in 1991 and sold it to Wal-Mart for £6.7bn in 1999. But underlying this phenomenal success was not the work of an isolated individual genius but a talented team including, at board level: Justin King (subsequently CEO Sainsbury), Richard Baker (subsequently CEO Boots), Andy Hornby (sub-sequently CEO HBOS), and Allan Leighton (subsequently Chair Royal Mail). In short, Asda'a success was built on collective intelligence not individual genius. This approach is particularly important to Wicked Problems because they are not susceptible to individual resolution. In other words, Wicked Problems demand the collective responses typical of systems not individuals – it is the community that must take responsibility and not displace it upon the leader (Heifetz). This brings us to the next aspect of Egalitarian techniques: building a community of fate.

E2: Community of Fate not a Fatalist Community

Anne Glover, a local community leader in Braunstone, Leicester, is credited with turning her own fatalist community into a community of fate when she mobilised her local neighbours to unite against the gang of youths engaging in anti-social behaviour and ruling their council estate through fear. Such fear effectively demobilised the community, turning it into a disparate group of isolated individuals – a Fatalist Community – all complaining about the gang problem but feeling unable to do anything about it. When Glover persuaded a large group to go out – as a group – and confront the gang, the gang moved on and were eventually removed from the estate. As Glover insisted, 'It never ceases to amaze me how a minority can control an area where a majority of people live... all because of the fear factor. If you stick together on an issue they can't intimidate you.' There is more to this than simply being brave enough to do something and willing to take the risk that it will not be easy; it is about recognising the importance of building social capital to develop an identity that generates a Community of Fate – the identity must be collective, but the responsibility must be individually shared for Wicked Problems to be addressed.

E3: Empathy not Egotism

Finally, the last Egalitarian technique lies in the ability to step into another's shoes, to generate an empathy that facilitates understanding of the other and is a pre-requisite for addressing Wicked Problems, but how might we acquire it? Jones' (2008) answer is to become an anthropologist of your own organisation, to walk a mile in the shoes of those of the shop floor, to become a mystery customer of your own bank or hospital, to experience the life of those with whom you want to engage in the collective effort because if you cannot understand how they see the problem how can you mobilise them? This is radically different from our usual methods for acquiring knowledge about how our organisations work because we know that what people say in focus groups or in surveys does not represent how they normally see the world – they are artificial environments and provide artificial data. Many CEOs and corporate leaders already do this – but many more do not, and then find themselves surprised when the bottom of the hierarchy doesn't respond in the way that the focus group or latest staff survey had predicted. For example, several Chief Constables in the UK ensure that they and their senior officers go out on patrol once a month, not to check up on more junior officers but to remind themselves of the kind of problems they face on a daily basis.

Conclusion

I began this chapter by suggesting that the high proportion of organisational change failures might be the result of assuming that all kinds of change were susceptible to the same kind of change programme when, in fact, change is often radically different. A typology to facilitate this understanding was then outlined that differentiates Tame, Wicked and Critical Problems and linked them to Management, Leadership and Crises. I suggested that while Tame Problems could be solved by adopting the Standard Operating Procedures that have worked before for managers, Critical Problems were the responsibility of Commanders who had to act decisively to provide the answer to the problem, but Wicked Problems were often either novel or intransigent and were the providence of Leadership.

This then took us in the cultural theory of Mary Douglas whose Grid/Group dimensions allow us to plot four different cultures: Hierarchist, Egalitarian, Individualist and Fatalist. These cultures tend to be internally consistent and self-supporting such that different groups understood the world differently and generated different responses to the same apparent problem. However, these Elegant modes of understanding, while often satisfactory for addressing the Tame or Critical Problems that cultures face, were unable to address the complexities of Wicked Problems. For Wicked Problems the role of leaders was to acknowledge that they did not have the answer to the Wicked Problem and to engage the community to address the problem. That meant adopting the role of the *bricoleur*, the makeshift craft worker who eschews the blank paper beloved of architects starting *de novo*, and made do with whatever was to hand, stitching together a pragmatic – nay Clumsy – solution using all three Elegant modes of understanding.

The techniques relating to Wicked Problems tend to emerge from one of the three Elegant frames, thus from the Hierarchists we considered the role of asking questions not providing answers, the issue of relationships over structures, and of reflecting on rather than reacting to Wicked situations. From the Individualist we considered the importance of Positive deviance not Negative Acquiescence, the encouragement of Constructive Dissent over Destructive Consent and the role of Negative Capability. Finally, from the Egalitarians we considered the use of Collective Intelligence not Individual Genius, the building of a Community of Fate not allowing a Fatalist Community to prevail, and to adopt an empathetic rather than an egotistic approach. I will finish with this quote attributed to Laurence J. Peter: 'Some problems are so complex that you have to be highly intelligent and well informed just to be undecided about them.'

References

Bligh, M.C. and Schyns, B. (2007) 'The Romance Lives On: Contemporary Issues Surrounding the Romance of Leadership', *Leadership*, 3(3): 343–360.

Bratton, J., Grint, K. and Nelson, D. (2004) *Organizational Leadership*. Mason, Ohio: Thomson/Southwestern.

Douglas, M (2003[1970]) *Natural Symbols*. London: Routledge.

Etzioni, A. (1964) *Modern Organizations*. London: Prentice Hall.

Fairhurst, G. (2005) 'Reframing the Art of Framing: Problems and Perspectives for Leadership', *Leadership*, 1(2): 165–186.

Jones, A. (2008) *The Courage to Innovate*, 2008. Axminster: Triarchy Press.

Gabriel, Y. (2002) 'Essay: On Paragrammatic Uses of Organizational Theory – A Provocation', *Organization Studies*, 23(1): 133–151.

Grint, K. (2005) 'Problems, Problems, Problems: The Social Construction of Leadership', *Human Relations* 58(11): 1467–1494.

Grint, K. (2007) 'Learning to Lead: Can Aristotle Help Us Find the Road to Wisdom?', *Leadership*, 2(2): 231–246.

Heifetz, R.A. (1994) *Leadership Without Easy Answers*. Cambridge, MA: Harvard University Press.

Jackson, P. (1995) *Sacred Hoops: Spiritual Lessons for a Hardwood Warrior*. New York: Hyperion.

Levi-Strauss, C. (1996) *The Savage Mind*. London: Weidenfeld and Nicolson.

Nye, J.S. (2004) *Power in the Global Information Age: From Realism to Globalization*. London: Routledge.

Nye, J. (2008) *The Powers to Lead*. Oxford: Oxford University Press.

Rittell, H. and Webber, M. (1973) 'Dilemmas in a General Theory of Planning', *Policy Sciences*, 4: 155–169.

Rosenzweig, P.M. (2005) *The Halo Effect & Eight Other Business Delusions that Deceive Managers*. (London: Simon & Schuster)

Stein, M. (2004) 'The Critical Period of Disasters: Insights from Sensemaking and Psychoanalytic Theory', *Human Relations*, 57(10): 1243–1261.

Verweij, M. (2006) 'Is the Kyoto Protocol Merely Irrelevant?', in Verweij, M. and Thompson, M. (eds) (2006) *Clumsy Solutions for A Complex World: Governance, Politics and Plural Perception*. Basingstoke: Palgrave Macmillan.

Verweij, M., Douglas, M., Ellis, R., Engel, C., Hendriks, F., Lohmann, S., Net, S., Rayner, S. and Thompson, M. (2006), 'The Case for Clumsiness', in Verweij, M. and Thompson, M. (eds) *Clumsy Solutions for A Complex World: Governance, Politics and Plural Perception*. Basingstoke: Palgrave Macmillan.

Weick, K. (1973) *Sensemaking in Organizations* (2nd edition). London: Sage.

Weick, K. (1995) *Sensemaking in Organizations* (2nd edition). London: Sage.

Zeitlen, M. (1990). *Positive Deviance in Child Nutrition*. New York: United Nations.

Zimbardo, P.G. (2008) *The Lucifer Effect: How Good People Turn Evil*. London: Rider & Co.

12

Knowledge and Capabilities for Leadership Across the Whole Public Service System

John Benington and Jean Hartley

Introduction

This chapter addresses the question: 'What are the knowledge and capabilities necessary for effective leadership across the whole public service system?'

This question is not new, and has been the focus of much discussion within academic circles and in many parts of the public service system over many years. However a variety of factors means that this may be an important moment of opportunity – a tipping point with the chance to turn thinking and talking into action.

The current economic crisis provides a significant catalyst for this debate because the pressure to be 'doing more with less' will become more strident as public sector spending comes under renewed scrutiny and is expected to decline in real terms over the next few years. During times of cut-back more effective leadership is often seen as one of the best ways of reducing transaction costs between separate organisations, of improving productivity and performance outcomes, and of releasing more public value for users, citizens and communities.

However, the need for better leadership across the whole public service systems does not derive solely from the current economic crisis, far-reaching though this is in its own terms. The world is in the throes of an even more fundamental and far-reaching restructuring of the ecological, political economic, technological and social context, which requires a 'Copernican revolution' in the basic paradigms for governance and public service. This requires a 'whole systems' approach to thinking about public services, and a radical redesign of provision for leadership development.

The need for new paradigms and practices

The complex cross-cutting problems facing citizens and communities require governments to develop new paradigms of whole systems thinking, and new patterns of inter-organisational working for outcomes.

Citizens and communities are increasingly confronted by a whole series of complex cross-cutting problems (e.g. ageing and community care; child protection; climate change; crime and the fear of crime), for which there are no simple solutions – and indeed where there is no clear or settled agreement about either the causes or the best ways to address the problems.

Government policies also push public managers to address cross-cutting issues in a joined-up way, and from the point of view of citizens and communities – recent examples in the UK include Every Child Matters; Community Area Assessments; Public Service Agreements.

These complex, and often contested, issues have been described by John Stewart (2001) as 'wicked' problems, and by Ron Heifetz (1994) as 'adaptive' problems. 'Wicked' or 'adaptive' problems of this kind are increasingly seen to require a qualitatively different kind of response from governments from 'tame' or 'technical' problems (Grint 2005; Heifetz 1994).

First, they require a recognition of the problems as part of a complex, polycentric, multi-causal, dynamic, inter-active and adaptive system, rather than as a simple, structured, uni-causal, mechanical chain of cause and effect (e.g. Byrne 1998; Marian and Uhl-Bien 2001; Stacey 1996; Waldrop 1992; Wheatley 1992).

Second, they require a commitment by government at all levels to work across the boundaries and silos which traditionally separate policies and programmes, in order to provide more 'joined up', citizen-centred and personalised public services.

Third, they require a qualitatively different kind of 'joined up' thinking and action by public policy-makers and managers, involving a capacity to work across many different boundaries.

The profound restructuring of the ecological, political economic social and technological context reinforces the need for the whole public service system to work in a more coherent and coordinated way. For example, as the UK and its regions and localities confront the consequences of the recession and the restructuring of global financial markets, the public leadership role has to extend beyond 'place-shaping' to 'place-shielding' – providing a 'holding environment' within which citizens and communities can be helped to think through the risks and uncertainties they face, to confront different interests and perspectives, to debate difficult choices, to engage in deliberative democratic forums to develop their identity as a local public, and to find a common purpose and direction during a period of fundamental change (Beck 1992; Benington 1996; Lyons 2007; Quirk 2008).

Leadership across complex polycentric networks

Complex cross-cutting problems require not only whole systems thinking and joined up policy-making and service delivery but also different patterns of leadership and action – which can address the inter-connections between issues, negotiate coalitions between different stakeholders, orchestrate inter-organisational networks and partnerships, harness disparate resources behind a common purpose, and achieve visible and measurable outcomes with and for citizens, communities and other stakeholders. This involves the exercise of leadership outside and beyond the organisation, often through influence rather than through formal authority, in addition to leadership inside the organisation.

Leadership of this kind has to resist the pressure from followers to act as a god or guru who can provide magical solutions to complex problems, and instead has to persuade stakeholders to accept themselves as part of the whole system, and therefore part of the problem, and to engage in the painful process of grasping difficult nettles, working through tough problems, and adapting one's own thinking and behaviour (Heifetz 1994; Benington and Turbitt 2007).

This kind of action-centred problem-solving leadership is being pioneered in practice by many policy-makers and practitioners, as they work in inter-organisational networks and partnerships and tackle complex cross- cutting problems (e.g. crime and disorder reduction partnerships, local area agreements; cross-cutting public service agreements). There is now an urgent need to reflect on, analyse, evaluate and learn from this experience, to assess the conditions under which leadership leads to practical improvement, innovation and measurable outcomes.

We also need to develop conceptual frameworks to help to make better sense of this experience. This requires leadership theories and models which reflect the complexities of working across sectoral and organisational boundaries, with varied groups with diverse interests, and which do not take individuals as the only unit of analysis, but also 'leadership constellations' which may consist of a team, a partnership group or other stakeholders who can work across a whole system (Benington and Moore, in press; Benington and Turbitt 2007; Hartley and Fletcher 2008; Grint 2005; Denis, Langley and Rouleau 2005; Moore 1995; Heifetz 1994).

Research evidence also suggests that it is possible to develop ways of sharing, comparing, disseminating and transplanting this emerging knowledge and experience more widely across the whole public service system, and that some of the most powerful learning both within and between organisations occurs when leadership failures or performance errors or mistakes are analysed self-critically but without blame (Hartley and Rashman 2007; Hartley and Benington 2006).

The skills, mindsets and capabilities which underpin effective leadership across the whole system, include political acumen or awareness: the capacity to negotiate between different interests, overcome inertia, and foster and mobilise coalitions between disparate organisations (Hartley and Fletcher 2008).

Dimensions of whole systems working

Whole systems thinking and action includes the capacity to analyse and understand the inter-connections, inter-dependencies and interactions between complex issues, across multiple boundaries:

- between different sectors (public, private, voluntary and informal community)
- between different levels of government (local, regional, national, supranational)
- between different services (e.g. education, health, housing, policing; social security)
- between different professions involved in tackling a common problem within a single agency (e.g. within the Academy for Sustainable Communities, or the Homes and Communities Agency)
- between political and managerial leaderships and processes
- between strategic management, operational management and front-line delivery
- between producers and users of services (in new patterns of co-creation between producers, users and other stakeholders outside the governmental system).

Leadership across the whole public service system therefore requires strengthened capabilities to think and to work along several different dimensions, often simultaneously:

- horizontally, between different sectors, organisations, disciplines, professions stakeholders, and partners
- vertically, along all the links in the value chain, from policy design in Westminster and Whitehall right through to service 'delivery' or intervention at the front-line in local neighbourhood communities – with movement in both directions, from top to bottom, bottom to top, and middle up-down
- diagonally, across the decision-making networks, linking together political leaderships, strategic managers, operational managers, front-line delivery staff, users and communities.

This requires a more sophisticated analysis of the changing external context – not just the policy context provided by central government but also the wider ecological, political, economic, technological, social and organisational context.

It may also require a different approach to policy analysis and development, and the need to link policy to implementation in an end to end process, which delivers practical action on the ground, at the front-line with communities.

Leadership development programmes need to join up to address whole system challenges

Leadership development programmes in the public and voluntary sectors increasingly therefore need to cultivate the knowledge and capabilities necessary to work effectively across the boundaries and networks of the whole public service system, in order to tackle the complex cross-cutting issues which concern citizens and communities.

Of course, in addition, there will always continue to be a need for specialist knowledge and skills in many areas of public service – the fire service, the health service, the police and schools still need to be led by people with expert mastery of the technical skills appropriate for their specific area of activity. Indeed it is arguable that this kind of specialist knowledge is even more necessary as a pre-condition for being able to engage effectively in cross-cutting work.

Whole systems working is not a playground for generalists, or network groupies! Our research suggests that inter-organisational networks and partnerships are strongest when they are formed by organisations and actors who are clear about their own specific roles and bodies of knowledge and expertise; but who have managed to negotiate a coalition across their different interests and a common purpose which draws on their different specialisms (Geddes and Benington 2001).

It might be helpful in analytical terms to consider a continuum from, on the one hand, a single public service with a single leadership development approach (c.f. The Ecole National (ENA) in France) to, on the other hand, specialist leadership bodies and leadership development for particular services (the current UK system). In using this continuum, the key question is what aspects of leadership require joint or generic development across the whole public service system, and which aspects require separate development because of their specialist technical bodies of knowledge.

However, there are many areas where greater collaboration in leadership development between different public services makes good common sense, and is already beginning to be explored.

Five main forms of cross-cutting public leadership programmes seem to be emerging in practice:

- Where there is overlapping expertise or specialism between services. For example, the police, fire, ambulance, local authority and army are developing joint leadership training for civil emergencies.

- Where leaders within a particular profession which has members in different sectors, services, and levels of government come together to discuss and develop their contribution to corporate strategic leadership (e.g. CIPFA/ Warwick courses for Leaders in Finance).
- Where leaders from different sectors, services and levels of government are brought together on leadership development programmes specifically within whole system aims and perspective (e.g. Warwick University's MPA and Diploma in Public Leadership and Management, and the Modern Leaders programme run by the National School of Government, both of which draw in managers from across the whole public service system, and consciously explore leadership of inter-organisational relationships and networks across different sectors, levels and services).
- Where leaders from different services come together to share, compare and develop their knowledge and expertise so that they can respond in more holistic ways to the needs of a particular group within the population (e.g. children or old people). The National College for Leadership of Schools and Children's Services runs a Multi-Agency Team Development programme to address the challenges of joint working posed by the Every Child Matters agenda.
- Where leaders from across the whole system in a particular place (neighbourhood, local authority area, region or sub-region) come together for joint leadership development programmes. Whole system, inter-organisational, cross-service leadership in a particular locality is increasingly not an option but a necessity, as agencies are required to respond both to the complex fast-changing needs of their communities, and also to the need at local and regional level to somehow 'join up' the wide range of disparate national government policies and programmes. The Leicestershire Leadership In Partnership Programme run jointly with Warwick Business School, is an imaginative and innovative example of whole system leadership development generated from below, bringing together the county and district local authorities, the health, police and fire and rescue services, and voluntary organisations for joint leadership development.

We can learn what supports or inhibits leadership development across the whole system by reflecting on initiatives which have gone well and those which have gone less well, including the need to review the lessons from major previous attempts at leadership development across the whole system.

Two barriers have been highlighted by several commentators. The first is the need for 'financial architecture' that is fit for purpose, with an incentive structure that supports whole system rather than silo-based leadership development – cross-service leadership programmes are undermined by funding streams which came down through vertical stovepipes.

The second is the need for strong high level corporate championship (e.g. by the Cabinet Secretary and the Permanent Secretaries' group), in the same way that the UK Government's Capability Review process has been led successfully from the corporate centre of the civil service, since this both created commitment to, and ownership of, a whole systems approach and also created a potential 'holding environment' (Heifetz 1994) in which tough questions and tensions between siloed services could be explored and addressed.

Leadership development programmes need to translate individual learning into organisational and inter-organisational action and improvement

One of the biggest challenges facing public sector leadership programmes is how to ensure that investment in learning by individuals is translated into improvement in the performance of their parent organisations. This is even more challenging when the unit of analysis is not a single organisation but an inter-organisational network or a complex inter-connected system like a neighbourhood, or particular group within the population (e.g. children, or older people).

There is little research into, or evidence about, the impact of leadership development programmes upon either individual or organisational performance (Hartley and Benington 2010). Most research in this field has been based upon self-reporting by participants of their own individual learning, rather than assessment by their employers or peers (though 360 degree assessments can go some way towards this). There are very few studies of the impact of leadership development programmes on organisational performance, let alone upon the whole public service system.

Instead of starting with individuals as the unit of analysis for leadership development programmes, and then attempting to translate their individual learning into changes in performance within their parent organisations, it may be more effective to start with an organisation or inter-organisational network as the unit of analysis, and to aim to develop the whole leadership team as a working unit (Day 2001).

Similarly, instead of starting leadership development with theory and then trying to apply it back into practice, it may be more effective to start with the practical challenges facing an organisation or network and then search for leadership theories and concepts which help the practitioners to make better sense of the complexity of the specific whole system in which they are working – and therefore be able to offer clearer leadership and strategic direction.

Similarly, instead of running leadership development programmes away from the workplace, and then trying to apply the learning back into practice in the parent organisations, it may be more effective to start leadership development at the workplace or in the community, and to move continuously between the battlefield and the balcony – as they do in medical education, with student doctors spending the morning doing ward rounds

Table 12.1   An Alternative Model for Whole System's Leadership Development
©John Benington 2009

	A traditional model for leadership development	A possible alternative 'whole systems' model for leadership development
Unit of Analysis	The Individual	The Workgroup/Team
Starting Point	Theory	Practice/Problem
Location	The Retreat	The Front-Line

at the hospital with the consultant, and then spending the afternoon at the medical school, studying the cases they have observed in the morning. This is in tune with the 'learning by doing' and 'dynamic capability' approach espoused by the Cabinet Office Capability Building team. See Table 12.1.

Strengthening leadership skills and capabilities for working across the whole public service system will require radical innovations in practice. The public sector leadership academies and the other main providers of public leadership education and development appear to do a good job in their own service sectors. A number of them are developing bi-lateral or tri-lateral discussions with other leadership academies about the possibilities for collaboration in leadership development between their services (e.g. fire, police, local government, schools, health). However, we doubt whether these relatively small scale incremental initiatives (worthwhile as they undoubtedly are) are going to develop sufficient momentum or critical mass to match the scale or urgency of the need for more effective leadership across the whole public service system.

We therefore suggest for debate a more radical set of innovations based upon intervention at three key stages in the leadership development process and in two key arenas.

Fast Track Graduate Entry: There is an opportunity to review each of the main fast track graduate entry schemes (e.g. into the civil service, local government, the health service, the police) and design in a requirement for some cross-service education and training (e.g. through some shared cross-over modules, and through ten week placements in other services).

Top Teams: It would also be beneficial to review each of the main top leadership and management schemes in the public service sector and design in some cross-service education and training, shoulder to shoulder working exchanges in other organisations, joint multi-agency project work, and stretching university-based thinking. It is critical that leadership across the whole public service system is led from the top, and modelled by early visible changes in leadership development behaviour and practice at this level.

Mid-Career Movers and Shakers: The most movement however is likely to come from mobilising a major national leadership programme for mid-career movers and shakers from among middle-managers across the whole public service. This would help to create a strong sense of this group being the leadership cadre for the next generation of top leaders for the whole of the public service – with a status equivalent to the top 200 in the UK civil service, but drawn from across the whole public service system. There would need to be rigorous national competition and tough selection for this programme which must be highly innovative in its leadership development and learning methods, and university accredited at the highest level. This is the group most likely to rapidly transform mind-sets and practices across the public service system.

Multi-Agency Teams and Leadership of Place: It would also be useful to launch a national programme of local pilot projects (perhaps ten to 20) in leadership development for cross-service partnership teams working at the front-line. The UK Government has recently announced a Total Place programme with 13 pilot projects, which have analysed and coordinated the flow of public money into the pilot areas, and are considering how to provide whole systems leadership across the geographical area. One example which is ahead of the field is the Leicestershire Leadership in Partnership programme, which brings together senior managers from across the whole public and voluntary sector (e.g. the County Council, district councils, NHS, police, fire, and voluntary organisations), to train and learn together on a tailored Diploma programme jointly designed with Warwick Business School, and to begin to develop as a leadership cadre capable of tackling complex cross-cutting problems facing local communities, and to develop inter-organisational strategies and responses.

The pilot projects might be selected through open national competition, with the successful projects being offered government seed money or match funding of their own local investment. The programme and the pilots should be monitored and formatively evaluated so that their learning can be captured and disseminated. The national programme might be linked into some kind of national Beacon scheme to disseminate learning through sharing, comparing and transplanting of experience.

Taking the plunge: Deep immersion for top civil servants

Several of the people we consulted in our research say that they see the civil service as the main laggards in terms of joined up government and leadership across the whole public service system (Benington and Hartley 2009). The civil service, it is alleged, does not practice what it preaches about joined up government, and continues to channel policies and funding streams down vertical stove-pipes, with little understanding of the horizontal connections to (or incompatibility with) the policies of other departments and agencies, or the vertical connections with other parts of the value and delivery chains. The senior civil service has also been criticised by other public service managers for being far too insulated from the complex realities of local communities, and for the fact that it is still too easy to get promoted within the civil service without any substantial experience of front-line work outside Westminster and Whitehall.

This is contrasted with the pattern in other key public services where, for example, all chief constables are expected to have served time on the beat at neighbourhood level; head-teachers are expected to have gained a good deal of class-room teaching experience; local authority chief executives are expected to have operational experience and/or front-line service delivery, as well as strategic management experience.

A bold high profile way of correcting this impression, (which undermines the leadership credibility and effectiveness of the civil service in some multi-agency situations), might be to start a deep immersion scheme which would require all potential senior civil servants, before admission to the Senior Civil Service, to have spent at least ten to 12 weeks working (not observing) at the front-line outside London – in a night shelter for homeless people; as an orderly in an accident and emergency ward of a hospital; on the counter of a benefits agency office; as a class-room teaching assistant; in a neighbourhood team.

Such an approach to action-oriented leadership development to encourage working across the whole public service systems needs to be counter-balanced by an equally strong commitment to critical analysis of the changing context, and rigorous reflection on the experience of leadership in practice (both success and failure).

There is, therefore, a crucial role for good universities with experience of engaged research, development and teaching, to work in partnership with the leadership academies and other leadership programmes to provide:

- theories and concepts that help to make sense of the complex experience of leadership challenges in practice
- evidence from research and from both formative and summative evaluations to help establish what kinds of leadership development make the maximum impact on both individual, organisational and inter-organisational performance (and which have little impact)
- a safe but stretching 'holding environment' in which difficult questions and issues can be asked and grappled with, and in which the insights of both theory and experience can be brought to bear on leadership practice
- rigorous independent accreditation of leadership thinking and practice

The rationale for such an approach is noted by Glatter (2008: 6):

Raw experience is not a sufficient guide to learning: leaders may need help in structuring and analysing experience to be able to use it as a resource for learning. For example, visits included in programmes need to be carefully prepared, clearly structured and purposeful to maximise their value.

Our research suggests that academic ideas and learning are critical to helping provide the theoretical and conceptual base to make sense of action within complex systems. Many sponsors of leadership development programmes are turning to university-accredited programmes to ensure critical reflection on experience, and because leaders are wanting rigorous independent assessment of their learning, and a high quality, and portable Diploma and Masters qualifications. Where university accreditation is pursued, it needs to draw on and engage with practical experience, to challenge established thinking and practice, and also use practice to develop and extend theory.

Conclusion

Our judgement is that the time is now ripe for a major new initiative to promote and cultivate leadership capabilities for working across the public service system. There is widespread agreement that this needs to be done strongly and quickly, so the key question is not 'whether' but 'how'. This brief review suggests that innovative ideas for cross-service collaboration in leadership development are already being explored and tested. The critical success factor will be strong championship of a whole system, multilevel, cross-service approach to leadership development at the highest level within government, and a funding regime to incentivise this rapidly. *Carpe Diem!*

Note

This chapter is based on research commissioned by the National School of Government and the Public Service Leadership Alliance.

References

Beck, U. (1992) *Risk Society: Towards a New Modernity*. London: Sage.

Benington, J. (1996) 'New Paradigms and Practices for Local Government: Capacity Building Within Civil Society', in Kraemer, S. and Roberts, J. (eds), *The Politics of Attachment*. London: Free Association Books.

Benington, J. and Hartley, J. (2009) *Whole Systems Go! Leadership Across the Whole Public Service System*. London: Sunningdale Institute and National School of Government.

Benington, J. and Moore, J. (in press) *Public Value: Theory and Practice*. Basingstoke: Palgrave Macmillan.

Benington, J. and Turbitt, I. (2007) 'Policing the Drumcree Demonstrations in Northern Ireland: Testing Leadership Theory in Practice', *Leadership*, 3(4): 371–395.

Byrne (1998) *Complexity Theory and the Social Sciences*. London: Routledge.

Day, D. (2001) 'Leadership Development: A Review in Context', *Leadership Quarterly*, 11: 581–613.

Denis, J.-L., Langley, A. and Rouleau, L. (2005) 'Rethinking Leadership in Public Organizations', in Ferlie, E., Lynn, L. and Pollitt, C. (eds), *The Oxford Handbook of Public Management*. Oxford: Oxford University Press.

Geddes, M. and Benington, J. (2001) *Local Partnerships and Social Exclusion in the European Union*. London: Routledge.

Glatter, R. (2008) 'Of Leadership, Management and Wisdom. A Brief Synthesis of Selected Reports and Documents on Leadership Development', *Report*. Nottingham: National College for School Leadership.

Grint, K. (2005) 'Problems, Problems, Problems: The Social Construction of "Leadership"', *Human Relations*, 58: 1467–1494.

Hartley, J. and Benington, J. (2006) 'Copy and Paste, or Graft and Transplant? Knowledge Sharing Through Inter-Organizational Networks', *Public Money and Management*, 26(2): 101–108.

Hartley, J. and Fletcher, C. (2008) 'Leadership with Political Awareness: Leadership Across Diverse Interests Inside and Outside the Organization', in James, K. and Collins, J. (eds), *Leadership Perspectives: Knowledge into Action*, pp. 157–170. London: Palgrave.

Hartley, J. and Rashman, L. (2007) 'How is Knowledge Transferred Between Organizations Involved in Change?', in Wallace, M., Fertig, M. and Schneller, E. (eds), *Managing Change in the Public Services*, pp. 173–192. Oxford: Blackwell.

Heifetz, R. (1994) *Leadership Without Easy Answers*. Cambridge, MA: Belknapp Press.

Lyons, M. (2007) 'Lyons Inquiry into Local Government. Place-Shaping: A Shared Ambition For The Future Of Local Government', *Final Report and Recommendations*. London: The Stationery Office.

Marion, R. and Uhl-Bien, M. (2001) 'Leadership of Complex Organizations', *Leadership Quarterly*, 12(4): 389–418.

Moore, M. (1995) *Creating Public Value*. Cambridge, MA: Harvard University Press.

Quirk, B. (2008) 'Quirk Calls for Place Shielding', *Local Government Chronicle*, 23 October. Accessed on 2 December 2009 at http://www.lgcplus.com/barry-quirk/1902324.article

Stacey, R. (1996) *Complexity and Creativity in Organizations*. San Francisco: Berrett-Koehler.

Stewart, J. (2001) *Modernizing Government*. Basingstoke: Palgrave Macmillan.

Waldrop, M. (1992) *Complexity: The Emerging Science at the Edge of Order and Chaos*. New York: Simon and Schuster.

Wheatley, M. (1992) *Leadership and the New Science*. San Francisco: Berrett-Koehler.

13
The Challenge of Change for Public Sector Leaders

Carina Paine Schofield and Mark Pegg

Introduction

The 'need for leaders' in a complex and challenging public sector

The UK government perceives leadership to be at the heart of public sector reform. In 1998, the then Prime Minister Tony Blair asked the government's Performance and Innovation Unit (PIU) to carry out a project on 'effective leadership in delivering public services'. This report, 'Strengthening Leadership in the Public Sector', places leadership at the core of its modernisation agenda (PIU 2001). The last decade has seen a growing and sustained interest in the importance and nature of leadership in the public sector. Several texts refer to the 'need for leaders' in the public sector at the start of the 21st century and many Organisation for Economic Cooperation and Development countries (OECD 2009), including the UK, assume that leadership plays a significant role in achieving both enhanced management capacity and organisational performance (Prime Minister's Strategy Unit 2004). Milner and Joyce (2005) state that this emphasis on leadership is in part a result of the problems created by the way the public sector appeared to fall behind developments in society and that public services now need to catch up (or to 'modernise' or 'improve'). This particularly relates to customer service standards, performance management, strategic commissioning and the design, development and implementation of information systems (Cabinet Office 2006).

There is widespread agreement regarding the complexity of leadership in the public sector: the public sector is highly diverse in character, governance and size (Charlesworth, Cook and Crozier 2003); there are competing needs within and expectations from diverse stakeholders (Brookes 2007); and tasks involve different types and sizes of organisation. Therefore, leadership in the public sector varies greatly. The challenge of defining leadership in this sector is further exacerbated by the numerous challenges of current times.

Over recent years a plethora of articles list the challenges for leaders in the public sector and describe how the number of challenges will increase over coming years and make leadership even more difficult. A key finding from the PIU Report (2001: 4) was that 'Britain's public services face unprecedented challenges at the start of the 21st century'. Public sector organisations are under pressure to be more responsive, reliable and accessible, and to focus on performance in the face of rising public expectations; demographic change; and globalisation and information technology advances (KPMG/Economist Intelligence Unit 2007). Charlesworth *et al.* (2003: 8) describe how 'the boundaries have changed in recent years and will undoubtedly change again as a steadily stronger consumer culture, rising living standards and a more diverse society lead to greater expectations of responsiveness, reliability and accessibility'. As the public sector is continually challenged to be more effective, efficient and innovative; to provide quality service and to put people first whilst at the same time to reduce costs; and to improve systems and processes in order to streamline delivery, 'more is being asked of public sector leaders than ever before' (PIU 2001: 7).

As real growth in UK public spending comes to an end in the 2010s, there is a more intense need for even better leadership skills – for leaders to bring a more enabled, more creative and more innovative public service workforce with them. Indeed, the whole public leadership agenda will shift markedly as we enter the new decade; old friends like 'doing more with less', 'value for money', performance management and a more strategic approach – 'the 20:20 vision for government' – will be even more important. However, they must be supplemented by a greater focus on connectivity – joined-up government, more personalisation of services, more e-Government and a changing role for government as the enabler. This will become increasingly necessary as more and more public services are provided by the private and voluntary sectors on behalf of the state. In particular, the aging population demographic may force the state to withdraw completely from some elements of delivery and limit its role to the regulation of commercially provided services.

Despite all of these changes and challenges, a recent review of the literature identified that public sector organisations (at all levels) have been largely neglected as a focus for empirical research and pointed to a need for this to be addressed (Paine Schofield 2008a). This chapter seeks to inform the data in this area by providing insights into the opinions of managers and leaders on the issues and challenges they face. Specifically, by exploring how managers and leaders working in the public sector see the state of their organisations today and their roles within them, and how far their private sector counterparts share their attitudes.

As providers of world class leadership development, Ashridge Business School and the National School of Government (NSG) wanted to collect data on management and leadership thinking in public service. Doing so would help make better sense of Faculty experience in the classroom delivering executive education to key public sector managers, to expose trends to inform future learning and development and to build capacity to meet the demanding leadership agenda in the future. Ashridge and the NSG set out to gather managers' and leaders' opinions on the issues and challenges they face using the newly-developed Public Management Index (PMI) survey. Based on the views of almost 1,400 public sector managers, the Index provides a fascinating insight into the issues and challenges facing managers and leaders involved in public service. This chapter will be based on the findings from the PMI. It will explore how managers and leaders are operating in the public sector; describe the issues and challenges they feel they face; make comparisons to responses from a companion survey used with private sector managers and leaders and draw on evidence from Faculty experience in the classroom. The chapter will particularly focus on the challenge of change: change in the public sector; changing management roles; and a changing workforce (specifically leadership and career development).

The public management index

The PMI was inspired by the design of the Ashridge Management Index (AMI), launched in 1994 as part of a continuing programme of research into the real lives of course members, those key managers and leaders studying at Ashridge. Repeated on several occasions, most recently in 2008 (Holton, Dent and Rabbetts 2008), the AMI has produced unparalleled insights into the challenges private sector managers face in business life and the rapid changes that are taking place over time. Reflecting Ashridge's client base in global business, the respondents to the AMI are predominantly drawn from the senior and high potential manager cadre in the global locations of their private sector organisations. Ashridge works extensively with global business but, as befits the growing interest the UK government has in leadership, also has a strong presence in the public and third sectors. In 2008 it was decided that it would add more value if a PMI, a new survey devoted to participants working in public services, was developed to widen the knowledge about management and leadership within the UK public sector, and to see if there were differences and similarities between managers in different sectors. Therefore, the PMI was launched in a spirit of enquiry, because both Ashridge and the NSG saw the data gathered as valuable in its own right both to help develop better teaching and learning for better leadership development and to act as a comparative benchmark. Specifically, the main objectives of the PMI survey were to: i) explore how managers and leaders are operating in the public sector; ii) understand more about the issues and challenges managers and leaders in the public sector currently face; and iii) provide valuable comparisons between managers and leaders working in the different sectors (public and private). The survey provides baseline data on the opinions and attitudes of public sector staff which help identify areas for improvement as well as areas of good practice. The survey results also offer valuable comparisons with individual departmental and public intelligence and survey data on managers and leaders.

The PMI was aimed at practising leaders and managers from any job role, at any level and in any part of the public sector. Many central government departments undertake staff surveys on a regular and routine basis. What makes the PMI unique is the breadth of coverage and the ability to make comparisons with participants working in global business, comparing responses to a range of consistent questions. Reflecting the Ashridge and NSG client base it is weighted towards the high potentials, the newly promoted or assessed as ready for promotion in a wide range of UK central and local government, agencies and non-departmental public bodies (NDPBs). The survey was designed to closely follow the most recent version of the AMI to allow comparisons between the public and private sectors. Using a variety of question formats, the survey explored several topics related to leadership and management issues in the UK public sector. Key topics identified in the public leadership literature (Paine Schofield 2008a) and in case studies provided by public sector workers (Paine Schofield 2008b) informed a number of additional questions. Almost 1,400 managers and leaders working in the UK public sector responded.[1] A comparable sample of over 700 managers and leaders working in the private sector responded to the AMI in 2008.[2]

Findings from the public management index

In the following sections, findings from the PMI data will be described and reflected on alongside the related published literature. Relevant quotations made by respondents to the Index will be used where available to highlight specific topics being discussed. Comparisons to the private sector findings from the AMI will be made where appropriate.

Change in the public sector

There have been many periods of major change in public services since the Northcote Trevelyan reforms in 1854. The post-1945 Attlee Government and the 1980s Thatcher Government transformed the way public services are provided and used. However, a strong perception persists that transformational change is more characteristic of the lives of those working in the private sector, and the contrasting image of the public sector is staid, with traditional and unchanging systems (as described by Head of the Civil Service Sir Andrew Turnbull in 2004 when announcing the Professional Skills for Government (PSG) Programme). The public sector in the 21st century is facing new pressures to learn, innovate and keep up with many changes (such as changes in public expectations, personalisation, citizen empowerment, globalisation and so the list goes on). A Capability Review published in 2007 describes the need for departments to be flexible, quick to respond, 'excellent at strategic development and alignment, and swift and pragmatic at aligning delivery mechanisms and models to new and evolving changes' (Capability Reviews: Tranche 3 2007: 5). The concept of change is nothing new; however, it is the increasing pace of change that is a particular challenge. Many of the public sector respondents commented upon the level, the breadth and the complexity of change which has become a standard feature for their organisations. Managers' opinions in the PMI reflect this and survey responses provide some rich illustrations of their current opinions:

'My organisation has been going through a transformation programme since early 2006 but with little investment of cash or people development. However – most of what has happened so far is simply job cuts without accompanying changes to ways of working or reduction in workloads, coupled with continual changes of leadership at the top of the organisation. While the impact on me personally could be said to be positive in that I have a post linked to the transformation, the continual change, lack of direction from the top, lack of opportunities for learning and development, lack of funding to support the change make working here immensely frustrating and inhibit implementation of improvements to ways of working.'

'There has been a plethora of organisational change and sometimes it feels as though one set of changes hasn't had time to bed down before the next ones come along! Clearly there are some changes one cannot influence since they are taken at top management level so I take the view that I have to get on with it and make it a positive experience rather than a negative one.'

'Constant change following change is becoming detrimental to overall performance. Change is good, change is healthy but periods of consolidation are required to allow people to orientate themselves and to perform to their maximum efficiency.'

Ashridge and NSG Faculty have rich experiences working with key managers in the public sector and can draw on reflections from experience in the classroom, but wanted hard evidence to support these perceptions. For example, senior management participants attending programmes tailored for the Ministry of Defence at Ashridge in the 1990s would often argue with their leaders Sir Richard Mottram and Sir Roger Jacklin about the need for a period of stability where change was put on hold. Sir Richard said 'it is not on offer – change is the norm, I can't stop the world and allow you get off' (Mottram 1996). In contrast, their successors in the 2000s as Permanent Secretaries, Sir Kevin Tebbit and Sir Bill Jeffrey, were subject to detailed and sophisticated scrutiny of the change, the robustness of the vision and the pace and alignment of change programmes – to negotiate the impact of the change and bring this key cadre with them. Participants now seem to reflect an understanding that change *per se* is not bad but that more effort and planning is required on the process of change. Change requires resources rather than simply creating additional work to what are already challenging workloads for individuals and for organisations. A change team can help drive progress forward but a number of public sector organisations are trying to balance several initiatives focused on different aspects of change; which makes it harder to be successful. Leaders who design the change process need to be closer to those who implement the change and actually appreciate the practical day to day reality of what staff experience. A report published by the Chartered Institute of Personnel and Development (CIPD 2003) describes how the greater the amount of change, the more negative people working in the public sector feel. Managers, and staff, need to make time to reflect – to see what has worked and what has not worked – before moving on to another change initiative. Therefore, it is important to ensure that at the same time as managing change and reform, it can be important to maintain continuity and routine (Benington 2000).

Management and leadership

Table 13.1 indicates the percentage of public sector and private sector respondents agreeing[3] with survey items which focused on management and leadership issues.

From Table 13.1 it can be seen that survey responses regarding line management were generally positive: over three quarters of respondents believed that their immediate line manager was effective and made sufficient time for them. Again, the topic of change arises as many of the less positive comments from respondents regarding line managers related to changes in line management and, in some cases, the impact of these changes. For example one manager commented: 'I have had four line managers in the past twelve months due to constant "modifications" to our team structure. I have raised my concerns about how ineffective I feel I have become, but I feel that I am not taken seriously.'

Table 13.1   Percentage of Public Sector and Private Sector Respondents Agreeing with Line Management and Leadership Survey Items

Survey Item	% Agree	
	Public	Private
I believe my immediate line manager is effective	77	80
My manager makes sufficient time for me	71	69
I believe top leadership in my organisation is effective*	55	74
I believe top leadership in my organisation spends sufficient time communicating with staff	46	49

*See footnote 3.

However, in contrast to respondents positive views regarding their line manager, views regarding top leadership in the public sector were less encouraging: with only just over one half of public sector respondents viewing top leadership in their organisation as effective. An earlier research study by Horne and Stedman-Jones for the Chartered Management Institute (2001) revealed similar concerns. They found that the quality of leadership in UK organisations did not receive high ratings, with public sector organisations receiving the lowest ratings of all.

These findings are also consistent with the government's own view of leadership in the public sector, and the recognition that more work needs to be done to develop leaders, as described in the Departmental Capability Reviews (launched in 2005) and the PSG framework (2005) (and more recently, the Skills strategy for central government (2008)). On taking office in 2005, Sir Gus O'Donnell (head of the UK Civil Service and Cabinet Secretary) set out his vision for leadership and leadership development in UK government and formed the '5 Ps' to spread his key messages – a theme he highlighted in speeches to senior staff, and also to staff at the 'sharp end' on visits to government offices throughout the UK:

5 'P's for Public Service

Pride – proud of being a public servant who creates wealth or the conditions for wealth creation – teachers, doctors, similar professionals – a focus on 'customers' not 'producers'.

Pace – overcoming 'the treacle that slows you down'. Most public servants work outside London in operations that need simplification, process re-engineering – an environment that should look for inspiration more to industry and 'kaizen' than to government.

Passion – objectivity does not have to mean cold – if you can't get passionate about child poverty and 'save the planet' what can you get passionate about?

Professionalism – a personal success measure would be that his successor came up through the ranks by success in operations not just policy-making – 'If you want to get on get out' means more secondments, better leadership development – to bring in new ideas.

Personal – the glue to link the other 4 Ps – be a visible role model, live the values, develop leadership skills – be part of a 'brand' that delivers excellent customer services – a service people can be proud to be a part of.

Some authors describe how organisations, particularly public sector organisations, need to be clear about the difference between management and leadership. For example, Dunoon (2002) argues that public sector organisations have a tendency to over-emphasise management at the expense of leadership, with potential adverse results for leadership development. Issues surrounding leadership development will be described later in this chapter.

Respondents from the private sector were significantly more positive than those from the public sector regarding leadership. One reason for the difference between the public sector respondents and their private sector counterparts may relate to the term 'leadership': is this term more ambiguous for public sector respondents? Although leadership in the public sector has been widely written and spoken about it is still unclear in the literature precisely what this refers to. Horne and Stedman-Jones (2001: 15) observe the lack of clarity around the perception of leaders. They describe a tendency among public sector managers to 'mix their perceptions of the concept of leadership as a specific role in an organisational process, with the characteristics of leadership as displayed by individuals'. Although there is a consensus in the literature that there is no single agreed definition of leadership (and certainly not of public sector leadership) it is clear from the differences between the PMI and AMI responses that there is an issue surrounding the effectiveness of 'leaders' (however leadership is perceived) in the public sector.

There was a strong suggestion in both the PMI and AMI data that senior leaders are perceived as being too remote: less than a half of public sector respondents felt that top leadership spends sufficient time communicating with staff. This seems a surprising finding in a mass communication world where the surveys show both public and private sector workforces often feel bombarded with information (over two thirds of public sector respondents feel that the growth of information technology and communications has improved communications in their organisations over the past three years, but a similar proportion feel that this growth has resulted in them feeling 'snowed under' by email and voicemails). Communication with staff is an important aspect of good leadership and it assists organisational knowledge. The key to improving communication may be distinguishing between quantity and quality: communication methods also include face to face discussions and if top leaders do not engage with staff but rely on impersonal paper-based or email messages then they are likely to seem distant and remote to the workforce and to most managers beyond the senior team.

Respondents from the public sector want an organisational climate in which they feel that they matter; that their concerns are of importance to those at the top. The data suggests that they get some of this from their immediate managers but, equally clearly, it suggests that this is not enough. Is leadership being seen as essentially the province of senior staff? Does the excuse of 'organisational distance' absolve senior leaders from the need to 'bridge the gap' between themselves and their staff: surely, this is a key duty of the leadership role?

Changing roles

Table 13.2 shows the percentage of public sector and private sector respondents agreeing with survey items which focused on changing management roles.

The work of the public services is steadily increasing in complexity and in the number of demands made. This is partly because departments and agencies need to employ matrix management to deliver large 'mission critical' projects, and partly because the delivery of outcomes consistent with increasing public value usually relies upon several agencies working together – so called 'joined-up government'. As such, there is a greater demand for collaborative, partnership working and joined up working across departments in the public sector, as well as between different sectors (public, private and voluntary): 'Partnerships are currently the most imperative, significant and institutionalised form of collaborative working in the public services in the UK' (Broussine and Miller 2005: 389). A 2007 Capability Review also refers to the need for partnership working in the UK public sector: 'government departments need to work in partnership consistently and dynamically.....to shift their mindsets between the global and the local and individual, working jointly to deliver integrated solutions to some of the biggest challenges facing the world today' (Capability Reviews: Tranche 3 2007: 5).

As Table 13.2 shows, the data from the PMI reflects these descriptions in the literature. The majority of public sector managers stated that increasingly they are required to manage cross-functional and virtual teams (this figure was significantly higher for private sector managers). Some managers

Table 13.2 Percentage of Public Sector and Private Sector Respondents Agreeing with Survey Items Relating to Changing Management Roles

	% Agree	
Survey Item	*Public*	*Private*
Increasingly I am required to manage people in cross functional and virtual teams*	70	82
My organisation provides sufficient support for virtual team-working*	35	46
In my organisation management roles are increasingly about influencing people over whom managers have no authority	74	74
Influencing people in my organisation is relatively easy to do*	35	43
I feel more involved in the decision-making process than I did 3 years ago*	51	69
I feel that top leadership in my organisation has moved towards a more consultative approach to decision-making*	39	48

*See footnote 3.

felt that this change had a positive impact. For example a public sector manager explained that: 'the [organisational change] that has had the best impact has been matrix working and the ability to lead across the organisation'. Another manager (working internationally) stated how: 'Far more matrix working and management with cross-cultural teams across the region of Europe and North America [has had a] positive [impact].'

The growth of virtual teams is identified in both the AMI and PMI with only just over one third of public sector managers feeling that their organisation provided sufficient support for virtual team-working. As one manager described, virtual team working: 'doubles the person management role for many'. This figure was also low for private sector respondents.

The majority of public sector respondents said that management roles in their organisation are increasingly about influencing people over whom they have no line management responsibility (this figure was the same for private sector respondents). While influencing is increasingly a necessary skill for success, organisations need to be aware of the challenges this creates for managers as only around one third of respondents stated that influencing people in their organisation is easy to do. One public sector manager summarised this issue:

> Being able to influence where one has no authority is an important skill but there is a danger that too much reliance is placed on individual skills in this area without providing the necessary support structures to enable it to happen as effectively as it should.

The percentage of private sector respondents stating that influencing people in their organisation is easy to do was also low.

Table 13.2 shows that with regard to decision-making, approximately half of public sector respondents reported that they felt more involved in the decision-making process than they did three years ago (this figure was significantly higher for private sector respondents). However, a significantly lower percentage of public sector respondents felt that top leadership in their organisation were moving towards a more consultative approach to decision-making, when compared to the private sector respondents.

Collectively, the PMI data firmly places a reliance on the traditional approach of authority, hierarchy and command in the past, as it no longer reflects the reality of today's public sector. Instead there is a need to turn towards non-hierarchical ways of working, as a result of which there will be a greater demand for involvement, influence, collaboration and distributed leadership. There is now a strong perception that leadership skills need to be developed and strengthened as indicated by The Capability Review Programme and the PSG competency framework.

Leadership and career development

Respondents to the PMI questioned the commitment of their organisations to leadership development. Table 13.3 shows the percentage of public sector and private sector respondents agreeing with survey items which focused on leadership and career development.

If senior leaders are perceived as too remote, this could be exacerbated by the related perception that not enough is being done by these leaders to organise the talent management of their organisations. Since the 1990s, more and more Departments have moved towards open competition for appointments and the use of assessment and development centres to populate key grades in their management structures. Together with a move towards shared services for HR and reforms in human resources management, this places more responsibility on individuals to manage their own personal and career development. The findings in Table 13.3 illustrate a perception that in making these changes not enough is being done to assure the future leadership provision, and a generally poor perception of the support available for individual career development in the public sector.

From Table 13.3 it can be seen that leadership development was an area of concern for both private and public sector organisations, but particularly for the latter. Although less than a half of private sector respondents reported enough was being done by their organisation to develop the next generation of leaders, the percentage of public sector managers agreeing with this statement was significantly lower.

The survey data suggests that most public sector managers are expected to take responsibility for their own career planning. Almost all managers polled agreed that 'career planning is mostly down to me' and this figure was significantly higher for PMI respondents. Although there may be exceptions to this for key groups of staff (e.g. through talent management or graduate programmes) the majority of managers must be active in managing their own career. In addition, it is a concern that about half of public sector managers and leaders claimed they do not receive any support for career development

Table 13.3 Percentage of Public Sector and Private Sector Respondents Agreeing with Leadership and Career Development Survey Items

Survey Item	% Agree	
	Public	Private
My organisation is doing enough to develop the next generation of leaders*	36	48
Career planning is mostly down to me*	94	81
There is little support for career development within my organisation*	51	40

*See footnote 3.

from their organisation. Whilst individuals are responsible for directing their own careers, where an organisation provides support both individuals and organisations benefit. Support allows managers to see how they can develop their career ambitions within an organisation and the organisation to create a pool of potential leaders. It may help to ensure that formal career development is available to all managers rather than elite groups.

The PMI findings indicate that, in spite of the current awareness about the importance of talent management, succession planning and leadership development, these are being neglected in the eyes of managers in both the public and private sectors. Research into both sectors supports these findings and concludes that managers see little in the way of a systematic or coordinated approach to developing and nurturing the next generation of leaders (Society of Chief Personnel Officers 2006).

The published literature describes the need for developing recruitment and retention strategies in order to attract and keep the best leaders in the public service. One of the main aims of the PIU project was to improve understanding in the public sector of how it can attract the leaders – and the leadership – to deliver public services for the 21st century. A key finding from this report was that although 'there is much excellent leadership in the public services today, there is evidence to suggest that the public services are not attracting or keeping the best leaders, and do not have sufficiently robust strategies for recruiting them to the posts that matter most' and that 'too few organisations seek actively to recruit the best leaders' (PIU 2001: 4).

Additional comments from both public and private sector respondents indicated an impression that organisations may overlook potential candidates already working in the public sector, and that there is an unfair preference to look externally for senior level appointments. This means that career progression can be limited and that succession planning and talent management are only taken seriously where external managers are involved. Buying-in much needed talent to fill current gaps in skills may send a strong negative message to those already working in the organisation that there is no plan to develop them above a certain level of management. Internal candidates can feel overlooked for senior roles in favour of someone from outside the public sector. Several public sector managers described the negative effects of bringing in managers who do not appear to appreciate the public service ethic. For example: '[the] influx of appointees from the private sector who are not properly inducted and do not understand either the constitution or ethos of the organisation and have a black/white view of public sector bad/private sector good led to confusion and lowered morale' and 'The employment of private sector workers has brought a very negative influence on the organisation. It has brought a lot of dissatisfaction into the organisation rather than a good influence.'

Bringing in external candidates can also mean that those working in the public sector may see this as being at the expense of their own career progression. Other managers described the need to look for suitable internal candidates before looking outside of the public sector, to use the talent that is potentially available to them:

'It is beneficial to pull people in from the Private Sector to add value, though it seems we often do not look to our own expertise or that of other government departments. I think it would be useful to have a "government network of excellence" with details of staff expertise and not just use external consultants all the time.' … 'It could improve the management skills of senior managers, to introduce a talent management and learning and development support for middle and senior managers rather than bring people in from the private sector who are perceived to be "higher calibre individuals".'

Several public sector managers also commented on the need to provide training for all employees, not just those in senior roles. For example: 'There has been a lot of leadership development for Heads of Department and I think this should be extended to the next level of managers who are trying to develop their leadership skills' and 'there is opportunity to learn and develop but little time due to priorities and little budget for external courses and conferences unless you are a member of the senior management team'.

Another comment illustrates the problems that can arise with long periods of interim appointments:

the resignation of our Chief Executive has provided me with an opportunity to step up into a different role but the length of time it has taken to recruit a replacement has meant a long period of instability under interim leadership when the organisation could have been enabled to grow rapidly if a successor had been groomed to take over.

Public sector workers are now being encouraged to receive leadership training and development earlier in their careers as it is realised that it is important to view leadership at all levels in an organisation, and develop the skills of all those working in the public sector, not only those at the top: 'leadership lies at all levels in an organisation…while top leaders are important, they are only one part of the jigsaw. People further down the organisation can have as much impact as senior leaders' (Sedgmore 2005). Wooldridge (2005) would like to see the public sector improve its approach to succession planning to ensure a level of continuity at the head of vital public sector organisations: 'we are trying to improve the quality of high level management but an important aspect of this is tackling the earlier stages in an individual's career – the time when you need to nurture and develop the leaders of tomorrow.' Departments, encouraged by the Blair Agenda, have created Leadership Academies typified by the members of Public Service

Leadership Alliance – academies to stimulate leadership development in defence, the police, fire, health, education and local government organised to build leadership capability set in its service context (Wallace and O'Reilly 2009).

Finally, public sector organisations are urged to develop their leadership strategies in a different way. As the public sector becomes increasingly complex it needs to devolve power and resources from the centre to those delivering public services. This has profound implications for the ways in which we develop our leaders (Benington 2006). It is now argued more and more that the search for an individual charismatic, inspirational and transformational leader to turn an organisation around – be it a school or an agency – is misguided; a wider cultural change is needed rather than a focus on initiatives aimed at enhancing leadership skills within the sector (Grint 2005).

Conclusion

Surveys of staff attitudes in government departments are not new. What is unique about the PMI is the ability to make direct comparisons between public sector and private sector data on a consistent basis and thereby inform new thinking on leadership and management and better executive development of public and private sector leaders wherever they are found. The results from the PMI confirm many existing impressions, but also offer fresh knowledge about leadership and management issues within the UK and provide a valuable insight into the specific challenges leaders and managers in different parts of the public sector face. Whilst the results reveal some encouraging findings, illustrating a positive picture of how managers and leaders are operating in the public sector, it also highlights issues and challenges for public sector organisations and their managers. The PMI points to issues that leaders in public organisations can now see with new perspectives. It also highlights leadership challenges in the public and private sectors that leaders can address to enhance public service delivery.

The increase in virtual team working and matrix management described suggests that the traditional approach of authority, hierarchy and command does not reflect the reality of today's public sector. As there is a need to turn towards non hierarchical ways of working there will be a greater demand for involvement, influence, shared (collaborative) and distributed (collegiate) leadership. In addition the findings indicate the importance of influencing others over whom one has no direct control and the difficulty respondents described with this. As a result, there is a strong perception that leadership skills need to be developed and strengthened. In response to changing roles, leadership development programmes are having to adapt from a single-department focus to cross-institutional leadership, and therefore place a greater emphasis on learning across sectors: drawing on best practice, and with a stronger emphasis on joining-up across sectors. Brookes (2007) describes the need for 'multifaceted leadership development' in today's 'multi-disciplinary, multifunctional and multi professional public sector world'. A statement from Hagen and Liddle (2007: 331–332) supports this view: 'modern day public sector leadership takes place within a very different global context than that of past decades and the capacity to solve societal problems and act independently has eroded'.

In addition to following up both the AMI and the PMI as a joint survey in the next two years to track changes in results, a future study will explore both public sector and private sector managers' views in more detail, specifically focusing on what 'effective public leadership' is and leadership development opportunities. Finally, the findings from the survey are being used to inform future requirements and priorities for executive development and to inform the design and development of learning processes, new programmes and individual sessions.

The global credit crunch and the huge growth in UK public borrowing points towards the end of growth in real terms in health and education spending and the real prospects of significant spending cuts in many areas of public services and we can expect considerable turmoil in public services in the next decade (as described by Rt Hon Alistair Darling in a speech on 17 June 2009 at the Mansion House). It will be interesting to explore whether the comparative data from future AMI and PMI surveys point to major changes in attitudes in the years ahead.

Acknowledgments

The authors would like to thank all colleagues from Ashridge and the NSG who were involved in the PMI. Particular thanks go to Viki Holton, David Sweeney and Julian Rizzalo.

Notes

1. A total of 1,394 respondents working in the UK public sector responded. This group included an even split of males (52%) and females (48%), with an age range from under 30 to over 50 years of age. Respondents were located all over the UK, with almost one half based in London (46%). Just over one half described themselves as senior or middle management (40% and 12% respectively), with the remaining 48% classifying themselves as professionals/specialist managers. Just over one half of respondents were working in a central government department (53%); around one in ten for a Local Authority (LA) (11%) and 14% for an executive agency.

2. A total of 708 respondents working in private sector organisations responded to the AMI. The profile of the private respondents was similar to the profile of public sector respondents in age; length of time in organisation; number of people working in organisation. However, just under one half of private sector respondents were based outside of Europe (28%). A further difference is in the gender divide: whilst the public sector survey had approximately even numbers of males and females responding the private sector respondents were made up of more males than females

(77% and 23% respectively). In addition, private sector respondents were made up of more senior managers (60%).

3. Levels of agreement referred to throughout the chapter were calculated by combining 'agree' and 'strongly agree' responses. Asterisk indicates significance at the 1% level when a chi-square test was used to test for statistical differences.

References

Benington, J. (2000) 'The Modernisation and Improvement of Government and Public Services', *Public Money and Management*, Volume 20, Issue 2, pp. 3–9.

Benington, J. (2006) 'Approaching Public Service Reform: Overview of the Conference Themes', *Reforming Public Services, Putting People First*, pp. 8–27. Sunningdale: National School of Government.

Brookes, S. (2007) '360 Degree Leadership in the Public Sector: Developing an Approach to Collective Leadership'. Paper presented at *Leading the Future of the Public Sector: The Third Transatlantic Dialogue*, University of Delaware, Newark, Delaware, USA.

Broussine, M. and Miller, C. (2005) 'Leadership, Ethical Dilemmas and "Good" Authority in Public Service Partnership Working', *Business Ethics: A European Review*, 14(4): 379–391.

Cabinet Office (2006) *Publication of First Capability Reviews Steps up Civil Service Reform*. Available from: http://www.cabinetoffice.gov.uk/newsroom/news_releases/2006/060719_capability.aspx (Accessed June 22nd 2009).

Capability Review (2007) *Tranche 3: Findings and Common Themes Civil Service – Strengths and Challenges*. Available from: http://www.civilservice.gov.uk/Assets/Tranche_3_summary_ tcm6-1074.pdf (Accessed May 13th 2009).

Charlesworth, K., Cook, P. and Crozier, G. (2003) *Leading Change in the Public Sector: Making the Difference*. London: Chartered Management Institute.

Chartered Institute of Personnel and Development (2003) *People and Public Services. Why Central Targets Miss the Mark. The Change Agenda*. London: Chartered Institute of Personnel and Development. Available from: http://www.cipd.co.uk/NR/rdon-lyres/650C1204-FA86-482C-908B-F326706A24BA/0/peopleandpublicservices.pdf (Accessed: February 9th 2008).

Dunoon, D. (2002) 'Rethinking Leadership for the Public Sector', *Australian Journal of Public Administration*, 61(3): 3–18.

Horne, M. and Stedman-Jones, D. (2001) *Leadership: The Challenge for All?* London: Chartered Management Institute/DTI/DEMOS.

Grint, K. (2005) *Leadership: Limits and Possibilities*. Basingstoke: Palgrave Macmillan.

Hagen, R. and Liddle, J. (2007) 'Changing Strategic Direction for Executive Development in the Public Sector', *International Journal of Public Sector Management*, 20(4): 325–340.

Holton, V., Dent, F. and Rabbetts, J. (2008) *Ashridge Management Index: Meeting the Challenges of the 21st Century*. Berkhamsted, UK: Ashridge.

KPMG/Economist Intelligence Unit (2007) *Performance Agenda: An International Government Survey*. Canada: KPMG International.

Milner, E. and Joyce, P. (2005) *Lessons in Leadership. Meeting the Challenges of Public Services Management*. Oxford: Routledge.

Mottram, R. (1996) *Speech to Senior Management Foundation Training Programme*. Ashridge Business School, June 1996.

OECD (2009) *Government at a Glance 2009*, Paris 22 October 2009 OECD.

Paine Schofield, C.B. (2008a) *Public Sector Leadership: A Literature Review*. Ashridge, Berkhamsted, UK: Ashridge Public Leadership Centre.

Paine Schofield, C.B. (2008b) 'Key Challenges Facing Public Sector Leaders: Themes from the Ashridge Public Leadership Centre Essay Competition 2007', *The Ashridge Journal Public Sector Issue*, pp. 33–38. Autumn 2008.

Performance and Innovation Unit (PIU) (2001) *Strengthening Leadership in the Public Sector*. London: Cabinet Office.

Prime Minister's Strategy Unit (2004) *Strategy Survival Guide*. Available from: http://interactive.cabinetoffice.gov.uk/strategy/survivalguide/dev/index.htm (Accessed June 22nd 2009).

Professional Skills for Government. Available from: http://www.civilservice.gov.uk/people/psg/PSG-framework.aspx (Accessed May 13th 2009).

Sedgmore, L. (2005) Public Sector Leadership Conference, Queen Elizabeth Conference Centre. London, April 21 2005.

Skills Strategy for Central Government (2008). Available from: http://www.government-skills.gov.uk/skills-strategy/index.asp (Accessed May 13th 2009).

Society of Chief Personnel Officers (2006) *Talent Management: The Capacity to Make the Difference*. London: SOCPO.

Wallace, M. and O'Reilly, D. (2009) 'Developing Organisation Leaders as Change Agents in the Public Services'. ESRC Report – Research Award No RES-000-23-1136. Cardiff University Business School and University of Bristol.

Wooldridge, E. (2005) Public Sector Leadership Conference, Queen Elizabeth Conference Centre, London, April 21 2005.

Part III
Public Leadership in Action?

14

Testing Adaptive Leadership Theory in Practice: The Policing of the Drumcree Demonstrations in Northern Ireland

Irwin Turbitt And John Benington

Introduction

This chapter is a case study of radical change in the leadership strategy for the policing of the annual Drumcree Sunday demonstrations in Northern Ireland between 2002 and 2004. It is co-authored by a practitioner and an academic, who were both involved in different ways in the development and implementation of the alternative strategy in practice. Benington researches and teaches public leadership and public value on the Warwick MPA degree (a public sector MBA) and other courses. Turbitt was (then) a chief superintendent in the Police Service of Northern Ireland, the silver commander for the policing of the Drumcree demonstrations, and a participant in the Warwick MPA degree course from 2000 to 2003.

Turbitt decided to test an alternative approach to the policing strategy for Drumcree, based upon an application and development of theories of Public Value (Moore 1995) and of Adaptive Leadership (Heifetz 1994) to which he had been introduced by Benington at Warwick.

He invited Benington to shadow him and the police and the army during the annual Drumcree Sunday demonstrations in July 2002, July 2003 and July 2004, and in various parts of the preparation and de-briefing for the July events. They discussed the events as they occurred and in many subsequent discussions over the years.

This chapter is therefore based upon Turbitt's first hand experience as the Police Silver Commander for the whole operation and upon Benington's participant observation and field notes taken at Drumcree weekends each July over three successive years, and upon years of joint reflection on these events. The chapter draws on a previous joint article published in Leadership, Volume 3 (4) Nov 2007, but in this case Turbitt, as a new breed of 'pracademic', has taken over as the lead author!

Heifetz's framework for adaptive leadership

This chapter applies and tests Heifetz's ideas about adaptive leadership in the complex situation surrounding the Drumcree demonstrations in Northern Ireland. This is an annual demonstration that for many years has hit the national and international news as a result of the disorder and violence associated with it. One of the groups in the demonstration (the Unionist and protestant Orange Order Lodge and its protestant supporters) would describe it as the exercise and defence of their religious freedom to worship and to parade. Another of the main groups in the demonstration (the Nationalist and Catholic community of the Garvaghy Road, down which the Orange Order want to march) would describe it as the abuse of that freedom, in an attempt to make political capital out of an event that has little to do with worship but much to do with sectarian provocation and coat trailing.

In his book Leadership Without Easy Answers, Heifetz (1994) sets out a framework for 'adaptive leadership' which can act as a compass for public managers facing complex problems – a compass rather than a map because 'adaptive leadership' applies to circumstances in which the future is uncertain, unclear and even unseeable. The journey on which the public leader has embarked has a destination that may not be obvious, and may not even be definable at the point of embarkation. So this is very different from the traditional view that sees the work of the leader as being first and foremost to establish a clear direction and destination – and to make it so appealing to followers that they are energised to act in a way that moves the organisation (or system) towards that destination. However, many situations do not fit this traditional view; they are messy or complex and/or contested – there is little or no agreement about what are the causes of the problem being faced, and even less agreement about the solutions necessary. In fact in such situations there may be no easy answers at all. For example, there may be no easy answers to the problem of men physically abusing women in the privacy of their home or personal relationships. There may be no easy answers to climate change or world poverty. However that is not to say that no useful work can be done that makes progress in the situation faced by victims in those circumstances, and also that adds value to the public sphere.

The adaptive leadership framework

Heifetz begins by distinguishing between people in positions of authority, and people in positions with no formal authority, who nevertheless choose to exercise leadership as he defines it. Even though we know intellectually that these are two discrete categories, often in day to day life we conflate the two. So there are senior authority figures who while occupying the formal position of a 'leader' do not exercise much if any 'leadership'; and equally people with much less formal executive authority who clearly exercise 'leadership' in many circumstances.

Secondly Heifetz distinguishes between technical work and adaptive work. A technical problem is one for which an agreed definition or diagnosis can be assembled, and to which an already known solution can then be applied. An adaptive problem is one where there is little or no agreement about the causes or nature of the problem, and where there is no available technical solution – indeed there may not be in existence a technical solution for the situation. In such situations technical work becomes an enabler of adaptive work rather than the way the problem is fixed. In addition an adaptive challenge is one where there is a gap between the expressed value system of the protagonists in the system, and their behaviour in the system as observed by others.

Heifetz argues that the first piece of work required by the public manager seeking to exercise adaptive leadership is to 'get onto the balcony' – the analogy here being to a balcony and a dance floor in a dance hall. The balcony is a place where instead of being able to view only the person you are dancing with, or a small group of dancers around you, you can get a wider view over the whole system contained by the dance hall (e.g. all the dancers, the dance band and the bar). You are then able to make observations and subsequent interpretations that will better inform you when you decide to rejoin the dancers on the dance floor.

In the Drumcree situation the balcony work involved a great deal of preparation and analysis of the history and of the context – including reading Ryder and Kearney (2001) and others who set out to explain the history of the Drumcree parade – an annual event that dates back to 1807 when the first Orange Order march and service took place at Drumcree church.

In addition to studying the history and the context, 'getting on the balcony' involved meeting many of the protagonists ('dancers') in the Drumcree scenario to understand their differing perspectives on the situation – for example, the Orange Order leadership, the leadership of the Garvaghy Road residents coalition, and the leadership of the two main political groupings (Unionist and Nationalist) that worked in the local council district.

This kind of preparatory balcony work is an essential requirement for someone planning an intervention in a messy complex dangerous situation like the Drumcree demonstrations. Heifetz's idea is that managers should move frequently, if not continuously, between the dance floor and the balcony – between action and reflection, with all action being the subject of reflection from the balcony and all reflection from the balcony better informing the next piece of action on the dance floor.

Having made some preliminary judgements about the nature of the context and of the system, the next piece of work suggested by Heifetz is to identify whether the problem to be tackled is a technical (or 'tame') problem or an 'adaptive' (or 'wicked') problem. So for example within the Drumcree situation the Orange Order see and present themselves as a religious institution enabling members, primarily men, to understand better what the Bible says, and providing them with an organisation that supports and encourages them to live their lives according to those Biblical standards. Yet from a 'balcony' perspective many observers see great variance between this self-perception and Orange Order behaviour in practice at Drumcree. Since 1985, each year, following a church service a period of disorder occurs, sometimes involving the use of firearms and explosive devices.

This is Heifetz's second principle of 'identifying the adaptive challenge'. The very act of verbalising any observed gap between espoused beliefs and actual behaviour is often found to cause some distress. The initial reaction of the 'dancers' is often to attempt to deny, or avoid the observation, to challenge the observer, to resist the interpretation that the observer has made, and sometimes to attack the observer as the problem. In some circumstances there is a strong and dysfunctional set of responses, strengthened by the dancers closing themselves off not just from a capacity to be reflective about their dancing but also from other groups of 'dancers'. They therefore continue to reinforce their own view that sees their behaviour as being in alignment with their value set and that the problem lies outside their group, rather than within themselves.

The third principle of adaptive leadership which Heifetz refers to is 'cooking the conflict'. The aim here is to generate sufficient felt distress amongst the protagonists that they become prepared to work on the adaptive challenge that has been identified. Too little distress, and complacency will not be disturbed; too much distress and the situation can boil over, or for example, at Drumcree, burst out, in terms of extreme violence. Leaders should aim to create a zone (or 'holding environment' – see below) where distress is used productively to enable or obligate a change in the behaviour of the protagonists so that there is (re)alignment between the expressed or required value set and the actual behaviours observed from the balcony. Thus protagonists are maintained within a 'productive zone of distress'. It is often difficult to get participants to be self-critically reflective, and to maintain disciplined attention to the challenge of bringing about the changes in thinking and behaviour that are required. One of the features that is often apparent during adaptive leadership is 'work avoidance'. The protagonists may argue not so much that adaptive work does not need to be done, but that there is other important technical work that needs to be done sooner – if not right now. It may even be that this other work is escalated to a position where it is critical and so having to deal with it now becomes unavoidable.

Another key feature of the leadership of adaptive work is that it is the people facing the challenge that need to do the work that is required to make progress on, or to bring about a solution to, the problem – to see themselves as part of the problem as well as part of the solution. This work requires leading and learning while doing – working together often in complex and difficult circumstances to navigate a way forward in the fog, with only a compass and no map. This is challenging as 'followers' often have a strong desire to give their problems over to heroic 'leaders' whom they expect to solve the problems without any adaptive work being required of them as followers. This is very seductive to both sides of course. The authority figure, the leader, can bask in followers' fantasies about their magical skills; the followers can stand back and simply observe the leader's work and receive the benefits of it (or criticise it when it goes wrong). Refusal by the leader to collude with this fantasy about their own magical skills, will often lead to disappointment among followers and a labelling of the leader as weak or a failure.

In Heifetz's phrase, the adaptive work has to be given back to the people with the problem (but at a rate that they can stand). So adaptive leadership involves getting the entire system to work on the problem, to obligate the protagonists and 'followers' to work jointly on the problem – in a process that many will find distressing. However if that distress can be maintained in its productive zone and if disciplined attention to that work can be maintained, then progress can be made in tackling the adaptive challenge. In this chapter the focus in the case study will be on giving back the work to the Orange Order leadership responsible for the Drumcree parade.

Another feature of Heifetz's adaptive leadership framework is the need to involve the voices of leadership from below – those people who, because of their lack of formal authority in the system, or because of their position at the periphery of the organisation, find it difficult to get their voice heard, to have their point of view taken seriously, or to have their observations recognised and validated. Often leaders hear the voices from below as voices of complaint, voices of whingeing, voices of destructive dissent and so on, rather than as voices which may be 'speaking truth to power'. Heifetz suggests that adaptive leaders need to learn to 'listen to the music beneath the words' – to sense the underlying feelings about key issues at the frontline. Taking a balcony perspective, seeing beyond the immediate presenting problems, looking below the cosmetic surface, hearing the painful messages and difficult truths – all these enable adaptive leaders to gain fresh insights into the changes that need to be made. The example given here will be the front-line public order police for whom Turbitt was a senior authority figure but of course there are also many other 'voices of leadership from below' in the 'Drumcree' system.

The way forward in these complex adaptive situations is a path that is not yet known, a route that has not yet been mapped. What is required therefore is a process of experimentation, a continuous process of trial and error, a process of learning by doing, of 'failing and falling forward faster'. This will require much experimental work across the system involving many of the 'voices of leadership from below'. Much of this adaptive work is likely to be distressing and possibly distasteful to many of the participants in the process and so it is necessary to provide a safe but challenging environment within which painful work can be accomplished. This holding environment clearly has physical dimensions to it, in the sense that the adaptive work has to be done by groups of people who need to be in some kind of physical relationship with each other. The physical spaces created for this work (e.g. location, layout, size, shape, and symbolism of the places chosen for the engagement) can have a major impact on the results. However, the creation of a holding environment for adaptive work is much more dependent on the social construction of those relationships and interactions that are necessary for the adaptive challenge to be identified and the painful nettles to be grasped. Those exercising adaptive leadership therefore have to do two different kinds of work in parallel – both the substantive work in moving the system forward, and also the process work of creating a sustainable capacity to do the substantive work (which includes the creation, development, and maintenance of an effective 'holding environment').

There were many meetings (with the Orange Order, the Garvaghy Road Residents Coalition and others) and other social encounters where the

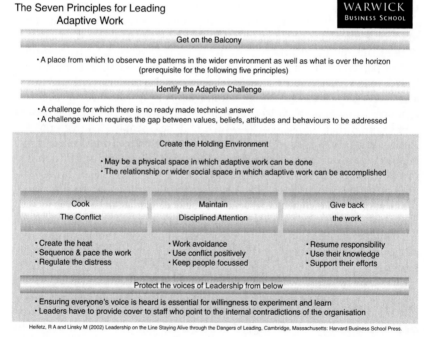

Figure 14.1 The Seven Principles for Leading Adaptive Work (derived from Heifetz 1994)

primary work being done was not to move the system forward in a concrete manner but to strengthen and develop the holding environment so that in future, at the next meeting perhaps, more substantive difficult work, challenging work, adaptive work within that productive zone of distress could be accomplished.

This adaptive leadership framework is illustrated below. Note that while it looks like a route map for solving problems in a linear fashion this is only because of the two dimensional nature of the paper it appears on. In practice the principles will be used in many different configurations both concurrently and sequentially.

So how does this adaptive leadership framework work out in practice? The next section describes and discusses the conscious application of this theoretical framework in the policing of the Drumcree demonstrations in Northern Ireland over the three year period from 2002–2004.

Testing the adaptive leadership framework in policing Drumcree

Turbitt first decided to experiment with the adaptive leadership framework when he was part of the command team responsible for the policing of a public order situation known as the Holy Cross school dispute in Northern Ireland. Using the adaptive leadership ideas as a way of reframing the policing of the Holy Cross school dispute (which previously seemed to have required 1,500 police and soldiers to protect children on their journey to school) he found that the situation could be changed and the violence reduced as the two protagonist communities were helped to find new ways of living sufficiently peacefully with each other to enable the primary school children to travel to and from school safely. (The Holy Cross dispute deserves a separate case study of its own, but there is no space to analyse this here).

A few weeks later Turbitt was promoted to be the District Police Commander in Craigavon, a police district that included Drumcree parish church, an event that had been troublesome in Turbitt's own police career for at least 20 years. Turbitt had spent many hours policing Drumcree over successive years, although he had never before been permanently stationed in the area in which this Drumcree church was situated. So he decided that from the beginning of his intervention into the Drumcree situation, as the local area police commander, he would seek to be guided by the adaptive leadership framework – he would seek to navigate his way forward and try and create a public value outcome using Heifetz's ideas as a compass. He began by researching and reading the history of Drumcree, and meeting as many of the protagonists and experts, self-proclaimed or otherwise, relevant to understanding the situation. He did not focus only on the technical work required of the police in their public order policing capacity but also more widely on trying to understand the complex dynamics within the situation.

He decided that of the adaptive challenges he observed there were two that would require work in the immediate future. The first was an adaptive challenge within policing and the second was an adaptive challenge for the Orange Order leadership in Portadown. Taking the adaptive challenge for the police first, Turbitt was puzzled as to why despite the great deal of violence over at least 20 years, there had been an extremely low level of prosecutions and convictions, particularly of Orange Order members, for rioting at Drumcree. His initial assumption would have been that the police only needed to improve their technical capacity to collect evidence, process it successfully and to present it against criminals in the court process to secure convictions. However he was now alert to a second possibility, that there might be adaptive work to be done. The adaptive challenge (the gap between the espoused values of the police force in Northern Ireland and their actual behaviours) was that the Orange Order is a protestant organisation and the Northern Ireland police service has traditionally been (not exclusively but mainly) a protestant organisation in terms of its staffing. An observation from a catholic nationalist (balcony) perspective might be that the police would not want to prosecute the Orange Order because in spite of their publicly espoused values, privately they supported the Orange Order and were never likely to prosecute them. This was a concern that Turbitt also shared, never having served in this area before. However, it turned out to his relief that this was not the case and that the reason for the low level of prosecutions was in fact a poor technical application of the procedures that would lead to the better collection of evidence leading to convictions. That meant that while there was work to be done within the police, it was technical work rather than adaptive work, at least with regard to improving the prosecution rate at Drumcree.

Turbitt then turned his attention to the Orange Order – an institution that claimed to be deeply religious in terms of its value set, and loyal to the Bible and to the Crown. However from the balcony many people, including Turbitt, observed that at Drumcree they were engaged regularly and repeatedly in public disorder at a level that would be called rioting – the most serious challenge to the state's authority short of terrorism. This clearly posed an adaptive challenge for the Orange Order leadership, and one that Turbitt chose to make his focus in his first period of working on and within the Drumcree situation.

This meant that a holding environment would need to be created if adaptive change was to be achieved – not just a holding environment for Turbitt and the Orange Order but a holding environment that could contain the adaptive work with many of the factions that made up the Drumcree system. One way of beginning the process of establishing that holding environment was for Turbitt to set up a series of regular and ongoing meetings with the various protagonists. Previous police practice had not been to engage so intensively in such meetings in advance of the disorder, but rather once disorder broke out and got to a critical level. Instead Turbitt decided to try and establish a regular series of meetings as part of the process leading up to Drumcree and so set up four groups (loyalist or unionist politicians; nationalist or republican politicians; the Orange Order local leadership; and the Garvaghy Road residents group who represented the largely Catholic population in the disputed area where the Orange Order were not now allowed to march) Turbitt reached agreement with all these four groups that they would meet regularly in the run up to Drumcree.

Turbitt's intention was to involve these groups as much as possible in the pre-planning of the policing of Drumcree in a way that had not previously been done, but also to seek agreement that during the actual Drumcree operation (usually a period of ten days), these groupings would meet every day to review the situation, to reflect on what had happened in the previous 24 hours and to try to co-produce what might be possible in the up and coming 24 hours. The establishment of these four groups was not of course by itself the development of a holding environment but it provided a forum that could be used, a set of emerging relationships that could be built on and strengthened to create a holding environment within which the adaptive work could be done.

The first bit of adaptive work that needed to be done was to discuss the adaptive challenge for the Orange Order leadership i.e. the gap between their values and their behaviours – the fact that they claimed to be God-fearing and law abiding, but some of them were engaged regularly in rioting. In discussions with the Orange Order and with their political representatives it became clear to Turbitt that they had not yet seen or accepted this challenge. Their view was that yes of course there was rioting at Drumcree but it was not the Orange Order or their supporters that were involved or responsible; they argued that it was other elements, perhaps unwanted elements, perhaps paramilitary elements, but certainly it was not themselves, it was others, it was 'them not us'. So rather than looking 'in the mirror' and recognising the adaptive challenge for themselves and for their group, their response was to 'look out of the window' and to blame other groups for the rioting and also to suggest that part of the difficulty was that the police did not act properly, did not act professionally, did not design their operation very well and therefore it was partly the police's fault the rioting occurred.

It was obvious that until the Orange Order leadership and their politicians recognised this challenge they were not going to be able to work on it. It was clear that they had become deeply attached to the view that they were not the problem and therefore there would be a significant level of distress when they were forced or obligated to recognise that they were part of the problem and therefore had to be party to finding a solution. Turbitt's view was that it was necessary to start finding ways of giving back the work to the Orange Order leadership and their loyalist unionist politicians as well as to the Garvaghy Road residents and their nationalist republican politicians.

One way in which this might be accomplished was to alter the big barrier that was used to block the parade from crossing the bridge at Drumcree just down from the church. This bridge was the legal line established by the independent Parades Commission, who ruled that the Orange Order parade should not pass over this bridge and should not march back into Portadown town centre down the mainly Catholic Garvaghy Road. It was the responsibility of course of the parade organisers and demonstrators not to pass over this bridge, but the police had taken on this responsibility, supported by the military, by putting up a huge concrete and steel barrier that was constructed of shipping containers 20 feet long, eight feet high, eight feet wide and weighing 30 tons. This very definitely blocked the bridge and stopped the parade from marching down the Garvagy Road.

In a sense the big barrier was symbolically saying to the Orange Order you do not have to do any work here; we the state and its agents (the Northern Ireland police and the British army) will do the work for you. We will put up this big barrier, there is not any way in which the parade can get past that, and so you do not have to do the adaptive work. The big barrier did not stop the rioting of course; it did not stop missiles, bullets and nail bombs being hurled across and injuring police officers and soldiers. However, paradoxically, the big barrier did stop the police from being able to disperse the crowd, or to arrest those people who had committed serious public order offences, so even in a technical sense it was not terribly successful. It was successful in stopping the parade but not successful in stopping the disorder. It prevented the police from enforcing the law, and it allowed the Orange Order to escape their responsibility for demonstrating within the framework of the law.

Turbitt thought that a lighter lower barrier would share the work of policing the parade more equally between the state and the citizens. The small barrier might become a means by which co-production would be required, would be obligated. It was clear that the Orange Order and the unionist politicians were not going to initiate this adaptive work; it was comfortable for them to allow the state to do it. So Turbitt started conversations around the fact that if the Orange Order's parade was lawful and peaceful, then a very large 30 ton barrier seemed to be rather over the top, a disproportionate response by the police and army, which did not recognise the Orange Order's ability to act lawfully and peacefully. So the smaller barrier was presented as a positive way of demonstrating to the world, through the media, that the Orange Order were lawful and peaceful. There was resistance to this change but it was not clear in any of the meetings what was the substance of the resistance. While Turbitt and his police colleagues were trying to do their balcony work in those meetings, trying to understand what the issues were, it was clear that the Orange Order leadership particularly were distressed about this idea of a smaller barrier, but not why. When Turbitt showed them a picture of what it might look like they were very distressed, but Turbitt was not able to read the reason for their distress at the time and so pushed ahead with the plan.

Turbitt did a lot of work technically with the police and the army; a lot of new tactics were required around public order policing, around arrest tactics, around dispersal tactics and so little by little the 'voices of leadership from below' within Turbitt's policing community and military community became more comfortable with the idea of the smaller barrier. They recognised that the big barrier did not work – it did not stop the rioting but it did stop people from being arrested who had hurt police and army personnel physically with their missiles, rocks, bombs, and bullets. The small barrier presented a much greater opportunity for arresting offenders. Perhaps it increased the risk of police injuries but it would also certainly increase the possibility for a much more flexible, dynamic public order operation. And so this work was done, and agreement was reached with the voices of leadership from below within the police and army. This provided Turbitt with an increasingly strong level of authorisation from below as well as from above, when he went to have this new set of technical tactics approved by his gold commander and chief constable.

So on Drumcree Sunday July 7th 2002 the new tactics were used for the first time. About 1,200 Orange men marched with their bands of pipes and drums, from Portadown city centre out to the Drumcree church (about three miles) where they held their traditional church service. After the service, the Orange Order paraded down to the Drumcree bridge which was blocked by this new much smaller barrier. There the Orange Order leadership made their ritual protest and handed a letter of complaint to the assistant chief constable, the gold commander for the operation.

However the crowd very quickly became aggressive – people spat in the faces of the assistant chief constable and a colleague with him, others threw rocks and branches at the police, while others smashed the smaller lighter barrier down, and surged on the police who were wearing full riot protection gear and shields, but were no longer protected behind a big barrier. This very quickly spilled over into a high level of rioting, involving not just the hangers on but also some of the people who had just come out of church, dressed in their Sunday suits, some wearing black bowler hats, and Orange Order collarettes. It was almost as if they could not contain themselves and the distress and anger burst out, and vented itself in breaking down the holding environment. Over 30 police officers were injured, plastic baton rounds (bullets) were fired by the police, and their hand-held batons were used, and the situation moved into a period of crisis. Eventually the big barrier was put back, in place of the smashed smaller barrier, by army drivers, water cannons were brought in, and command and control was re-established. The rioting stopped, the Orange Order and their supporters pulled back, but by this time the police had collected a large amount of mainly video-evidence of the build up to the rioting, the preparation for the rioting and the rioting itself. The police and the army were therefore equipped to start arresting people using their airborne surveillance, and their mobile communications, stopping offenders leaving the area of the riot, arresting them as they left Drumcree on foot and in cars and buses, and charging them with the criminal offences for which they had good video-evidence.

The distress was felt strongly by the Orange Order. For the first time the TV news reports showed that it was not just dysfunctional elements within the crowd, or paramilitary groups, who were rioting, but also Orange Order members themselves. These television pictures of Orange Order brethren just out of church on a Sunday lunchtime, personally involved in rioting and causing serious injuries to police officers, struck deep at the value set of the Orange Order, and caused great distress in the Orange Order institution across Northern Ireland. That distress caused many Orange Order members to withdraw support from the Drumcree demonstration, and even to leave the Orange Order. Many reflected deeply, and maybe for the first time they saw themselves as many other people had seen them for a long period of time.

When Turbitt and his colleagues met with the Orange Order leadership and with the Unionist councillors following this riot, it was their initial intention to increase the level of distress in the Orange Order community. They felt that they had got the attention of the people in authority positions within the Orange Order and that they could now turn up the heat and transform the distress into productive energy and actions to improve their behaviour i.e. make it lawful. However it became apparent very quickly that the Orange Order leadership and the councillors were already overwhelmed by their distress and what was required instead at this conjuncture, as an act of leadership from the police, was to lower the level of distress, not to increase it. What was required metaphorically was for the police to sit down shoulder to shoulder with the Orange leadership and to figure out how to work jointly together on the adaptive challenge – how to demonstrate lawfully and peacefully. The adaptive challenge was now a shared challenge. The arrests, the remands in custody, the negative publicity, and the detention of Orange brethren in custody and then on remand within the criminal justice system for several months, helped to maintain the Orange Order's disciplined attention to this adaptive challenge. The Orange Order were interested to know what sort of sentences their brethren might get if they were convicted of rioting and were distressed to learn that they could get serious prison sentences. This was particularly distressing for middle class professional people, who had good jobs and who had never previously been in trouble with the police, and so the distress was felt not just in the Orange Order leadership but also had a ripple effect throughout the wider Unionist community.

So Turbitt decided to regulate and reduce that distress, by suggesting to the Orange Order and to the unionist politicians that there was an opportunity for them to exercise adaptive leadership by working with the police, the local community, the church and other stakeholders to make the 2003 Drumcree parade lawful and peaceful. To make it in reality what it had been in the minds of the Orange Order leadership.

The distress felt by the Orange Order at being brought face to face with the gap between their own private image of themselves as God-fearing, law abiding citizens, and the public reality of their behaviour at Drumcree was quite shocking to them. So by using that distress productively, keeping the Orange Order focused on what might happen if there was similar trouble the next year, Turbitt aimed to 'give back the work to the people with the problem but at a rate which they can stand' Notice that this was not to abandon the Orange Order, or to dump all of the work on the Orange Order, but to engage in a careful process of adaptive leadership that resulted in the Orange Order starting to work alongside the police to help regulate the 2003 demonstration.

The main adaptive work was about getting the Orange Order to start taking more responsibility for what happened at Drumcree, not necessarily because they were intellectually convinced of the need for radical change in their thinking and behaviour but because they also saw that not to do the adaptive work might be even more damaging to their members still facing court cases. State authority (the police's power to arrest and prosecute offenders) was here being used not only to deal with individual offenders but also to stimulate wider changes in thinking and behaviour within the Orange Order and the local community.

This was quite difficult for the police as well of course, given that working closely with the Orange Order could easily be misinterpreted either genuinely or malevolently by the nationalist community, the Garvaghy Road residents and their politicians. So Turbitt and his police colleagues also kept meetings going with the nationalist communities and organisations and their representatives, and discussions were started about what would need to be done if the Orange Order did have a lawful peaceful parade. If that happened then many of the objections that the nationalist community had to the Drumcree parade would start to weaken – it would be more challenging to present the parade as something that was inherently unlawful and destructive of community relations.

And so adaptive work was being done at different stages and at different levels and around different elements within different factions within the overall system that was Drumcree. In the run up to the 2003 parade the intensity of the work increased and discussions started about how much work the Orange Order would do, how much policing the official state police would have to do, and how much policing the nationalist community would do with regard to their own community, on Drumcree

Sunday 2003. As these conversations continued they became much more practically focused, looking at what different options on the ground might look like in July of 2003. Some of this was around whether the small barrier would be there in 2003 as it had been in 2002. Of course there was a lobby from the Orange Order to return to the big barrier. Turbitt interpreted this as a desire to avoid doing the adaptive work of taking responsibility for the lawfulness of the demonstration, and instead to let the big barrier do this work as it were. However, by maintaining disciplined attention on the adaptive challenge and by holding steady and resisting that pressure to go back to the big barrier, Turbitt tried to move forward but also to support the Orange Order – to maintain them in a productive zone of distress. One way this new ability and willingness of the Orange Order to do some adaptive work manifested itself was for them to decide to put a line of orange tape in front of the small barrier – a symbol that they intended to demonstrate within the boundaries of the law. The police provided the Orange Order with this orange tape and with posts to put in the ground to hold it, but the signs that said 'Portadown Orange Order Do Not Cross' were the Orange Order's own. So anyone who chose to cross that line was separating themselves from the Orange Order. They were putting themselves beyond the Orange Order and so the Orange Order could symbolically separate themselves from anyone who did that. In this way anyone who broke through the Orange line and found themselves in conflict with the state would have made an active decision to leave the Orange Order community, so a clear visible separation could be made between those who were legitimate, lawful, peaceful God-fearing members of the Orange Order and those that were not. That was just one example within the whole process of giving back the work to the Orange Order. A lot of other work was done at many different levels in many different ways.

In many ways the parade and the policing of the parade in 2003 were co-produced, by the church, by the Orange Order and by the police – the police instead of doing all the work, backed up by the big barrier and other heavy military hardware, were creating a set of relationships, a holding environment within which the adaptive work was being facilitated. It was adaptive work facilitated by the obligation that had been created by the arrests and the public shame of the previous year's rioting, and by the ongoing distress of knowing that Orange Order members were still being held on remand and within the criminal justice system awaiting trial for their riotous behaviour the previous year.

In July 2003 the Drumcree parade passed off lawfully and peacefully and for the first time in over 20 years there were no disturbances at Drumcree either on the Sunday after the church service or on the Sunday evening, or the Monday or on any day following, right up until the time of writing. In 2004 much more of the policing work was done by the Orange Order and much less of it by the state police – and so on through 2005, 2006, 2007 and 2008 until it is now almost totally policed by the Orange Order with the police acting much more in a standby capacity, to back up the Orange Order should that be necessary but not standing any more on the front line; it is clear that this is the Orange Order's responsibility and they have accepted it and have developed a capacity to do it enabled over that period by successive police commanders and a whole variety of strengthening relationships.

Conclusions

The work described above is a discussion of the use of the theory of adaptive leadership in practice – not a *post hoc* application of the theory following a reflection on the practice, but an example of a practitioner consciously using and testing the theory, proactively navigating his way forward into the complex environment of Drumcree, guided by the compass of Heifetz's framework. Using trial and error, action and reflection, experiment and review, Turbitt was able to take some small and not so small steps in new directions, and to discover and lead some innovative approaches to the situation, which have helped to unfreeze some deeply ingrained patterns of behaviour. Notice that the problem is not solved; Drumcree is still a complex problem but it is not now so draining for the public nor for the police nor for the two divided communities.

It is right to question whether and how far there is any cause and effect linkage between the actions Turbitt took to reframe the Drumcree problem as one requiring adaptive leadership and the reduction in violence over a three year period. There were of course many other factors influencing the external context, including the Good Friday agreement and the establishment of the new institutions arising from it. 2002 was the first year the Police Service of Northern Ireland, as opposed to its predecessor, the Royal Ulster Constabulary (RUC), had policed Drumcree. The power sharing Northern Ireland Assembly had been established (but was in trouble and collapsed in the autumn of 2002) with a Unionist First Minister and a Sinn Fein Deputy First Minister in charge.

Our suggestion however is simply that there has been an observable change in the patterns of behaviour in and around Drumcree as a result of a thoughtful series of experiments in adaptive leadership, initially by and through the police and the army and then increasingly through various stakeholders within the community – first within the Orange Order leadership at Drumcree/Portadown and then increasingly deeper within the Orange Order community and within the wider loyalist and Unionist community.

There is also evidence of adaptive learning through engagement with the wider nationalist community to the extent that in the run up to the Drumcree parade in 2008 the Orange Order leadership met with Gerry Adams, the president of the nationalist party Sinn Fein. The Orange Order's narrative had been that Drumcree had never been a problem until Gerry Adams decided to make it a problem, that Gerry Adams was the main cause of the problem and they would never meet him or anyone associated with him. Now they find themselves able to sit in the same room and have a conversation with that person. Did the use of adaptive leadership set up a set of observable and non-observable changes in the dynamics of the system that eventually led to this breakthrough? We think so.

Our experience suggests that the adaptive leadership approach can be applied usefully to many complex problem situations. Such situations will not be solved by technical knowledge alone. However such problems might just be subject to progress if we adopt an experimental value-creating exploratory mindset, navigating our way forward into the fog using the compass of adaptive leadership, observing and acting, reflecting and experimenting, failing and reflecting and trying again. Always trying again.

References

Benington, J. and Turbitt, I. (2007) 'Policing the Drumcree Demonstrations in Northern Ireland: Testing Leadership Theory in Practice', *Leadership*, Volume 3(4), Nov 2007.

Heifetz, R. (1994) *Leadership Without Easy Answers*. Cambridge, Massachusetts: Harvard University Press.

Moore, M. (1995) *Creating Public Value*. Cambridge, Massachusetts: Harvard University Press.

Ryder, C. and Kearney, V. (2001) *Drumcree the Orange Orders Last Stand*. London: Methuen Publishing Ltd.

15
Leadership of Change Narratives: An Alternative Voice

Mervyn Conroy

Introduction

Public sector reform initiatives have had a chequered history with probably more black squares than white. The private sector has not fared much better. According to some researchers the failure rate of change initiatives across the board is 60–80% (Kallio *et al.* 2002). This suggests that current conceptualisations of change and their applications are missing something significant in their understanding of what organisational change means. The research summarised sets out to discover what is missing by drawing directly on the accounts of managers in the midst of leading the latest round of reforms to the NHS in England.

The chapter draws on empirical data derived from an analysis of NHS mental health service managers' narratives viewed through the lens of MacIntyre's virtue ethics theory (1981). The initial interest was to understand what it means to managers to be leading change and what they need to support them in improving the services they manage. As the study progressed the potential for an alternative ethical and sustainable public service improvement approach emerged not necessarily as a replacement to mainstream structural and programmatic approaches but as an additional choice for policy-makers and practitioners to consider. An ethical dimension to the understanding of organisational change and an alternative way of theorising resistance within change is proposed. A new term is suggested – *'ethical resistance'* – to the corruption of healthcare practices by reform leadership and policies with weak or inherently conflicting ethics.

The chapter has three main sections. First, dominant conceptualisations of change are reviewed along with some of their existing critique. Alistair MacIntyre's virtue ethics (1981) are introduced as part of this critique. Second, an alternative narrative view of change is introduced and theories of resistance are discussed from this viewpoint. Third, managers' narratives of change are explored and analysed using MacIntyre's concepts to draw out conclusions and implications.

Dominant theories of reform

Much of the organisational change management discourse that NHS managers are subject to and in some cases are part of is structural functional in nature (e.g. Iles and Sutherland 2001; Iles and Cranfield 2004). The support produced by structural functional approaches is often a set of qualitative factors or models of change that offer a guide to practitioners of what 'levers' to focus their attention on. The belief is that by pulling or pushing on these levers change can be controlled and stable outcomes predicted. Organisational change management theory utilised in public administration has been criticised as managerialist (e.g. Smith *et al.* 2001) or as Watson (1982) suggests as serving a managerial ideology. Patrick Dawson (2003) has criticised this type of theory for misdirecting attention towards best practice recipe guidelines that actually do little to improve the management of organisational change. Sandra Dawson in writing about change as experienced by managers in the NHS suggests that:

> We need to understand the practitioners' world, to see it through their eyes. Only then can we hope to be able to develop a dialogue in which the findings of the research can enlighten practice. (Dawson 1999: 23)

This infers that the 'practitioners' world', what it means to practitioners to lead and implement change, still remains elusive to researchers and theorists. This point is emphasised by Cameron *et al.* in a companion guide to that produced by Iles and Sutherland (2001) on the management of change specifically for the NHS:

> Substantial numbers of managers and clinical professionals argue that much of the evidence about effective change management is located in the heads of practitioners and has yet to find its way into the scholarly journals. (Cameron *et al.* 2001: 5)

Further challenges exist to the underlying assumption of a 'ubiquitous' (Sturdy and Grey 2003) mechanical model of organisational change management (OCM) framed within an 'epochal' discourse of change being inevitable, desirable and something that can be managed (du Gay 2003). Sturdy and Grey (2003) argue a case for research that provides 'alternative (additional) voices and therefore choices' (*ibid*: 659). Social constructionist and discursive approaches in particular, according to Sturdy and Grey, have the potential to 'provide alternative (additional) voices and therefore choices' (2003: 659). They draw on MacIntyre (1981) to challenge theories that underpin OCM.

MacIntyre's (1981) contention (is) that the social sciences have completely failed to develop predictive generalities, and moreover, that they will never do so. OCM [Organizational Change Management] has no such inhibitions. For example, in Pettigrew *et al.*, although there is a familiar recognition of a 'complex, dynamic and internationally conscious world', a 'search for general patterns of change' remains (2001: 697). If OCM is, as we have suggested, both managerialist and universalist, what might be done to articulate a different kind of understanding of change? (Sturdy and Grey 2003: 657).

MacIntyre's theorising, according to Sturdy and Grey (2003: 657), 'corrodes the assumptions upon which (traditional) OCM is built' and they add 'this is crucial because, if change is not inevitable and desirable but contingent and contested, then the organizational and political consequences are potentially profound'.

MacIntyre's After Virtue (1981) contribution contains, according to (Moore and Beadle 2006) a narrative based virtues-goods-practice-institution schema. MacIntyre proposes that the goods[1] of a practice or practices, in this case excellence in mental health practices, can only be achieved through attention to virtues. MacIntyre argues that narrative plays a central role in the formation and reformation of the virtues of the institution. The role of managers at all levels in socially constructing those virtues (or vices) is demonstrated in this chapter. MacIntyre emphasises the significance to the wellbeing of the institution of there being a set of virtues negotiated through a communal narrative that informs practice improvement. This is how MacIntyre describes the relationship between virtue and the internal goods of practice.

> A virtue is an acquired human quality the possession and exercise of which tends to enable us to achieve those goods which are internal to practices and the lack of which effectively prevents us from achieving any such goods. (MacIntyre 1981: 191)

The way MacIntyre envisages the collective relationship of practices, narratives of the institution and its link to a common purpose (*telos*) and a potential disruption is summarised by McCann and Brownsberger (1990):

> The normative character of MacIntyre's definition of a social practice … is secured within a larger account of the moral life as a whole. There must be some *telos* to human life, a vision anticipating the moral unity of life, given in the form of a narrative history that has meaning within a particular community's traditions; otherwise the various internal goods generated by the range of social practices will remain disordered and potentially subversive of one another. Without a community's shared sense of telos, there will be no way of signifying 'the overriding

good' by which various internal goods may be ranked and evaluated. (McCann and Brownsberger 1990: 227–228)

As will be shown later in the chapter, when managers' narratives are viewed in this way a multitude of ethical conflicts in their accounts are revealed. This chapter argues that an ethical dimension contributes a missing piece of the jigsaw in understanding why so many change programmes do not meet their objectives and is important for leaders of change in the public sector to consider because it offers an alternative framing and approach to achieving the desired outcomes of their improvement projects.

Narrative understanding of reform

A subset of social constructionist (Berger and Luckmann 1967; Weick 1979) studies of organisations contends that narrative approaches are an appropriate means to study organisational change (e.g. White 1981; Skoldberg 1994; Boje 1995; Czarniawska 1997; Gabriel 2000). The contention is that groups comprise individuals and as individuals come together to form organisations they construct their social reality in narrative form. Through narrative they construct a mixture of individual and shared meanings (Bruner 1991). Ford's (1999) position is that the accumulation of sufficiently consistent narratives can objectify 'reality' for the people who author them within organisations. Ford further suggests that organisational change can be viewed as shifting conversations and that conversations set the stage for what will and will not be done.

In relation to change the task of managers and leaders, according to Downing (1997), is to manage and solve the conflicts caused by change stories. A different approach was taken in this study, which was to understand the narrative enactments rather than 'solve' them. MacIntyre (1981) suggests that some of the conflicts practitioners experience are irresolvable since the 'sides' are rooted in different moral traditions, built on different premises, presenting perfectly reasonable but incompatible rational arguments. For MacIntyre, unless the virtues carried in the narratives are built on the same moral premise then they will be irresolvable. Does this offer insight as to why change programmes rarely achieve their intended outcomes? This suggestion will be examined further through the accounts of managers and from the perspective of ethics and resistance as the story in this chapter unfolds. First, a brief look at theories of resistance to change currently used to understand resistance to reform.

Resistance to reform?

Resistance as cynicism interpreted from a mechanistic perspective (Lewin 1951) is a force pressing against change, something to be weakened. From a humanist perspective Casey (1999) suggests that 'cynicism protects against both commitment to the company and its encroachment into the private realm of (relative) individual choice'. From a post-structuralist perspective Willmott (1993), drawing on Kunda (1992), suggests that workers actually collude with the relations of power they seek to escape because the very possibility of them being able to express their cynicism and resistance is evidence of the institution's commitment to openness and freedom. There is also the notion that resistance reinforces the structures of domination that were the object of resistance in the first place (Piccone 1978) and provides an element of vitality termed 'middle-class radicalism' without seriously threatening the domination (Fleming and Spicer 2003). These authors develop this theme by drawing on Zizek (1989) and suggest that in emphasising the external nature of subjectivity the 'stressed worker' becomes the 'stressful workplace', the 'tired employee' becomes the 'exploitative organisation'. Attention is then focused on these negative HRM categories and we lose interest in the 'realistic' response of individuals in the midst of external circumstances.

In Learmonth's comprehensive review of NPM critique (2003: 106) he suggests that critical management studies are sympathetic to 'understanding managers' worlds' type studies, however, he says they 'rarely invite us to reflect upon whether or not management practices may be complicit with wider sociological structures.' This study is enabled by MacIntyre's *After Virtue* thesis (1981) to extend reflection into wider society by highlighting the ideological horizons reflected in the virtue conflict enacted narratives of the participants. In a particularly relevant excerpt Learmonth also raises concerns about *a priori* assumptions about what managers do derived from standard texts rather from empirical material and therefore could also be taken as a particularly loaded view of what managers do. Learmonth's conclusion is that 'managerial values (and arguably virtues) remain more or less in the background and, whilst they still influence the work, the assumptions themselves are not subject to rigorous theoretical and empirical consideration' (2003: 106). This chapter attempts to bring managerial virtues, conveyed in their narratives to the foreground and in doing so open up a hidden dimension to scrutiny that it is hoped will offer some very interesting and worthwhile contributions to public sector reform policy, leadership and practice. It builds on Learmonth's conclusion to offer an ethical dimension to the theme of resistance which further challenges the theory that organisational change can be managed, measured and manipulated. In order to begin that challenge, voices from some of the managers interviewed over a 12-month longitudinal study of change to mental health services in the North of England are introduced.

Stories of reform

Fifty managers were interviewed over a period of 12 months in three rounds of in depth interviewing with some of the managers being interviewed twice and three times. All those interviewed were leading the implementation of a range of government and local change initiatives with the aim of improving mental health services. Examples of some of the typical stories told by the managers are provided below. The poetic mode (epic, tragic, comic or romantic) *a la* Gabriel (2000), title and the central virtue clash discerned in the story are included in the table.

Four of the above stories are included below, one from each category, to show how they were understood and analysed using

Table 15.1 Examples of Narratives of Change

Poetic Story Mode	Story Title	Central virtue clash in the story
Epic (successful change story	*Finding the flow*	leadership education vs. no education
	Subversive	evidence based management vs. partnership based clinical work
	I'm not having it!	manager decides vs. staff decide
Tragic (suffering loss through change)	*Cuckoo Reform*	doing a good clinical job vs. individual self interest
	Wasted Talent	using skills and talents vs. putting people in boxes
	Nobody to get angry with	Respecting that humans need time and resources to do a good job vs. efficiency measures and effectiveness standards
Comic (entertaining/ farcical/tragic)	*Bite on the bottom*	meeting needs vs. meeting targets
	I shred it	manager and clinician led vs. bureaucratic edicts from government
	Gone Shopping	locally managed case data and accountabilities vs. nationally managed case data
Romantic (showing care or love for another)	*Rose tinted glasses*	caring for people without caring about the cost vs. caring for the cost of caring for people
	My staff need me	for the greater good vs. personal needs
	Just absorb that crap!	buffering staff vs. bullying staff

MacIntyre's virtues-goods-practice-institution schema (Moore and Beadle 2006).

1. *Subversive:* Jane's epic story of successful change
2. *Cuckoo Reform*: Jo's tragic story of suffering loss through change
3. *Shred It*: Tim's comic story of how he 'leads' change
4. *My Staff Need Me*: Pat's romantic story of caring for her staff

In the analysis following each transcript, three primary questions are being asked. Firstly 'What does change mean to the manager concerned?'; secondly, 'What do the stories construct into the social reality of the organization?'; and thirdly, 'What ethics of leading change do they construct and perpetuate?'

1. Subversive

Context: Jane (J) is a senior manager with clinical responsibilities in her late 40s. She has a dual managerial/clinical role: she sits on the senior management team and manages a group of clinicians in addition to carrying her own case-load of patients. She is describing her approach to implementing a change which started with a small group of people and a common interest in a certain type of mental health disorder.

J: I think it's this split between how management see the organisation and what it's actually like at the coalface and that's certainly not unique to this organisation, because since I met with you last I've done a Health Care Commission Review which was absolutely fascinating and there was the same very different organisation, but yet so many aspects that resonated and particularly this thing about this split between working clinically, it's like you've got these two sorts of currents you've got your top current that's going one way and then there's this sort of clinical one that goes on and flows on and thinks we'll be here anyway whatever happens. The patients don't change and the clinical issues don't change, and it's not necessarily that that bottom current is flowing in the opposite direction, but it may be going slightly differently. It's not that things are standing still and not changing or progressing at the coalface it's doing it to a different agenda to the agenda that drives the rest of the organisation.
Interviewer (I): You're in a position of experiencing both these currents.
J: There are areas in which I know I've set up my own little current to achieve something and a group of us have done this for people with mood disorders and we've been very successful. Like metaphors we've like flowed off along our own channel which has been supported in the organisation but in a strange sort of way and now we're flowing back and almost flying ahead of the current, in terms of sort of engagement

developing a service which is very much engaged with people with the disorders.

I: Making your own path down the same river.

J: Yes it's being subversive but to achieve a goal that I feel is what the spirit of the service is about.

I: In practice what was happening? What were the managers saying and what did you do in your subversion?

J: It started off as an interest in mood disorders and somebody else needed to change their role as an outpatient nurse, they wanted to change the role of the outpatient nurse to be more challenging and as we talked we saw the common goals and then I was aware of other like-minded people and we got together a group of people who had no common base, apart from their interest in mood disorders who came together and that group changed over time and eventually became a coherent little group who came from very different places in the organisation. We had various ideas about how we wanted to develop services for people with mood disorders, we wanted to establish better practice to make sure people who had skills were able to use those and we also were very keen to develop a partnership style of working. I think what we all had in common was that we saw our clinical work as being working in partnership with patients, clients or whatever we personally called them and we wanted the service to develop in that way and then we had the opportunity to go into the Clinical Governance Development Programme, which basically was I think six days that we had away working with some training, but more than that it gave us the space and time out of the organisation to meet up, plan out what we were doing and to achieve various steps on the way towards our goal. We were fairly subversive in that we sat and listened to the presentations which were very useful and were then given tasks and then we just did our own thing.

'Rivers', 'flows' and 'currents' feature in this story to describe what it means to be leading organisational change for this manager. She says that she has deliberately set up her own little 'subversive' current to achieve something with others and claims to have been very successful – to the point of almost flying ahead of the main (government driven) current of change. She names the management current as '*evidence based management*' and her own as '*clinical*', flowing in different directions but not entirely opposed. Because of her position, straddling management and clinical, she can see both currents and the sense is that they do not really flow together.

For Jane she sees her clinical role as working in partnership with the client and used time away on a 'Clinical Governance Development Programme' to develop that way of working with her group of like-minded professionals who all had a common interest: '*I think what we all had in common was that we saw our clinical work as being working in partnership with patients*'. In this account, they did their 'own thing' on the course and used the time away to plan out the steps to their goal. She claims this process was successful.

Following MacIntyre (1981) it is argued that the 'evidenced based' and 'practice based community approaches' are based on different principles and moral traditions, and therefore incompatible. This manager does not attempt to try to join the two, instead she does her own thing with a group of like-minded others. She is like the leader of a peaceful rebellion: recognising there is a conflict of approaches but finding a quicker way down the river to meet and get ahead of the evidenced based approach in terms of what they both want to achieve. So a shared sense of purpose (or *telos*) exists but very different virtues, one acting on evidence and the other acting through partnering, they don't clash head on but they do remain separate with a sense of competition between them.

What might this story construct into the social reality of the organisation under change? The story offers inspiration: it is like listening to a leader of an underground movement, who was working both with the management as a spy and returning to her band of outlaws, the latter were the heroic ones who found a way to beat the system without directly opposing it. The virtue of clinical and patient partnership wins through in the end but to get there you have to be subversive and do your own thing. This runs counter to the notion of the communal narrative and would suggest a proliferation of people being subversive and doing their own thing in the face of prescriptions on how to implement change.

2. 'Cuckoo' reform

Context: Jo, a Service Manager, is in her mid-40s and has seen many changes in her career but says she is finding recent demands for organisational change particularly difficult to reconcile. She has had to implement a significant change to the way the mental health services she is responsible for are delivered. The Mental Health National Service Framework, a government policy document that describes what the service should be providing, requires the changes. Relocation of her team has also been necessary. She starts by describing how she feels and then moves on to describing the relationship between the organisation and the clinical work she manages.

> J: I keep getting illnesses, no immune system, even though I look after myself I go to the gym, eat healthily, try and have holidays doing the normal self-care stuff...talk to staff and really good supportive relationships within our service, so I feel as though I'm in a really good balance with the rest of my life. There's this thing about having to manage, in the olden days I was a bridge to the organisation so we got on with what we were meant to be doing so I bridged – there was this two way process of linking in with the wider organisation, but now the organisation is like a cuckoo it's just consuming it.

I: So what does the nest represent?

J: The nest is the work, getting on doing a good clinical job and the demands of the organisation is eroding our time, energy it's getting rid of staff our staff have left. It sounds very emotive, the staff have said you can't sustain this...I mean it sounds very emotive.

I: That's how it feels?

J: Yes, one of my staff is trying to get secondment out for two years into a different field, another one is saying she wants to reduce her hours because she's just not coping...

Two very clear metaphors are used in Jo's description which describe what implementing change means to her: Jo originally feeling like she personally was a two-way 'bridge' to the wider organisation and now feeling like the organisation is like a 'cuckoo' eroding time and energy and getting rid of her staff. The nest means the clinical work, doing a good job is what she values. What she describes might be seen by MacIntyre as the virtues of practice that offer a nest for the 'internal goods'[2] – the eggs. In this short excerpt we have a sense of a very dramatic and in her own words 'emotive' story of the government agenda of change fed through the organisation like it is arriving in her nest of work like a cuckoo chick and tossing her eggs, internal goods, out of the nest.

The cuckoo is a very powerful metaphor for a bird that appears only to care about itself and is ruthless, willing to steal and murder to get what it wants – nest and nurture for its own chick. Willmott's (1993) notion of the ideological colonisation of workers' affects and subjectivities has some resonance with this metaphor. The metaphor is interesting and illuminating in its depth – as first the cuckoo lays its egg in the nest and the nest owning bird just sees another egg and raises it as its own – only when the chick grows into a cuckoo is the destructive force truly unleashed as the imposter throws the rightful offspring out of the nest. Similarly the modernisation and managerial programme of change seemed reasonable, just another government initiative but later its ideological force is revealed and the tragedy unfolds.

What this story is doing, like Propp's (1928) folklore of oppression under Stalin, is conveying the feelings of oppression and an inability to cope with a ruthless *'cuckoo'* type virtue set that is successfully competing against a virtue set that this manager sees is about her *'work, getting on doing a good clinical job'*. 'Bridging' with a cuckoo would indeed be impossible given the massive difference in ethics they uphold. Conversing again between MacIntyre and this data we see what might be an example of a breakdown in what he describes as the 'narrative unity'[3] (1981: 226) and a corruption to practice (1981: 223) when two different ideologies meet at the point of practice. Her story evokes anger and outrage and is experienced as tragic. Other managers in the same environment told similar stories of loss.

What does this story construct into the social reality? It demonises the source of the changes and demands on her, in this case the 'organisation', and exhibits an explanation of the organisation, as cuckoo, being responsible for eroding our 'time and energy' and making people sick and leave. This kind of story has the potential to construct anger and cynicism towards change amongst peers and unfold organisational change meanings of tragedy and suffering into the social reality. As Ricoeur (1983–85) observes the reader or listener completes the cycle (mimesis 3) and has the potential to act on their interpretation and therefore narrative can become ethics in practice.

3. 'I shred it'

Context: The service manager, Tim, recounting this story is responsible for a group of practitioners who provide one-to-one therapeutic treatment for people suffering serious mental health conditions. He is explaining how he handles the continuous flow of practice changes he is asked to make:

> T: I couldn't quite see the relevance to my work at having to ask somebody about their allergies or other physical questions. It's that kind of thing we're supposed to respond to and be relevant and so we change our practice accordingly and as a result of that I tell my staff, 'Look what we're having to do here' and they stormed in angrily saying 'That's ridiculous' so we go back to the source and she says 'Well it's a national requirement'. So we have to do it then. We get a lot of this it feels like the old cliché of bureaucracy gone mad...audit could be done by an administrator. I choose to leave gaps between paragraphs, but you're not allowed to leave lines and it's this kind of pedantic attention to detail, unnecessary in my point of view.
>
> I: By meeting all the detailed requirements it takes away from your central role?
>
> T: That came out of the bombardment of having to attend to so many requests, how many more piles of paper do I have on my desk that are connected with ongoing things can I cope with and as a result I sometimes put a letter at the bottom of the pile and hope they'll go away or get forgotten about or people will forget they've asked and then six months have gone and nobody's asked so I shred it.

An account that conveys what it means to this manager to be handling change to services that he does not believe in. The story was accompanied by the poetics of gesture and movement: he picked up a piece of paper representing a 'must do' change to practice and placed it under a pile of other papers on his desk then extracted it and actioned an arc of movement towards the shredder with his hand. He laughed with relish at being able to shred what he considered to be another bureaucratic and irrelevant 'must do'.

Like the previous story, this one could be interpreted as an expression of resistance driven by a personal belief in what is worthy to be spending time on – certainly not the national requirements that increase bureaucracy 'it's this kind of pedantic attention to detail, unnecessary in my point of view'.

The essence of the story contains a clash of virtues associated with the level of bureaucracy that is required to run a service. For this manager what it means to be implementing reform is finding ways to reduce the number of things that he believes are unnecessary. What kind of social construction and virtues might this story unfold? The story itself contains some reactions from this managers' staff group 'they stormed in angrily saying "That's *ridiculous*"'. The source of the change is framed as a kind of meddling bureaucrat. The edicts, partly due to their nature and partly due to their volume are not to be taken too seriously and not to be acted upon immediately. The way you handle change is to ignore it for a while, hope that it will go away and you can then shred the edict. The virtue of keeping things simple and not being distracted by 'unnecessary' disruptive influences to practice such as the next great change idea from meddling bureaucrats disconnected from our reality seems to be the moral tale.

4. My staff need me

Context: Pat is a ward manager in her early 30s and reform projects to her mean extreme stress. During one such programme of change called 'Agenda for Change'[4] she describes reaching the point of feeling that she just could not cope any more. The whole programme was tightly controlled with a set of 'must do' deadlines and salaries could be affected by the outcomes. She knew that what she really needed was to take time off and recover but the care she felt for her staff outweighed her personal needs:

> If it were not for my staff needing me I would have gone off sick definitely.

This manager cried whilst she told her story of the dilemma she felt inside. The tears convey the strength of loyalty she felt for her staff during this period: she wanted to care for them because they were caring for vulnerable patients on the ward but the cost to her personally was significant. Loyalty to staff by managers and *vice-versa* was a common theme in the stories told of organisational change.

What is this type of story doing? For this manager the virtue of being there for her staff, meeting their needs, was paramount, overriding her need to recover, and gave her the incentive to come in to work. The message is I am not prepared to sacrifice what I believe to be the right thing to do which is to be there for my staff. This type of folklore has a sense of 'Change programmes might make me ill but I will not be beaten' and again is reminiscent of counter culture of the oppressed as described by Propp (1928).

Kallinikos (2006) speaks about the roles and responsibilities that the institution defines to meet its own ends and therefore directs people to operate towards the ends and external goods, as defined by those roles. Through being an agent of change the manager can unwittingly be an agent of the ideology underpinning that change. Taking the MacIntyre line, it could be argued that practice is therefore corrupted unwittingly by the practitioners who adhere to managerialist solution constructions to service improvement. Reports from these managers suggested that some people came out of 'Agenda for Change' winning financially others lost out and had their jobs downgraded. Many reported that it pitted people against each other and created competition, fear, anxiety and mistrust. The job panel reviews were designed to be objective with reams of criteria documentation to assess jobs and people against. Some claimed the pressure to deliver reduced the whole process to a fiasco and turned the impossibility of objectivity into something like a 'Reality TV' assessment of whether someone should be given the grade or not.

In this story there is a duality in the romance. Firstly seduction in the aims of the change: equality of pay and therefore on first impressions very appealing. Secondly a manager pushing herself to attain the 'internal goods' of feeling good about caring for her staff through the virtue of courage to push against her own needs. For managers, the social reality of implementing the change means competition and suffering. Again, this type of romantic tragedy was a very common construction amongst the managers interviewed.

Conclusion

MacIntyre (1981) asserts that humans are narrative animals who can share a sense of purpose for the overriding good through virtues that are constructed in a communal narrative about practising our crafts. For this NHS mental health service reform programme what do we see constructed into the social reality by these typical stories of leading change? Further, how does the analysis help with understanding more about why so many change programmes fail to meet their objectives?

The interpretation of resistance follows Fleming and Spicer's (2003) view of a 'healthy' contestation of corrupting influence on their working lives. It is argued that this is a form of 'ethical resistance' and is a socially constructed outcome from enacted virtue conflict narratives that seek to protect healthcare practices and care for the patient from being corrupted. 'Ethical resistance' is intended to resist vicious change – that is change that has a weak ethical status, inherently conflicting ethics or that has ethics primarily in service of the attainment of external goods of money (or saving money), status or power. As we see in the accounts of the participants and as suggested by MacIntyre these are ethics that have a corrupting influence on the social reality of practice and foster narrative disunity and moral disarray. The managers narrate their virtue-to-virtue combat with ethics that in some cases are reflections of wider ideological battles (e.g. market vs. common good) and that are only reconcilable with the violence of assertion.

The primary aim of NHS reform is currently quality or excellence in healthcare practices (and equal access to that quality) along with afford-ability of services (DoH 2008). In the social reality of the NHS undergoing change that we have sampled, what chance do managers as leaders have to understand what it means to be delivering excellence in mental health practice? Where will staff draw on narratives of the institution that carry these principles? Ironically, this study finds that the narrative message is to subvert or defend practices from the very reform programmes that are trying to achieve quality. MacIntyre's analysis is that we have been deflected from our ability to maintain a unity in moral debate by the liberal individualistic influences from the enlightenment onwards. Further, that we are unable at this point in history to properly reconcile the collision of different ideological horizons and moral traditions that are battled for daily in the workplace. A more optimistic stance would be that it might be possible to (re)construct the moral debate on the 'basic principles' in the context of service reform through facilitated peer group debate in certain localities with new or forming com-munities of practice. However it is argued that those people engaged in the moral debate also need to be informed on the antecedents of the reform dis-courses that form their subjectivity. MacIntyre advocates a similar form of education in his sequel to *After Virtue* (1981), *Whose Justice Which Rationality?* (1988). This chapter argues that the ethical dimension has, to date, been missing from organisational change theorising and has profound implications for (re)forming public institutions such as the NHS. If this analysis is correct, and practice is corrupted or insulated by 'ethical resistance' from efficiency and effectiveness change discourses, then this is urgently needed not just in the NHS but in all our public services.

Implications

In summary, this chapter highlights a missing ethical dimension to organ-isational change theory and has identified a strong, healthy 'ethical resistance' in public sector reform programmes which should not be underestimated. This finding could go some way to understanding more about why so many change programmes fail to meet their objectives. Further advances in this area may start from the following three questions. Firstly, 'If current reform approaches engender cynicism and mistrust, what are the alter-natives?' Secondly, 'What does ethically informed organisational change mean in practice?' Finally, there is a need to inform policy-makers leaders of change on the ground about the antecedents of their ethical clashes and ask 'What kind of health service morality (and world) do they wish to build and fight for together?' – a considerable and new public leadership challenge.

Notes

1. Internal goods (of excellence): both the excellence of products/ services and the perfection of the individual in the process. According to MacIntyre the achievement of both are reliant on a communally agreed set of virtues acquired through participating in practice.
2. MacIntyre's (1981: 273) account of the virtues proceeds through three stages: a first which concerns virtues as necessary to achieve the goods internal to practice, second as qualities contributing to the good of a whole life, and third which relates them to the pursuit of a good for human beings the conception of which can only be elaborated and possessed within an ongoing social tradition.
3. 'Narrative unity' is the notion that like narrative our lives have a beginning, middle and ending and they only make sense as a unity of life. MacIntyre argues that the virtues find their point and purpose not only in seeking the good of life as a whole but in sustaining those traditions which provide practices and individual lives with their necessary unity and context. Lack of the virtues is corrupting of practice and therefore, it might be argued, of a person's narrative unity
4. Agenda for Change, a government initiative, that was designed to benefit staff by evaluating every post and giving everyone a job description and ultimately pay equity for people in equivalent roles so that nobody is paid less or more than they should be.

References

Berger, P.L. and Luckmann, T. (1967) *The Social Construction of Reality: A Treatise in the Sociology of Knowledge*. Allen Lane.

Boje, D.M. (1995) 'Stories of the Storytelling Organisation: A Postmodern Analysis of Disney as "Tamara-Land"', *Academy of Management Journal*, 38/4: 997–1035.

Bruner, J. (1991) 'The Narrative Construction of Reality', *Critical Inquiry*, 18: 1–21.

Cameron, M., Cranfield, S., Iles, V. *et al.* (2001). *Managing Change in the NHS: Making Informed Decisions on Change: Key Points for Health Care Managers and Professionals*. Booklet produced by NHS NCCSDO. London: LSHTM.

Casey, C. (1999) '"Come, Join Our Family": Discipline and Integration in Corporate Organizational Culture', *Human Relations*, 52(2): 155–178.

Czarniawska, B. (1997) *Narrating the Organisation: Dramas of Institutional Identity*. Chicago: UCP.

Dawson, P. (2003) 'Organisational Change Stories and Management Research: Facts or Fiction', *Journal of the Australian and New Zealand Academy of Management*, 9(3).

Dawson, S. (1999) 'Managing, Organising and Performing in Health Care: What Do We Know and How Can We Learn', in Mark, A.L. and Dopson, S. (eds), *Organisational Behaviour in Health Care: The Research Agenda*. London: Macmillan.

Department of Health (2008) *High Quality Care For All: NHS Next Stage Review Final Report*, known as the 'Darzi Report'. London: DoH.

Downing, S.J. (1997) 'Learning the Plot: Emotional Momentum in Search of Dramatic Logic', *Management Learning*, 28(1): 27–44.

du Gay, P. (2003) 'The Tyranny of the Epochal: Change, Epochalism and Organizational Reform', *Organization*, 10(4): 663–684.

Fleming, P. and Spicer, A. (2003) 'Working at a Cynical Distance: Implications for Power, Subjectivity and Resistance', *Organisation*, 10(1): 157–179.

Ford, J.D. (1999) 'Organisational Change as Shifting Conversations', *Journal of Organisational Change Management*, 12: 480–500.

Gabriel, Y. (2000) *Storytelling in Organisations: Facts, Fictions and Fantasies*. London: OUP.

Iles, V. and Sutherland, K. (2001) *Managing Change in the NHS: Organisational Change – A Review for Health Care Managers, Professionals and Researchers*. Literature Review produced by Cambridge University Judge Institute for the NHS SDO. London: LSHTM.

Iles, V. and Cranfield, S. (2004) *Managing Change in the NHS: Developing Change Management Skills – A Resource for Health Care Professionals and Managers*. Literature Review Sponsored and Distributed by NHS SDO. London: LSHTM.

Kallinikos, J. (2006) *The Consequences of Information: Institutional Implications of Technological Change*. Cheltenham: Edward Elgar.

Kallio J., Saarinen, T. and Tinnila, M. (2002) 'Efficient Change Strategies: Matching Drivers and Tracers in Change', *Business Process Management Journal*, 8(1): 80–92.

Kunda, G. (1992) *Engineering Culture: Control and Commitment in a High-Tech Corporation*. Philadelphia: Temple University Press.

Learmonth, M. (2003) 'Making Health Services Management Research Critical: A Review and a Suggestion', *Sociology of Health & Illness*, 25(1): 93–119.

Lewin, K. (1951) *Field Theory in Social Science*. London: Tavistock Publications.

MacIntyre, A. (1981) *After Virtue: A Study in Moral Theory*. London: Duckworth.

MacIntyre, A. (1988) *Whose Justice? Which Rationality?* London: Duckworth.

McCann, D.P. and Brownsberger, M.L. (1990) 'Management as a Social Practice: Rethinking Business Ethics after MacIntyre', in Yeager, D.M. (ed.), *The Annual of the Society of Christian Ethics*, 223–245. Washington, D.C.: Georgetown University Press.

Moore, G. and Beadle, R. (2006) 'In Search of Organisational Virtue in Business: Agents, Goods, Practices, Institutions and Environments', *Organisation Studies*, 27(3): 369–389.

Pettigrew, A.M. *et al.* (2001) 'Studying Organisational Change and Development: Challenges for Future Research', *Academy of Management Journal*, Vol. 44, Issues 4, p. 697, 17p.

Piccone, P. (1978) 'The Crisis of One-Dimensionality', *Telos*, 35: 43–54.

Propp, V. (1928) *Morphology of the Folktale*. Austin: University of Texas Press.

Ricoeur, P. (1983–1985) *Time and Narrative (Temps et Récit)*, 3 vols. trans. Kathleen Laughlin and David Pellauer. Chicago: University of Chicago Press.

Skoldberg, K. (1994) 'Tales of Change: Public Administration Reform and Narrative Mode', *Organisational Science*, 5(2): 219–238.

Smith, J., Walshe, K. and Hunter, D.J. (2001) 'The "Redisorganisation" of the NHS', *British Medical Journal*, Vol. 323: 1263–1264.

Sturdy, A. and Grey, C. (2003) 'Beneath and Beyond Organizational Change Management: Exploring Alternatives', *Organization*, 10(4): 651–662.

Watson, T.J. (1982) 'Group Ideologies and Organisational Change', *Journal of Management Studies*, 19(3): 259–275.

Weick, K.E. (1979) *The Social Psychology of Organizing*, 2nd edition. Reading, Mass.: Addison-Wesley Pub. Co.

White, H. (1981) 'The Value of Narrativity in the Representation of Reality', in Mitchell, W.J.T. (ed.), *On Narrative*. Chicago: Chicago University Press.

Willmott, H. (1993) 'Strength is Ignorance; Slavery is Freedom: Managing Cultures in Modern Organizations', *Journal of Management Studies*, 30(4): 515–552.

Zizek, S. (1989) *Sublime Object of Ideology*. London: Verso.

16

Section 17 Crime and Disorder Act 1998: A Missed Opportunity for Public Leadership?

Kate Moss

Law, leadership and local action

This chapter examines one of the critical conditions for the emergence of effective public leadership – namely the need to engage in both shared and distributed leadership. It suggests that the enactment a decade ago of the Crime and Disorder Act 1998 (hereinafter referred to as CDA) but specifically section 17 of that Act, provided an excellent opportunity to put this type of leadership into practice and to conjoin national and local public leaders to improve the quality of life for citizens. The legislation placed an obligation on local authorities and the police (amongst others) to cooperate in the development and implementation of a strategy for tackling crime and disorder. Section 17 fits well with the modernisation of public institutions in that it requires local authorities and police authorities to consider crime and disorder implications within their decision-making. However, what this chapter will demonstrate is that the implementation of these legal provisions has been at best, lukewarm and at worst, non-existent. The chapter also explores the potential that this legislation offered for public leaders to openly display their collaborative efforts in improving responses to and strategies for tackling crime and disorder at the local level. It also assesses the implications of the legislation for specific local authority departments and police forces, both legally and strategically, and outlines some of the possible reasons for the inaction of public leaders – at all levels – in relation to the important task of improving community wellbeing. The relevance of public leadership to the improvement of community safety is explored in relation to a) the need for collective action in tackling crime and disorder; b) the notion that such collective action should seek to develop shared aims and objectives and c) the notion that it should also aim to deliver improved social wellbeing utilising crime and disorder strategies as a medium.

The chapter suggests that this legislation was poorly articulated from its inception. Primarily conceived as an enabling device for the promotion of effective crime reduction in the everyday activities of police forces and local authorities, it has far reaching implications in terms of drawing together the collective efforts of a number of different agencies. As such, it also has relevance to the enabling nature of public leadership. However, the chapter suggests that its effectiveness has been hampered because central government has not itself followed the principles that it laid down in this legislation for the agencies named therein. It concludes that although the legislation could have been (and perhaps still may be) a mechanism for bringing together the diverse range of Local Authority functions, the failure of its full implementation is potentially quite damaging and could be viewed as a worrying form of inaction by public leaders.

Public leadership and crime reduction

It is probably pertinent at the outset to acknowledge and define the notions of public leadership, crime reduction and the idea of legislating to reduce crime, and to explain why these ideas – which may at first glance seem fairly disparate – are relevant to community safety. Other chapters outline more comprehensively what is meant by public leadership. For the purpose of this chapter, the approach that is used is that offered by Brookes and Grint in Chapter 1 which argues for collective leadership across a range of public institutions.

Legislating to reduce crime is not a new idea but interest and relevant research in relation to crime reduction has increased in volume and quality over the last 30 years. Moss (2006: 1) states that:

> The 'idea' of preventing crime predates this period by a substantial amount. In his Statute of Winchester 1285, the reforming English King Edward I tried to control highway robbery by forcing property owners to clear the verges of highways (by cutting down trees and bushes alongside it) so that robbers would have nowhere near the road to hide, from which to surprise passers-by. Property owners who failed to do this were held legally liable for any robberies which occurred along their uncleared verges. So the idea of legislating for crime reduction has a long history. What have changed over the years (alongside the nature of crime itself) are the methods employed to give effect to crime reduction and ideas about who should be responsible for it.

Ekblom (1994: 1) has famously stated that: 'Crime prevention involves the disruption of mechanisms which cause crime events'. Given this statement, it appears that he presumes some sort of clarity about what constitutes a crime. Unfortunately, with most things legal no such clarity in reality exists. I have said before (Moss 2006) that a crime comes into existence at that point when government legislates to make something a crime. Whilst there is some consistency between jurisdictions as to common crimes (for example murder) there are many differences too. To complicate matters further, definitions of crime change over time alongside changes in society. Acts which used to be crimes are no longer (such as consensual adult homosexuality), and acts which used not to be crimes (such as the rape of a wife) now are. The scope of crime reduction must change over time because crime itself changes too. One of the more interesting suggestions posited by some modern criminologists has been that to disrupt a crime does not necessarily require either police, criminal justice or other legal intervention. Those of us who count ourselves as rather old fashioned liberals might say that it is just as well that crime prevention does not only seek legal intervention but also concentrates on a much more diverse range of disruptive techniques because as Pease (1997: 963) states:

A society in which more crime is prevented is not necessarily a more pleasant society. The burdens and restrictions imposed on people to prevent crime must be balanced against the harm caused by the crime prevented.

Moss (2006: 2) also highlights that:

...there are two basic aspects to legislating to reduce crime. The traditional way has been to prescribe punishments so that people are deterred from committing acts that were crimes already. The second way is demonstrated by the more recent return to legislating to enable a sharing of the responsibility for reducing crime...and is embodied in section 17...of the CDA 1998...

Responsibility and leadership

The last decade has seen major shifts in thinking about who should be responsible for preventing crime. Traditionally, the police had been assigned primary responsibility for that task. More recently, however, the Morgan Report 1991 sought to allocate responsibility for crime reduction to local authorities. A less radical option was legislated in the CDA 1998. This designated, under section 17, local authorities and the police as jointly responsible for crime reduction, and thus presented a good opportunity to practise collective leadership in an important area of public policy. Section 17 specifically imposes a duty on each local authority to exercise its functions with due regard to the need to do all that it reasonably can to prevent crime and disorder in its area. The Home Office Consultation Document 'Getting to Grips with Crime: A New Framework for Local Intervention'

(1997: ch. 3, para 33) stated that the purpose was to 'give the vital work of preventing crime a new focus across a very wide range of local services...It is a matter of putting crime and disorder at the heart of decision making...'.

In terms of public leadership, Brookes (Chapter 1) states that it is:

> A style of collective leadership in which public bodies and agencies collaborate in achieving a shared vision based on shared aims and values which seek to promote, influence and deliver improved and sustained social, environmental and economic wellbeing within a complex and changing context.

So why does public leadership have relevance to community safety? First, as we have seen from these brief introductions to both crime reduction and public leadership, they both rely on collective action. Second, they both seek to develop shared aims and objectives and finally they also aim to deliver improved social wellbeing. With regard to the statutory duty imposed by section 17 of the Crime and Disorder Act 1998, arguably this section could be perceived as fairly radical, producing as it did the notion of shared responsibility for crime reduction across a wide range of local authority services. As previously posited, section 17 was primarily conceived as an 'enabling device' for the promotion of effective crime reduction in the everyday activities of the police and local authorities. Specifically it imposed a duty on each local authority to 'exercise its functions with due regard to the need to do all that it reasonably can to prevent crime and disorder in its area.' In terms of the thrust of this paper, the most interesting issues are; how has section 17 influenced practice on the ground and what has been the practical application of section 17 for public leaders?

Missed opportunities for leadership

Moss and Pease (1999) have argued previously that the true potential of this legislation has not been recognised within government and amongst local authority officials. Although conceived of as an enabling device for the promotion of effective crime reduction in the everyday activities of agencies, it appears that it has not drawn together the collective efforts of these agencies. Moss and Pease (*ibid*) have speculated that one of the problems is that ideas of crime reduction are popularly reduced to the problem of what do to about the criminal, and thus the relevance of local decision-making could be overlooked. Moss (1999, 2000, 2001) has also indicated that in spite of its far reaching implications for the work of local authorities, section 17 has been poorly articulated. In spite of the fact that it could assist in ensuring that local authorities share their leadership with other agencies, including the police, and moreover distribute it within their own organisation, this potential for effectiveness has been hampered because central government are not bound by the same criteria and thus fail to share and distribute their own leadership. It is pertinent to explain this further.

At the time of the implementation of the Crime and Disorder Act 1998, its potential to assist with the sharing of responsibility for crime reduction through shared and distributed leadership was acknowledged by some local authorities. The more proactive of these even arranged specific training in respect of section 17 in an attempt to mainstream it. It was acknowledged – perhaps not as widely as it should have been – that most local authority decisions might be affected by section 17 considerations and that the range of issues to which it could potentially extend was enormous. In one area of local authority responsibility however, there was particular interest in section 17. From the author's extensive experience of working nationally with the police, town planners and local authorities, it had become clear that in relation to planning legislation, section 17 was perceived of as a means of effectively reducing crime. Unfortunately, section 17 did not have the impact in this sphere that was hoped. It is relevant to explore this in more detail.

Subsequent to the enactment of the CDA 1998 and in line with the requirements of section 17, some police forces and local authorities endeavoured to implement this in the decision-making processes which concerned planning. Specifically, section 17 was seen by some of the more proactive architectural liaison officers and crime prevention design advisors as an enabler to incorporating more crime prevention measures in town centre planning applications or change of land usages where that use was specifically related to restaurant, bar or club use, with all the potential attendant crime problems of 'attractive nuisances'. It is probably true to say that section 17 was seen initially as a Godsend by worried police officers and local authorities contending – alongside changes in licensing laws – with the push for a 24-hour-a-day, seven-day-a-week town or city centre economy. The hope was that given the move towards a shared responsibility for crime reduction under this section, all agencies would come together to 'sing from the same hymn sheet' in relation to creating a balanced economy in the town centres of the UK which could be well planned and adequately policed.

Against this background, developers were also aware that changes in the licensing laws signalled the facilitation of a potentially lucrative period for them and many moved in on town and city centres across the country to develop franchised nightclubs and to request permissions for changes to the classification of existing premises to class A3, which indicates use for a pub or club. In the cases where a change of use or a request for planning permission was denied at the local level on the grounds of crime prevention under section 17, some developers were prepared to appeal that decision to the Planning Inspectorate, a central government department. What is particularly interesting, given the reasons for the enactment of section 17 in the first place – as a crime reductive tool – is the outcome of these cases and the reasons given for the decisions which, in most instances, went against the local agencies and led to the Planning Inspectorate stating quite firmly that section 17 – the very basis under which the planning applications had been refused in the first place – was *not* a factor it was prepared to take into consideration. Indeed, to the Inspectorate, section 17 was not even a material consideration in its decision-making processes. It is relevant to describe some examples of this in order to explain how and why this could occur, and in doing so, to elucidate one of the main reasons why section 17 has so far failed both as an enabling device for the promotion of effective crime reduction in the planning context, and as an enabler for collective public leadership.

The case of Aquarium Entertainments Ltd v Brighton and Hove Council [2000] is famous (or infamous) for two reasons. First, it was a test case for appeals of this kind. Second, it was not unusual in the trend it set in decision-making in relation to the use of section 17 as an enabler for crime reduction. In this case, a developer (Aquarium Entertainments) had applied for, and was granted, planning permission for a night club development for up to 900 people. The developers then applied for permission to extend this initial development into two adjacent units which would house a maximum of 1,740 people. After consultation with the police and local residents, and mindful of the new statutory duty that section 17 had recently placed on them to 'exercise their functions with due regard to the need to do all they reasonably could to prevent crime and disorder', Brighton and Hove Council refused the second application. The developers appealed this decision and the appeal was upheld by the Planning Inspectorate. Some important issues can be teased out of this decision.

Without doubt, the local council and the police in this case felt that they were acting (and indeed were) within the boundaries of the statutory responsibility which had so recently been imposed upon them in the form of section 17. They had interpreted this responsibility (quite correctly) as enabling them to act in ways which would reduce crime in their locality and protect citizens from the types of nuisance, crime and disorder that is associated with the night club culture and an extended night-time economy. This has been evidenced most recently by Finney (2004). In the face of this, to receive such a decision was to say the least a disappointment and it is worth looking in more detail at the reasons which were given for the Inspector's decision. The Inspector accepted that licensed premises had a connection with crime and disorder; she also accepted that the council and the residents were right to be concerned about crime and to prevent it wherever possible. She also demonstrated that she was aware that recent statistics had shown that violent crimes in Brighton were at that time twice the national average per head of population. In spite of this however, she implied that section 17 was not relevant to this particular appeal. How could this be the case?

Leading from the top: Do as I say, not as I do

The explanation for the case described above appears straightforward. In the drafting of section 17, the responsibility it imposed on local authorities to reduce crime had simply not been extended to central government in any way and therefore, the Planning Inspectorate, representing an arm of central government, was simply not bound by the same criteria as local government departments. In hearing the appeal the Inspectorate was under no compunction to apply section 17 criteria. This represented (and still does since this Act has not been amended) at best – a legal loophole which had unfortunately not been foreseen and thus had inadvertently led to a situation in which central government found itself not bound by its own law. At worst it represents (for the cynic or the realist – depending on your point of view) an intentional lead in which central government was really saying 'do as I say rather than do as I do'. Recommendations for the extension of the section 17 duty to central government have been made, for example, by the second Foresight Panel Crime Report (2000) but these recommendations have yet to be implemented formally and the missed opportunity for central government to displays *its* commitment to collective leadership remains.

In making her decision on the basis that section 17 did not apply to the Planning Inspectorate, the Inspector in this case could be deemed to be legally quite correct. However, several other issues were not taken into consideration. Section 17 actually emphasised the legally binding principles of a previous Home Office Circular. Circular 5/94 'Planning Out Crime', had already established that crime prevention was capable of being what is called a 'material consideration' and therefore on this basis at least the Inspector should have given weight to such considerations, duly re-emphasised by section 17. Circular 5/94 acknowledges that successful crime prevention depends on a wide range of coordinated measures which, used collectively, can work to discourage anti-social behaviour and make it harder for criminals to find targets. It also encourages sensitive use of the planning system and its guidelines to urge developers to take into account the security of both people and their property when decisions concerning the siting of new residential, commercial or leisure developments are made. Where there was potential to reduce crime as demonstrated by the Aquarium Entertainments case, this rightly featured in the collective discussions that the authority had with the developers and the local police. It is also something which should have been taken into consideration in the appeal process. In this particular case, the local authority and the police were mindful of their statutory duty under section 17 to 'consider crime prevention in all their decision making processes' and felt duty bound to work together to get this right. What they did not foresee – nor could they reasonably have done – was that this would be at odds with the guidelines to which the Planning Inspectorate would continue to operate – arguably a clear case of leadership inaction. Understandably this made many people operating at the local level feel that the Inspectorate was putting 'development' firmly before security, safety, community and partnerships. This quite rightly begs the question; where is public leadership really played out?

In a letter to Brighton and Hove Council following the appeal decision, the Inspectorate contended that the CDA was not material to its decision. Its legal advisers informed the Inspectorate that section 17 was not in itself a material planning consideration. Having established that the Inspectorate was not under the same duty imposed by section 17, it remains pertinent to draw attention to exactly what constitutes a material consideration and why section 17 should already have been construed as such, rendering the fact that the Inspectorate were not specifically bound by the section itself immaterial.

Supporting the principle of collective leadership

Moss (2000) outlines that crime prevention is one of the social considerations to which regard must be given in development plans and highlights that it is important that crime prevention schemes are designed to meet specific security needs on a location basis. The Aquarium Case, like many such cases since, demonstrates that in every town or city there are particular trouble spots, highly vulnerable to opportunistic crime, for which effective and simple crime prevention measures are available. The people best placed to determine what these are, are the police working in partnership with local councils and the community. So when the Inspectorate states that section 17 is not a 'material consideration' this is a very narrow view, particularly since case law already exists which determines what types of crime and disorder issues can be material.

Whilst it is true that there is still no case law specific to the CDA itself, as any self-respecting lawyer will tell you, it is not the subject matter of a particular case which is important, but the legal principle embodied in that decision. Cases such as Stringer v Minister of Housing and Local Government [1970] and Ladbroke Rentals Ltd v Secretary of State for the Environment [1981] established some time ago what sorts of crime and disorder issues are capable of being material. These include issues impacting on; a greater need for policing; residents; the feasibility of policing at key times; the consideration of health and safety and law and order, and on amenities with attendant law and order problems. Because these are all crime and disorder issues *and* material considerations, according to existing legal precedent, it could realistically be argued that it is neither appropriate, nor legally correct, to suggest that the crime prevention issues raised by section 17 are *not* similarly material. It would also be logical to suggest that section 17 serves to emphasise these requirements and if not taken into account, this could be *ultra vires* on the grounds of unreasonableness as established in the case of Associated Provincial Picture Houses v Wednesbury Corporation [1948].

So what is the impact of this interpretation of section 17 on its feasibility as a legislative crime reductive tool and as a mechanism for the promotion of shared and distributed leadership in relation to social wellbeing? Decisions like the Aquarium Entertainments case and others, such as that in Warrant Investments [2000] have demonstrated that whilst many police forces and local authorities nationally have endeavoured to implement section 17 of the CDA in line with government policy, they have been frustrated in their attempts to do this effectively by the Planning Inspectorate which, as an arm of central government, are not themselves bound by this statutory requirement and which have maintained that section 17 is not a material consideration in spite of legal precedent which justifies numerous crime and disorder issues as material. This interpretation of the statute by the Inspectorate has created a bizarre situation where local authorities make decisions based on the crime and disorder criteria they are bound by statute to consider but if these are appealed the Inspectorate is at liberty to claim that these criteria are irrelevant because they are not operating to the same guidelines. Any appeal for the judicial review of such decisions would, no doubt have to be undertaken at a public cost which would be difficult to justify and would have no certain outcome.

Moss and Seddon (2001: 25) have highlighted that:

> Whilst it is true that some initial appeal decisions were not favourable to the use of section 17 as a crime and disorder material consideration, more recent decisions have been more supportive of this trend. Crime prevention is capable of being a material planning consideration – but is probably not being given the profile it deserves in planning decision-making. Using crime prevention considerations as a reason, or supplementary reason for refusing planning permission ultimately develops case law through the appeal system. Recent appeal decisions support this.

For example, in the Jackson's Farm Case [2001] an appeal was made against the requirement for lighting on a public driveway. The appeal was dismissed because the Inspector agreed that the condition had been imposed in the interests of crime prevention and community safety. Similarly in the Grove Vale Depot Case [2000] the main issue concerned a residential development of 93 houses and whether the design and layout would provide a safe and attractive environment for future residents. The Inspector noted that a through route for pedestrians and cyclists would permit access for strangers; that underground parking would produce a gloomy and unsafe atmosphere and that overall there were substantial shortcomings in crime prevention and defensible space which were sufficient to dismiss the appeal. It has also been established in a number of cases (such as Gateshead MBC v Secretary of State for the Environment [1994] and West Midlands Probation Committee v Secretary of State for the Environment [1997]) that the fear of crime can be a material planning consideration.

Whilst problems of interpretation have prevailed in relation to section 17, the main guidance that has been used in respect of crime prevention and planning has been Home Office Circular (1994) 'Planning out Crime' (referred to as 5/94), which did give some advice about crime prevention. However, problems of interpretation and the anomalous situation with regard to section 17 led in part to a recent revision of the guidance in 5/94. It has been argued, however, (Moss 2003) that the drafting of this has still not given priority to crime prevention issues. Neither has it rectified the fact that whilst local government is still bound by section 17, central government remains unbound. The current situation remains such that there is still a lack of awareness of section 17 on the ground and still a need for further leadership and training for local authorities in respect of its merits and potential implications. Perhaps the most unfortunate drawback is that the anomalous situation highlighted here and the lack of will to rectify this sooner has meant that section 17 has not had the impact that it could have had in terms of being a radical and innovative crime reductive tool.

Collective crime reductive efforts

Notwithstanding this, the bottom line with modern crime reductive legislation has been to recognise that agencies other than the police routinely make decisions with crime consequences and that they should therefore all be involved in crime reduction through a collective responsibility for community safety. The legislation highlighted within this chapter is a radical repositioning of responsibility for crime reduction and does require some trade-offs between crime reduction and privacy. What is needed above all, however, is an emphasis on agreement which would afford a level playing field for all the agencies involved in these processes. The fact that this has not been made clear has hindered the progress that might have been otherwise made.

What can be drawn from all of this? The drafting of legislation is complex and mistakes can be made but it remains important to respond to any mistakes or inadvertent anomalies quickly in order for that legislation not to become meaningless or impossible to respond to. Practitioners and all those involved in issues like these have to respond to many demands on their time and to many changes in legislation and policy which necessarily affect their working lives and the ways in which they operate. For new ideas to be successful, they must be implemented with sufficient guidance and must be seen to apply to all, rather than just those working at the local level. Successful implementation of what are, in essence, innovative and ground breaking ideas with the potential to change the face of crime reduction altogether also depends on those on the ground having the certainty that everyone is singing from the same hymn sheet.

The Home Office accepted some time ago that the anomalies which remain with regard to the CDA and the Data Protection Act 1998 merit another look at the legislation with a view to amending it in some way. It remains to be seen, however, given the generalist nature of the Home Office and in particular of career civil servants which may be tasked to take the lead on this, whether future amendments, if made by non-specialists in the field, will amount to any significant and meaningful changes. To date, in spite of such promises, this legislation remains unamended and lacking in clarity.

To summarise, this chapter has argued that there is a need for collective action in tackling crime and disorder and that this should seek to develop shared aims and objectives across a range of public sector institutions. This form of collective leadership is particularly relevant to the police and local government who have the opportunity to play a key role in the improvement of social wellbeing. Section 17 could be considered to be a missed opportunity in relation to public leadership specifically and in collective efforts to improve social wellbeing more generally. It represents an example of the government's attitude being one of 'do as I say rather than as I do'. Is this therefore an example of good leadership? It demonstrates that there is little or no collaborative leadership in relation to the need to work together to improve crime, disorder and community safety. The resultant inaction of public leaders in this important part of improving community wellbeing means that little has been achieved. Added to this, there is little or no political will to amend the legislation in spite of promises to do so by the Home Office. Without strong leadership being displayed from the heart of central government, how can Ministers realistically expect strong leadership at the local level of public service delivery?

References

Aquarium Entertainments Ltd v Brighton and Hove Council. Appeal Ref: T/APP/Q1445/A/99/1025514/P2, 22nd February 2000, 1–2 and 15–18.

Associated Provincial Picture Houses v Wednesbury Corporation [1948] 1 KB 223.

Ekblom, P. (1994) 'Proximal Circumstances: A Mechanism-Based Classification of Crime Prevention', in Clarke, R. (ed.), *Situational Crime Prevention Studies*. NY: Monsey.

Finney, A. (2004) *Violence in the Night Time Economy: Key Findings*, Home Office Key Research Findings No. 214. London: HMSO.

Foresight Crime Prevention Panel (2000) *Turning the Corner*. London: DTI.

Gateshead MBC v Secretary of State for the Environment [1994] JPL 432.

Grove Vale Depot Case. Appeal Ref: APP/A5840/A/00/1041744. Grove Vale Depot, Vale End, East Dulwich, 25 October 2000.

Home Office (1994) *Planning Out Crime*, Circular No. 5. London: Home Office.

Home Office (1997) *Getting to Grips with Crime: A New Framework for Local Intervention*. London: Home Office.

Jackson's Farm Case. Appeal Ref: APP/E2530/A/00/1054000. Land adjoining Jackson's Farm, off Middle Street, Skillington, Lincolnshire, NG33 5ER, 28 February 2001.

Ladbroke Rentals Ltd v Secretary of State for the Environment [1981] JPL 454.

Moss, K. (2006) 'Legislating to Reduce Crime: Rhetoric or Reality?', in Moss, K. and Stephens, M. (eds), *Crime Reduction and the Law*. London: Routledge.

Moss, K. and Pease, K. (1999) 'Crime and Disorder Act 1998: Section 17. A Wolf in Sheep's Clothing?', *Crime Prevention and Community Safety: An International Journal*, 1(4): 15–19.

Moss, K. (2000) 'Crime Prevention v Planning: Section 17 of the Crime and Disorder Act. Is it a Material Consideration?', *Crime Prevention and Community Safety: An International Journal*, 3(2): 43–48.

Moss, K. and Seddon, M. (2001) 'Crime Prevention and Planning: Searching for Common Sense in Disorder Legislation', *Crime Prevention and Community Safety: An International Journal*, 3(4): 25–31.

Moss, K. (2003) 'The Good, the Bad or the Ugly? What Will the New Planning Out Crime Guidance Be Like and What Should It Be Like?', *Community Safety Journal*, Vol. 2, Issue 1, January 2003.

Pease, K. (1997) 'Crime Reduction', in Maguire, M. *et al.* (eds) *Oxford Handbook of Criminology*. Oxford University Press.

Stringer v Minister for Housing and Local Government [1970] 1 WLR 1281.

Warrant Investments Ltd v Newcastle-under-Lyme Borough Council. Appeal Ref: T/APP/P3420/A/00/1036269/P2, 3 May 2000.

West Midlands Probation Committee v Secretary of State for the Environment [1997] JPL 323.

17
Partnerships: Rhetoric or Reality?

Sue Goss and Paul Tarplett

Introduction

In recent years, everyone in government has been talking about partnerships. Every initiative, every new target seems to require a new partnership. Collaboration has become an accepted way of working. And yet, almost everyone agrees that the rhetoric has outstripped the reality. While there have been real partnership success stories, almost every senior manager or politician has a story to tell about spending unproductive hours in tedious, directionless partnership meetings. Are partnerships really necessary? And if so, how do we make them more effective?

There are many different sorts of arrangements described as partnerships across the whole of the vast public service delivery 'system'. Collaboration is often required between organisations or individuals at the same level within the system e.g. between a local authority and a PCT; or between organisations/others at different levels within the system e.g. central and local government, district and county councils or between government offices for the regions and localities. In addition there are many arrangements described as 'partnerships' e.g. between the public and the private or voluntary sectors which are essentially commercial contracts. A useful definition of partnership describes it simply as 'Collaboration between people in different organisations in pursuit of shared goals' (Brookes, 2007).

In this chapter, because of the importance that has been ascribed to them by government, we have chosen to focus on Local Strategic Partnerships (LSPs). We will look at the learning emerging from our evaluation of and our work with LSPs and what this tells us about the differences between organisational leadership and leadership in partnership settings. We identify some of the problems that sometimes are encountered in partnership working and the reasons why nonetheless it is important to find ways to make them effective. We argue that LSPs are complex networks requiring 'systems leadership' and begin to set out some of the capabilities those emergent systems leaders are beginning to display.

Recent developments in partnership working

In considering partnership working, probably the most important development over the past decade has been the creation in every locality in the country of a LSP. These have brought together for the first time all the key public service agencies within that area and usually representatives from business, the voluntary and community sector and faith groups. LSPs provide the basis for a 'Sustainable Community Strategy' that identifies and tries to tackle the most important needs of a whole community – and makes possible a shared responsibility across agencies for what some have called 'the leadership of place'.

Local authorities, as the organisations with direct democratic legitimacy, have in most cases played the leading role in these partnerships. However by bringing together statutory, business and voluntary sectors LSPs have offered an opportunity to build on the electoral legitimacy and accountability of local authorities. Shared legitimacy for agreed plans and the actions of other agencies has been developed by gaining consent for them through public consultation processes. Also LSPs provide a means by which all the agencies can hold each other to account for shared goals, through a performance management process. This has helped some LSPs to 'come alive' and move from being talking shops, to turning 'strategy' into action.

This improvement in collaboration and delivery has in recent years been reinforced by a second important development. The government has introduced Local Area Agreements (LAA), which, in theory, offer the opportunity for a negotiation between the locality and central government about the priorities for spending. Since government funds most of the public agencies in an area they will inevitably want to direct some of the priorities, but the LAA process sets up an evidence based dialogue between the needs of the area as identified by local agencies, and the priorities of government. While it is still early days, an opportunity now exists for a more adult dialogue between the centre and localities than simply 'top down management'; and a framework has been created for agreed action-plans between agencies that have very different accountabilities. By allowing localities to pool funding, by introducing the 'duty to co-operate' for other public service agencies, by reducing the number of overall targets to a manageable negotiated set (currently the government are expecting 35 negotiated targets plus an additional 16 educational targets) and by introducing a new regulatory regime that looks at the effectiveness of all the agencies working together in a locality, government hopes to build effective partnerships capable of acting decisively to tackle local problems.

The list of 23 'named partners' that have a duty to cooperate in the LAA process (Local Government and Public Involvement Health Act 2007) gives a sense of the potential scale of the system which LSPs have to manage. Some of the bodies on the list such as PCTs have well developed local structures that are co-terminus with some local authorities. Others such as National Park Authorities are national or regional bodies that don't have standardised local structures and their importance will vary markedly between localities. LSPs themselves therefore vary considerably in scale. Depending on the nature of the locality they can be relatively simple groupings of co-terminus agencies or highly complex inter-related structures across large counties.

LSPs have become important to central government because national policy only 'joins up' at local level. The need for so much partnership working is an indirect consequence of the fragmentation of decision-making at both national and regional level. Regional agencies include Government offices of the regions, Regional Development Agencies and Strategic Health Authorities, while at local level services are provided by police authorities, PCTs, hospital trusts, local authorities, learning and Skills Councils, funding bodies such as English Partnerships, the Housing and Communities Agency, Natural England, and so on. Despite promises by Conservative and Labour governments to reduce the number of quangos this fragmentation of delivery agencies seems set to continue.

While on the one hand the current government has created more quasi-independent bodies, on the other, it has emphasised a commitment to ensuring that services are not simply delivered efficiently by each agency, but are integrated to ensure positive social outcomes – such as reductions in obesity, or improvements in community cohesion. Since no single agency has the power to achieve complex social outcomes, collaboration becomes necessary.

'Common sense, the evidence base, perhaps even our genetic code tells us that collaboration makes sense. The big complex social problems cannot be tackled within the fragmented public sector delivery systems' (Parker and Gallagher 2007).

The focus on outcome goals and the fragmentation of agencies has encouraged collaboration around shared strategies and clarity of contribution to these plans. At the same time the financial difficulties faced by many public sector agencies has led to a more determined attempt to share service provision and delivery mechanisms across boundaries. This is reflected in the ways in which partnership working has developed in recent years.

Evidence of progress?

Over the past five years, partnership working has developed considerably. In many parts of the country we can now point to shared delivery systems. Some have involved co-locating services, for example Bradford have developed combined one stop shops/customer service centres, where a range of local and national agencies share the same building and in some cases offer a single point of contact for the public. The drive for greater efficiency has also led to some examples of shared management and internal organisation e.g. two district councils sharing a chief executive; Herefordshire Council and PCT have a joint management team and some shared functions. Swindon is also developing integrated working between the council and the PCT. The West London Alliance is well-advanced in sharing a number of services. Cities such as Leeds have a long track record of successful partnership working, leading to substantial economic regeneration. Croydon has worked in partnership with the local community and with the business community, using its town centre business improvement district to raise over a million pounds to invest in the area. South Tyneside and Wigan have used their Local Strategic Partnerships to develop radical, innovative thinking about intractable local problems. In other areas, authorities have worked together on ambitious infrastructural and regeneration projects; the Association of Greater Manchester Authorities (AGMA) shares many services, jointly owns Manchester Airport and all the authorities work closely together to develop the regional economy, and in particular to develop a transport infrastructure for the greater Manchester area. The East Kent Partnership brings together four councils wanting to develop a shared long-term vision for the prosperity of their sub-region.

Local Area Agreements (LAA) are leading to the delivery of new shared projects with pooled funding. Innovative multi-agency projects are being set up all over the country, in response to new targets on healthy eating, childhood obesity, reducing the carbon-footprint and improving community cohesion.

In two-tier areas, successful working between counties and districts is beginning to bear fruit, a shared agenda is beginning to integrate the work of districts, counties and partner agencies in counties such as Suffolk and Devon, and in some areas districts are taking the lead as the 'delivery arm' of the county LSP.

But progress elsewhere has been slow. The gap in performance between the most successful partnerships and the least successful is widening. After five years, many LSPs argued that they were 'on the cusp' of moving from planning to delivery (Goss 2005). Five years on, some partnerships are still finding the transition difficult to make. In some areas, given the history of distrust between many of the organisations involved, the transition was never going to be easy. The apocryphal cynic who describes partnerships as 'the suppression of mutual loathing in pursuit of government money' is often quoted. For every success there is another story where even the lure of new funding, the threat of intervention and the reality of financial pressures have not been enough to overcome the obstacles to partnership working.

Practitioners often argued that partnership is slower and less effective than single agencies working alone, processes are cumbersome and unwieldy, with often a sense of drift and lack of clarity of purpose (Goss 2001).

However, the fragmentation of service provision within each locality means that partnerships are here to stay.

It seems very unlikely that power will be transferred back to local authorities, indeed under either of the two main parties; policy is to create more single purpose organisations with their own local electoral legitimacy, which will intensify the need for integrated working.

The financial difficulties ushered in by the credit crunch could make agencies retreat back into their silos and abandon experimental work that cannot demonstrate instant results. But as resources become more scarce, and social outcomes become harder to achieve – the need for partnership working will arguably become stronger in the future.

The unique qualities of partnerships

As Barry Quirk (2007) has noted:

> Collaboration is a style of thinking and acting at the level of practice and operation. This does not come easily; it is an unnatural activity – often seen as the antithesis of getting things done.

Working with others involves a 'transaction cost', typically time spent discussing and agreeing what to do and how to do it. Experience teaches us that the more people we involve the greater these 'transaction costs' tend to be. It is this that leads to much of the frustration with partnership working.

However, rather than seeing these additional costs as a problem, it is possible to see 'the cost' of additional time spent thinking and understanding each other as a benefit. Partnerships offer the possibility of breaking out of the assumptions and constraints that lock member agencies into traditional solutions – creating the potential of 'unoccupied' or 'experimental' space where organisational obstacles and 'group think' are less strong. It is the collision of the different mind-sets, assumptions and professional practices that can create a breakthrough – finding solutions to problems that have never been solved within organisational boundaries.

Many of the difficulties LSPs have faced are a consequence of not properly exploring the characteristics of partnerships that make them different from individual organisations. By recognising these differences and finding new ways to work to respond to them, many of these 'problems' can become the source of fruitful new thinking.

Our study of LSPs teaches us that it can often take successful partnerships five to ten years to develop to the point where they begin to work successfully. Perhaps this should not be surprising – since partnerships require very different skills and mind-sets, and radically different ways of working. Achievement of short-term goals needs to be balanced against building relationships and achievements in the long term.

Partnerships are a powerful example of situations that Ron Heifetz identifies as 'adaptive' (Heifetz 1994) – in which the solutions cannot be found within the mental frameworks that were created to deal with problems within single organisations. The problems faced are rarely 'technical' problems for which there are known solutions. The solutions require new creative thinking which operates at the point of interface of different organisational perspectives – and it is the collision of these ideas and mind-sets that can create a breakthrough.

The differences between working in partnership and working within single organisations need to be recognised, and new approaches developed in response. Many of the typical problems faced by partnerships are really a failure to develop these new adaptive responses.

Typical problems facing partnerships

The problems that emerge within LSPs seem to derive from one or more of the following factors and often from several at once.

Absence of shared goals

Partnership working cannot be successful without agreeing collectively to a set of shared goals. The negotiation of shared goals is made harder when objectives are imposed from the centre, or from a single partner organisation – since this encourages other partners to play passive roles of compliance or acquiescence. If partnerships are 'required' to act in a particular way in order to comply with government guidance, or to fit a neat LAA structure rather than being driven by the real priorities of the individuals or organisations concerned, partnership working is unlikely to move from information sharing or planning to action. In one partnership meeting we facilitated between a SHA and a county council, for example, participants identified a list of 20 goals for the partnership. But when the two agencies were each asked to pinpoint their five highest priorities – no goal appeared on the list of both organisations. They had simply strung together two separate lists. No wonder collaboration never really took off!

Without shared goals, partnerships often exhibit what we have called the 'leadership paradox' – a partnership full of proven and successful leaders in which no one is demonstrating leadership (Goss 2005). Unless powerful individuals within a partnership are personally highly committed to the partnership goals, they often choose not to take responsibility for dealing with problems within the partnership, making a judgement that their time and energy is better invested elsewhere.

Agreement to shared goals is not inevitable. There is an assumption that with enough hard work, a consensus can be built between all the organisations in an area. Sometimes however, interests and priorities conflict. Recognising this will be important if time and resources are not to be wasted, since if partnerships fail to agree on shared goals, they are unlikely to succeed at anything.

The wrong people – or the wrong structure

For partnerships to work effectively, they need a structure that is fit for purpose, and the right people involved to achieve their aims. So key decisions are about how to organise the partnership, about who attends and what they are allowed to decide. In the beginning there was a tendency to go for inclusiveness which may have helped resolve the issues around representation but led to complex structures that made meaningful dialogue and decision-making very difficult.

Many LSPs underwent a radical restructuring to become fit for purpose for the new LAA process, moving to smaller decision-making boards, comprised mainly of those who could commit resources, often balanced by occasional large-scale events to which larger numbers of stakeholders are invited. Getting structure and membership right will never be easy, and as partnerships evolve will require constant attention.

Some of the more intractable problems are experienced in two-tier areas, where it is difficult at county level to engage effectively with all the district councils without unbalancing the partnership towards local government and making other agencies feel peripheral. The structural problems facing LSPs remain difficult to resolve within two-tier government. Nevertheless there have been some innovative networking and whole systems thinking, for example in Devon, Gloucestershire, Lancashire and Hertfordshire. Furthermore as we will argue below it is often more a question of building good relationships than trying to finesse ever more complex governance structures.

Governance and accountability

Problems often arise because of uncertainty about accountability and governance arrangements. Worries have been expressed about the accountability of LSPs to the public – they are largely invisible to the public, but are expected to commit resources and take decisions. Accountability is 'fractured' with partners being accountable in many different ways – some to central government departments, some to their boards and members, some to local elected members and central government. This fractured external accountability can make it hard to reach and keep agreements about goals and the allocation of resources to achieve them.

In 2005 the Audit Commission took a broad view of accountability (Audit Commission 2005) taking account, giving account, being held to account and providing redress when things have gone wrong. While individual public sector organisations have defined systems for each of these aspects of accountability, partnerships have to evolve a process which offers sufficient legitimacy and accountability to the public. Most operate by 'borrowing' the legitimacy and accountability of the partner agencies, and in particular the democratic legitimacy of the Local Authority, rather than creating cumbersome new procedures and systems. As argued earlier the Sustainable Community Strategy offers a useful 'umbrella' of legitimacy, so that private, community and third sector agencies have legitimacy for actions that fulfils a Sustainable Community Strategy, which has been consulted on and agreed. However as partnerships move from planning to doing, it becomes more important for partners to be able to hold each other to account and to organise 'consequences' for failure to deliver.

With the greater degree of discretion over spending as envisaged by LAAs and a general shift from strategy to delivery then external accountability across the four Audit Commission dimensions also becomes increasingly important. We believe that this offers an opportunity to overcome the criticisms that have been levelled at partnerships by many elected members. Unless they are members of the executive they are unlikely to have been personally involved and have often received little information. Yet they are the point through which members of the public are likely to voice their concerns. In the early days of LSPs, the role of politicians was often unclear, and backbench and opposition politicians often feared 'power creep' towards unaccountable partnerships and away from democratically elected councillors. As LSPs have developed and as the LAA process has evolved, the cabinet and leaders of local authorities have begun to play a more central role. There is however considerable scope for improved involvement of backbench members, through the overview and scrutiny process. When this works well it not only helps to connect members to partnerships and improve democratic accountability but also provides opportunities for members of the public to play a role via attendance at scrutiny panels.

Management and agency

Lack of resources to support partnership working was reported as a problem by some LSPs in the early years. The lack of dedicated partnership resources has been and will continue to be a barrier to success, which may well be why in our evaluation of LSPs we found that those partnerships in Neighbourhood Renewal (NR) areas that had specific additional funding tended to be more sophisticated than those that didn't (CLG 2007).

Some partnerships have set up their own funding and management arrangements, with a chief executive or director working directly to the LSP with their own staff. While this can make day-to-day running of the partnership far easier, most partnerships, have to 'bend' the mainstream budgets of the partner agencies, in order to achieve their goals; so that much of what is done depends on the relationships between and the commitment of the key partners.

Some LSPs have floundered because they don't yet have the power of 'agency' (Argyris and Schon 1996). While individual organisations have the power to make things happen, partnerships often remain 'inert' unable to command or deploy resources unless decisions are linked directly into the delivery systems of participating organisations. To implement their plans, partnerships need the power of the decision-makers within the partnership to commit to actions – and make things happen.

Cultural differences and 'defensive behaviours'

Relationships inside a partnership can be damaged by processes or assumptions that don't take account of the fact that partnerships have to work differently to single organisations; and by the failure of partners to recognise their own cultural assumptions about what is 'normal'. Each organisation has a 'default' mode of operating, which can be imported into the partnership without the underlying assumptions being examined and without this being obvious to those doing it. This may take a number of forms but typically will relate to sensitivities around such issues as status, values, working practices and ways of giving and receiving information. For example, a council leader, used to being treated deferentially by managers in his/her organisation, may find that he or she needs to work differently in a partnership setting. A meeting around a typical board table may be interpreted by some as a signal for a formal committee style approach but by others as simply somewhere to park their papers.

Of course as well as unintended problems of cross cultural working partnerships may also be unsuccessful because key players are attending in a 'defensive' role, making sure that nothing happens that gets in the way of their organisational objectives, rather than making a commitment to achieve partnership goals. The absence of shared goals often leads to confusion and a feeling of lack of direction, but even where they exist partners may not see them as being as important as their own. They may indulge in defensive behaviours for example trying to get others to accept or to contribute to goals that their organisation has already established rather than genuine partnership goals, or being inflexible in changing or reshaping existing activities.

Central-local relationships

Partnerships can also be adversely affected by the impact of expectations or demands from central government. Since partnerships always have to involve the voluntary coming together of key decision-makers – too much government interference can prevent the agreement of truly shared goals, and turn a partnership into a 'paper exercise'. Civil servants in central government often genuinely want to encourage effective partnerships at local level, without understanding that their own actions can add to the problems.

We can identify two different models of central-local relationships that are often assumed by civil servants and by local managers.

Figure 17.1 shows the relatively successful relationship that can develop between a directive centre and a compliant locality.

Figure 17.1   Relationship Between a Directive Centre and a Compliant Locality

Relationships between the two go smoothly if the centre can be clear and directive about the performance it requires and the processes it is expecting and key partners at local level are happy to comply with these expectations, have the necessary evidence, systems and performance management systems in place and the skills and knowledge necessary to achieve the outcomes through the processes suggested to them through government guidance.

Figure 17.2 shows a second model, with a different set of relationships, between a creative, purposeful local partnership and an enabling, supportive centre.

Here, relationships go smoothly if the locality is clear about shared goals, has negotiated actions between key agencies, identifying the evidence and resources necessary and is willing to experiment with new approaches on a multi-agency basis. Success here relies on a non-interventionist centre, willing to allow local experimentation, recognising that effective solutions are most likely to emerge at local level and willing to support and work alongside localities, helping to locate necessary resources and remove obstacles.

Problems emerge when the two 'implicit systems' collide, for example where a weak locality loses its way in the context of complicated and confusing guidance from the centre, or where poor local partnerships remain directionless because they are unsupported. Equally, a purposeful and creative local partnership can be constrained by national policies that are not joined up, or by central guidance or inflexibility that undermines local attempts to see problems holistically.

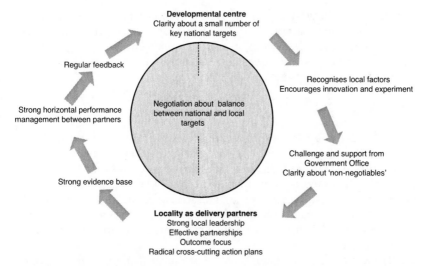

Figure 17.2 Relationships Between a Creative Purposeful Partnership and an Enabling Supportive Centre

Some of the most successful LSPs have been willing to challenge government assumptions – determining their own objectives and targets, and designing their own solutions and ways of working, unwilling to be 'boxed in' by government process. It seems to be a mark of a strong partnership that partners are willing to take control of their own governance and delivery arrangements rather than simply 'following guidance'.

Leadership in partnerships

Not all the problems set out above can be 'solved' through good leadership, although sometimes in the literature and in conversations both the problems and the solutions are presented as one of leadership. In this context it seems as if 'leadership' is being used as a synonym for 'being effective' and consequently says more about our lack of understanding than our insight. As Jim Collins pointed out in Good to Great (Collins 2001):

> Every time we attribute everything to leadership we are no different from the people in the 1500s who attributed everything they didn't understand (such as famine and plague) to God.

Nevertheless, we have observed, over the past five years, that effective partnership working requires good leadership, and that good leadership in a partnership context is different to the leadership needed within a single organisation.

A research study undertaken by OPM into what makes leadership effective within a partnership identified four clusters of competencies: (OPM 2007) – these were *focus on purpose: working with other organisations; building relationships and managing self.* Below, we set out the key findings in relation to each of these clusters.

Focus on purpose

A good leader in a partnership setting helps to focus the attention of the partnership on shared goals. In our research, interviewees stressed the importance of a leader being able to articulate a vision that could inspire partners, articulated in ways that helped them see the linkages between partnership goals and their own organisational goals. The purpose needed to be expressed in ways that identified the changes that would be achieved for the wider community, and helped everyone focus on outcomes rather than on process.

It is the existence of shared goals that makes it possible to release the leadership potential in a partnership. A good partnership leader is therefore able to explain how these goals fit within the wider policy context, both in relation to central and regional government demands, and in relation to the priorities for partner agencies. By understanding the context of the different organisations involved in the partnership, and accurately 'reading' the situation of individual partners and the wider context at regional and national level, it is possible to ensure that partners are not placed in impossible situations or faced with unrealistic demands.

Getting the best out of multi-agency working

Even when goals are shared, achieving them in a multi-agency context will always be challenging. All the individuals and agencies involved in a partnership will face their own challenges and constraints. Despite shared goals, real tensions are likely to surface over willingness to allocate resources. Different organisations have very different ways of doings things, and different room to manoeuvre. Leadership interventions therefore also involve building a shared set of 'rules of engagement' – and a shared set of values and ground rules for behaviour that will guide the work of the partnership both in and out of meetings. This shared agreement about the 'what' and the 'how' means that there is a basic contract between members of the partnership, which is essential to any notion of internal accountability. This agreement provides a basis from which the partnership can be built and any challenge to what the partnership is spending time on or how people are behaving can be resolved. It also provides a means to access the leadership energy and commitment of those involved.

Another dilemma for partnerships can stem from the current organisational emphasis on value driven leadership (Bundred, Grace and Taylor 2007). 'leadership should be values driven, a visible commitment to their organisation, which transcends their ego, but if a clash of values occurs in a partnership setting and makes partnership unworkable what of leadership then?'

The answer to this challenge lies in the ability of successful leaders to create a process through which the values that bind them as a partnership can be negotiated, without expecting anyone to simply carry all their organisational goals or values into the partnership. Shared values within the partnership should provide a basis for a dialogue about diversity and difference.

The ability to negotiate goals and values in multi-agency settings seems to depend on the creation of good physical and psychological spaces where exploration and dialogue can take place. This means that a critical leadership task is helping to design structures and processes that work well, encouraging experimentation, innovation and new ways of working. A good leader ensures that processes are fit for purpose and is willing to challenge and change them when they are not. For example they might suggest new ways of working, such as using maps and other evidence in workshop settings, to undertake creative visioning; or simply ensure that overfull agendas don't prevent the discussion that is needed.

A crucial leadership role is to help the partnership understand the creative tension between different organisations as a source of productive thinking, rather than as an obstacle. Differences between members of the partnership can provide opportunities for learning about other ways of thinking through problems. An important leadership role will be to encourage a positive view of that diversity.

Building relationships with others

A key leadership role is to build the relationships within a partnership that enable plans to be turned into action. Strong relationships are characterised by mutual trust. However trust needs to be built over time and in the early days of many partnerships 'the history' may have got in the way.

Good leaders create an environment within which relationships and trust can safely be built. This can be done in many ways, but some of the behaviours we have observed include welcoming new members into the group, responding positively to the suggestions of others, exploring the views of everyone in the room, understanding their hopes and expectations, and reflecting back accurately what others have said, or how others feel. Good leaders also help partners to feel comfortable, by making clear the purpose of meetings, setting timetables for work so that people can see where they can contribute, and working with partners informally outside meetings to check their commitment and ensure their problems are recognised.

If the partnership is to be meaningful, good leaders may sometimes have to challenge inappropriate behaviour and that will almost certainly mean helping members of the partnership to have robust discussions and arguments. However few partnerships have reached the point of actually 'calling' behaviour that contravenes their own ground rules. If they were to do so, as Heinemann (2007) has argued it would send an incredibly powerful message.

Managing self

The absence of formal authority puts more emphasis on personal style and in particular the ability to behave in ways that build relationships and influences others. A good leader in a partnership setting can adapt to the needs of the partnership, playing the role that will make the greatest contribution.

The skilled leader in partnerships will be more interested in achieving the right result than being seen to be in charge. These are the type of skills associated with Daniel Goleman's work on emotional intelligence (Goleman 1998); an emotionally intelligent leader will have the ability to read a situation and to make an informed choice about how to intervene. This will involve self-awareness about the sort of impact one is making on others, on the consequences of different sorts of interventions, and about how to respond appropriately to the needs of others. At the micro level this may mean being able to read when a meeting isn't working and suggesting an alternative process, rather than making a speech. It is more like skilled facilitation than formal leadership. Some of the skills needed are close to good coaching skills; i.e. an ability to listen carefully and really hear what is being said, understand the language in its context and to ask good questions that throw light on a problem.

A leader can also help to create the conditions for success through modelling the partnership values, by taking personal responsibility for actions, for example, and by ensuring that they are actively held to account by their partners. Chesterman and Horne (2002) see a key role of leaders in partnerships as 'brokering between different belief systems'. The role of the leader is to help people to listen to, and hear, others who have different ways of thinking and different perspectives on shared problems.

Ralph Stacey (1992) makes a very helpful distinction between the leadership required when there is agreement about what to do and relative certainty about what will work; as opposed to situations where there is far less agreement and no-one is sure what will work, The former lend themselves to what has been termed 'transactional leadership' (Kotter 1990) or what others think of as tight management of performance. However, when the goals of a partnership require exploration, and there is considerable uncertainty about what to do next, nothing is gained by someone taking charge and trying to direct others. In these circumstances, it is much more important to encourage others to take the time to explore ideas. In this context a critical leadership role may be to create a safe space in which others feel able to explore the problem before they jump to action, to 'open things up' by investigating and experimenting and allowing time for "solutions to evolve"'. Once it is clear what works then it becomes appropriate to 'close things down' through action planning and performance management.

The way forward: Developing a leadership system

Over the last century leaders, managers, theorists and consultants have all invested considerable time and effort into improving organisational working and performance. Despite this effort there is still a considerable gap between theory and practice. People are desperate for 'simple solutions' and there is a constant stream of management literature providing new approaches (or more commonly reworked 'old' ideas). Yet as Phil Rosenzweig (2007) said 'Nothing really works, at least not all the time. In spite of our desire for simple steps the reality of management is much more uncertain than we would often like to admit, searching for the secrets of success reveals little about the world of business but speaks volumes about the searchers, their aspirations and their desire for certainty'.

If this is true in the case of single organisations how much more must it be so for partnerships that have had relatively little time to develop and have received relatively little attention?

LSPs, present even greater challenges, since they are not simple partnerships, but are, in effect a network within a locality linking, public, private and voluntary organisations and the communities they are serving.

It is helpful therefore to see the leadership required in partnerships as more like a 'leadership system' requiring leadership from many individuals and organisations to be exercised from several different points within the system. It is often as important in leadership terms to maintain relationships through the informal spaces between meetings as it is to intervene effectively in the partnership meetings – as useful to create processes in which the leadership of others can be encouraged as it is to lead oneself. A key 'leadership role' is to build the capacity of the whole system – making it possible for others to invest their leadership – developing the 'capacity of networked relationships' (Chesterman and Horne 2002) and developing the conditions within which solutions are 'negotiated, not imposed'.

If partnerships are to succeed, they have to build both the authority and the power to act. Crucial to success is the connection of political leadership, through elected councillors, to those with the delivery power of a range of public, private and voluntary bodies, and to the support, energy and goodwill of the wider community. Most importantly, networks need an 'orchestrating leadership' able to link together purposefully the endeavour of the many different leaders within the overall system.

Effective leaders in this setting recognise that their role is to work with others to provide integrated leadership – so that the whole becomes greater than the sum of the parts. It is this role of helping to orchestrate and optimise the leadership of others that makes leadership in partnership settings so challenging, and so inspiring. Leaders do this in many different ways, but we have identified some of these within this chapter. System leaders help to agree clear goals and they explicitly contract with partners to shape and clarify expectations. They are willing to act and work with diversity to create spaces for genuine dialogue and build effective governance, structure, processes and leadership behaviours in others. They actively design 'safe space' for partners to experiment together and learn; and they create an environment where relationships can succeed through their own behaviours and their willingness to support others. Finally, they are able to inspire others, keeping a focus on outcomes, and holding the anxiety of colleagues long enough to allow new possibilities to emerge.

References

Argyris, C. and Schon, D. (1996) *Organisational Learning II*. Reading, Mass: Addison Wesley.

Audit Commission (2005) 'Governing Partnerships Oct 2005', *Public Sector National report*.

Brookes, S. (2007) '360° Leadership in the Public Sector', paper presented to the third transatlantic dialogue University of Delaware, May 31–June 2, 2007.

Bundred, S., Grace, C. and Taylor, S. (April 2007) Forward to 'Local Leadership for Global Times', Solace foundation imprint.

Chesterman, D. and Horne, M. (2002) *Local Authority Demos 2002*.

Collins, J. (2001) *Good to Great*. Random House.

CLG National Evaluation of LSPs Report on 2006 (2007) *Survey of All English LSPs*.

Goleman, D. (1998) *Working with Emotional Intelligence*. Bloomsbury.

Goss, S. (2001) *Making Local Governance Work Networks, Relationships and the Management of Change*. Basingstoke: Palgrave.

Goss, S. (May 2005) 'Leadership in Local Strategic Partnerships', Issues Paper, *National Evaluation of Local Strategic Partnerships*. London: ODPM.

Heifetz, R.A. (1994) *Leadership Without Easy Answers*. Belknap: Harvard University Press.

Heinemann, B.W. Jnr (April 2007) *Avoiding Integrity Land Mines*. HBR.

Kotter, J.P. (1990) *A Force for Change: How Leadership Differs from Management*. Free Press.

Local Government and Public Involvement in Health Act 2007 Part 5 Chapter 1.

OPM (2007) *Characteristics of Effective Leadership in Partnership: A Self-Assessment Tool*. OPM website.

Parker, S. and Gallagher, N. (2007) 'Introduction', in Parker, S. and Gallagher, N. (ed.), *The Collaborative State Demos*. London.
Quirk, B. (2007) 'Roots of Cooperation and Routes to Collaboration', in the *Collaborative State Demos*. London.
Rosenzweig, P. (2007) *The Halo Effect*. Free Press.
Stacey, R. (1992) *Managing the Unknowable*. San Francisco, CA: Jossey Bass.

Part IV

Outlining a Public Leadership Approach

18
The Challenge for Public Leadership Arising from Mixed Modes of Governance

Dominique Lelièvre-Finch

Introduction

This chapter explores the challenges faced by public leaders within changing modes of governance in public service delivery by focusing on selected aspects of the way they construe their role and enact their practice.

Increasingly, public services in many areas of public life are delivered through multiple organisations linked in partnerships that straddle the public and private divide. However, the rhetoric of partnership and joined-up service delivery masks dissimilar situations in empirical settings. The oversimplified portrayal of the dynamics of governance of such entities fundamentally limits our understanding of the context in which public leadership is enacted and how it can impact on the creation of public value.

In an attempt to clarify the nature of the evolving environment within which public leaders operate, the first part of this chapter examines critically three conceptualisations of the changing forms of public service delivery chains.

Public leaders and senior executives are heralded by many as the coordinating force behind such partnerships. Drawing on existing empirical studies, this chapter then explores the challenges faced by public leaders. It suggests some of the ways leaders address the dilemmas in these complex environments and highlights elements that are likely to promote effective leadership in a mixed mode of governance.

In conclusion, the chapter will outline avenues for further research towards a comparative agenda that allows for a better articulation of the complex links between the conceptualisation and practice of leadership and the characteristics of public-service delivery chains.

The issues

Conceptualisations of leadership and governance regimes

Changing modes of governance represented by a move from bureaucracies to networks, itself resulting from fragmentation of the value chain at the delivery end of public services, pose substantial challenges for the study of leadership. This applies to both the definition and practice of leadership. In governance terms, public leaders have to deal with a broad range of organisations – public, non-profit as well as private/ for-profit organisations. In a bureaucratic environment, leadership was traditionally linked to a hierarchical organisational structure but now public leadership is more often linked to a market and networked environment.

As noted by Newman (2005a) and others, each governance arrangement constructs its own image of a leader, an image clearly formed in the case of either bureaucratic or market governance. In hierarchical regimes, it is the traditional administrator, based on the bureaucratic principle of the separation of office from personal preference, the ethos being associated with neutrality, accountability upwards and professional autonomy. By contrast, in market regimes, the leader is portrayed as an entrepreneur (embodied by vision, charisma and clearly displayed values). The person's values are an integral part of the office and leadership in this context is linked to organisational turn-around and change management (Du Gay 2000, 2005; Salaman 2005).

Assuming that network-based forms of coordination are displacing both market and bureaucratic modes of governance and in the context of the growing salience of the discourse of transformational leadership, what then characterises new public leaders? Issues of governance come to the fore, and in keeping with earlier chapters, contextualising leadership is important. In particular, there is a need to consider the links between the (so-called) logic of network forms of governance and notions of shared and distributed leadership (Brookes 2007) such as those discussed and exemplified in previous chapters in this book and the following questions:

What are the situational characteristics (such as the contested nature of issues and the complexity of environment) that specifically impinge on the definition and practice of leadership?

How do leaders explore and construct their identity as transformational leaders, as well as deploy their practice of leadership?

To which extent can leaders favour the construction of meanings, and/or co-construct meaningful explanations of change?

How do they demonstrate entrepreneurial behaviour and promote organisational innovation and the development of collaborative capacity?

Changing contexts of public service delivery

In addressing these questions it is useful first to consider the characteristics of the context in which public leaders are increasingly active. The 'Third Way' policy agenda (Newman 2001) and networked forms of public-service delivery often accompany the notion of collaborative practice involving the public, private and not-for-profit sectors. Partnerships constitute the new, preferred way of delivery for public services. In the first instance we need to move away from simply invoking vague labels, such as networks and partnerships, and more towards analysing the environment, relating its features and dynamics to the actions of embedded actors – namely leaders and managers.

Networks and network forms of governance have generated considerable interest and a large body of literature (e.g. Rhodes 1997; Kickert, Klijn and Koppenjan 1997). Norms of trust and reciprocity are generally considered the central regulating mechanism although this view is questioned by some authors. Indeed, according to Ackroyd *et al.* (2004), Bachmann (2001), Hardy *et al.* (1998) and others, inter-organisational control relies on a mixed pattern that also involves authority and other forms of coercion.

Network governance remains a diffuse notion and there is a tendency to emphasise the learning benefits of network forms of organisations. In the majority of the literature on networks, the social processes that enable actors to create specific and stable spaces of exchange, and that are deemed effective in promoting inter-organisational learning seemingly apply in a blanket fashion. A normative view of network effects of governance (i.e. the network is considered a superior organisational form or principle) is implicit in these approaches. This may be because, as Podolny and Page (1998) stress, many authors implicitly consider the network in a functional perspective and assume that networks automatically favour exchange and generation of knowledge and the building of competencies.

The rhetoric about trust and network effectiveness stems primarily from research on private sector networks (where networks tend to be self-initiated) and may have limited transfer value to the public sphere where often networks tend to be mandated or contracted. This has considerable implications for the dynamics of governance of these entities, and trust is not necessarily present or easy to build. Beyond trust, their mechanisms for governance and regulation are rarely considered in the available literature, and never in a comparative way.

When we try to understand the dynamics of the context of public service delivery one problem encountered is that public networks and collaborative inter-organisational arrangements are often discussed too broadly. The notions of *governance* (a coordinative structure), *mode of governance* (logic of coordination through hierarchy, market, network), and *governance arrangement* (specific form of corporate structure such as public-private partnerships) (Skelcher and Mathur 2004) are often conflated in analytical terms. This has the potential for obscuring many of the ensuing debates.

The interface between public and private organisations and public-private partnerships

What is the distinct, institutionalised context in which leadership is increasingly enacted for the delivery of public services? Public-private partnerships (PPPs) are particular organisational arrangements used as a vehicle for change in the context of the wide-ranging public sector reforms and at the forefront of the renewal of public delivery channels. This empirical phenomenon has generated considerable interest, both in theoretical and normative terms over the last decade or so. Described as an 'innovative approach to public management', they are seen as a 'risk-sharing relationship between the public and private sectors based on a shared aspiration to bring about a desired public policy outcome' (IPPR 2001: 40). In practice, however, it loosely describes arrangements where the public and private sectors deliver services cooperatively (Grimshaw *et al.* 2002; Skelcher 2005) and many of these partnerships represent unusual institutional forms (Brereton and Temple 1999).

A large part of available research heavily focuses on analysing the economic and financial outcomes rather than the nature and organisational dynamics of such partnerships. Some normative studies continue to produce arguments and counter-arguments on the desirability of such arrangements (e.g. financing risk between public and private sectors and benefits of market driven logic on public sector management approaches). More often than not, therefore, this object of study is discursively constructed through opposed rhetorical stances but our knowledge of the organisational characteristics and understanding of the dynamics of such a 'hybrid' remain minimal. Nevertheless, critical case studies analysing private sector involvement across different areas of public services highlight the nature of a broad range of barriers to the successful implementation of PPPs (Marchington *et al.* 2005).

However, these entities have become central to the delivery of public value. The main justification for their existence rests on the benefits that arise from combining the resources of government with those of private entities to deliver societal goals as partners draw on their complementarities. In organisational terms, their hybridity is allegedly characterised by a form of organisation that has both a public and private orientation and an indistinct boundary between public and private interests.

Readily identified in the literature are the problems connected to the ability of such a form of organisation to foster a mutual sense of purpose and joint strategic direction and goals among the main parties involved. There is inherently a deeper seated problem; whether there is a distinctive logic of functioning that underpins this particular mode of governance. If so, what element is it primarily based on (Market principles or administrative fiat)? As discussed earlier, trust is more a normative assumption than an intrinsic value of networks and network governance (particularly at the interface of the public and the private).

Additionally, accountability structures normally associated with this form of organising remain unclear, and for some authors, democratic considerations appear to have limited impact on the governance arrangements of PPPs (Grimshaw and Hebson 2005). Responsibility to ensure that community values are considered within such hybrids weighs heavily on the shoulders of public managers and leaders (Batley 1996; Ghere 2001) as they constitute the main mechanism of inter-organisational coordination (Agranoff and McGuire 2003; Newman 2005a).

The reality of public service delivery chains

Some authors reject the unified logic of network governance for the multiple and conflicting logics of organising present in evolving public service delivery chains. In this sense governance is not perceived as relying on the pure principle of heterarchy associated with networks, nor is it understood in terms of an opposition, or uneasy accommodation, between the public and private spheres.

Scarbrough (2000), Reed (2005), Newman (2001; 2005b) and others highlight the uncomfortable coexistence within public environments of divergent organising principles; markets, hierarchies and networks. Rather than a new 'organizational form' with a different logic (Powell 1990), evolving service delivery chains often involve 'hybrid' elements within existing organisational forms. The coexistence of several forms of organisation with divergent organising principles brings about complex and contradictory logics of governance (Marchington *et al.* 2005; Grimshaw and Hebson 2005), and interactions and working patterns that are proving difficult to institutionalise. In fact, bureaucracy and bureaucratic principles of organisation have not necessarily departed to give place to a new logic of collaborative practice extending across organisations and sectors (Reed 2005; Salaman 2005). The 'variable' geometry of network organising has not yet entirely displaced the 'fixed geometry' of bureaucratic organisation (Reed 2005: 133). What emerges is a 'hybridisation' rather than a paradigm shift as authors acknowledge the enduring presence of vertical 'control and command' structures (Ferlie *et al.* 2003); hybridisation that contains its own internal inconsistencies (Newman 2001).

In some settings professional power is to be reckoned with through knowledge segmented by specialisation and the dominance of a professional logic of hierarchy (e.g. Clinicians in healthcare). Thus, in environments such as the NHS, professional agency is at least as critical as managerial agency. The interplay between organisational and professional boundaries in public service networks can be particularly complex, and less powerful professional groups may find it difficult to enact boundary-spanning roles associated with new organisational forms (Currie, Finn and Martin 2008b). Overall though, the issue of strength of professional control can vary from one public environment to another and this will have an impact on the way networks of service delivery function. Furthermore, strong direction in the form of performance regimes reasserts a form of state control, albeit in an externalised form. Tensions between the logic of network governance and the presence of state intervention through targets, audits, etc. emerge.

In sum, and despite acknowledgement of complex and dispersed fields of power, the conceptualisation of public service delivery chains in theoretical terms is not strong. It suffers from too much description, labelling and rhetoric and not enough comparative analysis across sectors, types of services and core processes involved. In particular, it is not clear what constitutes the dominant principle of regulation, and issues of coordination and control continue to elude researchers faced with considerable complexity and variety in terms of organisational dynamics. As Brandsen and Van Hout observe in relations with partners within networks: 'providers find that they must both compete and co-operate, trust and distrust' and that the requirements for accountability – each of them reasonable in itself – become a threat to the organization's integrity when they come together in complex and contradictory configurations' (2006: 548).

The observations resulting from finer-grained studies of these organisational spaces – considered in parallel to the strong discourse of transformational leadership – emphasise the role of agency. This positions public sector executives as the main coordinating force in these organisational settings (Salaman 2005; Newman 2005a; Williams 2002). Similarly, Provan and Kenis (2008) argue the role of management is critical for effective governance, 'especially regarding the handling of tensions inherent in each governance form' (2008: 233). The implication for agents (managers and leaders) operating in these diffuse and stratified fields of power and under contradictory logics of organising are substantial, their efforts primarily focused on addressing the resulting tensions. For many authors effective leadership is deemed, amongst other things: 'To provide a sense of cohesiveness, (...) an overarching sense of direction and vision, a healthy mechanism for innovation and creativity, and a resource for invigorating the organizational culture' (van Wart 2003: 215).

The next section draws on existing empirical studies and examines three illustrative dilemmas concerned with cross boundary management. This includes the way in which leaders perceive and construct their roles, how they work across value-systems and the extent to which they can facilitate the development of collective organisational capabilities.

Public leaders' challenges and dilemmas

Leaders' perception and construction of their roles

Notwithstanding the acknowledged multiple, overlapping and at times conflicting goals that public leaders have to contend with at the boundary of public and private provision, they also have to respond to other tensions. This includes the way in which performance is evaluated, authority deployed, human capital managed and the way in which leaders themselves are held accountable. Challenges faced include eliciting common goals, creating an atmosphere of trust, acting as a broker and mobilising different actors, harnessing and deploying collective resources in order to deliver public value. This supports the creation of interagency collaborative capacity but potentially exposes leaders to a number of fundamental dilemmas whilst their steering ability remains perceived as critical in holding the 'network' together (Agranoff and McGuire 2003).

A key challenge is the extent to which leaders agree and achieve a cohesive vision when faced with divergent cognitive sets. How do they favour the construction of meaningful explanations of change? How do they succeed in managing competing values and/or in incorporating divergent rationalities and values in emergent organisational strategies? From where do they draw their authority and legitimacy to act? Examples and insights are drawn from recent case studies of leadership (and public service delivery) in different sectors and settings. This assists an understanding as to how leaders construe and approach their role and the processes they deploy when exercising their leadership in context. Leaders are both agents as well as objects of change and it is important to see how they construct their roles and their understanding of the dilemmas they face, as articulated through the notion and discourse of the transformational leader.

Considering the fractures brought about by changing modes of governance and evolving state policy, Newman draws on a multi-sector sample to explore the micro-politics of public policy delivery. She shows how the discourse of 'transformational leadership' offers the possibility of new positioning and new forms of identities for public leaders. While this discourse did not appear to produce a fundamental change in leaders in terms of their role, identities and alliances were shifting. Most of respondents were becoming more active agents, although the juxtaposition of feelings such as 'confusion and loss' with those of 'freedom and excitement' were often reported. There was a growing concern about the tension inherent between government stated goals of collaboration and partnership and the intensification of external control through targets. These tensions were negotiated by different actors in different ways, the study highlighting the importance of discourse in both developing new forms of identities and in framing the dilemmas leaders were confronted with:

> There are a lot of conflicts between what you know and believe will make things different for patients from a local perspective and what you are being told. We are looking at the spaces within government priorities to legitimize issues that will make a difference to local populations.
>
> (Senior Manager, Health Service [Newman 2005b]: 204])

Some used government discourse as a means of enhancing managerial power. Others took some of the dominant policy discourse and coupled it with alternative views that were more reflective of a public service ethos. However, the space for 'transgressive' meaning making appeared limited. Nevertheless by reappropriating both political and policy discourses and using them to reframe meaning, such actors legitimised their position in a way that did not fundamentally depart from their ethos and focus on public value goals and outcomes.

This more dynamic view of leadership reflects the notion of entrepreneurial leadership. A study by Currie *et al.* (2008a) drew a sample from the national health sector, secondary schools and further education colleges. It showed the latter concept was readily (if cautiously) embraced by the leaders interviewed. They were able to position themselves within such discourse and translate it within their context. Indeed, many appeared frustrated at professional intransigence towards innovative reconfiguration of service delivery (health sector) and this new model of leadership appeared suitable in their eyes with other policy developments such as public-private partnerships (2008: 995). Whilst recognising that the scope for entrepreneurial behaviour needed to be understood in the light of public sector organisational aims, the main limitations on the subjects arose – not from how they viewed their role – but from organisational constraints on the way in which they could enact it.

A contrasting study in the educational sector details how the policy rhetoric of transformational leadership was seemingly resisted or ignored by school heads and senior actors in this environment (Currie and Lockett 2007 and see also Gunter and Forrester, chapter 4 of this volume which raises the interaction with the socio-historical context as a central issue). Similarly, Stokes and Clegg argued that while expected to align themselves with a highly specific rhetoric of change, the senior managers they studied 'experienced this rhetoric as confused, ambiguous and political' (2002: 234) and promoting contradictory and competing policy decisions. Managers seemed unable to reconcile the conflicting priorities, as well as the dilemmas of identity that they experienced, but displayed instead an orientation purely to political survival. Instead of replacing the old public service ethos with a new ethic, the authors claim that the process of public sector reform had a different impact. It 'produced new power games centred on the unresolved and contradictory dualism that the reform process introduced' (2002: 241).

Overall the evidence highlights the difficult task leaders – as agents of change – face in translating policy discourse into a vision that both preserve the legitimacy of their position and accord with their ethos. One of the challenges for public leaders remains that of retaining the 'publicness' of public-private partnerships (Skelcher 2005) and to ensure their accountability in terms of the public interest and the delivery of public value.

Bridging value systems

As identified by many authors, leaders in public service organisations 'often work with actors belonging to different institutional spheres and supporting divergent viewpoints, interests and values' (Denis *et al.* 2005: 455) and leaders have to find means of bridging value-systems and enabling collaboration between groups holding competing values. Emphasising the need to focus on the processes in which compromises are made between competing values-sets and associated legitimacies, Denis *et al.* (2005) bring to bear recent theoretical work by the conventionalist school on these issues. In conventionalist terms, a leader seeks to stimulate a set of processes that generate accommodation or compromise between competing values. This occurs through invention or negotiation of conventions (an artefact or an object that is supposed to crystallise the compromise between various logics in a specific context, e.g. a quality improvement policy, an organisational strategy, etc.). According to Denis *et al.*, special organisational devices such as committees, internal contracts, incentive schemes and performance indicators represent institutional mechanisms that may help leaders mediate between different values sets. An illustration of their argument is provided through the examination of strategy formation and evolution at the National Film Board of Canada (NFB), a cultural agency financed by the Federal Government of Canada. Through the action(s) of different leaders at different points in time, design and conventions, such as a new film, were successfully used to facilitate a compromise between the divergent logics of the 'inspirational' and the 'industrial' world, and to deal with the on-going tensions between these two worlds.

However, other studies featuring strategic endeavours and practices, designed to bring closer, different logics or value-sets, draw a more complex picture. Similarly set in the context of cultural organisations, Townley's (2002) longitudinal study examines the impact of business planning and performance measures into Cultural Facilities and Historical Resources (CFHR), a division of the provincial government of Alberta. It compared responses to competing and inconsistent logics brought about by a clash between the cultural and economic values spheres. The former concerns knowledge, practice and ethos of museum staff and management and the latter, business planning and performance measures. Formally, there was acquiescence or compliance with the requests to introduce a strategic performance measurement system. However, the embedding of private sector values that this initiative carried were resisted by staff such as this division manager, who expressed moral dilemmas between their mission as a 'values-based organization' and the need to think in a market-driven way:

> There is certainly a concern internally about maintaining historic integrity. I mean we are a mission driven organization but we are now having to [be] market-driven. If there is a continuum ... if there is mission and market ... people would prefer us closer to mission. We are concerned about historical integrity and the validity of the message. I mean, how far do you go before you start threatening the message? (Townley 2002: 178)

Instead of trying to accommodate the different cultural and market logics – and behind a façade of compliance – introducing business planning and performance measures re-emphasised a clash between fundamentally different logics. This increased ambiguity for the actors in the system.

The difficulty in reconciling competing and inconsistent logics based on different sets of values is echoed in a study carried out by the present author. This concerns promoting and implementing a service quality initiative within a large transport system in the UK involving public and private partners (Lelièvre-Finch and Murphy 2002). This service delivery chain was characterised by complex sets of interactions at operational and strategic levels and overshadowed by commercial and technical regulatory pressures (the latter instrumental in promoting common technical standards). The service quality initiative was strongly and publicly supported by the leader and board of management of the public organisation and its value readily recognised by senior executives in the private partner organisations. It was promoted through several organisational devices and management tools (forecasting, joint promotional campaign), consultation, negotiation and setting up service level agreements, and integration of data and information. Nevertheless, divergence in corporate goals, and organisational values and orientation between the 'partners' across the public-private divide inhibited the effectiveness of this communication and coordination. In particular, the specific norms and values prevalent within the public partner company and consistent with the nature of its corporate governance promoted certain work patterns and orientation that affected the decision-making process (slow decision-making) and the internal coordination of action (lateral or downward delegation). To private partners, these appeared to encourage a reactive and risk-avoidance stance.

> They talk, they talk but they don't know how to walk the talk. They don't know what it means to do service delivery jointly. They like talking, but actions: no. They are very scared of actions. (General Manager, Supplier Company).

Thus, high-level support and use of substantial communication and coordination to advance an initiative designed to promote joint ways of working did not help in bridging divergent value-sets. In fact, organisational devices such as those mentioned above were not effective in mediating between different spheres and value-sets, and appeared to undermine the central actor's (public organisation) own status as network coordinator. Each group of partners instead crystallised around their individual sets of norms and practices. This hampered the development of a service quality initiative as a strategic concern and the promotion of a system wide-perspective on this issue – a case of 'collaborative inertia' (Huxham and Vangen 2000).

Other studies consider how new contractual approaches and practices to delivering public service through public-private partnerships transform traditional values underpinning the public sector ethos and enable new sets of values to emerge that are not in opposition to either approaches. Hebson *et al.* (2003) show how public sector principles of accountability and bureaucratic behaviour were displaced under PPP by contract-led decision structures that required intense negotiations. This eroded initial high trust relations and encouraged public sector managers to mimic private sector techniques to secure 'value for money'. Similarly, Grimshaw *et al.* (2002) found that, far from a common understanding and definition of issues being forged, it was the norms and rules of the private sector management that underpinned reforms. Private partners' greater experience in working with contracts put public managers at a disadvantage.

Brereton and Temple (1999) offer an alternative view. In their study of such partnerships, an outcome-oriented service ethos was increasingly emerging as the managerial and decision-making style in the local authorities, and the local and regional organisations. Resembling some aspects of private sector values, this style disguised a complex redefinition of what frames service to the public. The authors describe this as a new public service ethos with consensus based on a synthesis of a new managerial culture. More traditional notions of good conduct were forged across public-private divides.

An inconsistent picture emerges. It illustrates the difficulty in reconciling values and suggests that often there is a superficial buy-in or that one set of values dominates the other. Whether this mixed picture reflects leaders' limited ability in analysing the sets of values and navigating credibly between different worlds, or their difficulty in overriding constraints inherent in the environments in which they are embedded is a moot point.

Developing the network organisational capabilities: Innovation and learning

Beyond the articulation of a vision that takes account of prevalent discourses and the bridging of competing value systems, a priority for leaders in a multi-organisational setting is to develop organisational capabilities within the network. This involves three aspects of skills and abilities:

- enhancing leadership throughout the network
- effective decision-making
- facilitation of learning and transfer of good practice.

Complex and intractable multi-agency issues often construed as wicked problems (Grint 2005 and see chapter 11) are common barriers to the effective delivery of public services. Breaking down these barriers requires innovative approaches. Combining partnership resources, for example, to stimulate innovation in the delivery of public services as well as to enhance the learning capacity of the partnership itself is a powerful demonstration of public leadership. Huxham and Vangen (2000) discuss a holistic view of leadership that can arise from any level or location among a network of organisations. This is what can be described as both shared and distributed leadership (see Chapter 1). Currie *et al.* (2008a) indeed note that the most effective chief executives or principals distribute entrepreneurial leadership beyond those in formal leadership positions, enabling others to lead and innovate. However, as alluded to earlier, innovative behaviour is predicated on the perception of risk and propensity to take risks. This is considerably different between the public and private sector (Currie *et al.* 2008a; Grimshaw and Hebson 2005). Often attributed to differences in organisational 'culture', a differing approach to risk-taking in the public sector is conditioned by a higher public visibility (in case of failure) as well as differing employment and reward systems, accompanied by tight state control. Changing perceptions of, and facilitating risk-taking requires leaders to exercise a degree of control over some of these factors; this varies substantially according to individual public sector and forms of partnerships. Intervention at the level of HR systems and the development of new competence structures, for example, are instrumental in promoting a basic change of focus. Conversely, 'the development of simultaneously more fragmented and more networked organizational forms raises issues of how to understand potential conflicts and contradictions around the "employer" dimension to the employment relationships' (Rubery *et al.* 2002: 645–646). These constitute immovable constraints that considerably limit the room for manoeuvre of public leadership in networks. It is a major challenge.

A leader's ability in guiding effective decision-making when seeking to promote and implement innovation is also important. The large number of stakeholders and the lengthy and convoluted decision-making process in public sector environments impact on the ability to co-design or promote innovative service delivery solutions within a suitable time-frame. Leaders need to be skilled at navigating the complex system of rules while holding a strong negotiating stance with partners within the network. Often, the coordination needs are complex and too much time is spent negotiating the system rather than delivering; partnerships may consume more than they produce (see Tarplett and Goss, Chapter 17 of this volume). Leaders need to promote the network itself as a collective entity and its needs while also negotiating the bureaucratic mechanisms to garner the necessary approval and support.

Learning and the transfer of good practice is an identified benefit of working across boundaries. However, some public-private contracting disproportionately results in the transfer of ready-made expertise to private suppliers, particularly staff transfer (Marchington *et al.* 2005). Rigidities in contractual terms as well as differing work practices may hinder learning. In their comparative case analysis of public-private cooperation, Grimshaw and Hebson found that 'the process of interorganizational learning was decidedly one-way – from the public to the private sector' (2005: 121).

These organisational realities are fundamental to leadership. Beyond the rhetoric of partnership, it also suggests that public sector collaboration is often externally imposed rather than internally developed by the collaborating members themselves. This constitutes constraints on the actors, although leaders sometimes play a role in the evolution of these structures by designing and strengthening communication and coordination mechanisms (Vangen and Huxham 2003).

This discussion shows that under some circumstances, leaders were pro-active agents, absorbing the tensions created by conflicting policy requirements, and reinterpreting the message in a way that suited the circumstances. Demonstrating and enacting public leadership in networks of service delivery requires an ability to rearticulate policy discourse in a way that rebuilds and preserves the legitimacy of the actors in their leadership roles while co-constructing explanations of change.

Leaders must be able to engage with dissimilar stakeholders and mobilise support for defined causes acceptable to all. Garnering support also means that they need to operate efficiently within the complex systems of rules that are prevalent in some environments to promote effective and timely decision-making.

Skills in handling and devolving power, in encouraging the emergence of informal leadership and building organisational capabilities within the network are equally important. This benefits the organisation of collective action by creating communication and coordination structures through the network.

Nevertheless, care must be exercised in order not to fall back into a voluntaristic stance and explanations that are too polarised on actors and actors' volition, as the nature and complexity of environmental constraints impact on leaders in a substantial manner. Variation in mechanisms that influence leaders' behaviour and decisions across different sectors and individual sectors characteristics, such as professional power in healthcare settings, are highly instrumental in conditioning actors. This type of power may well be absent from other environments (e.g. social work/local housing services), engendering different political dynamics within multi-organisational partnerships. These shape decision-making processes and the way leaders construe and enact their role.

Conclusions and further research

Managing or co-constructing meaning, reconciling divergent value-systems and developing capabilities of service delivery chains to enhance public value are behaviours that can all be generically related to effective public leadership. However, what is less well understood is how the specificity in organisational terms of individual service delivery chains impinges on leaders' actions. Contextual complexity has long been acknowledged in broad terms as one of the difficulties in leadership studies (van Wart 2003). There is an absence of a clearly articulated conceptualisation of public service delivery chains in studies of leaders working across boundaries. This makes it difficult to derive strong or prescriptive propositions that systematically link actors' behaviour to constraints and opportunities generated by these specific and fast-evolving contexts. Networks of public service delivery continue to be treated as black boxes. Yet, public leadership is exercised in different ways in different 'network' configurations.

In conclusion, there is a need to account for basic differences in the scale, scope and complexity of the service delivery chains observed, as well as the nature of the task they undertake, in evolving discussions of public leadership. Understanding the dynamics of governance of public-private service delivery networks is of particular significance. There is a need to identify more clearly and systematically the nature and origins of the tensions observed, the way in which they constrain actors, the way they are construed and reformulated and how this impacts on leaders' subsequent actions.

One preliminary task is to develop middle-range theory that aims to systematically identify and explain variations in structural and regulative terms between superficially similar organisational forms and governance arrangements. This may help us to answer more comprehensively questions such as, how:

- is the 'public sphere' reconstructed in these hybrid arrangements?
- do leaders go about construing and attempting to create and deliver public value?
- can leaders through their practice in turn modify the context, both in terms of how they interpret their role as transformative leaders but also how they influence the make-up of the network?

There is a need to consider the extent to which the stability and evolution of such governance arrangements are in turn contingent on the exercise of leadership. Can and does leadership impact on the long-term structuring and regulation of these governance arrangements?

Refining understanding of the nature and practice of leadership in collaborative spaces shared by the public and private spheres needs more theoretical and empirical inquiry. This chapter identifies directions for further research that include the need for a comparative agenda rooted in a better understanding of the contextual dynamics of shared and distributed leadership within collaborative settings.

References

Ackroyd, S., Batt, R., Thompson, P. and Tolbert, P. (2004) *The Oxford Handbook of Work and Organization*. Oxford: Oxford University Press.

Agranoff, M. and McGuire, M. (2003) 'Big Questions in Public Network Management Research', *Journal of Public Administration Research and Theory*, 11: 295–326.

Bachmann, R. (2001) 'Trust, Power and Control in Trans-Organizational Relations', *Organizations Studies*, 22(2): 337–365.

Batley, R. (1996) 'Public-Private Relationships and Performance in Service Provision', *Urban Studies*, 33(4–5): 723–751.

Brandsen, T. and Van Hout, E. (2006) 'Co-Management in Public Service Networks. The Organizational Effects', *Public Management Review*, 8(4): 537–549.

Brereton, M. and Temple, M. (1999) 'The New Public Service Ethos: An Ethical Environment for Governance', *Public Administration*, 77(3): 455–474.

Brookes, S. (2007) 'Bridging the Gap Between Theoretical and Practical Approaches to Leadership: Collective Leadership in Support of Networked Governance and the Creation of Public Value', *6th International Studying Leadership Conference*. Warwick 2007.

Currie, G., Humphreys, M., Ucbasaran, D. and McManus, S. (2008a) 'Entrepreneurial Leadership in the English Public Sector: Paradox or Possibility?', *Public Administration*, 86(4): 987–1008.

Currie, G., Finn, R. and Martin, G. (2008b) 'Accounting for the "Dark Side" of New Organizational Forms: The Case of Healthcare Professionals', *Human Relations*, 61: 539–564.

Currie, G. and Lockett, A. (2007) 'A Critique of Transformational Leadership: Moral, Professional and Contingent Dimensions of Leadership Within Public Services Organizations', *Human Relations*, 60(2): 341–370.

Denis, J.-L., Langley, A. and Rouleau, L. (2005) 'Rethinking Leadership in Public Organizations', in Ferlie, E., Lynn, L.E. Jr. and Pollitt, C. (eds), *The Oxford Handbook of Public Management*. Oxford: Oxford University Press.

Du Gay, P. (2000) *In Praise of Bureaucracy*. London: Sage.

Du Gay, P. (2005) *The Values of Bureaucracy*. Oxford: Oxford University Press.

Ferlie, E., Hartley, J. and Martin, S. (2003) 'Changing Public Service Organizations: Current Perspectives and Future Prospects', *British Journal of Management*, 14(S): S1–S14.

Ghere, R. (2001) 'Ethical Futures and Public-Private Partnerships: Peering Down the Track', *Public Organization Review*, 1(3): 303–319.

Grimshaw, D., Vincent, S. and Willmott, H. (2002) 'Going Privately: Partnership and Outsourcing in UK Public Services', *Public Administration*, 80(3): 475–502.

Grimshaw, G. and Hebson, G. (2005) 'Public-Private Contracting: Performance, Power and Change at Work', in Marchington, M., Grimshaw, D., Rubery, J. and Willmott, H. (eds), *Fragmenting Work: Blurring Organizational Boundaries and Disordering Hierarchies*. Oxford: Oxford University Press.

Grint, K. (2005) 'Problems, Problems, Problems: The Social Construction of "Leadership"', *Human Relations*, 58(11): 1467–1494.

Hardy, C., Philips, N. and Lawrence, T. (1998) 'Distinguishing Trust and Power in Inter-Organizational Relations: Forms and Façades of Trust', in Lane, C. and Bachmann, R. (eds), *Trust Within and Between Organizations*. Oxford: Oxford University Press.

Hebson, G., Grimshaw, D. and Marchington, M. (2003) 'PPPs and the Changing Public Sector Ethos: Case-Study Evidence from the Health and Local Authority Sectors', *Work, Employment and Society*, 17(3): 481–501.

Huxham, C. and Vangen, S. (2000) 'Leadership in the Shaping and Implementation of Collaboration Agendas: How Things Happen in a (Not Quite) Joined-Up World', *Academy of Management Journal*, 43(6): 1159–1175.

Institute for Public Policy Research (2001) *Building Better Partnerships: The Final Report of the Commission on Public-Private Partnerships*. London: IPPR.

Kickert, W., Klijn, E-H. and Koppenjan, J. (eds) (1997) *Managing Complex Networks: Strategies for the Public Sector*. London: Sage.

Lelièvre-Finch, D. and Murphy, J. (2002) 'Inter-Organisational Work Systems: A Case Study', *British Academy of Management Conference*. London, 9th–11th September.

Marchington, M., Vincent, S. and Cooke, F.L. (2005) 'The Role of Boundary-Spanning Agents in Inter-Organizational Contracting', in Marchington, M., Grimshaw, D., Rubery, J. and Willmott, H. (eds), *Fragmenting Work: Blurring Organizational Boundaries and Disordering Hierarchies*. Oxford: Oxford University Press.

Newman, J. (2001) *Modernizing Governance: New Labour Policy and Society*. London: Sage.

Newman, J. (2005a) 'Enter the Transformational Leader: Network Governance and the Micro-Politics of Modernization', *Sociology*, 39(4): 735–753.

Newman, J. (2005b) 'Bending Bureaucracy: Leadership and Multi-Level Governance', in Du Gay, P. (ed.), *The Values of Bureaucracy*. Oxford: Oxford University Press.

Podolny, J. and Page, K. (1998) 'Network Forms of Organization', *Annual Review of Sociology*, 24: 57–76.

Powell, W. (1990) 'Neither Markets Nor Hierarchies: Network Forms of Organization', in Staw, B. and Cummings, L. (eds), *Research in Organizational Behavior*, 195–336. Greenwich, Conn.: JAI Press.

Provan, K. and Kenis, P. (2008) 'Modes of Network Governance: Structure, Management, and Effectiveness', *Journal of Public Administration Research and Theory*, 18: 229–252.

Reed, M. (2005) 'Beyond the Iron Cage? Bureaucracy and Democracy in the Knowledge Economy and Society', in Du Gay, P. (ed.), *The Values of Bureaucracy*. Oxford: Oxford University Press.

Rhodes, R.A. (1997) *Understanding Governance*. Buckingham: Open University Press.

Rubery, J., Earnshaw, J., Marchington, M., Cooke, F.L. and Vincent, S. (2002) 'Changing Organizational Forms and the Employment Relationship', *Journal of Management Studies*, 39(5): 645–672.

Salaman, G. (2005) 'Bureaucracy and Beyond: Managers and Leaders in the "Post-Bureaucratic" Organization', in Du Gay, P. (ed.), *The Values of Bureaucracy*. Oxford: Oxford University Press.

Scarbrough, H. (2000) 'The HR Implications of Supply Chains Relationships', *Human Resource Management Journal*, 10(1): 5–17.

Skelcher, C. (2005) 'Public-Private Partnerships and Hybridity', in Ferlie, E., Lynn, L.E. Jr. and Pollitt, C. (eds) *The Oxford Handbook of Public Management*. Oxford: Oxford University Press.

Skelcher, C. and Mathur, N. (2004) 'Governance Arrangements and Public Service Performance: Reviewing and Reformulating the Research Agenda', *AIM Research Working Paper Series*.

Stokes, J. and Clegg, S. (2002) 'Once Upon a Time in the Bureaucracy: Power and Public Sector Management', *Organization*, 9: 225–247.

Townley, B. (2002) 'The Role of Competing Rationalities in Institutional Change', *Academy of Management Journal*, 45(1): 163–179.

Vangen, S. and Huxham, C. (2003) 'Enacting Leadership for Collaborative Advantage: Dilemmas of Ideology and Pragmatism in the Activities of Partnership Managers', *British Journal of Management*, 14: S61–S76.

van Wart, M. (2003) 'Public-Sector Leadership Theory: An Assessment', *Public Administration Review*, 63(2): 214–228.

Williams, P. (2002) 'The Competent Boundary Spanner', *Public Administration*, 80(1): 103–124.

19
The Challenge of Leadership for the Third Sector

Alex Murdock

Introduction

Leadership in the third sector has some distinctive characteristics which marks it out from the other sectors. In the private sector the implicit (if not explicit) existence of a bottom line is a factor of life for leaders. For the public sector most public managers are ever aware of the political dimension with an ultimate accountability to elected politicians who in turn are held accountable by electorates. There are also other factors which differentiate the nature of leadership in the third sector which will be explored at the outset of this chapter.

Recent developments in the UK and other countries have seen a change in the relationship between the public and third sector. The third sector has increasingly come to be a provider of public services and the funding basis of that provision has moved from a traditional grants funded mode to a contract based mode. Now the state is keen for the third sector to take a more active role in delivery of many of these services through contracts, grants or other arrangements. There are commentators on the third sector which have also explored this (Blake, Robinson and Smerdon 2006; Cairns, Harris and Young 2005).

These developments have been regarded by each sector from somewhat different perspectives. The public sector view on third sector provision is based upon such factors as public value, equity and choice in provision. Some public officials regard the third sector as representing a lower cost option than that of state provision or private providers.

The third sector perceives the growth in service provision and contractual relations with the public sector with mixed feelings. For some – especially the larger and more commercially orientated organisations – it is seen as an opportunity. For others it is seen as jeopardising deeply held organisational values and organisational independence. This is exemplified in the UK by a debate over whether the third sector should take contracts involving loss of liberty or benefits to clients (such as running custodial facilities or assessing disability).[1] This chapter will significantly focus upon the implications of public service delivery but it is important to stress that much of the third sector does not engage in any public service delivery.

This diversity of the third sector stands in some contrast to that of the public sector. This diversity covers many aspects. Size represents a particular aspect with the vast majority of third sector organisations being far smaller than the typical public sector one. Few public sector organisations are 'led' by their founder but this is not uncommon in the third sector. Though a significant proportion of third sector organisations have a service provision role which arguably provides a similarity to that of the public sector this is by no means the case for the majority.

For third sector organisations which have a campaigning or advocacy role accepting government contracts is often seen as restricting (either implicitly or explicitly) their freedom of action to engage in this aspect of their role.

A key characteristic accepted as defining the nature of the third Sector is that of independence. This independence is often construed in terms of a mission which has an underpinning set of values. Charities which work with, for example, pregnancy may have a value set which acknowledges the woman's 'right to choose' a termination. Yet if such an organisation is to seek government funding or contracts then a clash of values may appear – as was identified by Etzioni writing about the USA. In the UK and much of the English speaking commonwealth there has been the growth of devices such as 'compacts' to try and acknowledge the independence issue.

The value differences may appear not just at a 'mission level' but also in terms of operational practices. Public servants are expected to adopt a position of 'neutrality' and professional detachment in the conduct of their activities. Indeed this may even extend to their activities outside the workplace and joining the boards of outside organisations may lead to questions of their impartiality. In contrast the third sector makes widespread use of networks and 'cross memberships' are part of the organisational landscape.

The values orientation might be seen as representing a common ground for leaders in both the public and the third sector. However the leadership orientation in the third sector represents aspects which are clearly different in nature. The words 'passionate leadership' carries a sense of personal commitment which, for example attracts people willing to sacrifice a substantial amount of salary (and perhaps as importantly the final salary pension benefit) (Kirchner 2006). This, it is argued, can create a very significant difference between the features of leadership in the third sector and that of the public sector.

At the strategic level non-profit organisations tend to run on a high level of informal contact and trust as opposed to the rules and accountability which are part of the public sector landscape. Indeed members of charity boards are called 'trustees' – a term not used to describe their political equivalents in the public sector.

Leadership in the third sector

Third Sector organisations typically start with an idea which takes time to form and find its expression in formal organisational structures. Many third sector organisations initially employ no-one and indeed the majority of such organisations continue in this form. This marks a profound difference to public sector organisations which typically arise from existing structures with paid staff. The voluntary element for the third sector is almost invariably present in their origins and for many persists throughout their growth and maturity. The Caravan and Camping Club is a large voluntary organisation which has delegated planning powers akin to many public sector bodies. Yet it runs very largely on the enthusiasm and commitment of unpaid members.

The founder element in leadership

Many charities were founded by charismatic and driven individuals whose leadership style was highly appropriate – indeed possibly essential – for their initial success and growth. However as the organisation becomes more structured and formal then a different kind of leadership style is typically needed. The tension which arises as the original founder fails to recognise this has been variously described as 'founder folly'. The Open University in research on 'On Being a Chief Executive' summed this up as follows:

> As organisations develop, there is a risk of encountering 'founder syndrome', where individuals whose passion and raison d'être can be so tied up with what they have started that they find it difficult to let go and allow the distribution of responsibility. Different skills sets are required to establish, develop or sustain an organisation and also for the development of collaborative working arrangements.[2]

This particular phenomenon is also found in private sector settings – especially in the context of family firms. It is comparatively rare in the public sector where typically public leaders move into pre-existing organisations with formality, staff and structures (albeit ones which may need change).

To an extent it can be argued that initially the founder needs to be a leader first and a manager second (if at all). The history of founding leaders in the third sector such as Abbe Pierre of Emmaus or Leonard Cheshire is not so much a saga of organised and efficient management but rather one of inspirational leadership. It is not unusual for such leaders to engage in activities which – were they in the public sector – would have almost certainly led to dismissal. Sue Ryder (founder of Sue Ryder Care) openly and publically opposed the management and board of the very organisation she created whilst forming an alternative organisation.[3] The founder role is highlighted as giving face credibility to third sector leaders. At a Third Sector Leadership summit in 2007 Craig Dearden-Phillips, CEO of SpeakingUp noted:

> Being a founder-CEO does give me credibility in the eyes of others. I think staff know that I have earned the role, done what they have done and am personally committed to our mission. This credibility really helps me to lead effectively (quoted in Kirchner 2007).

Few public sector managers can lay claim to have founded the organisation that they lead starting the organisation with no budget, no salary and no resources. The founder mythology can present a challenge to people moving into lead pre-existing third sector organisations. It has been described as passionate leadership:

> A strong emotional affinity with the raison d'être of the organisation. A passion for its beliefs. A desire to succeed for the greater good of the organisation. A high degree of personal energy and enthusiasm for the cause (Cormack and Stanton 2003).

Such passion is found in some aspects of the public sector – in particular the NHS would spring to mind. However in the public sector 'passion' takes a place alongside a range of other pressures and imperatives. Sometimes passion is regarded with some caution in the public sector. A policeman with a passion for catching criminals without regard for process, for example.

Size and diversity matters?

If a charity in the UK was chosen at random the likelihood would be that a very small organisation would be selected. The reality of the charity sector as depicted by the NCVO Annual Survey of the Sector is that the typical CEO of a Third Sector organisation is leading a small (sometimes very small) organisation. To paraphrase a popular car advert 'size matters' and this means that leadership in the third sector is dominated by the majority of relatively (in public sector terms) small organisations. A typical secondary school in both staffing and budgetary terms would be a very substantial third sector organisation.

In the third sector there is a great diversity in the degree of complexity, the nature of operations and the source of funding. Cormack and Stanton identify that these factors make it very difficult to arrive at a common basis for the requirements of a CEO in the third sector. They suggest, however, that certain basic categories can be proposed as a basis for distinguishing varieties of leadership in third sector organisations. They propose a two dimensional model generating a series of clusters (Cormack and Stanton 2003).

The question of scale is one dimension (which is linked to the degree of complexity of the organisation).

A second dimension is represented by the main focus of activity (which could be fundraising, campaigning, service delivery or membership). For smaller organisations a very substantial part of a typical CEO role is fundraising. In larger organisations this may well be devolved to other staff.

Leader or leadership?

The preceding sections have focused upon leadership as something possessed by – or attributed to – the individual. The concept of the leader is invested in a person. However where an organisation or movement has a value set which exists independently of the individual then it can be argued that leadership is a separate concept. As Day notes:

> Leadership emerges with the process of creating shared meanings, both in terms of *sense making* and in terms of *value-added'* (Day 2001).

Third Sector organisations can possess very strong values and academics and researchers have long commented on the binding force offered by norms or ideology often offering religious based organisations as exemplars (Mintzberg 1989). Where an organisation possesses such a strong binding ideology or set of norms then leadership is as important as the leader. The sharing of a strong ethos can enable such organisations to survive and even flourish despite an apparent absence of a clear shaping leader and indeed without the management systems expected in large formal organisations.

This is also characterised by an organisational form particular to the third sector – that of the federated organisation. In organisations such as MIND the centre does not control the organisation. Rather each local organisation is constituted as an independent organisation which belongs to the National body and – very probably – regards the national body as responsible to the individual MIND organisations. In federated organisations leadership is typically 'distributed'. It is a model with a lot of appeal – the sum is greater than the individual parts. This concept is picked up elsewhere in this volume but also has relevance for third sector organisations.

Contracting and public service delivery: The changing environment

There is an active debate ongoing with the Third Sector as to public service delivery. The attitude of the government is that the Third Sector is to be encouraged to engage with public service delivery.

Provision of public services by the third sector has been a major focus in recent years in the UK. National Audit Office (2005). The Government sees the third sector as a potential 'partner'.

Many charities have a history of an identification of a need for service provision followed by the actual provision to meet that need Kendall (2003). Indeed there is one major organisation in the UK which provides a rescue service for those at peril on the sea and does it without recourse to public funds (The Royal National Lifeboat Institution). However in general the pattern has been of a charitable provision being set up to meet a particular need (hospitals and orphanages, for example) and over time the state steps in to take over the provision.

Now the state is keen for the third sector to take a more active role in delivery of many of these services through contracts, grants or other arrangements. There are commentators on the third sector which have also explored this. (Blake, Robinson and Smerdon 2006; Cairns, Harris and Young 2005).

Richard Best, writing in a forward to a Joseph Rowntree Foundation report set out the reasons why the government would engage in public service delivery by the third sector.

> First, to modernise public services by bringing in the pluralism, competition, variety, innovation and flexibility associated with this sector; second, and linked, to engage more citizens and more communities directly in the process of service delivery, reform of state-funded services and more widespread civil renewal' (Paxton *et al.* 2005).

The Third Sector is not united in its' response to the concept of public service delivery. Leaders of sector representational bodies exemplify this lack of unanimity.

On the one hand Stephen Bubb of ACEVO is open in his support for the third sector to be involved in public service delivery.[4] In a statement to the Public Administration Committee of the House of Commons in 2007 he observed:

> The expanding role of the third sector in public service delivery is both inevitable and desirable. This is the time for Government to deliver

on promises that have been made to improve conditions for third sector organisations. It is also a time for third sector leaders to feel energized by the opportunities that are unfolding and to rise to the challenges that these opportunities bring.[5]

Mr Bubb sees public service delivery as representing a clear (and welcome) opportunity for the Third Sector. However he noted the importance of government to fulfil promises made and, to a large extent, this is associated with resolving issues such as Full Cost Recovery on contracts and also longer term security of funding. We will return to these later in this chapter.

On the other hand Debra Alcock Tyler of the Directory of Social Change expresses concerns about the implications of public service delivery contracts.

> This Government needs a few tricks to balance the books. One trick is competitive tendering for short-term contracts. This drives down costs, shifts the liability to the contractor and does it all without ceding control. For charities this means that prices for delivering public services are driven below their true cost. More interested in the cause than the contract they sign, they often quote artificially low overheads, effectively trading profit for passion, but the result can be that they use their own resources (including your donations) to pick up the tab (*The Times* 2006).

Alcock Tyler is particularly concerned about the ability of smaller organisations to compete in the public service contract arena. This is particularly relevant for Social Enterprises which like charities in most cases, tend to be small organisations.

The background of policy for public service delivery is redolent with reports from a range of government departments and regulatory agencies (HM Treasury 2002, 2005 and 2006; Cabinet Office 2006; National Audit Office 2005, 2007). It also has been the subject of reports sponsored or written by a range of stakeholder organisations such as UNISON (Davies 2007) and The National Consumer Council (2007).

The tenor of the government policy has been to regard delivery of public services by third sector (including social enterprises) as to be encouraged. The sector is, under the terminology of the Voluntary Sector Compact, to be seen as a full partner and not subservient in the relationship. However the operation of the Compact in practice has been subject to critical comment. The fine words set out on paper do not always translate themselves into practice on the ground, (Murdock 2005a,b; Osborne, S. and McLaughlin 2002 and 2004).

The voluntary sector compact

Recent developments such as the Compact can be traced from a major review of the voluntary sector in 1996 (Commission on the Future of the Voluntary Sector 1996).

The Commission highlighted changes in the nature of the relationship between government and the third sector. It recognised moving towards contractual relationships between government and the third sector was having a major impact upon the way in which third sector organisations had to work. The Commission also highlighted the diverse nature of the third sector, offering enormous potential and challenge to the both government and the third sector.

The Voluntary Sector Compact – a formal memorandum setting out the nature of the relationships between government and the sector – was perhaps a tangible result of this history (Osborne and McLaughlin 2002 and 2004). The compact has had implications not just for the UK but has had significant policy impacts in other countries (Murdock 2006). The Compact, could be described as an attempt to enable the government and third sector to agree a set of rules for behaviour. In particular it could be regarded as an endeavour to ensure that as contracts become more embedded the third sector is recognised as having 'rights' and also a degree of independence of movement. Though the government may be the partner 'who leads' in terms of funding the third sector is not a passive partner but one seen as worthy of respect (NVCO 2005, 2006; Osborne 2005).

The compact principles recognised that the third sector had a right to be consulted and indeed to criticise in terms of both the current and proposed relationship. Indeed the sector was recognised as possessing areas of expertise (Osborne and McLaughlin 2002 and 2004; Murdock 2006).

The critical question is whether the development of contractual relationships between the government and the third sector is affected by a fundamental difference occasioned by the different value and ethical sets brought by the respective parties. The third sector is described as 'diverse' by Deakin and as a 'loose and baggy monster' by academics and researchers[6] (Deakin 2006; Kendall and Knapp 1995). It is important to note that the term is not necessarily used in a negative fashion to describe the sector. However it does create the image of sector diversity and problems in establishing clear categories and defining rules of behaviour. It implies a lack of predictability and conformity. This imagery is not commensurate with the formalism of regulated government.

The issues associated with public service delivery by social enterprise and third sector organisations

Independence

Nick Seddon, in a recent Civitas publication, questioned the independence of charities which derived a substantial proportion of their income from the state (Seddon 2007).

<table>
<tr><td colspan="2">How Civitas would classify charities</td></tr>
<tr><td>CLASSIFICATION</td><td>EXAMPLE CHARITIES</td></tr>
<tr><td>Independent charities
(receiving less than
30% of their income
from the state)</td><td>NSPCC
National Trust
RNLI
The Salvation Army</td></tr>
<tr><td>State-funded charities
(receiving between 30 and
70% of their income from
the state)</td><td>Save the Children
Oxfam
Shelter
British Red Cross</td></tr>
<tr><td>Statutory agencies
(receiving 70% or
more of their income
from the state)</td><td>Turning Point
NCH
Barnardo's
NFPI</td></tr>
<tr><td colspan="2">Source: Who Cares? by Nick Seddon</td></tr>
</table>

Figure 19.1   Classification of Charities

He asserted that beyond a significant proportion a charity lost its independence and when that proportion reached a certain level (he used 70%) then the charity become a *de facto* state agency and should cease to be a charity (see Figure 19.1). His views were challenged – especially by the charities he defined as *de facto* state agencies. However the challenge was in part denying the proportion of funds received by the state.

ACEVO (whose CEO, Stephen Bubb, favours public service delivery by the third sector) understandably took exception to Seddons' conclusions. In a riposte they stated:

> We maintain that strong and independent governance, sound leadership and the clear exercise of accountability are the essential components of organisational independence in maintaining public trust, rather than the exact proportion of statutory funding received by the organisation.[7]

Wittenberg, writing from a Directory of Social Change (DSC) perspective, asserts that independence can be assured if it is the larger organisations which engage in public services delivery contracts. These organisations possess the critical mass and structures necessary to ameliorate the risks associated with such contracts.

The DSC contends that a contracting relationship for delivery of public services is probably best concentrated on the top 2% who have the capacity to negotiate effectively, where turning down a contract does not threaten the organisations existence and where the structure of the organisation is sufficiently close to state structure to make the relationship easier to manage. (Wittenberg 2007)

The reality is more complex in that some organisations (such as Turning Point) assert with evidence the fact that they derive a high proportion of income from the state does not impact on their independence. Lord Adebowale, Chief Executive of Turning point, was pressed on this when he gave evidence to the Public Administration Committee on 7 June 2007. He described Turning Point as a 'not for profit social enterprise' which derived about 95% of its income from statutory sources and asserted that such funding had not impeded their independence. However the size of Turning Point and the fact that it operated in 250 locations with over 400 contracts almost certainly insulates it from the risk attendant with an organisation which is heavily dependent on only one or two public service contracts.

The Baring Foundation was particularly concerned about this and has produced two recent reports which highlight the issues. Smerdon writing about charities defined independence in some detail (Smerdon 2006). He saw these as representing a number of 'freedoms' as follows:

Freedom to:

- agree values based on their own experience and vision and not external pressures
- carry out work that delivers the stated purpose of the organisation
- negotiate robustly with funders and partners
- challenge others and engage in public debate

(Smerdon 2006: 5)

The Baring Foundation was sufficiently concerned to set up a grants programme to assist charities to maintain independence. Subsequently Pharoh, in a later Baring publication, analysed the 525 applications received for these grants. The results enabled a thorough analysis of the issues of public service delivery upon independence. Pharoh concluded:

> The value of service delivery contracts make government a major 'shareholder' in today's voluntary sector, and constitute a tranche of sector income at least equal to that from voluntary sources (and likely to overtake it). It is in the dominance of government as a funder that today's threats to independence are seen to lie, whether in its power to give or withhold contracts, or to restrict the scope of contracts. (Pharoh 2007: 5)

The results showed charities identified a number of threats to independence of which policy changes, targets excluding key activities and restrictive contracts figures as the three prominent threats.

This threat to independence was manifested by threats to particular abilities of the organisations to carry out their activities. The main threats were to provision of core services, actual survival and to the organisational values.

The loss of independence and threat to organisational abilities from public service delivery contracts is a very real one. The Charity Commission in its report 'Stand and Deliver' also found that organisations felt affected by contract pressures (Charity Commission 2007).

The charity commission – A key player

The Charity Commission, the regulatory body for charities in England and Wales, published a key report examining the effects of charities accepting a greater role in public service delivery. A large number of charities took part (approx 3,800). The report perhaps quixotically entitled 'Stand and Deliver' was published in February 2007 and the findings make disturbing reading.

Over 60% of the charities who responded have an income of over £0.5 million and were involved in public service delivery. Of the charities involved in public service delivery a third were dependent on this for 80% or more of their total income. However only 12% reported that they were getting full cost recovery (Charity Commission 2007). Figure 19.2

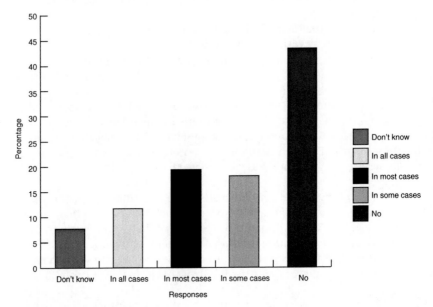

Figure 19.2   Full Cost Recovery
Source: Charity Commission (2007b) *Stand and Deliver* Charity Commission of England and Wales, February 2007.

Table 19.1 Full Cost Recovery

| | Does funding cover the full cost of services provided? | | | | | | | | | |
| | Don't know | | In all cases | | In most cases | | In some cases | | No | |
	Number	%	Number	%	Number	%	Number	%	Number	%
Under £10,000	19	19	16	16	9	9	9	9	47	47
£10,000–£100,000	37	11.97	44	14.24	43	13.92	44	14.24	141	45.63
£100,000–£250,000	14	5.71	19	7.76	43	17.55	34	13.88	135	55.1
£250,000–£500,000	7	3.7	17	8.99	44	23.28	48	25.4	73	38.62
£500,000–£1 million	4	2.17	22	11.96	52	28.26	43	23.37	63	34.24
£1 million–£10 million	4	4.26	14	14.89	24	25.53	21	22.34	31	32.98
Over £10 million	2	9.52	1	4.76	6	28.57	8	38.1	4	19.05
Total	**87**	**8**	**133**	**12**	**221**	**19**	**207**	**18**	**494**	**43**

Source: Charity Commission (2007b) *Stand and Deliver* Charity Commission of England and Wales, February 2007.

Table 19.2 Full Cost Recovery by Type of Funding Agreement

| | Type of funding agreement | | | | | | | | | | | |
| | Don't know | | Grant(s) | | Contract(s) | | Service level agreement(s) | | A mixture/ more than one | | Other | |
Full cost recovery?	No	%	No	%	No	%	No	%	No	%	No	%
Don't know	17	51.52	13	7.78	5	2.99	10	5.24	12	2.82	30	18.87
In all cases	3	9.09	19	11.38	32	19.16	33	17.28	28	6.59	18	11.32
In most cases	3	9.09	23	13.77	37	22.16	37	19.37	110	25.88	11	6.92
In some cases	2	6.06	21	12.57	28	16.77	23	12.04	114	26.82	19	11.95
No	8	24.24	91	54.49	65	38.92	88	46.07	161	37.88	81	50.94
Total	**33**	**100**	**167**	**100**	**167**	**100**	**191**	**100**	**425**	**100**	**159**	**100**

Source: Charity Commission (2007b) *Stand and Deliver*, Charity Commission of England and Wales, February 2007.

shows this and also shows that by far the largest proportion (43%) report that they did not recover full costs in any case.

It could be assumed that the stronger (i.e. Largest) third sector organisations might be more likely to achieve full cost recovery. Table 19.1 suggests that this is not the case for the very largest (though they are less likely to report not getting any full cost recovery). What is also surprising is that the very largest organisations appear more likely to report not even knowing if their funding had covered their costs.

Possibly the nature of the service delivery arrangement was a factor. Maybe there might be a difference between contract, grants, service level agreements[8] and a 'mixture' of these? The results reported in Table 19.2 prove interesting. Grants are most likely to be associated with a failure to meet full cost recovery with service level agreements coming second. The commentary on the report suggests that it may be possible that some respondents were unclear as to what were the nature of the agreements they had with the public sector. In any event it suggests that participation in this particular arena had not benefitted the third sector.

One argument advanced by third sector leaders is a plea for longer duration funding. This seems eminently sensible. However the Charity Commission findings suggest that longer duration contracts may be associated with poorer financial returns. Figure 19.3 shows that contracts longer

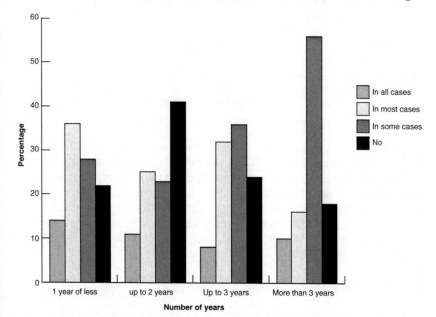

Figure 19.3   Length of Agreements Held by Charities Showing Full Cost Recovery
Source: Charity Commission (2007b) *Stand and Deliver*, Charity Commission of England and Wales, February 2007.

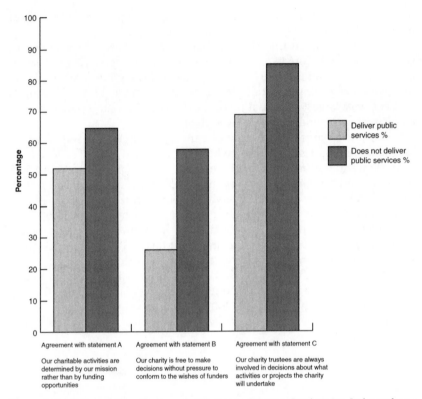

Figure 19.4   Agreement on Statements Relating to Mission Conformity, Independence and Trustee Involvement
Source: Charity Commission (2007b) *Stand and Deliver*, Charity Commission of England and Wales, February 2007.

than three years appear to be a worse deal than those which are shorter. It looks like 'long commitments' may not necessarily benefit the third sector.

Finally there is the question as to whether the third sectors' independence has been compromised through public service delivery. The findings from the survey suggest that respondents do feel this is the case. Organisations which did not deliver public services were more likely agree to statements showing mission conformity, independence and trustee involvement in key decisions. Figure 19.4 shows the extent of the differences.

The provision of service: Quality and the user experience

The Public Administration Committee was interested to learn whether third sector organisations actually delivered a better service – either through actual or perceived quality. It was hardly surprising that there was no unanimity of response here. The third sector organisations offering evidence to the Committee tended to aver that there was a clear indication of improved quality and focus of service. To use an overused quote 'they would say that, wouldn't they'. The Audit Commission, in its evidence to the Committee was more careful in its judgement:

> Our research on choice in public services found that what matters most to users is the quality of the service they receive, rather than who provides that service. Citizens do not always know who provides their services – sometimes they have no idea whether it is the local authority, the health service, or another public or private organisation. What matters to users is having choice in how the service is delivered, and it is particularly important for them to have choice in personal social services.[9]

The National Consumer Council, a registered charity, has undertaken more specific research which indicates that the user perception varies depending on the nature of the service provided (Hopkins 2007). The third sector was most likely to be regarded more positively by users in the context of employment services.

> In employment services, third sector providers were more likely than either public or private sector providers to deliver all nineteen service factors in the study, and third sector users were more likely to say their provider was very good or excellent in this respect (Hopkins 2007: 5).

The private sector was in some respects seen as better than either the third or public sector. This study represents a possible indicator as to user views on public service delivery by the various sectors. Hopkins noted that further work is being undertaken. If the conclusions of the National Consumer Council research are upheld by subsequent work then this may challenge some of the assumptions held by third sector organisations about user preferences:

> We also discovered a potential divide between public and non-public sector delivery of public services in terms of user-responsiveness across a wide range of factors. This was especially true for the delivery of flexibility and choice within a service. The evidence in this report also indicates that private sector providers show distinctiveness in the way users experience public service delivery, presenting a challenge to the third and public sectors to improve (Hopkins 2007: 79).

The National Consumer Council research included organisations which had specifically identified themselves as social enterprises (though it is not possible to extract them individually). Assuming Social Enterprises as entities accept the concept of the market then the prospect of competing against the private sector should not be an issue (Paton 2003). However the prospect of being outperformed by private sector competitors in key aspects should give pause for thought. The research suggests that though third sector organisations outperform their public sector counterparts they find their match with private sector companies in the domiciliary care service arena. The increasing concept of consumer choice is part of government policy.

Does public sector contracting matter if the third sector and public sector share their values?

Both the public sector and the third sector have been described as possessing strong value sets. Writers such as Anheier and Etzioni have examined the nature of the values and mission of the third sector (Anheier 2005; Etzioni 1973). The public sector value literature is extensive and Beck Jorgensen and Bozeman provided a useful bibliography for the Public Value panel at the 2006 EGPA Conference (Beck Jorgensen and Bozeman 2006).[10] The question of public values has been linked to the reform agenda (Van de Walle 2005). Public Values are also seen as associated with 'taking tough choices' (O'Kelly and Dubnick 2005) and are comprehensively discussed elsewhere within this volume.

Organisational values sometimes get wrapped up with the idea of culture and indeed this is true for all three formal sectors (private, public and third) (Aiken 2001). The conception that values are transmittable – in effect tangible objects – implies that they can be controlled by leaders and managers. This, however, understates the importance of the tacit and intangible quality attached to value. Nevertheless governments and the public sector bodies associated with government have sought to expressly set out what the 'public sector values' are in tangible form (HM Treasury 2004).

Concern in the early 1990s in the UK about standards of public officials led to what has become known as the Nolan report (Cm 2850-I).[11] For the UK it represents perhaps a common denominator of what should guide the behaviour of those in public office. The Nolan principles are illustrated in Figure 19.5.

It is worthy of note that these principles have also been accepted by some of the major third sector umbrella organisations in the UK Third Sector as relevant for their members in the exercise of their third sector responsibilities. Therefore there is a case for arguing that the Nolan principles may represent a base set of guidelines which can be referred in this context as the 'rules of behaviour for managers and leaders as well as for their organisations'.

A number of these principles are in fact explicit in the governance of charitable bodies and in particular with respect to the board members

---

THE SEVEN PRINCIPLES OF PUBLIC LIFE

Selflessness

Holders of public office should take decisions solely in terms of the public interest. They should not do so in order to gain financial or other material benefits for themselves, their family, or their friends.

Integrity

Holders of public office should not place themselves under any financial or other obligation to outside individuals or organisations that might influence them in the performance of their official duties.

Objectivity

In carrying out public business, including making public appointments, awarding contracts or recommending individuals for rewards and benefits holders of public office should make choices on merit.

Accountability

Holders of public office are accountable for their decisions and actions to the public and must submit themselves to whatever scrutiny is appropriate to their office.

Openness

Holders of public office should be as open as possible about all the decisions and actions that they take. They should give reasons for their decisions and restrict information only when the wider public interest clearly demands.

Honesty

Holders of public office have a duty to declare any private interests relating to their public duties and to take steps to resolve any conflicts arising in a way that protects the public interest.

Leadership

Holders of public office should promote and support these principles by leadership and example.

Source: Cm 2850-1(1995) First Report of the Committee on Standards in Public Life (The Nolan Report), HMSO UK

Figure 19.5   The Seven Principles of Public Life

(trustees) of such organisations. Selflessness, integrity, accountability, honesty and objectivity are enshrined in the legal expectation of how trustees of charities will conduct themselves. Openness and leadership are implicit (Hudson 2004).

So third sector values – Do they differ?

Aiken in a couple of key articles has set out what he regards as distinctive about the values of voluntary and cooperative organisations. He indicates that for such organisations their values are often the core of their being. There is no private sector 'business bottom line' to fall back on (Aiken 2001, 2002). The values cannot be maintained by reference to an 'official government line' – they need to be sustained and renewed or the organisations concerned will deteriorate. Aiken notes that such organisations do not operate in a social and political vacuum and refers to commentators who question the continued distinctiveness and independence of the sector (Six and Vidal 1994).

A working paper from the London School of Economics undertook a review of the nature of the values in the voluntary sector (Elson 2006). This is reproduced from the working paper as Figure 19.6.

Figure 19.6   The Nature of the Values in the Voluntary Sector

Source (reference)	Values	Context
Cheung-Judge, M-Y. Henley, A (1994) Equality in Action – Introducing Equal Opportunities in Voluntary Organisations	Fairness, (social) Justice, Accessibility Accountability	Foundation for equal opportunities UK legislation
* Gerard, D. (1983) Charities in Britain: conservatism or change?	Authority, Hierarchy, Equity, Compassion, Freedom, Beneficence	Context organisations – social order (adherence to moral and spiritual values) [stability, unity, cohesion] and service to those in need
	Democracy, Participation, Equality, Tolerance, Individual rights, Solidarity	Social change – (secular and material values) and *identify with* those in need
Jeavons, T.H. (1994) Ethics in nonprofit management: Creating a culture of integrity	Integrity, Openness, Accountability, Service, Charity, Reciprocity	Organisational ethical values
Jeavons, T.H. (1992) When the Management is the Message: relating values to management practice in non-profit organisations	Organisational honesty, Accountability, Service (to public good), Dignity and respect (for workers and volunteers)	Critical importance of consistency between values in organisational purpose and management
Leat, D. (1995) Challenging Management: An exploratory study of perceptions of managers moving from for-profit to voluntary Organisations	Sociability, Equality, Participation, "business-like", Trust, altruism	perceptions of managers moving from for-profit to voluntary Organisations
Mason, D.E. (1995) Leading and Managing the Expressive Dimension	Accountability, Caring, Citizenship, Excellene, Fairness, Honesty, Integrity, Loyalty, Promise keeping, Respect	Managing nonprofit organisations
O'Connell, B. (1988) Values underlying Non-profit endeavour	Commitment beyond self (altruism), Worth and dignity of individual, Responsibility, Tolerance, Freedom, Justice, Responsibilities of citizenship	Values espoused by independent Sector (US)
O'Neill, M. (1992) Ethical Dimensions of Nonprofit Administration	Societal responsibility, Service to vuinerable, Honesty, Environmental protection	Ethical aspects of nonprofit management (US)
*Otto, S. (1997) Comparative Study of role issues and structures in voluntary and statutory organisations	Power combined with commitment to public good, Personal and professional development, Empowerment, Collaboration	Trustee Chairs and senior managers in agencies for the homeless and statutory schools (UK)
Paton, R. (1996) How are values handled in the voluntary sector?	Equal opportunity, User empowerment Social Justice	Social ideals Organisational values Personal conduct
Paton, R. (1992) The Social Economy: Value-based Organisations in the Wider Society	Devotion, Compassion, Enthusiasm, Solidarity, Defiance	Commitment to a common or public benefit
*Tonkiss, F. Passey, A (1999) Trust, Confidence and Voluntary Organisations: Between Values and Institutions	honesty, fairness, trust	Trust-base relations in civil society

*Empirical evidence provided

(Cheung-Judge et al., 1994; Gerard, 1983a; Gerard, 1983b; Jeavons, 1992; Jeavons, 1994; Leat, 1995: Mason, 1995; Massie, 1987; O'Connell, 1988; O'Neil, 1992; Otto, 1997; Paton, 1992; Paton, 1996; Tonkiss et al., 1999)

Source: Elson 2006.

Many of the values adduced from the literature by Elson echo the Nolan principles set out above. Indeed in Governance terms some authors have successfully written to encompass both sectors in the same text (Cornforth 2003).

However there are a number of values which are not associated with the Nolan Principles and indeed are arguably potentially in conflict with them. Paton refers to values of 'devotion, compassion, enthusiasm, solidarity and defiance' (Paton 1992). These are values which may not sit well with such Nolan principles as 'objectivity and accountability'. Other values referred to in Elsons' impressive collation of authorities include 'Sociability', 'Reciprocity', 'Collaboration', 'Loyalty' and 'Trust'. Such values are highly pertinent to many charitable and voluntary organisations.

The actual concept of 'Charity' itself is worthy of exploration as a value. One definition describes it as 'an unlimited loving-kindness towards all others'.[12] For some charities this is inherent in the way in which they conduct themselves.

The relationship with the public sector – Separation

If the third and public sectors operate separately and their paths do not cross then the potential for value conflict is quite limited. Some charities do not take any money from the public purse whether in the form of grants or contracts. They observe the legal formalities and are relatively detached from the public sector. It is as if they are separate but are only jointly affected if a major event happens. Where a charity engages in an activity where the public sector would not become involved (such as the meeting of specific religious needs) then the relationship can be distant unless the values of the organisation impinge on public law or cause public disquiet. In the UK post-9/11 there has been a greater public concern about the nature of the activities of imams in mosques, for example. However the activities of other religious sects may pass without public comment.

The relationship – The third sector takes the lead

For some third sector organisations the inherent aim is to leverage some kind of change from a potentially labile or unwilling public sector. This may take a number of forms. The third sector organisation may possess an asset or attribute which can be used to effect change. Some medical charities in the UK have a large donor base and use the financial leverage to pressure the government to change policy and enhance service provision. They are in effect the dominant partner and the public sector may have to change to accommodate them. In short the third sector is able to 'pay the piper and influence the tune'.

In other situations the third sector possesses resources – perhaps access to celebrities or to a large membership base which enables it to influence or even threaten the public sector in order to get what it wants. The impact of individuals such as Bob Geldorf and the power of media and music are well understood by charities. The public sector is not immune to being seduced by fame and glamour.

If seduction does not work then in some cases the third sector is able to exploit the threat of exposure and political vulnerability. A local issue raised by a charity may threaten the security of re-election of a politician who then accepts the need to 'dance to a different tune'. This has been exemplified by the spectre of government ministers joining protests against policies which they had, in cabinet, acquiesced in. Campaigning charities are often adept at applying pressure through carefully targeted media coverage and letter writing. Amnesty international is able to bring considerable pressure on apparently intransigent foreign governments over the treatment of prisoners by such means.

The attraction of full cost recovery

One lure to the third sector in the UK has been something described as 'full cost recovery' – This means not just the disbursement of the immediate costs of provision of the service but also what has been described by sector organisations as 'core costs' such as:

- Management and leadership
- Infrastructure and accommodation
- Finance, governance and controls
- Strategic development[13]

The third sector would argue that in order to join in such contracts for the public sector they feel that it is not just the immediate participation costs which need to be met but also the longer term expenses such as infrastructure and development.

There are also those who feel that the loss of independence associated with joining in contractual relationships determined by the public sector is a price too great to pay. The constraints of government contracts are seen as restricting the ability of charities to offer a range of services and also may limit the choice of beneficiary. Furthermore many charities see themselves as agents of societal change. The ability to criticise and pressure the government may be affected by having a substantial dependency on that same government for income.

Conclusion

Leadership for the third sector encompasses a wide range of contexts. Some of these are very similar to that of the public sector. For large third sector organisations with a high degree of formality and structure engaging in public sector contracts there may be much in common in terms of both leadership and leaders.

However the founder syndrome marks out a possibly significant area of difference and also the large number of small yet highly independent organisations in the sector generate a wide range of leadership demands. There are a significant proportion of third sector organisations which operate with little relationship to the public sector (beyond complying with legal requirements). The position of federated organisations also marks them out as having a different set of leadership challenges.

The relationship between the public sector and the third sector is a varied one. There is a sharing of values in that many of the public sector values (as represented by the Nolan Report in the UK) would be found in the charitable sector. However voluntary and charitable organisations in many cases espouse values which are potentially at variance with public sector ones.

This may not be a problem. In some cases the parties do not interfere with each other beyond the usual civilities. In other cases the third sector may be more influential and possess desired resources. However the increasing involvement of the third sector in the delivery of public services seems to be associated with both inadequate resourcing and a perceived loss of independence. This is clearly a source of concern to the Chair of the Charity Commission, Dame Suzy Leather, who made the following observation as part of her speech introducing the findings of the survey.

> Under-funding threatens the very survival of charities delivering public services. Charities themselves, commissioning authorities and Government all have to address this urgently. If they don't, they will end up killing the very thing they believe in...Much as John Donne's bell tolled for everyone, so one charity's loss of reputation, mission or integrity could have an impact on the way in which charities are generally viewed. Reputation at best is a fragile thing and must be protected.[14]

Third sector organisations may be engaging in 'high risk' behaviour in taking on public service contracts. It is likely that some may leave saddened through financial losses which may – at the extreme – threaten their viability.

Perhaps however the more insidious threat is the 'loss of virtue' which as some might argue is priceless since once lost it cannot be repurchased. Furthermore such loss may serve to damage not just the repute of the immediate owner but to erode the repute of other third sector organisations seen as partaking in a similar activity.

Notes

1. Presentation by Stuart Etherington, CEO of NCVO at London South Bank University Oct 2005.
2. See: http: //www.open.ac.uk/oubs/onbeingachiefexecutive (accessed June 28 2009).
3. See http: //news.bbc.co.uk/1/hi/uk/1004400.stm (accessed 28 June 2009).
4. Association of Chief Executives of Voluntary Organisations www.acevo.org.uk

5. See: Report on statement by Stephen Bubb to Public Administration Committee 16 May 2007 https://www.acevo.org.uk/index.cfm/display_page/news_press/control_contentType/news_list/display_open/news_849 (accessed 16 June 2007).
6. The original term was probably attributed to the novelist Henry James who referred to Tolstoy's War and Peace as a 'loose and baggy monster'.
7. See acevo web site (accessed 16 June 2007) https: //www.acevo.org.uk/UserFiles/File/Acevo_Reponse_to_the_Civitas_Report_-_Who_Cares.doc.
8. Service level agreements are typically agreements where professional services (such as expert social work input or legal advice) is being provided. They are usually costed on a different basis to conventional contracts.
9. Audit Commission evidence To be published as HC 340 *Third Sector Commissioning* Public Administration Committee, Parliament. Note that references to this report in this paper are based on uncorrected evidence submissions.
10. See URL for EGPA 2006 (accessed 27 Feb 2007) http://soc.kuleuven.be/io/egpa 2006/
11. See URL http://www.archive.official-documents.co.uk/document/parlment/nolan/nolan.htm
12. Source wikipedia.com
13. For more information on the nature of full cost recovery see www.acevo.org.uk
14. Dame Suzy Leather (Charity Commissioner) speech to NCVO Annual Conference 21.2.2007.

References

Aiken, M. (2002) 'What Strategies Do Value Based Organisations Adopt to Resist Incursions on Their Organisational Values from Public or Private Sector Markets?', Paper at 6th 'Dilemmas Facing the Public Sector', International Research Conf. Sept. 2002. London, UK. Dilemmas Conference: 6th International Research Conference Can be Round at http://technology.open.ac.uk/cru/Dilemmas2002.pdf

Aiken, M. (2001) 'Keeping Close to Your Values: Lessons from a Study Examining How Voluntary and Co-Operative Organisations Reproduce Their Organisational Values', Open University (accessed by web 14/2/2007) http://technology. open.ac.uk/cru/NCVO%20Paper.pdf

Anheier, H. (2005) *Non Profit Organisations: Theory, Management, Policy*. Routledge.

Beck Jørgensen, T. and Bozeman, B. (2006) 'The Public Value Universe: An Inventory', *Administration and Society* (in press).

Blake, G., Robinson, D. and Smerdon, D. (2006) 'Living Values: A Report Encouraging Boldness in Third Sector Organisations', *Community Links*. UK.

Cabinet Office (2006) *Partnership in Public Services: An Action Plan for Third Sector involvement and Social Enterprise Action Plan: Scaling the Heights*.

Cairns, B., Harris, M. and Young, P. (2005) 'Building the Capacity of the Voluntary Nonprofit Sector: Challenges of Theory and Practice', *Int. J. of Public Administration*, Volume 28: Number 9–10.

Charity Commission (2007) *Stand and Deliver* Charity. Commission of England and Wales. Feb. 2007.

Cm 2850-I (1995) *First Report of the Committee on Standards in Public Life* (The Nolan Report). UK: HMSO.

Cormack, J. and Stanton, M. (2003) *Passionate Leadership: The Characteristics of Outstanding Leaders in the Voluntary Sector*. Hay Group and ACEVO.

Commission on the Future of the Voluntary Sector (1996) *Meeting the Challenge of Change: Voluntary Action in the 21st Century*. London: NCVO.

Cornforth, C. (2003) *The Governance of Public and Non-Profit Organisations*, Routledge.

Davies, S. (2007) *Third Sector Provision of Government and Health Services*. UNISON.

Day, V.D. (2001) 'Leadership Development: A Review in Context', *Leadership Quarterly*, 11(4): 581–613.

Delivering public service. A report to the Office of the Third Sector by the National Consumer Council, Alison Hopkins, April 2007.

Deakin, N. (2006) 'Gains and Strains: The Voluntary Sector in the UK 1996–2006', Baring Foundation Lecture, Dec. 2006. London, UK. www.baringfoundation.org.uk/

Elson, P. (2006) 'Ties that Bind: An Empirical Exploration of Values in the Voluntary Sector: Value Importance, Hierarchy and Consensus in Independent Hospices in the UK', Working Paper, Centre for Civil Society, London School of Economics.

Etzioni, A. (1973) 'The Third Sector and Domestic Missions', *Public Administration Review*. July/August 1973.

HM Treasury (2004) *Regularity, Propriety and Value for Money*. HM Treasury UK, Nov 2004.

HM Treasury (2002) *The Role of the Voluntary and Community Sector in Service Delivery: A Cross Cutting Review*.

HM Treasury (2005) *Exploring the Role of the Third Sector in Public Service Delivery and Reform*. London: HM Treasury.

HM Treasury (2006) *The Future Role of the Third Sector in Economic and Social Regeneration: An Interim Report*.

Hopkins, A. (2007) *Delivering Public Services: Service Users Experience of the Third Sector*. National Consumer Council.

Hudson, M. (2004) *Managing Without Profit*. Directory of Social Change.

Kendall, J. and Knapp, M. (1995) 'A Loose and Baggy Monster: Boundaries, Definitions and Typologies', in Davis Smith, J., Rochester, C. and Hedley, R. (eds) *An Introduction to the Voluntary Sector*. Routledge.

Kendall, J. (2003) *The Voluntary Sector*. Routledge.

Kirchner, A. (2006) 'Value-Based Leadership: A Third Sector View', *The British Journal of Leadership in Public Services*, 2(4): 30–33.

Kirchner, A. (2007) *Leading Leaders: A Snapshot into the Minds of CEO's*. UK: ACEVO.

Mintzberg, H. (1989) *Mintzberg on Management*. Hungry Minds.

Murdock, A. (2005a) 'Who Pays the Piper ... Voluntary Sector Reform and the New Service Delivery, Devolution and Localism Agenda', ISTR-EMES, Paris, April 2005.

Murdock, A (2005b) 'The Voluntary Sector Compacts and Localism in the UK: Third Sector Service and Co-producer Implications of Variations between England, Scotland, Northern Ireland and Wales'. EGPA Berne 2005.

Murdock, A. (2006) 'Lessons from the Delivery Of Public Services by the Third Sector and the Increasing Links to Citizenship: The Emergence and Development of Contractual Partnerships between the Third Sector and Government', Paper to 3rd Sino-US International Conference for Public Administration, June 8–9 2006, Beijing P.R. China (in publication by China Renmin University Press).

National Audit Office (2005) *Home Office: Working with the Third Sector*.

NCVO (2006) *The UK Voluntary Sector Almanac 2006: The State of the Sector*. London, UK: NCVO.

NCVO (2005) *Voluntary Action: Meeting the Challenges of the 21st Century*. London, UK: NCVO. Feb 2005.

O'Kelly, C. and Dubnick, M. (2005) 'Taking Tough Choices Seriously: Public Administration and Individual Moral Agency', Working Paper: Queens Univ., Belfast, Inst. of Governance , Public policy and Social Research.

Osborne, S. and McLaughlin, K. (2002) 'Trends and Issues in the Implementation of Local Voluntary Sector Compacts in England', *Public Money & Management*, Jan–Mar 2002.

Osborne, S. and McLaughlin, K. (2004) 'The Cross Cutting Review of the Voluntary Sector: Where Next for Local Government – Voluntary Sector Relationships?', *Regional Studies*, 38(5): 573–582.

Osborne, S. (2005) 'Voluntary Action in a Changing Europe: Critical Perspectives', *Int. J. of Public Administration*, Volume 28: Number 9–10.

Paton, R. (1992) 'The Social Economy: Value-based Organisations in the Wider Society', in Cornforth, C. and Paton, R., *Issues in Voluntary and Non Profit Management* (ed. Balsleer J.). UK: Adddison Wesley.

Seddon, N. (2007) *Who Cares?* Civitas.

Paxton, W. *et al.* (2005) 'The Voluntary Sector Delivering Public Services Transfer or Transformation?', Joseph Rowntree Foundation.

Paton, R, (2003) *Managing and Measuring Social Enterprises*. London: Sage.

Pharoh, C. (2007) *Sources of Strength*. Baring Foundation.

Six, P. and Vidal, I. (ed.) (1994) *Delivering Welfare: Repositioning Non-profit and Co-operative Action in Western European Welfare States*. Barcelona: Centre d'Iniciatives de l'Economica Social (CIES).

Smerdon, M. (2006) *Allies not Servants*. Baring Foundation.

The Times (2006) *Cheap Tricks or True Charity*, September 12th, Times Newspapers.

Van de Walle, S. (2005) 'The Impact of Public Service Values on Services of General Interest Reform Debates', Paper to IRSMP1X Bocconi Univ. Italy April 2005.

Wittenburg, B. (2007) *State, Private Sector and Voluntary Activity: A Vision for the Future*, Directory of Social Change.

20

Can Public Leadership be Evaluated?

Nick Tilley

Introduction

Most evaluations ask about specific policies or programmes. Policies and programmes are devised to deal with some state of affairs (say levels of poverty or ill-health) or behaviour (say patterns of criminal activity or truancy) that is deemed problematic. The success or failure of the policy or programme is measured in terms of the change in the targeted state of affairs or behaviour together with positive and negative unintended side-effects. The main interest is in learning lessons for future policy and practice.

An early advocate of systematic evaluation, perhaps the first, was Karl Popper who advocated 'piecemeal social engineering' (Popper 1945, 1957). Piecemeal social engineering comprises an experimental approach to the development of public policy and practice: in relation to specific harms (states of affairs or behaviours) it involves a) developing some hypotheses about what might reduce or remove them; b) implementing the required measures in a limited way; c) measuring the outcomes and; d) starting again, refining the theory, or broadening the application of the measures in accordance with the results.

Some programmes are relatively simple, for example the hand-washing regime introduced to reduce childbed fever in a mid-19th century Vienna maternity hospital (Semmelweis 1983[1860]; Nuland 2003), and some are relatively complex, say the Crime Reduction Programme introduced in Britain in 1999 to try to prevent a range of crimes of national and local concern (Maguire 2004).

It is possible that public leadership (or some variant of it) could be introduced as a programme to deal with a state of affairs or set of behaviours that was deemed problematic, say chronic interagency conflict that was believed to impede the achievement of social objectives requiring cooperation. This chapter explores whether evaluation is either relevant or practical in relation to 'public leadership' and what form it might take.

The approach to evaluation that will be drawn on here is 'realist', not only in the belief that this is the best evaluation methodology in general, but also because it is thought to be the only one what might be fit for purpose in looking specifically at public leadership (Pawson and Tilley 1997). Realist evaluations begin with different questions and adopt different methods from those used in traditional experimental evaluation.

Traditional 'gold standard' evaluations are concerned with the bottom line. Did the intervention work or did it not. And if it did work, how large was the 'effect size'? The favoured, experimental method generates answers to these questions. This method is the randomised controlled trial (RCT). RCTs identify potential recipient populations from which experimental and control groups are randomly selected. Standardised interventions are applied to the 'experimental' group whilst no intervention, a placebo or normal practice takes place in one or more control group. Before and after measurements are made in the various groups and the programme is adjudicated a success if the experimental group outperforms its rivals. This occurs if the difference in the differences between the before and after measurements in the experimental groups exceeds that of the control groups by an amount that is statistically significant. Making sure that the participants in the trial, those delivering the interventions and those making before and after measurements do not know who are and are not receiving the experimental treatment (so-called 'blinding' or 'masking') is deemed crucial in RCTs in medicine, in order to avoid systematic sources of bias. RCTs are uninterested in how programmes work. They are well suited to simple, standardised, invariant interventions, such as taking of medication for specific conditions. The lower level of control over the intervention, the impracticability of blinding and the inherent complexity of many social programmes makes the use of RCTs for their evaluation at best much more challenging and at worst impossible. The following discussion brings out a few of the specific ways in which the nature of programmes (and of leadership in particular) implicitly challenges the experimental orthodoxy. The details of the pros and cons of experimentation, however, lie beyond the scope of this short chapter. The interested reader is invited to consult other sources (for example Shadish *et al.* 2002).

Realist evaluation

The starting point for realist evaluation is the construction of theory. The reason is that all programmes are 'theories incarnate'. That is, they embody sets of hypotheses that a given measure or set of measures will generate changes producing an improvement in the problematic state of affairs of pattern of behaviours. The thinking of the architects of programmes is but one source of theory. Other sources include the literature, past evaluation studies, general social science, stakeholder views, and the views of those who are targeted by the programme.

Three generic attributes of programmes should also be mentioned here, as they bear both on the nature of programmes and on theories of them in ways that are crucial to evaluation. The first is that programmes rarely, if ever, remain static beyond demonstration phases and they often do not last even that long. Programmes adapt and change according to the attributes of the people involved in them, and their own internal dynamics. The second is that programmes produce complex patterns of outcome, with winners and losers, successes and failures. The third is that the external conditions for programmes are apt to vary and to change over time, sometimes in chaotic and inherently unpredictable ways. Folk programme theories, likewise, are unlikely to remain fixed. In particular, those individuals who are implicated, at whatever level, are liable to experience programmes in distinctive ways and thereby to formulate (and to deploy) fluid notions of what the programme is about and what is delivered as part of it.

From the welter of theory that is liable to emerge, in particular in relation to complex programmes, the evaluator has to select some for formalisation and testing. In most cases there will be too much for anything approaching comprehensive treatment. That selected will ordinarily be the most promising, interesting or significant in relation to the problem state of affairs and behaviour and any potential substantial side-effects. It may also in practice be shaped in part by the concerns of key stakeholders.

Having formalised the theory, the evaluation then chases down data sets that speak to the specific outcome patterns that would be expected in the light of the theory. These specific outcome patterns may relate to people, process, times, places, and sub-groups.

The way in which programme theory is formalised is quite distinctive in realist evaluation. The realist is interested in identifying and testing configurations, rather than one-to-one causal relationships. RCTs focus on whether the independent variable (the programme) affects the dependent variable (the intended change in the state of affairs or patterns of behaviour). Realists are interested, in contrast, in 'mechanisms'. The term 'mechanism' is used in answer to 'how' questions. Much of the study of medicine is concerned with disease mechanisms, how diseases are triggered, transmitted, develop over time and how treatments may disrupt the activation of disease generating mechanisms, the transmission of the disease and the pathological development of the disease. In regard to social programmes a key part of the theory, which evaluators try to elicit and formalise, has to do with how the intervention or interventions may be affecting the target behaviour or state of affairs. Mechanisms differ from programme interventions (or sub-parts of programmes) in that they are often invisible. Just as gravity, electricity and natural selection cannot be observed directly but nevertheless comprise important mechanisms in nature generating observable patterns, so in social programmes underlying mechanisms will often be unobservable whilst generating changes in behaviour or states of affairs. We shall come to further examples when we discuss the evaluation of public leadership. For the moment, consider 'inspiration.' Great leaders are often said to inspire others whose behaviour changes accordingly. We cannot directly observe this inspiration, even if we may be able to observe the behaviours that may be activating the inspiration and the behaviours that are produced as a consequence of that inspiration!

The second element realists are interested in, in developing programme theories, is context. The leadership literature is replete with references to context. Much of this is highly normative. It emphasised the need for the successful leader to adapt to context. The idea is that different circumstances call for different styles of leadership. Events change the issues to be addressed, different populations within the ambit of the leader call for different leadership qualities, and one task at hand may differ qualitatively from another, each making its own leadership demands. Implicit in this is the notion that the same leadership activities play out differently according to context. What works positively in one setting may be a disaster in another. It is instructive to see the sniggering disdain with which academics generally respond to most leaders' efforts at their emotional inspiration. They want to be persuaded (a kind of mechanism) by strong arguments and evidence (the intervention).

The coupling of context and mechanism produces the third element of the configuration: the outcome. In relation to a programme what matters in context is that which is relevant to the mechanisms that are activated. Much will be irrelevant or only very tangentially relevant. The fact that programmes, like leadership, tend to be introduced across populations that are relevantly heterogeneous, that target populations often change in significant ways over time, and that what is delivered is generally not fully consistent gives rise to a patchwork of interventions, contexts and mechanisms generating diverse outcome patterns, some of which tend to be positive and some negative. The task for the realist evaluator is to discern interesting, useful and significant configurations that can be identified, tested and refined for future use.

Consider perpetrator arrest and repeat domestic violence. Arrest activates anger amongst some, which can precipitate repeat events. It can activate contrition amongst others, which can inhibit repeat events. It seems that those who are less socially integrated are more susceptible to anger-activation and hence repeat patterns of behaviour while those who are more integrated are more susceptible to contrition-activation and hence suppressed repeat incidents. The same measure (arrest) activates different mechanisms (anger or contrition) that produce variations in outcome (more or fewer repeat incidents) according to context (less or more social integration) (see Sherman 1990; Tilley 2000).

Applying realist evaluation to public leadership

Leadership clearly differs from social programmes, which are introduced to address specific problem states of affairs or patterns of behaviour, in a number of crucial respects for its evaluation using traditional methods:

- Whilst there may have been acephalous groups in some simple small-scale societies, they are relatively rare.
- Leadership is a chronic feature of social life. There may be different forms of leadership. But leadership control or comparison conditions are unlikely to be available.
- Leadership may be important in determining what should be considered problem states of affairs or patterns of behaviour or what is done in response to them. It is not, however, a programme to deal with such issues directly with corresponding identifiable intended outcomes.

Leadership styles cannot be introduced in quite the same way as a specific social programme can, with relatively well-defined, controlled and sustained specific interventions. Let us see if realist evaluation can, nevertheless, help provide a framework for evaluating leadership. How would the realist begin to evaluate public leadership?

The starting point for realist evaluation, as already indicated, is theory. What is the realist theory of public leadership? Although the problem giving rise to a perceived need for a particular style of leadership is not that of a specific state of affairs or pattern of behaviour, it is presumably that of failure, absent adequate leadership, to identify and address harms of the kind Popper referred to in his discussion of piecemeal social engineering through conventional (non-public) leadership. It will be easier (for me and the reader) to focus the discussion on some specific public issue arena. I shall use crime because it is a domain with which I am familiar, although I think that many other areas, for example health, education, and urban regeneration, could equally have been used.

In relation to crime, three types of problem can be identified, following the general lines usefully described by Grint (2005), although unlike Grint these are not deemed here simply to be socially constructed categories. Critical problems are those that demand decisive action: a riot breaks out, a bomb is exploded, a hostage is taken, rival football supporters clash violently, or a fire starts. In some cases what needs to be done will be obvious to anyone competent to act. They can take charge and tell others what to do. In other cases what needs to be done will be less obvious, but there will be a strong sense that something needs to be done. Tame issues are those problems where there is an established set of responses that are accepted as effective by those competent in the given domain. Domestic violence may be a case in point. There are known ways of reducing risks of repeat domestic violence that will be effective if implemented properly (see Hanmer *et al.* 1999), although they will not work if not implemented properly, which may itself in part be a function of leadership (Hanmer 2003). Then there are 'wicked issues'. These describe unfamiliar problems where there are no known and accepted effective responses. It is not clear who should do what to address them, even though in the case of crime there may be plenty of stakeholders and plenty of opinions. In Britain, gang-related youth violence comprises a recent example.

The leadership needs vary by problem type. In the case of critical problems, control and quick decision-making are important. If catastrophe looms and action may avert it then the leadership needs are for rapid judgement, credibility and authority. The police can-do attitude and clear command structure equip them well for the exercise of leadership in relation to 'critical' problems. Their experience, intuition and training should enable tame critical issues to be addressed in a predictable, effective way and wicked critical issues to be addressed in at least a prompt and promising way, albeit that there will clearly be risks in the face of the unknown circumstances. In the case of tame non-critical issues, technical competence by the leader-ship is crucial. Authority is vested in the leaders' credentials that make their direction persuasive. Much of the work of crime scene examiners, and those who direct their behaviour, for example, falls into this category. In order for their work to have credibility, crime scene examiners must use their expert knowledge and must do so in well-recorded standard and standardised ways if it is to yield useful leads to investigators and if it is to stand up in court. Wicked issues are those for which no standard responses are known. As Donald Rumsfeld's put it in his famous (but unfairly derided) formulation, '(A)s we know, there are known knowns; there are things we know we know. We also know there are known unknowns; that is to say we know there are some things we do not know. But there are also unknown unknowns – the ones we don't know we don't know.' Wicked issues are those seen to have these attributes. We can also add a little more: some things may be known but who knows what with what certainty is unknown. The severity of the problem is unknown. Even when the knowns are known and there can be some confidence in these knowns, what can be done to reduce or remove the problem is still unknown. Understanding does not always yield obvious recipes for action. Indeed competing interests in a given problem may mean that those who want to act and those who can act most plausibly to address the problem may not overlap.

Let us try to make this clearer with an example: alcohol-related city centre late-night violence. Known knowns typically include the levels and locations of police-reported and recorded violent incidents where the victim or offender has consumed alcohol, and the kinds of event that precipitate violent acts. Known unknowns typically include patterns and rates of unreported alcohol-related violent incidents, the extent to which police reported and recorded alcohol-related incidents can be attributed to drinking in bars, cheap drinking in bars, drinking at locations other than bars, and levels of determination to consume alcohol. Unknown unknowns cannot in principle be known in advance by those implicated in trying to deal with the problem. They are likely to include the forms of adaptation employed by those in relation to whom interventions are applied. Suppose, for example, that we replace glass that breaks into sharp shards when smashed with toughened glass that breaks into small cubes that are relatively blunt (cf Warburton and Shepherd 2000; Tilley 2009). An unknown unknown for those contemplating this action is likely to include the forms of response to this that will be made by the assailant and those who might protect the victim. Finally, even if we understood the full dynamics of alcohol-related city centre violence (there were no known or unknown unknowns), that is unlikely to yield a single uncontentious intervention that will be implemented without question. There are strong and competing interests and priorities by those who might be competent to act, for example youth who might be encouraged to drink less but do not want to do so; bar owners (and supermarkets) who might increase prices producing less drinking but who do not want to or cannot afford to sacrifice custom; legislators who might increase the drinking age or restrict drinking hours but do not want to alienate voters or the drinks industry; local authorities that might oppose planning permission for developments that attract a lively night time economy but that want to bring people into the town centre for the revenue and popularity that brings; parents who might exert more control over young drinkers but who have other priorities and pressure from their children and their children's peer groups to treat them as responsible adults; schools that might sensitise youngsters to the risks of heavy drinking but have competing priorities for the education of young people; health services that might offer treatment to heavy drinkers but for whom there are more pressing (and maybe deserving) calls on their limited resources; and the police who might provide a strong presence at night when violence most often erupts but who have a host of other responsibilities and limited resources with which to discharge them. Those directly bearing the costs of alcohol-related city centre late-night violence and hence who also have the greatest material interest in their reduction – the police and health services – are not those best placed to act differently in ways that lessen the problem upstream, where the causes of the problem lie but where there are fewer interests in dealing with it and less accountability for addressing them. The contexts furnished for each stakeholder, including health and the police, help shape the priorities each has.

Because for most crime issues, whether they be tame or wicked, many organisations have a stake, as sources of information about them, ideas about what to do about them, capacity to exert leverage on the causes of them, and bearers of the costs of them, crime reduction partnerships have been advocated since 1984 (Home Office 1984). Local partnerships were put on a statutory footing in 1998 with the Crime and Disorder Act. The members of these partnerships have to balance their own individual agendas, which are often complex, diffuse and changing, with an obligation to attend to the partnership crime and disorder agenda that will coincide to a greater, or lesser, extent with their own individual priorities. Public leadership is exercised in relation to this messy world. Leadership has to be exercised both in relation to the internal workings of and aims of particular individual organisations and in relation to partnership workings and partnership aims.

In practice there is substantial evidence of failures to deal effectively with crime, one identified contribution to which has been leadership weakness, which suggests that this leadership needs to be reformed (see Read and Tilley 2000; Bullock *et al.* 2006). Identified requirements of effective public leadership in relation to crime have included, for example:

- Inspiration to kick-start change in orientation and enthusiasm throughout the organisation for problem-solving
- Articulation of a clear philosophy underpinning ways of working
- Championship of well-thought through problem-solving ways of working by identified individuals with sufficient tenure to see through their initiatives
- Continuity in approach where staff do change
- Knowledgeability (and hence credibility) in relation to the substantive issues being addressed
- Knowledgeability (and hence credibility) in relation to staff, local issues and partner agencies and organisations
- Empowerment of staff to use their own initiative and leadership qualities
- Routine management, oversight, support and coaching for junior, less experienced staff
- Scanning of the environment for changed situations and problems providing for adjustments where needed
- Openness and flexibility in relation to emerging and varying needs
- Facilitation of partnership links with other agencies required to deliver effective responses

Crime and disorder leadership theory needs might be summarised as follows.

In a context where a) presenting problems to be addressed remain unchanging and are well-understood, b) clearly-identified bodies are responsible for those problems and have the powers to apply measures known to be effective to deal with them, c) problems are discrete in that action in relation to one has no significant consequences for another, and d) role-occupants have the skills and understanding to deliver the measures for which they are responsible, then segmented, hierarchical top-down leadership will produce predictable intended outcomes. This is not the context for dealing with crime and disorder in modern societies. Yet much leadership presumes it is. Instead, a) presenting problems continuously morph as offenders and preventers adapt to one another and to changing opportunities or as changing priorities are set, and the problems to be addressed are only ever partially understood, b) responsibilities are shared between bodies that have different main missions and responsible bodies often lack the powers or incentives to apply promising measures to deal with problems, c) problems are highly connected to one another in that a measure producing an effect on one problem-domain may also produce beneficial effects on another, but may equally generate problems on other domains, and d) role-occupants often lack the subtle skills and understanding to deliver their measures. Change in leadership style is needed better to reflect the actual context for policy and practice to deal with crime and disorder. A realist theory would articulate what specifically would be involved and how reformed leadership would work.

Let us now step back specifically from the field of crime and disorder which illustrates the problems of public leadership. What mechanisms might a public leadership activate more generally? In principle there are many, a number of which may be activated in the leadership of private enterprises also. These are positive generic leadership mechanisms, in that they contribute to the achievement of objectives whether in the public or private domain. Realists tend to sort mechanisms into those that furnish resources in their broadest sense (people, objects, money, skills etc.) and those that affect reasoning in its broadest sense (values, feelings, priorities, ideas etc.). The broad categories are indicated in the following list of sample leadership mechanisms, which are littered through the leadership literature. They could variously apply in a business concern, sports team or charity as well as in any public sector organisation.

- Goal and strategy-setting: the specification of broad objectives and overall means for followers to help achieve (reasoning)
- Goal withdrawal: the decision to abandon hopeless causes, including follower activity (reasoning and resources)
- Inspiration: the emotional or normative motivation of followers (reasoning)
- Problem-solving: the identification of variations in problem type for relevant followers to work on, either to devise or implement attempted solutions (reasoning and resources)
- Questioning: fostering critical enquiry about potential sources of improvement in the activity of followers in the achievement of goals (reasoning)
- Encouragement: reassurance in the face of followers' doubts and difficulties (reasoning)
- Context-setting: the creation of conditions where followers act in preferred ways (reasoning and resources)
- Incentivisation: the deployment of benefits and costs to followers to elicit preferred behaviour (reasoning and resources)

- Enablement: the provision of physical, financial and technical resources for followers to act in intended ways (resources)
- Alignment: the coordination and harmonisation of different follower activities to achieve a given strategy (resources)
- Coaching: the transmission of necessary skills and understanding for followers to act in the achievement of objectives (reasoning and resources)
- Consultation: the elicitation of followers' ideas and understanding in identifying means to ends (reasoning)
- Recruitment: the acquisition of resources needed to achieve ends (resources)
- Dismissal: the removal of those who fail to follow or who threaten the attainment of objectives (resources)
- Team-building: the assembly of follower-groups capable of achieving collectively what cannot be achieved individually (resources)
- Command and coercion: the instruction of others to act in required ways (reasoning)
- Conciliation, arbitration, and division: the removal, creation or exploitation of internal tensions amongst followers, competitors and other third parties to encourage cooperation, competition and mutual obstruction as needed for the achievement of goals (reasoning)
- Authority bestowal: the legitimation of limited leadership rights and responsibilities for subordinates in the in the implementation of overall strategy (reasoning)

Though these may comprise a set of generic leadership mechanisms, the literature suggests that they may be activated in many different ways. Indeed, as we have already stressed those that are relevant will to some degree be a function of the problem being addressed. It also seems to be the case that individuals differ in their capacity to activate these mechanisms. Moreover, individuals have their own styles of leadership that allow them to activate distinct configurations of leadership mechanisms (Goffee and Jones 2006).

If the leadership is poor enough in the private sector and performance is sufficiently affected adversely, then economic competition provides a natural way for it eventually to be eliminated. The strategy has to include attention to profitability as a condition of success and the means have to be successful enough to keep the organisational head above water. In view of this, the leadership of thriving, large-scale sustained private sector enterprises by definition is fit enough for the conditions in which it is being exercised. In the public sector, this ultimate method of judgment over leadership is not available. This is one reason why its evaluation by other means might be appropriate as a basis for informing improvements, especially in view of the track record of failure that is sometimes found, as in the case of crime.

What additional positive mechanisms might be needed in public leadership, in addition to the generic ones of the kind mentioned so far? Consider the following, all of which relate back to the public rather than private interests that lie at the heart of publicly funded organisations and activities.

- Inspiration of public service orientation: exemplification, reward for, and emphasis on follower integrity in pursuit of the public good (reasoning)
- Balance of diverse public good objectives: recognition that followers must balance competing demands in organisations with multiple public service aims (reasoning and resources)
- Subordination of local or specific organisational objectives to the pursuit of the public good: redeployment of resources to steer followers to pursue public interests rather than private or single-sectoral ones (resources)
- Courage in the face of the selfish, unprincipled or impossible: refusing and encouraging followers to refuse to act in ways that contradict the pursuit of the public good (reasoning)
- Recognition of ultimate accountability to the electorate: acknowledgement that resources and legitimacy for leaders and followers are provided by the electorate, even if in the short term public opinion may be disregarded in the interests of pursuing the public good (reasoning and resources).

The attentive reader will have noticed that this chapter has concentrated mostly, although not exclusively, on 'leadership' rather than 'leaders'. Karl Popper explains why this is appropriate in the public sphere in a discussion of 'The Principle of Leadership' published in 1945. Popper rejects the question, 'Who should rule?' and advocates instead, asking, 'How can we so organize political institutions that bad or incompetent leaders can be prevented from doing too much damage?' (Popper 1945: 121) As Popper's chapter-heading indicates, by rulers he has in mind leaders and he favours an institutional approach that does not depend on the particular qualities of the individuals involved. Institutions, he argues, are needed to act as checks on the unbridled exercise of power and the risks that this brings. This does not mean that individuals do not matter. As Popper says, 'Institutions are like fortresses. They must be well-designed *and* manned.' (Popper 1945: 126, original italics).

A public leadership theory is one of institutions. This might include methods of selecting and fostering those who will man (or, better, 'staff') those institutions, but will not be one of the attributes of great individual leaders of the sort that is represented by some academic and much popular leadership literature. In public leadership public interest lies in the activation of mechanisms that will lead to sustained, democratically accountable achievements of public goods, of which the most uncontentious is probably harm-reduction of the sort sought in crime prevention and stressed by Popper.

Figure 20.1 sketches the bare bones of one broadly realist theory of public leadership, which draws inspiration from Grint's problem-types discussed earlier in relation specifically to crime although here is intended to be generic. The theory is realist in that it attempts to abstract what may be constellations of contextual conditions which are germane to the styles of leadership that, other things being equal, might be expected to generate better (or, by inference, worse) performance in the public sector. Two dimensions of leadership variation are identified. Horizontally, leadership may be spread more or less widely across a number of organisations or it may be located in only one. Vertically, it may be located in only one command position or it may be distributed more or less widely within any organisation. Four major quadrants are shown in Figure 20.1.

In the top left leadership is widely distributed vertically but not horizontally. This, it is conjectured, is liable to produce better performance where there is a single responsible and competent organisation, but where the issue at stake is a wicked one or one which is variable in its manifestation and hence poorly understood in its particulars. Here, it is expected that central direction would tend to produce sub-optimal outcomes and delegated authority better ones.

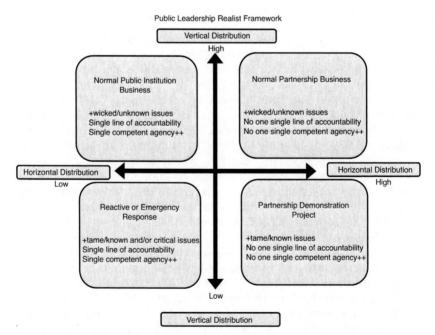

Figure 20.1   Potential Realist Evaluation Framework for Public Leadership

In the top right leadership is again widely distributed vertically but this time it is also widely distributed horizontally. Here, the hunch is that better performance follows where there is no single responsible and competent organisation, and where the issue at stake is a wicked one or one which is variable in its manifestation and hence poorly understood in its particulars. Here, it is expected that central direction would tend to produce sub-optimal outcomes and delegated authority better ones, but where that delegated authority is best spread across diverse organisations which collectively have a better chance of understanding and delivering effective responses than any on its own.

In the bottom left leadership is narrowly distributed both vertically and horizontally. In relation to critical issues that call for an immediate response, especially where there are well-tried strategies and a single organisation competent to address them, the hypothesis is that a single agency with a clear command structure will most effectively deliver positive outcomes. Someone needs to be in charge and able to direct resources and action to produce predictable results.

In the bottom right lies leadership which is widely distributed horizontally but narrowly distributed vertically. In relation to issues that lie beyond the competence or responsibility of any single agency but for which there are standard or agreed responses by multiple organisations, this is the form of leadership that is expected to produce the most successful outcomes.

This theory is, of course, not necessarily true. It comprises, at best, a plausible account of the ways in which conditions for leadership vary in ways that suggest that differences in structure and style will produce better (or worse) outcomes.

In relation to the frequently messy world of public leadership, where reform is proposed the evaluator's first task is to distil any specific theory being advanced (for example that of shared and distributed leadership sketched in Figure 20.1) in terms of the mechanisms believed to be activated that will contribute to improvements in the achievement of public benefits (ultimately leading to better or less harmful states of affairs and better or less harmful behaviour patterns). The distillation and formalisation of any such specific theory will involve talking to the architects of the theory, reading relevant literature, drawing on established broader bodies of theory, and talking to those who are implicated in that leadership either as intended leaders or intended followers or as intended leader-followers (those who are both led and lead according to the specified theory). These views will not in and of themselves let us know whether or not the leadership regime is working in the expected way. It will, nevertheless, inform the formulation of theory that can be tested in other ways, to which we come in due course.

Realist evaluation also requires that we identify ways in which the theory might not be working out quite as expected. This means trying to take into account ways in which the theory may work out in practice in unanticipated and unintended ways. Most actions, including most leadership styles, produce side-effects that are generally, although not always, unwanted. Ernst Gombrich's brilliant survey of world history from the beginning of time to the aftermath of the Second World War makes clear the limits of leadership, the fact that much goes on independently of leadership that throws intentions off course, as well as the ways in which leaders chronically tend eventually to fail even following initial achievement (Gombrich 2005). The last in a long line he mentions, is Hitler.

Here's a small sample of mechanisms that may be triggered by leaders to produce unintended and unwanted consequences:

- Over-extension: stimulating too much activity by followers across too wide an area so that much is undone or not done properly (resources)
- Over-delegation: enabling intermediary leader-followers to lead their own followers in ways that obstruct or challenge (reasoning and resources)
- Setting contradictory strategies: directing followers to pursue one goal that jeopardises the achievement of another (reasoning)
- Excessive change: loss of confidence (cynicism) in followers that a consistent strategy is being followed (reasoning)
- Inflexibility: failure to realise that conditions have changed and hence followers' interests are no longer being met (reasoning and resources)
- Excessive demands: provocation of mutiny or disloyalty amongst followers (reasoning)
- Insufficient ability or understanding or recognition of own limitations: loss of confidence amongst the followers that the leader had the capacity to lead them (reasoning)
- Over self-confidence: failure to listen to followers able to inform strategy and necessary to deliver strategy (reasoning)

These are unlikely to exhaust unintended unwanted mechanisms activated by leaders and new leadership regimes, but they illustrate the point that any evaluation needs to attend to what leadership might produce unintentionally as well as what is produced intentionally. Those participating as leaders and followers are liable to have a strong sense of what these might be in practice in relation to any given leadership regime.

Conclusion

This paper has tried to sketch out how realist evaluation might approach public leadership. The emphasis is on contexts, mechanisms and outcomes. The product would be context, mechanism outcome pattern configurations (CMOCs). What kinds of leadership work in what ways, according to what conditions, to produce what sorts of positive and negative outcome? For example, what kind of leadership structures generate the delivery of what kinds of activity effectively or ineffectively to reduce public harms or create public goods? Some of the findings would likely parallel those that could be expected from leadership in any setting. Others would be particular to the distinct conditions of public service.

The concrete study of any given public sector case would likely involve both an overarching examination of the leadership washing through the organisation or partnership as a whole and interrogation of the specific leadership activities, mechanisms and follower outcomes occurring within the organisation or partnership, resulting in differing patterns of service delivery. The latter, if related to a judgment over the patterns of public benefit (and cost) achieved, would ultimately yield empirically based guidance on what kind of leadership activity produces what kind of positive and negative outcomes in what conditions. It is difficult to gauge the level of abstraction that would emerge. Grint's classification of problem-types looks promising as a key basis for differentiating contexts where the activation of different leadership mechanisms would produce varying outcome patterns, but only empirical study could determine whether or not this is, indeed, the case.

Technically, any realist evaluation of public leadership is liable to be highly challenging and would require the use of diverse techniques, involving qualitative, quantitative, documentary and comparative research.

Given the fluidity and complexity of public service it is unlikely that an experimental approach would be practical. There could also be no guarantee that a realist approach would yield useful or valid findings. The argument of this chapter, however, is that it provides a promising starting point, offering some prospect of theoretically informed but empirically grounded reasons for promulgating one form of leadership or another according to the conditions faced.

Acknowledgement

Thanks are due to Steve Brookes for his most helpful comments on and suggestions for improvements to this chapter.

References

Bullock, K., Erol, R. and Tilley, N. (2006) *Problem-Oriented Policing and Partnerships: Implementing an Evidence-Based Approach to Crime Prevention*. Cullompton, Devon: Willan.

Gombrich, E. (2005) *A Little History of the World*. New Haven: Yale University Press.

Goffee, R. and Jones, G. (2006) *Why Should Anyone be Led by You? What it Takes to be an Authentic Leader*. Boston: Harvard Business School Press.

Grint, K. (2005) 'Problems, Problems, Problems: The Social Construction of Leadership', *Human Relations*, 58(11): 1467–1494.

Hanmer, J. (2003) 'Mainstreaming Solutions to Major Problems: Reducing Repeat Domestic Violence', in Bullock, K. and Tilley, N. (eds) *Crime Reduction and Problem-Oriented Policing*. Cullompton, Devon: Willan.

Hanmer, J., Griffiths, S. and Jerwood, D. (1999) 'Arresting Evidence: Domestic Violence and Repeat Victimisation', Policing Research Series Paper 104. London: Home Office.

Home Office (1984) 'Crime Prevention', *Home Office Circular 8/88*. London: Home Office.

Maguire, M. (2004) 'The Crime Reduction Programme in England and Wales: Reflections on the Vision and the Reality', *Criminal Justice*, 4(3): 213–237.

Nuland, S. (2003) Th*e Doctors' Plague: Germs, Childbed Fever and the Strange Story of Ignac Semmelweis*. New York: W.W. Norton.

Pawson, R. and Tilley, N. (1997) *Realistic Evaluation*. London: Sage.

Popper, K. (1945) *The Open Society and Its Enemies*. Volume 1 Plato. London: Routledge.

Popper, K. (1957) *The Poverty of Historicism*. London: Routledge.

Read, T. and Tilley, N. (2000) *Not Rocket Science: Problem-Solving and Crime Reduction*, Crime Reduction Research Series Paper 6. London: Home Office.

Semmelweis, I. (1983[1860]) *The Etiology, Concept and Prophylaxis of Childbed Fever*. Madison: The University of Wisconsin Press.

Shadish, W., Cook, T. and Campbell, D. (2002) *Experimental and Quasi-Experimental Designs for Generalised Causal Inference*. Boston: Houghton Mifflin.

Sherman, L. (1990) *Policing Domestic Violence: Experiments and Dilemmas*. New York: Free Press.

Tilley, N. (2000) 'Doing Realistic Evaluation of Criminal Justice', in Jupp, V., Davies, P. and Francis, P. (eds) *Doing Criminological Research*. London: Sage.

Tilley, N. (2009) 'What's the "What" in "What Works?"? Health, Policing and Crime Prevention', in Knutsson, J. and Tilley, N. (eds), 'Evaluating Crime Reduction Initiatives', *Crime Prevention Studies*, Vol. 24. Monsey, NY: Criminal Justice Press.

Warburton, A. and Shepherd, J. (2000) 'Effectiveness of Toughened Glasswear in Terms of Reducing Injury in Bars: A Randomised Controlled Trial', *Injury Prevention*, 6: 36–40.

21
Epilogue
Reform, Realisation and Restoration: Public Leadership and Innovation in Government

Stephen Brookes

Reform – NPM as the nemesis of leadership?

Chapter 1 suggests that understanding context is critical for public leadership. The more recent context is characterised by reform that is focused on 'delivery' (HMSO 1999) with an unprecedented obsession with measurement. The context of public services is also one of crisis, a lowering of trust and confidence and a growing acceptance of the need for collectiv*ity* (as opposed to collectiv*ism* – the former representing a quality or condition rather than the latter which denotes a movement (Allen 2004)). The overall outcome of good public leadership should be the creation and demonstration of public value and not the single minded pursuit of easily measurable but relatively meaningless targets.

Part I of this volume[1] reviewed the impact of reform on individual public services and each author identified the deleterious impact that the obsession with 'performance' and 'targets' has had on the ability of leaders to lead with a tendency to introduce structural reform rather than address underpinning values. At its worst, NPM can be viewed as one of an avenging nemesis for those organisations that do not 'perform' regardless as to the strength of their leadership or the institutional constraints that leaders operate within. At its best, NPM can be viewed as a foundation upon which public leadership can flourish. Of course, the authors identified some clear benefits in introducing means to continually improve performance, but the real challenge for public leadership is to determine whether the focus is on 'counting what counts' as opposed to 'what can be count*ed*' (to quote Albert Einstein).

Some commentators have boldly declared that New Public Management (NPM) is in crisis (Evans 2009: 48), and some even go as far as saying that it is dead. (Dunleavy *et al.* 2005: 3). Dunleavy and his colleagues argue that changes in public management regimes have resulted in increased levels of institutional and policy complexity but have reduced the level of autonomous citizen competence and levels of social problem solving, which were the aims of NPM. Others suggest that NPM and its impact have been overstated (Kickert 2001), that it fails to address the inter (as opposed to intra) governmental needs for delivery (Rhodes 2001; Osborne and McLaughlin 2008) that it's benefits are partial and contested (Pollitt and Bouckaert 2004) or that it has failed (Farnham and Horton 1996) – which brings us back to the declaration that NPM is dead! So – can a new public leadership approach supplant the worst of new public management while preserving its better attributes?

Realisation: NPL as the phoenix – Rising from the ashes of NPM?

'Realism' as a doctrine suggests that matter 'as the object of perception' has real existence and, as a philosophical theory, while agreeing that objects exist independently of the mind, that they differ in accounts of appearance, perception and illusion and are assessed in 'terms of their truth to reality, rather than in terms of their verifiability' (OED 2009). As Nick Tilley argues comprehensively in the last chapter, realistic evaluation (Pawson and Tilley 1997) holds real promise in helping us to both understand and assess the benefits and outcomes of effective public leadership. Tilley suggested that realistic evaluation helps us to understand 'what kinds of leadership work in what ways, according to what conditions, to produce what sorts of positive and negative outcomes'. For example, what kind of leadership structures or behaviours generates the delivery of what kinds of activity effectively or ineffectively to reduce public harms or create public goods?

In Part II, our authors examined the essential features of public leadership that may help in identifying this realisation and the mechanisms that can bring about the desired change. Although this volume argues strongly for a collective approach one cannot ignore the importance of individual agency which Lord Turnbull examined. This was followed by an examination of the different forms of leadership including political and community leadership mechanisms. Essential features of public leadership include the need for leaders to ask intelligent questions in a problem solving way rather than trying to portray themselves as the 'font of all knowledge'. The required skills are explored within the context of networks and whole system working and from the experience of current leadership development programmes which highlight the challenge of change for public sector leaders. In Part III, some practical applications of public leadership are highlighted to show respectively how competing values can be effectively harnessed in highly charged and emotive contexts and the extent to which narratives can help in elucidating the challenges that change brings. Missed opportunities through leadership-enabling legislation and the difficulty of making partnerships work better show some of the mechanisms that are available and the challenges that face public leaders. Part IV explored some of the lessons that can be learned in taking forward a public leadership approach including an acknowledgement of the strengths and lessons to be learned from mixed modes of governance and the third sector. Tilley's question in the penultimate chapter explored whether public leadership can be evaluated. This is a critical question and one that this epilogue places at the heart of a public leadership challenge for the future with innovation as its main goal.

Based on the arguments presented in the foregoing chapters, it is argued that a new public leadership challenge should be set for 2011 and beyond through the 'Purpose', 'Process', 'Praxis' and 'Public Value' of public leadership. Once again with the assistance of the Oxford English Dictionary, each of these will be briefly unpicked and can be traced back to earlier chapters.

Purpose

The 'purpose' of public leadership is to set out clearly what it is that public leaders seek to attain through clearly stated intentions or aims. It takes account of, and seeks to balance, the prevailing contextual conditions presented by the political, social, economic, technological, environmental and legal drivers and barriers. It also provides a discourse that articulates the reason for these intentions and aims, the result or effect intended or sought and the end to which the intentions and aims are directed towards, within a climate that is conducive to publicly valued outcomes. Within the context of public leadership the purpose will include the need for the active participation of both internal and external stakeholders, the development of a shared vision based on an agreed mandate and identifying the desired public good to be pursued or harm to be eradicated or minimised.

Process

The 'process' of public leadership represents the sequence of leadership actions that are required to transform the purpose of public leadership into practice and how activities are coordinated. The process commences with the development of policies and procedures based on the purpose and the principles to be adopted in the implementation of the purpose through problem oriented approaches. Heifetz argues that it is within the process of leadership that leadership activity can be evaluated and, further, that theories shed light on the practice of leadership. Heifetz (1994) argues that we 'forget our past at our peril'. Handy (1985) and others make similar points (Yukl 1989) and the importance of collective leadership within a partnership setting cannot be understated (Agranoff 1986, 1990; Agranoff and McGuire 2003).

Praxis

The 'praxis' of public leadership represents the actual practice of particular public leadership styles at all levels. This is in support of its stated purpose in the achievement of shared objectives and in a way that it is accepted as habitual practice through shared learning and insights. Personal impact is vitally important through the development of an effective personal leadership style, use of constructive challenge and the enhancement of trust although there is a need to consider the complex interrelationships, both synergies and conflicts (Young 2000). Heifetz and Laurie (1997) argue for the collective intelligence of all employees and that leaders should get away from the habit of providing solutions, and devolve this responsibility.

Public value

'Public value' as the outcome of effective public leadership requires an alignment between the social goals identified by stakeholders, the trust and legitimacy which leaders secure in the delivery of these goals and the extent to which organisational capability matches the stated purpose to practice through the process of public leadership (Moore 1995; Kelly *et al.* 2002). Benington and Moore (in press), Benington (Chapter 12), Evans (*ibid*) and Stoker (2006) argue that the time for PVM (Public Value Management) has come of age. The creation and demonstration of public value includes the need for probity in relation to delivery of public service agreement targets pertaining to all stakeholders in accordance with the mandate and wider value-related measures including perception and pride.

The framework is illustrated in Figure 21.1.

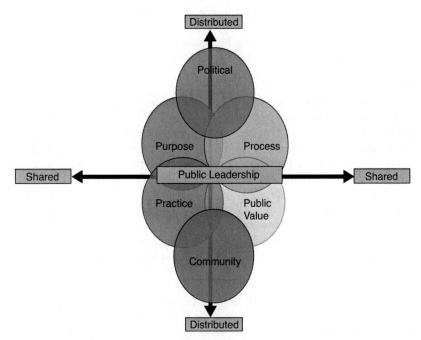

Figure 21.1   New Public Leadership Framework

The framework draws together the following elements:

- The differing forms of leadership represented by the upper and lower segments which respectively illustrate the inputs received through both political and community leadership and the four inner segments. These inner segments together represent the way in which these inputs are transformed through both organisational and individual leadership.
- Transformative leadership relies on the process of defining and implementing the purpose of leadership (based on political and community inputs) into publically valued outputs through the praxis of leadership.
- The collective leadership style is represented by the combination of shared (horizontal) and distributed (vertical) leadership.

Restoration: Public leadership and innovation

The volume will conclude by highlighting the role of innovation as a means of drawing together leadership, management and governance networks within a virtuous circle of collective leadership. This volume has spoken much of the distinction between leadership and management. The importance of inter and intra governmental networks is similarly critical (Rhodes 2001) and – some argue – understated (Conlon and Posner 2007).

With the assistance of the Oxford English Dictionary, 'Innovation' can be viewed as the introduction of new elements (of the phenomenon under review – in this case – public leadership), the alteration of what has already been established (public management) and the changes made in the nature or fashion of its delivery and its processes (different forms of leadership). Innovation can also be viewed as 'revolution' (in this case – a policy revolution) as a means of determining the practices (of public leadership). It can also be considered as the substitution of a new obligation for the old. If the old obligation was about NPM and the measurement of easily quantifiable outcomes then the new is about NPL with its focus on publically valued outcomes and leadership processes.

Interestingly the provenance of the word innovation derives from the formation of a new shoot at the apex of a stem or branch. This epilogue argues that to innovate in government against the crises described earlier, build confidence and trust in the public and to encourage collective approaches in doing so, requires more than just management and governance – it requires leadership in setting a vision and in showing the way to ensure that the 'green shoots' of recovery (economic and performance) and restoration of confidence (public and institutional trust) become the genesis of excellence and generate organisational learning (Senge 2006).

A time to think differently about public leadership

NPL versus NPM

There are three suggested areas of significant difference between New Public Leadership and New Public Management:

i. The role of public leadership in the context of reform which is about transformational rather than transactional change within a collective context. We thus argue for public leadership as a form of collective leadership.
ii. The importance of relationships through networked management. It is about collective influence not power. As Grint argues in Chapter 11 'We thus argue for a form of intelligent leadership that makes the most of knowledge and expertise across diffuse but collaborative networks'.
iii. The overall goal of public leadership *vis-à-vis* the overall goal of public management which is about the identification and balancing of, competing values in the creation and demonstration of socially useful outcomes (as described by Heifetz *ibid*). We thus argue for a value-oriented approach to leadership which defines the purpose and determines and delivers the public value outcomes based on the effective process and practice of public leadership.

If leadership is about 'doing the right things' and management is about 'doing things right' (Drucker 1966, 1975; Drucker and Zahra 2003) then governance, it is argued, is about ensuring that the right things are done by the right people, in the right way, in the right places with and for the right people. Quite simply then, governance can be described as the act of mediating among networks, markets and hierarchies (Stephenson 2008) in ensuring that practices and processes are fit for the purpose in delivering public values. This is illustrated in Figure 21.2.

Conclusion

Why should an approach that advocates new public leadership as opposed to new public management be any different from its predecessor? Based on the four P's of public leadership (described earlier) the following distinctions are offered:

*   Purpose: It goes beyond NPMs emphasis on disaggreation, competition and incentivisation (Dunleavy *et al.* 2005) and instead seeks to identify public priorities based on identified public values in which some of NPMs features are the means by which these wider aims will be achieved.

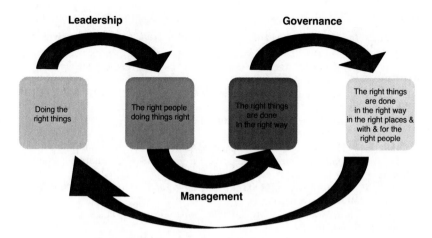

Figure 21.2 A Virtuous Circle of Collective Leadership

- Process: The process of NPL represents the means by which the values, strategies and aims of public leaders is transformed to delivery through a combination of shared, distributed and individual leadership rather than the managerial framework that NPM has so clearly encouraged. It has a potentially unique focus on networked governance as a form of ensuring adherence to shared values and the shared vision of collaborating partners.
- Practice: The NPL practices rather than NPM practices focus on value based leadership in the encouragement of adaptive approaches such as those proffered by Heifetz (1994). It similarly seeks to encourage an appreciation of the different forms of public leadership including community, political, organisational and individual leadership (in mitigating the links between the process of shared and distributed leadership).
- Public Value Management (PVM) moves the lens from one of performance regimes to one of a public value framework and a public value test.

In conclusion, this volume has illustrated that NPM has resulted in some positive impacts in modernising public services but that the negative consequences have resulted in an almost single minded pursuit of 'easy to measure' quantitative targets that do little for the long term improvement of public service delivery. The challenge for public leaders is to create a climate of public value through a process of transforming the purpose of leadership into practice through a collective leadership style that take due account of differing contexts and problems profiles and where evaluation of the effectiveness of public leadership is assessed against agreed standards to the same degree as the current focus on improved performance. This requires a more focused concentration on a new way of thinking about NPL in addition to the narrower focus on NPM.

Note

1. Includes findings from the ESRC Series (*The Public Leadership Challenge*) which led to this volume.

References

Allen, R. (2004) '-ism and -ity', *Pocket Fowler's Modern English Usage* (2004). *HighBeam Research*. <http://www.highbeam.com>, accessed 7 Jun 2009.

Agranoff, R. (1986) *Intergovernmental Management: Human Services Problem-Solving in Six Metropolitan Areas*. NY: SUNY Press.

Agranoff, R. (1990) 'Frameworks of Comparative Analysis', in Lynn, N. and Wildavsky, A. (eds), *Public Administration: The State of the Discipline*, 23–4. Chatham NJ: Chatham House.

Agranoff, R. and McGuire, M. (2003) *Collaborative Public Management*. Washington DC: Georgetown University Press.

Benington, J. and Moore, J. (in press) *Public Value: Theory and Practice*. Basingstoke: Palgrave Macmillan.

Conlon, T.J. and Posner, P.L. (2007) 'Intergovernmental Management and the Challenges Ahead', in Conlon, T.J. and Posner, P.L. (eds), *Intergovernmental Management for the 21st Century*. Washington DC: Brookings Institution Press.

Dunleavy, P., Margetts, H., Bastow, S. and Tinkler, J. (2005) 'New Public Management is Dead, Long Live Digital Era Governance', *Journal of Public Administration Research and Theory* (2006), 16(3): 467–494.

Drucker, P. (1966) *The Effective Executive*. New York: Harper and Row.

Drucker, P.F. (1975) *Management: Tasks, Responsibilities, Practices*. London: Heinemann.

Drucker, P. and Zahra, S.A. (2003) 'An Interview with Peter Drucker', *The Academy of Management Executive* (1993), Vol. 17, No. 3 (Aug. 2003). Briarcliff Manor, NY: Academy of Management.

Evans, M. (2009) 'Gordon Brown and Public Management Reform – A Project in Search of a Big Idea?', *Policy Studies*, Vol. 30, No. 1, 33–51. February.

Farnham, D. and Horton, S. (1996) *Public Management in Britain*. New York: Palgrave.

Handy, C. (1985) *Understanding Organisations*. London: Penguin Books Ltd.

Heifetz, R. (1994) *Leadership Without Easy Answers*. Cambridge, MA: Belknapp Press.

Heifetz, R. and Laurie, D. (1997) 'The Work of Leadership', *Harvard Business Review*, January to February 1997.

HMSO (1999) *Modernising Government*. London: HMSO.

Kelly, G., Mulgan, G. and Stephen, M. (2002) *Creating Public Value: An Analytical Framework for Public Service Reform*. London: Cabinet Office, accessed March 2005 on www.strategy.gov.uk.

Kickert, W. (2001) 'Public Governance in the Netherlands: An Alternative to Anglo-American "Managerialism" 184: 207', in Osborne, S., *Public Management: Critical Perspectives*. London: Taylor and Francis.

Moore, M. (1995) *Creating Public Value: Strategic Management in Government*. Cambridge, MA: Harvard University Press.

Osborne, S.P. and McLaughlin, K. (2008) 'The Study of Public Management in Great Britain: Public Service Delivery and Its Management', in Kickert, W.J.M., *The Study of Public Management in Europe and the US: A Comparative Analysis of National Distinctiveness*. London: Routledge.

Oxford English Dictionary (2009) *Oxford English Dictionary Online* available at http://oed.com accessed 29 May 2009.

Pawson, R. and Tilley, N. (1997) *Realistic Evaluation*. London: Sage Publications.

Pollitt, C. and Bouckaert, G. (2004) *Public Management Reform – A Comparative Analysis.* Oxford: Oxford University Press.

Rhodes, R.A.W. (2001) 'The New Governance: Governing Without Government, 208–227', in Osborne, S., *Public Management: Critical Perspectives.* London: Taylor and Francis.

Senge, P. (2006) *The Fifth Discipline: The Art and Practice of the Learning Organisation.* Auckland, NZ: Random House Business Books.

Stephenson, K. (2008) 'Rethinking Governance: Conceptualizing Networks and Their Implications for New Mechanisms of Governance Based on Reciprocity', in Williamson (ed.), *The Handbook of Knowledge-based Policing: Current Conceptions and Future Directions.* Chichester: John Wiley & Sons Ltd.

Stoker, G. (2006) 'Public Value Management: A New Narrative for Networked Governance?', *American Review of Public Administration*, 3691), Sage Publications.

Young, A. (2000) 'I'm Just Me', *Journal of Organizational Change Management*, Vol. 13, No. 4, pp. 375–388.

Yukl, G. (1989) *Leadership in Organisations.* Englewood Cliffs, NJ: Prentice-Hall.

Index